UNDERSTANDING DIFFERENTLY

Jo O'Donovan RSM was on the staff of Mary Immaculate College, Limerick, from 1966–2002. For over twenty-five years, her main engagement was with religious education for B.Ed. In line with further college developments, she worked with RE staff to establish the BA in Theology and Religious Studies. She was director of that programme from 1991 to 1999 and lecturer in theology until her retirement in 2002.

D1342319

UNDERSTANDING DIFFERENTLY

Christianity and the World Religions

JO O'DONOVAN

VERITAS

Realisation is the very life of religion.

CARDINAL NEWMAN

Published 2012 by

Veritas Publications

7–8 Lower Abbey Street

Dublin 1

Ireland

publications@veritas.ie

www.veritas.ie

ISBN 978 1 84730 367 7

10 9 8 7 6 5 4 3 2 1

A catalogue record for this book is available from the British Library.

Designed by Dara O'Connor, Veritas

Printed in Ireland by Turners Printing Limited, Longford

Veritas books are printed on paper made from the wood pulp of managed for-
ests. For every tree felled, at least one tree is planted, thereby renewing natural
resources.

Contents

Acknowledgements

While writing can be a lonely activity, I have not been without community and support. This has come in the form of the Mercy Sisters with whom I live, who have given me time to write and who have been long suffering and patient with my tardiness and abstraction. I've also been supported by the good memories left with me of working with colleagues and students of Mary Immaculate College from 1966–2002, and the current staff of the departments of Theology and Religious Studies and of Religious Education, whose queries of 'When will it be published?' kept me working. Thanks, too, to the library staff who have always been obliging and patient; to Eugene Duffy and Alan Hilliard of the college theology department who reviewed the manuscript and made helpful suggestions; and to my own family and many good friends who wondered why I did not visit more. I also thank Donna Doherty, who supported the project from the offset, and the other Veritas staff for their excellent editorial advice. Finally, I wish to thank the Midwest Interfaith Network, in whose refreshing company I discovered that dialogue is not necessarily all about beliefs and differences, but also about being human together.

Abbreviations

Magisterial Documents referred to may be found in Austin Flannery, ed., *Vatican II: Conciliar and Post-Conciliar Documents* (Dublin: Dominican Publications, 1975); Francesco Gioia, ed., *Interreligious Dialogue: The Official Teaching of the Catholic Church, 1963–95* (Boston: Pauline Books, 1994); and on the Vatican website (www.vatican.va).

AG *Ad Gentes*. Vatican II Decree on the Missionary Activity of the Church (1965)

DI *Dominus Iesus*. Statement of the Congregation for the Doctrine and the Faith. On the Unicity and Universality of Jesus Christ and the Church (2000)

DM *Dialogue and Mission*. Statement of the Pontifical Secretariat for Non-Christians. The Attitude of the Church Towards the Followers of Other Religions: Reflections and Orientations on Dialogue and Mission (1984)

DP *Dialogue and Proclamation*. Statement of the Congregation for the Evangelisation of Peoples and the Pontifical Council for Interreligious Dialogue. Reflections and Orientations on Interreligious Dialogue and the Proclamation of the Gospel of Jesus Christ (1991)

DV *Dominum et Vivicantem*. Encyclical Letter of John Paul II (1986)

EA *Ecclesia in Asia*. Apostolic Exhortation of John Paul II (1999)

ES *Ecclesiam Suam*. Encyclical Letter of Paul VI (1975)

FR *Fides et Ratio*. Encyclical Letter of John Paul II (1998)

GM *Gaudium et Spes*. Pastoral Constitution on the Church in the Modern World (1965)

LG *Lumen Gentium*. Dogmatic Constitution on the Church (1964)

NA *Nostra Aetate*. Vatican Council II Declaration on the Relationship of the Church to Non-Christians (1965)

OF *Orationis Forme*. Letter to the Bishops of the Catholic Church on Some Aspects of Christian Meditation (1989)

RM *Redemptoris Missio*. Encyclical Letter of John Paul II (1990)

The New Revised Standard Version (NSRV) is used for biblical citations unless otherwise stated, when the New Jerusalem Bible (NJB) is used.

PREFACE

The chapters of this book have come out of my experience teaching theology students and are presented as 'houses' – worlds of meaning which ask the reader to imaginatively and concretely enter through their doors. Chapters 1, 3, 5 and 7 present the essentials of four main religions. This is done with empathy rather than criticism. It's not that I am unaware of the limitations and partialities of the religions; it is because my aim has been to present them simply as '*theologies*', as ancient and vibrant visions of God at work in the world and in peoples. It is also because of an underlying desire to show them in their beauty – each religion having its own particular radiance, rationality and spirituality – with the hope that the reader might enjoy learning more about them and find them attractive as I have. In order to explore each religion in some depth, the book focuses on four traditions only – Judaism, Islam, Hinduism and Buddhism – which, along with Christianity, are the great world religions.

Writing about the Asian religions has proven the greatest challenge. It required a change of gear from my usual way of accessing truth. Nevertheless, some periods of exposure to Buddhism were fortuitous for me, in that I was pushed into dialogue beyond limits and boundaries. As *Dialogue and Proclamation* powerfully reminds us, the eschatological nature of Christian truth propels us forward to an ever greater fullness of knowledge, and Christians must be prepared to learn and to receive through other believers the positive values of their religious traditions (DP 49).

The reader will also find that the study of other religions will, to a degree, be a 'passing over' in the sense of allowing oneself to 'understand differently' and be changed in some way in relation to the other. And it will also be a coming back to a wonder at the originality and gift of one's own tradition. In becoming free from unnecessary attachments, one begins to hold the truth of God's presence in Jesus Christ for what it is, a gift and a call to a larger system of relationships.

The accompanying chapters 2, 4, 6 and 8 attempt to address this question of relationship. More historical, searching and tentative, they touch on some of the main issues, sadly conflicting and in need of healing, that have characterised the Church's relationship to non-Christians in the past and still do so today. And since these issues are constantly changing, and since they surface in the media every day, we get a sense of the cut and thrust of what it means to be Christian in a multi-religious world, and of what our Church leaders, and indeed each one of us, may say and must not say to avoid alienating other believers. For the truth of who God is in Christ and who we are as Christians can no longer be considered untouchable. We have to allow for the possibility that adherents of other religions will challenge us, even 'make us ashamed' as John Paul II said. The complementarities and differences of the religions themselves, coupled with their historical relationship to Christianity, will mean that the issues raised in dialogue can be diverse. Our relationship with Buddhists is not exactly the same as our relationship with Jews, and we know that Islam raises different questions again.

Nevertheless, since Vatican II especially, the Church has been formulating an overall programme for dialogue. The first chapter will deal with this and introduce interreligious dialogue in terms of its theological development through approaches and models. It will also briefly consider the main Conciliar and post-Conciliar teachings that have encouraged dialogue or, in some cases, that have been in tension with it. The final chapter will focus again on dialogue and on Christ and the religions. Obviously, the Christological question is central to a Christian theology of the religions. To enter the fray fully would not be possible in an introductory book such as this. I offer instead some concluding reflections – some as possibilities – that have come to me from 'favourites' in theology. I offer them also as the way I have come to think myself.

While it also has in mind the teachers of religious studies at second level, in the writing this book has developed mainly as a text for college students of theology, who may also find it a stimulus to take their studies further. I firmly believe that the religions must not be presented simply as bodies of belief and practice which, in their esotericism, can be more refreshing and intriguing to the imagination than the more familiar doctrines of Christianity. I believe these systems of faith are more than data. They each address us out of their own interiority and lead us to God. And for greater understanding they need also to be set in context of our past relationship with them and how, as Christians, we must journey together today. Hopefully, it may also be used by the general reader as a book to dip into, depending on one's interest, or by a parish group as a text for study.

INTRODUCTION

Understanding Differently

> *Instead of working out where we agree, maybe we should start learning from each other in an exchange of gifts.*
>
> CARDINAL KASPER

Christian faith has always developed through its reaching out to 'others' of all kinds. In the last fifty years these others have been mainly the worlds of science, atheism and religious indifference. In recent times the others at the door have been the poor, whose voices we have heard in Latin American theologies, and women, the 'poorest of the poor', as heard in feminist theologies. These voices continue to expand the interpretive framework of theology, but the time has now come to listen to the voices of other religious believers – Jews, Muslims, Hindus, Sikhs, Buddhists. No longer confined to exotic and remote countries, global economic and political interdependence and expanding opportunities for communications and travel mean they are now part of the society we live in. In short, the Catholic and Christian churches of the West are called to recontextualise themselves and open themselves to dialogue with other world religions.

THE TRIPARTITE MODEL

Christianity, even in its beginnings, was already seriously addressing other religions or philosophies, and the phrase 'seeds of the Word', which designated the rays of truth found in philosophers such as Socrates and Plato, dates from that period. This patristic insight surfaces again and again in Church teaching as a guiding principle whenever questions in interreligious dialogue are raised. The implication of the insight from third-century St Justin (d. 165), the most important of the early Christian apologists, is that all possession of truth, as well as of righteous conduct, comes through the personal manifestation of the Eternal Word (*Logos*), who is fully realised in Christ and in his sacramental presence in the Church.[1]

In the Middle Ages, it was generally assumed that the world as a whole had already been evangelised. If a person was not a Christian it was because they had explicitly rejected God's truth. Hence Jews and eventually Muslims (from the seventh century onwards) were seen as wilful sinners and heretics and not as 'other', as we see them today. After the discovery of the Americas and the Far East, the question of the salvation of non-Christian peoples was posed with greater urgency, yet with little interest in the beliefs of the colonised. It is only in the modern period that we find increased interest in other religions, due to a number of factors. Firstly, two world wars were fought in the heart of Christian Europe. One effect of this was that many Europeans ceased to have confidence in the resources of their own religion and began to look to other religions, new and old. Secondly, the enlightenment spirit of the time freed scholars to engage with religions simply as systems of meaning and studies were made in the monotheisms of Judaism, Islam and religions of the Orient, as alternatives to war and destruction. A third factor was the critique of Christian mission, which many liberal Europeans saw as bearing responsibility for the destruction of ancient and primitive cultures and as arrogantly valuing Christianity over other religions. Finally, it must be said that it was the Holocaust (the slaughter of nearly six million Jewish people) that moved the Church to look at its relationship to Judaism in particular. And as we shall see in Vatican II's *Nostra Aetate* (1965), this primary relationship was to pave the way for the wider engagement with Islam and religions of the East.

In response to the new interest in other religions and following on from the impetus provided by the Vatican Council, there was need for a framework for dialogue. The most helpful so far has been the well-known tripartite model of exclusivism, inclusivism and pluralism.[2]

Exclusivism

The model of exclusivism, which is strongly ecclesiocentric, runs simply as follows: it affirms that truth is found only in one religion, Christianity, for revelation and salvation are found only in Jesus Christ who is present to all peoples in and through the Church. The Christ event expressed in the Church is constitutive of any encounter with God always and everywhere. An extreme exclusivism would consider other religions as flawed human attempts at self-salvation; and since they are filled with error we have nothing to learn from them. For a time, the Catholic tradition, which is strongly ecclesial, popularly defended this view with the slogan: 'outside the Church, no salvation'. Interpreted literally, it meant that only if one was a member, institutionally and legally, of the Church, could one be saved. However, the literal interpretation of this doctrine was officially rejected by the Church in 1949.[3] Indeed, the true mind of the Church has always been that God's offer of grace and salvation is available to all, which implies an inherent openness in the exclusivist stance. For example, the Church taught that while belonging to the ecclesial community of Christ through baptism was necessary for salvation, it was also true that unbaptised infants were saved though the faith of their parents, and that non-Christian people were saved through 'baptism of desire'. Nor does this 'desire' have to be explicit, because God also accepts an implicit desire expressed in a good disposition of soul, by which a person wants his or her will to be conformed to God's will. The abiding value of the axiom is retained by Vatican II, and formulated positively, when it defines the Church as the 'universal sacrament of salvation' (LG 48).

Karl Rahner further developed this opening beyond a literal exclusivism with his theory of 'the anonymous Christian'.[4] Here he skilfully moved beyond exclusivism to a more Christocentric inclusivism. As we shall see, aspects of this more expansive circle of dialogue were to be espoused by the Church at Vatican II.

Inclusivism

Inclusivism means that the saving God, who is at work in Jesus Christ, is present and at work in *all* religions, at least implicitly or anonymously. There are some problems with Rahner's 'anonymous Christians', the most obvious being whether it is respectful of a Hindu believer to call him 'an anonymous Christian'. And what is our response to the same Hindu, who belongs to the most inclusive and tolerant of religions, when he says to us that he can accept Christ as an *avatar* of the Divine, as he accepts Krishna? Despite these objections, the value of inclusivism, with its Christocentric emphasis, is that it holds together two truths which are professed by most mainline Christian churches. These truths are aptly summed up by the author of the First Letter to Timothy, who tells us that God 'wants everyone to be saved and reach full knowledge of the truth' and that 'there is only one mediator between God and humanity, himself a human being, Christ Jesus, who offered himself as a ransom for all' (1 Tm 4:6).

Pluralism

The pluralist model attempts to move beyond exclusivism and inclusivism, but its exponents vary in the value they give to Christ. In general, it may be said that this model is mainly theocentric rather than Christocentric. It focuses on God as the unifying core of all religions. Its most well-known exponent has been the British philosopher-theologian, John Hick.[5] Pluralists acknowledge that there are concrete manifestations of God in all the religions – such as Jesus in Christianity, Krishna in Hinduism and the Buddha in Buddhism – but they do not give these manifestations substantive meaning. The pluralist model also has many agendas. Its main one possibly springs from a bad conscience over Christian missionary activity in the past, which we have to admit was accompanied by the intolerance of indigenous religions and a politics of colonial conquest. Hick's call for a universal religious tolerance has been criticised as a form of Western secular humanism, yet closer inspection of his writings shows that his call to resist religious fanaticism of any kind has deep roots in his own commitment as a Christian believer.[6]

Jesus' command to love is also evident in the writings of Paul Knitter, a courageous and lone voice of pluralism in the Catholic tradition, who has moved from purely theological-doctrinal questions to give priority to action for liberation, both human and ecological, as the only possible way of dialogue that will connect with believers of different religions without causing offence.[7]

The three models briefly summarised above have been the mainstay in a nascent theology of religions. And even still they provide a launching pad for where we go in the future. In recent writing, the inclusivist and pluralist models have come under fire. The assessment of theologians such as Stephen J. Duffy, Joseph A. Di Noia and Gavin D'Costa is that both systems of thought deal with the religions abstractly and generically, and engage in *a priori* paradigm building.[8] Both are typically modern. They are based on the unwarranted assumption that religions, even while espousing different aims, doctrines, patterns of life and rituals, are, in their deepest reality, the same. That, for example, the experience of God in Christ and in Zen *sunyata* or Hindu *nirvana* are not different. It is characteristic of modernity to respect the other simply as an image of oneself. It is also characteristic of modernity to explicate truth in an overarching way, desiring to leave nothing unsaid.

In favour of exclusivism, however, it must be said that it has been criticised too harshly, given what a particular religion and its practices mean to its adherents. Religions are incorrigibly plural in the sense of being particular and are, to that extent, exclusive. Religion is always *this* religion. No one dies for a generic religion. Stephen J. Duffy believes there is a truth to be redeemed from the old exclusivism that speaks to our times. He writes:

What we label exclusivism and equate with imperialistic adventure and colonialist abuse was in its origins not an expression of arrogance but of the absoluteness of religious commitment ... Perhaps yesterday's missionaries were more accurate observers of other religions, for even in their hostility and superiority they registered differences unseen by the glossing eye of open-eyed, tolerant moderns?[9]

And so the message to be learned from the frequently denigrated exclusivist model is that there is a valid pluralism of difference in religious truth claims, and that such pluralism is not just the result of the human mind's limitation in 'getting it all together'. Rather, it is an invitation to open ourselves to the religions as communication systems in all their diverse richness. A Christian theology of religions, then, will comprise, as far as possible, definite *a posteriori* elements, where differences in truth-claims, one's own and others', are acknowledged as real and are respected. We have moved beyond the stage where our theological interest in other believers is about questions such as who is saved and how. As Duffy says: 'Academics, too, must enter houses as others do, through their doors.'[10]

ENTERING HOUSES THROUGH THEIR DOORS

In the early stages of my work on interreligious dialogue with students of theology, I used the tripartite method. The students lost interest. They felt that adherence to the method robbed what promised to be an exciting course of its freshness and difference. They simply wanted to learn first about the religions as systems of meaning and ways of faith for other peoples. They resented what looked like overarching attempts to pre-empt how they must think as Christians. They wanted the freedom of being trusted with their faith, whatever its level, and, from Christian faith as they experienced it, to make a crossing over in a spirit of conversation and dialogue. In effect, they wanted an open-ended and adventurous experience of the difference of the other, to explore new terrain as if they were relating to persons who were also friends. There was so much to be discovered.

The Particularity of Religious Truths

Religious truth, while having a universal meaning, does not have to be abstract. Abstractions can let us off the hook of real meeting. When we first encounter another religion we are tempted to focus on similarities with our own. We hang on to and lift up familiar truths – such as incarnations, trinities and saviours – and we see them everywhere. This can be a temptation to a comfortable pluralism. Succinct summaries of religions can favour this, for they create generic patterns of meaning which invite one to jump prematurely to conclusions. Maybe Krishna is like or *is* Christ? Maybe Buddhist emptiness *is* the hidden God of the Judeo-Christian tradition? Maybe the Zen master's *satori* is but an alternative experience of Christian salvation? Whereas a religion invites us to enter into the language and symbols of *its* world. An alternative temptation is to see religions as purely geographical and cultural institutions pointing to the Absolute, locked within systems of meaning that matter to their adherents only, with nothing to say to the rest of us. Illusions such as these keep us within our own mental constructs. They blunt our natural human curiosity against the possibility that the aims and forms of the faith traditions of others might indeed have something to say to us.

Religious Truth as Manifestation

In our postmodern age, characterised as it is by a breakdown of synthesis, and exhibiting a love for the *a posteriori* and a wonder at difference, it follows that the mode of our articulation of truths also has to express this concern. It is with this in mind that David Tracy writes of the concreteness and particularity of religious truth: 'The truth of religion is like the truth of its nearest cousin, art, primordially the truth of manifestation.'[11] Truth-as-manifestation is aesthetic in quality. It is a truth one imaginatively participates in. More roundly communicated by narrative, ritual and art than by the analysis of ideas alone, religions are not competing ideologies. They are symbolic manifestations of different ways of being human, and as we expand our understanding of the ways of being human, our knowledge of the religions increasingly interpenetrate. With practice and over time we gradually begin to seek out, and indeed find, the Christian meanings in the other religions, while at the same time welcoming Jewish, Muslim, Hindu and Buddhist meanings as enrichments of our Christian self-understanding.[12] But there will always be gaps opening up, and we will also find ourselves wrestling with strangeness. Even the foreignness of the language, rituals and culture will accentuate this. David Tracy encourages us not to be afraid of difference. He reminds us that in ordinary relationships we do not understand unless we understand differently, that is, unless we are changed in some way by our meeting with or our knowing of the other.[13] When I make room for the other believer, then, there will be always something I can learn from my meeting with him/her. I may even risk having my self-understanding radically transformed.

Comparative Exchange: A Gift to Oneself

On exposure to another religion, we are led to see in a new way truths we already possess, because we are seeing them through the eyes of another and so with greater objectivity. Real dialogue occurs between persons who are grounded in their faith traditions. The sense of one's identity is not a limitation. Paradoxically, it is from the very particularity of one's faith that one is enabled to authentically relate to the other with freedom and choice. James Fredericks speaks of the invariable tension in interreligious dialogue, which he defines as the (i) vulnerability to the transformative power of the other and (ii) loyalty to the Christian tradition. He asserts that Christian theological formation today must give people the skills to deal responsibly with non-Christian believers. Fredericks is one of the contemporary theologians who has moved beyond the tripartite model to propose a comparative theology. By this he means that we need to be concerned with difference in interreligious dialogue – but not in the old exclusivist way. He envisions that we must deal concretely with the truths and doctrines of the religions, their texts and traditions, and open ourselves in friendship to those who embody these truths. It is obvious that such in-depth comparative studies are a generation away and that Christian theologians who are comparativists are still learning their trade.[14] But even in a limited exposure to other religions, one is invited to think comparatively. In doing so, the edges of identity are sharpened and in receiving the gift of the other, one is also receiving, in a new way, the gift of oneself.

There will be Spiritual Regret

While we will meet with many suggestive possibilities in exploring the 'house' of another religion, we will also have moments of 'spiritual regret'.[15] Spiritual regret recognises that there is a broad range of legitimate religious ideals and that no one person can encompass them all. The inner logic of the ideals of another religion may even serve to throw one back to where one belongs. This can happen again and again. This is not because as a Christian I am personally superior as a locus of truth. It is not that these other religions are watered-down versions of my own. Nor is it that, at last, I have proven that in relation to the them I have nothing to learn. What Karl Rahner said in his 1966 essay on interreligious dialogue still stands: the Christian must continue to engage with the non-Christian religions, doing so firmly with tolerance and humility. Humility lies in the accepting of the gift of faith as God's action in us, which has enabled us to confess his presence in Jesus as way, truth and life, and as a gift for others. In humility we know also that this truth is not one we possess, nor one we have lived up to, but a truth still being unfolded, because God continues to manifest the Divine Mystery in surprising ways.[16]

THE CHURCH AND DIALOGUE

The present concern of the Catholic Church for a more respectful, open and better-informed relationship with the world religions is due in large measure to the seminal document of the Second Vatican Council, *Nostra Aetate*, promulgated in 1965. The importance of this document was that it summarised and gave official encouragement and voice to the experience of bishops in multicultural Middle-Eastern and Asian countries, and to Christians who were neighbours to and religiously close to people of other faiths. It also took on board some aspects of the more expansive theological ideas that had been maturing among noteworthy theologians, such as Rahner, whose inclusivist theology is evident in the document: 'The Catholic Church rejects nothing that is true and holy in these religions ... they often reflect a ray of that Truth which enlightens all men'(NA 2).[17] The Council Fathers saw that an approach which concentrated only on the effort to convert the other would block the religious relationship of trust, openness and mutual respect which they felt should characterise the communication of Christians with other believers. An exclusively single-minded missionary attitude would mean there could be no ease or warmth in relationships with Muslims or Hindus who continued to live and die within their traditions and who did not wish to become Christian. Behind the vision of *Nostra Aetate* lay also a growing appreciation of the presence of holiness and goodness in the religions (NA 2). So while the Church continues to state that it has the right and duty to proclaim the gospel, it also recognises the value of what God is already doing in the lives of believers who are not Christian. *Nostra Aetate* communicates a more respectful approach, an attitude of listening that encourages Christians to learn how others are also encountering the mystery we call 'God'. As we shall see, this new openness is demonstrated in *Nostra Aetate*'s dealing specifically with the religions. It gives a special place to Judaism, but it also deals with Hinduism, Buddhism and Islam, encouraging the study of these traditions and the preservation of the spiritual and moral goods present in them.

While *Nostra Aetate* no longer formally implies that it is in spite of their religious institutions that Muslims and Hindus are saved, the document nevertheless shies away from overtly embracing the seeds of the open inclusivism found in Rahner's approach. In line with his theology of revelation-grace as the historical presence of the divine mercy in history in the 1966 article 'Christianity and the Non-Christian Religions', he concludes that their historical structures, scriptures and rituals are providentially the places where Muslims, Hindus and Buddhists meet with the mercy of God in Christ. Thus he goes on to speak of the 'lawfulness' of the religions.[18] Here Rahner appears to be moving beyond the view that the religions are 'preparations for the gospel' or that the believing Hindu is saved in spite of his religion and not through Hinduism. What is implied is that the very concreteness of the religious institutions are 'channels' of grace, and that while 'the ray of Truth which enlightens all men' (NA 2) is present in these traditions, however obscurely or incompletely appropriated, it is, nevertheless, *their* providential mediation of saving Truth. This brings a certain realism to interreligious relations, in that the 'other' is really there, meeting us from within the context of their culture and beliefs as dialogue partner, as is the Christian. In terms of interreligious dialogue, this was obviously new ground, which has been left to later theologians to develop. We will return to this question again in the last chapter.

Dialogue and Proclamation

The term 'dialogue' first appeared in official Church teaching in an earlier encyclical, *Ecclesiam Suam* (1964), by Pope Paul VI. What *Ecclesiam Suam* makes clear is that dialogue is more than mutual understanding between, and friendly relations with, other believers, and more than collaboration in social projects. At its deepest level, it is *theo*logical – it is a dialogue of salvation. That is, it seeks to discover and better clarify the signs of the age-long dialogue which God maintains with humanity (ES 98–9). This fundamental understanding of dialogue is taken up again by Pope John Paul II in his March 1984 address to the Secretariat for Non-Christians, who had formulated the document *Dialogue and Mission*. In a personal, confident and existential style, he reminds us that the overriding Christian obligation is the command to love (Jn 15:12-17), and that the Church, as a community of faith, does not exist for itself alone, its identity being found in the love it bears for others. Echoing Pope Paul VI's 'dialogue of salvation' and 'dialogue of love' of twenty years earlier, he says:

Dialogue is fundamental for the Church, which is called to collaborate in God's plan with its method of presence, respect and love ... Christ has joined every person to himself ... the Spirit works in each individual: therefore dialogue is also based on love of the human person as such, who is the primary and fundamental way of the Church ... and on the bond existing between culture and the religions which the people profess. (Address 2 in DM)

Too often in the past, John Paul II explains, religion has been made an excuse for polarisation and division. Dialogue is a matter of 'learning to forgive', of 'trying to understand the heart of others' and of 'putting oneself at the service of all humanity and the one God' (Address 4 in DM).

Dialogue and Mission has not been surpassed as a charter for the basics of interreligious dialogue.[19] The document's opening section sets out that dialogue is not only 'discussion, but all positive constructive interreligious relations with individuals and communities of other faiths which are directed toward mutual understanding and enrichment' (DM 3). Dialogue is referred to as a human encounter, which leads Christians to listen and strive to understand that which other believers communicate to us in order to profit from the gifts which God bestows so generously on believers in different religions. The most basic requirements are a true respect for the other as 'other', the ability to listen and a sense of 'one's own limitations as well as the possibility of overcoming them'.

A person discovers that he or she does not possess the truth in a perfect and total way but can walk together with others towards the goal. Mutual affirmation, reciprocal correction and fraternal exchange lead the partners in dialogue to an ever greater maturity, which in turn generates interpersonal communion. Religious experiences and outlooks can themselves be purified and enriched in this process of encounter. (DM 21)

The tension between proclamation and dialogue is sensitively expressed by the document's inclusion of the oft-cited instruction given in 1221 by St Francis of Assisi to his brothers:

The friars who through divine inspiration would desire to go among the Muslims ... can establish spiritual contact with them [the Muslims] in two ways: a way which does not raise arguments and disputes, but rather where they would be subject to every human creature for the love of God and confess themselves to be Christians. The other way is that if they see that it would be pleasing to the Lord, they would announce the word of God. (DM 17)

The more didactic *Dialogue and Proclamation*, issued in 1991, dealt with this double theme. Dialogue and proclamation represent different approaches to the evangelising mission of the Church. Each has a distinct aim, and there can be no question of choosing one and neglecting the other. 'Proclamation is a response to the human aspiration for salvation' (DP 67): there is a sense in which all religions are proclamatory in that they are directed to the human being who asks about the meaning of life – where do I come from, where am I going, what are suffering and death – all of which are questions of salvation: 'It should not be surprising, but quite normal, that the followers of other religions should also desire sincerely to share their faith … [because] love wishes to share' (DP 83). The proclamation of the gospel is not optional for the Christian. It has the necessity and urgency of love, and in this context it is fitting to remember the words of Paul: 'For if I preach the gospel, that gives me no grounds for boasting. For necessity is laid upon me. Woe to me if I do not preach the gospel' (1 Cor 9:16). And yet proclamation is not an imposition on the other. Not only must it respect the culture and spiritual traditions of those addressed but, as the Church in Asia is discovering, it must also be dialogical. The other who hears the gospel is not a *tabula rasa,* but someone in whom God's Spirit is already present.

Dialogue is more than a civilised means of proclamation. As a mirror of God's saving love in the world it is implicitly oriented to proclamation, but it is also distinct as a good in itself. It is a human process in which gifts are received as well as given. It is a reaching out to the other in 'love for the human person as such', it is also a reaching out because with their help, we also find out who we are. Its ultimate aim is the 'conversion of all towards God' (DP 41).

In Vatican documents, interreligious dialogue has come to be seen as a valid and necessary ministry within the broader mission of the Church. That mission is constantly under review, particularly so today because of the tension between proclamation and dialogue. While a more recent document such as *Dominus Iesus* (On the Unicity and Salvific of Jesus Christ and the Church, 2000) appears to be coming down strongly on proclamation, yet it is fair to say that what has been achieved in the early post-Vatican II period cannot be undone. The tempering of proclamation with dialogue is a fruitful one even in our daily lives. It brings to the certainties of Christian faith a healthy vulnerability, a remembrance that the gift of faith is not static, and that our journey toward and with the God who revealed himself in Christ remains always a journey and can be enriched by relationship with other believers.

Levels of Dialogue

The operative vision of dialogue in the mission of the Church is broad, comprehensive and holistic. As an expression of love and service of the other, it can have a number of forms. While *Dialogue and Mission* was the first to present the now well-known four forms of dialogue (DM 29–35), we also find them briefly and conveniently summarised as follows in *Dialogue and Proclamation*:

> The *dialogue of life*, in which people strive to live in an open and neighbourly spirit, sharing their joys and sorrows, their human problems and preoccupations.
>
> The *dialogue of action*, in which Christians and others collaborate for the integral development and liberation of people.
>
> The dialogue of *theological exchange*, where specialists seek to deepen their understanding of their respective religious heritage, and to appreciate each other's spiritual values.
>
> The dialogue of *religious experience*, where persons rooted in their own religious traditions share their spiritual riches, for instance with regard to prayer and contemplation, faith and ways of searching for God or the Absolute. (DP 42)

The actual content and order of these 'principal modes' of dialogue have significance. Primacy is given to the *dialogue of life* as it can be the first dialogue we experience in living with other believers as neighbours. It is more an attitude and spirit that guides one's conduct: 'It implies concern, respect, and hospitality towards the other. It leaves room for the other person's identity, his modes of expression and values' (DM 29). In short, it is the love of neighbour to which every disciple of Christ is called.

In second place, the document speaks of our common commitment to justice and human liberation, giving it precedence over theological discussion. This dimension of dialogue assumes great significance in Asian countries, where the multi-religious societies are culturally rich but suffer from extreme poverty and infringement of human rights. The dialogue of action springs from the dialogue of life and together they form a human substrate, without which theological discussion and exchange of religious experience would have little relevance.

Regarding the final two forms, veteran of interreligious dialogue, Jacques Dupuis, recommends that the order should be reversed:

> Actual experience shows ... that mutual understanding at the level of theological discourse remains difficult – if not impossible – unless it is preceded by a profound spiritual communion, which can be established only by a mutual exchange of religious experience. If that is absent, discourse runs the risk of turning into abstract debate, or even of degenerating into confrontation.[20]

Theological exchange or dialogue of doctrines does accentuate difference. But it is the *way* we hold these differences that matters. The dialogue of religious experience or spiritual exchange is fruitful because through it we already entrust ourselves to the communalities that we share. *Nostra Aetate* names these as the questions that arise from our common human pilgrimage:

> What is man? What is the meaning and purpose of life? What is upright behaviour and what is sinful? Where does suffering originate and what end does is it serve? How can genuine happiness be found? What happens at death? What is judgment? What reward follows death? And finally what is the ultimate mystery beyond human explanation, which embraces our entire existence, from which we take our origin and toward which we tend? (NA 1)

As we shall see, the trust in our common ground is fundamental in John Paul II's contribution to dialogue, and was reiterated at the end of the World Day of Prayer for Peace, held in Assisi in 1986:

> While we have walked in silence, we have reflected on the path our human family treads: either in hostility if we fail to accept one another in life; or as a common journey to our lofty destiny if we realise that other people are our brothers and sisters. The very fact that we have come to Assisi from various quarters of the world is in itself a sign of this common path which humanity

is called to tread. Either we learn to walk together in peace and harmony, or we drift apart and ruin ourselves and others. We hope that this pilgrimage to Assisi has taught us anew to be aware of the common origin and common destiny of humanity. Let us see it in anticipation of what God would like the developing history of humanity to be: a fraternal journey in which we accompany one another toward the transcendent goal which he sets for us.[21]

Benedict XVI

What is distinctive about John Paul II's energetic embrace of the Church's venture into interreligious dialogue is that it seems to draw from the wider base of our common humanity, desires and questions (NA 1). In his vision, the Spirit is mysteriously at work, not only in individuals, society, history and peoples, but also in cultures and the religions (RM 28). One can say he is possibly more like Rahner in his approach to the religions, underplaying the distinction between nature and grace and recognising the ubiquity of the Spirit's presence.

For Benedict XVI, the supernatural level is the deepest and most real level of existence. A characteristic distinction between natural and supernatural, reflective of his own Augustinian emphasis on the primacy of grace, seems to pervade his thinking.[22] But also important is the fact that, as a systematic theologian, Benedict is more given to detail and precision. He concerns himself with questions of truth and with respecting differences in the way truth is apprehended. In a homily given in 2002 to commemorate the 1986 Assisi Day of Prayer, he states:

> For a proper understanding of the Assisi event, I think it is important that we do not see it as a representative array of supposedly interchangeable religions. It was not the affirmation of any equality of the religions, which does not exist.[23]

While this text has been interpreted as a critique of an unmodified pluralism of the religions, it has also been seen as an implicit correction of the idea that while adherents of different religions may formally present themselves together before the Absolute, it does not mean they are praying to the same God.

In 2000, the Congregation for the Doctrine of the Faith, of which Cardinal Ratzinger was Prefect, published the controversial *Dominus Iesus*. In fairness, it has been said that it is not a document of dialogue as such, but rather a kind of in-house declaration for Catholics – 'Bishops, theologians and all the Catholic faithful' (DI 13) – in that it recalls for them certain indispensible elements of Christian doctrine in the face of the secularism and relativism of contemporary culture.[24] Yet this document is also considered to be an implicit response to the tensions between the Asian churches and Rome over how best to proclaim the gospel without relativising its truth.[25]

In a significant lecture in Mexico, given in 1996, Cardinal Ratzinger had spoken at length on relativism. Firstly, he said there was the pragmatic relativism of European thinking, arising from the Kantian caveat about truth – that we do not know truth, we only know phenomena. Accompanying this is the mindset that it is only when we are democratic, tolerant and humble in our grasp of truth that we are truly respectful of the truth of another person. Secondly, he spoke of a religious relativism, Asian in origin, which is allied to a false idea that we cannot know God, and that it is more respectful of the divine mystery to consign it to a vague unknowing, which means eventually that God ceases to impinge on our lives. Here he implies that the uncritical openness to this apophaticism in some Asian religions appears to give an aura of sacredness and spirituality to the philosophic relativism of westerners.[26]

Ratzinger's main concern here is that for the relativistic mentality, truth is the casualty. There is no truth that I can express to another as *the* truth, for to do so is to be intolerant. Thus, the multiple truths we live by become a play of mirrors – subjective, pragmatic, serving our egos and desires.[27] This situation is alienating for the human being, for the truth we all desire is ultimately sourced in the Truth, the *Logos*, and this is the truth that is saving for the human being. The threat of relativism to Christian faith is that it is an attack on its claim to truth, and for Christians to abandon this claim is to fail to uphold that the revelation of God in Jesus has universal meaning for *all* people.

For Benedict XVI, then, dialogue is a robust but respectful exchange:

> The religions can encounter one another only by delving more deeply into the truth, not by giving it up. Scepticism does not unite. Nor does sheer pragmatism … Mission and dialogue must no longer be antitheses, but must penetrate each other. Dialogue is not random conversation, but aims at persuasion, at discovering the truth. Otherwise it is worthless.[28]

The following is a précis of some of his guiding principles:

- That the encounter of the religions is not possible by renouncing truth but only by a deeper entering into it. We need a respect for the beliefs of others and a readiness to look for the truth in what strikes us as strange and foreign, for such truth concerns us and can lead us farther along the road to God who is ever greater.

- That we must always look for what is positive in others' beliefs and be willing to accept criticism of ourselves and of our own religion.

- That the process of dialogue does not replace mission. Mission and dialogue mutually interpenetrate, otherwise truth is being renounced (Benedict does not expect others to renounce truth, either). He implies that when interreligious relations are governed by a concern for truth, then dialogue does not become empty conversation, nor does proclamation/mission become an imposition. He concludes: 'the dialogue of the religions should become more and more a listening to the *Logos*, who is pointing out to us , in the midst of our separation and contradictory affirmations, the unity we all share.'[29]

In *Truth and Tolerance: Christian Belief and the World Religions* (2004), in which Ratzinger responds to criticisms evoked by *Dominus Iesus*, there is the usual insightful and sharp critique, but one can glean a reasonable positivity and a freshness of approach in some of the statements throughout. Mere pluralism of religions as blocks of meaning standing beside each other are discounted by him. He also states that if we are to use the term 'inclusivism', it cannot be simply inclusivism as the absorption of all religions by one. It must be 'an *encounter*, in a unity that transforms pluralism into plurality' as something necessary for today.[30] He goes on to say that religions that proclaim a finality of truth will tend to engage with plurality of some kind. It has been happening in Indian religions, which, in a surprising move, he says we must no longer dismiss as a *quantite negligeable*. Hinduism's classic spiritual monism allows all other religions to have their place and to have their symbolic significance, while at the same time it transcends them in an ultimate profundity. In the same context, a brief reference is made to Islam, although this is not developed. As a religion which proclaims a finality in its truth, Christianity also engenders an inclusive plurality of religions.

To return to the statement, then, and to Benedict's emphasis on 'plurality' rather than pluralism, and on 'encounter' rather than absorption, one detects a great positivity here. It seems that the communality envisioned by him is already the context of Christian life today experienced as a communion of plurality; but it is also a mandate for Christians to work toward this communion in their witness to the God of Jesus Christ as Truth in Love. Dialogue for Benedict is always located in Christian revelation (the supernatural level), in truth as God-given and in protecting the difference of Christian faith while honouring other religions in their differences. Within the vision of a communion of plurality, dialogue is a live issue for him. But as a listener and a realist, he has an instinct for what affects religious believers in their relations, humanly and socially, and tends to engage in dialogue pragmatically in terms of the issues and problems which arise.

SUMMARY

The Church has been concerned with other religions and idea systems from Patristic times. Also from that period comes the phrase 'seeds of the Word', which, for Plato and the Greeks, referred to elements of transcendence. Christendom through to the Middle Ages was a fallow period for dialogue. History records enmity with the then-known 'other' religions, Judaism and Islam. But the expansion to the colonies and the exposure of the Church in mission to religions in far-away places gave rise to theological questions, such as 'How were these people saved?'

With Vatican II, a new era of openness began. For theologians and teachers of the faith, the useful tripartite model of exclusivism, inclusivism and pluralism helped to give some order to the complexity of interreligious dialogue, but its weakness has been that it treats other religions abstractly, without personally engaging with them. Today, with greater global awareness and migration of peoples, we can do this no longer. We must 'enter the house of the religions through their doors', we must learn also from encounters with other believers and we must reflect on who God is for them, based on their texts and sacred scriptures. This more complex comparative approach will slow down the process of dialogue, but it will be ultimately more enriching and will demonstrate greater respect for others.

While the Church continues to state that it has the right and duty to proclaim the gospel, it also recognises the value of what God is doing in the lives of other believers and thus engages in dialogue with them. Such dialogue is more than a civilised way of proclaiming Christian faith, it is a human process in which gifts are given and received. Indeed, it is a good in itself, and its ultimate aim is the 'conversion of all towards God' (DP 41). It can take many forms: the dialogue of life, the dialogue of action/service, the dialogue of doctrinal exchange and the dialogue of religious experience.

One can say that the dialogue of common human experience (NA 1) and spiritual exchange was one of the hallmarks of John Paul II's energetic promotion of the Church's relation to the religions. In comparison, Benedict XVI appears more cautious, but he is very constructive. He brings a precise theological mind to the question, a concern for truth and a sharp critique of the current 'dictatorship of relativism' that robs people of their inalienable right to know truth and to claim it without being considered intolerant. Bringing together faith and reason, as in the Early Church, Benedict says that Christian faith is the truth and, as truth, it is universal in import. Yet the Christian is not an inclusivist in the sense of taking over all religions. He/she is on mission toward what Benedict terms 'an inclusivist plurality', born of encounter with the other. Whereas John Paul II moved toward believers of other religions from our common human search for the face of God, Benedict envisions a new communality in our future together. This communion, which will have plural elements, is what Christians are called to work toward as they witness to belief in God of Jesus Christ who is Truth and Love.

FURTHER READING

Barnes, Michael, *Religions in Conversation: Christian Identity and Religious Pluralism* (London: SPCK, 1989).

————, *Theology and the Dialogue of the Religions* (Cambridge: Cambridge University Press, 2002).

Berling, Judith A., *Understanding Other Religious Worlds: A Guide for Interreligious Education* (Maryknoll, NY: Orbis Books, 2004).

Cornille, Catherine, *The Impossibility of Interreligious Dialogue* (New York: Crossroad, 2008).

Fredericks, James L., *Faith Among Faiths: Christian Theology and Non-Christian Religions* (Mahwah, NJ: Paulist Press, 1999).

Hall, Gerard, 'Catholic Church Teaching on its Relationship to Other Religions Since Vatican II', *Australian eJournal of Theology* Vol. 3 (2003), 1–8.

Michael L. Fitzgerald and John Borelli, *Interfaith Dialogue: A Catholic View* (Maryknoll, NY: Orbis Books, 2006).

Gioia, Francesco, ed., *Interreligious Dialogue: The Official Teaching of the Catholic Church 1963–1995* (Boston: Pauline Books, 1997).

NOTES

1. See Jacques Dupuis SJ, *Toward a Christian Theology of Religious Pluralism* (Maryknoll, NY: Orbis Books, 1997), pp. 57–60. Saint Justin speaks of the divine Word existing with God; he does not make a distinction between orders of knowledge, natural and supernatural, in that all interventions of God in the universe are attributed to the Divine *Logos*. There is but one Truth, the Divine *Logos*, perceived in all things, either obscurely in shadows or clearly. Dupuis sees an anticipation of Rahner's 'anonymous Christianity' here, eighteen centuries earlier.

2. The tripartite model was first introduced by Alan Race, *Christians and Religious Pluralism* (London: SCM, 1983).

3. In response to a controversy which developed in the Archdiocese of Boston because of the literal interpretation of the principle 'outside the [Catholic] Church no salvation', by Leonard Feeney SJ (d. 1978), the Holy Office (now Congregation for the Doctrine of Faith) sent a formal letter to Cardinal Richard Cushing (d. 1970) in 1949. The letter affirmed that it is not always required that a person be incorporated in reality as a member of the Church, but it is required that the person belong to it at least in desire, though this desire need not be explicit. See J. Neuner and J. Dupuis, eds., *The Christian Faith in the Doctrinal Documents of the Catholic Church* (New York: Alba House, 1996), nos. 845–7. This teaching is also reaffirmed by Vatican II's Dogmatic Constitution on the Church, *Lumen Gentium*, 16.

4. Karl Rahner, 'Christianity and the Non-Christian Religions', *Theological Investigations*, Vol. 5 (London: Darton, Longman & Todd, 1966), pp. 115–34; and 'Anonymous Christians', *Theological Investigations*, Vol. 10 (London: Darton, Longman & Todd, 1973), pp. 390–8, in which Rahner defends the theory.

5. John Hick and Paul Knitter, eds., *The Myth of Christian Uniqueness: Toward a Pluralistic Theology of Religions* (Maryknoll, NY: Orbis Books, 1987). John Hick, *A Christian Theology of Religions: The Rainbow of Faiths* (Westminster: John Knox Press, 1995).

6. For Hick's own account of his spiritual pilgrimage, see *God Has Many Names: Britain's New Religious Pluralism* (London: Macmillan, 1980), pp. 1–9.

7. Paul Knitter, *One Earth, Many Religions: Multifaith Dialogue and Global Responsibility* (Maryknoll, NY: Orbis Books, 1995).

8. Stephen J. Duffy, 'Christianity in Dialogue: Jesus at the Circumference or the Center?', *The Living Light*, 32 (1995), pp. 61–72; 'Mission and Dialogue in a Pluralistic Global City', *Ecumenical Trends*, 12.60 (1996), pp. 9–11; 'The Stranger Within our Gates; Interreligious Dialogue and the Normativeness of Jesus', *The Myriad Christ*, T. Merrigan and J. Haers, eds. (Leuven: Leuven University Press, 2000), pp. 3–30. J. A. Di Noia, *The Diversity of Religions: A Christian Perspective* (Washington DC: Catholic University of America Press, 1992). Gavin D'Costa, 'Discerning Christ in the World Religions', *The Month* (1994), pp. 486–90.

9. Stephen J. Duffy, 'Christianity in Dialogue', pp. 64–6.

10. Stephen J. Duffy, 'Mission and Dialogue, p. 11.

11. David Tracy, *Dialogue with the Other: The Inter-Religious Dialogue* (Leuven: Peeters Press, 1990), p. 43.

12. Michael Barnes, *Religions in Conversation*, p. 131.

13. David Tracy, p. 44.

14. James L. Fredericks, *Faith Among Faiths: Christian Theology and Non-Christian Religions* (Mahwah: NJ: Paulist Press, 1999), p. 163; 'A Universal Religious Experience? Comparative Theology as an Alternative to a Theology of Religions', *Horizons* 22.1 (1995), p. 87; 'Interreligious Friendship: A New Theological Virtue', *Journal of Ecumenical Studies* 35.2 (1998).

15. Judith A. Berling, *Understanding Other Religious Worlds*, p. 56.

16. Karl Rahner, 'Christianity and the Non-Christian Religions', *Theological Investigations*, Vol. 5 (London: Darton, Longman & Todd, 1966), p. 134. See Catherine Cornille on humility as one of the human qualities needed in our dialogue with other believers in *The Impossibility of Interreligious Dialogue* (New York: Crossroad, 2008), pp. 9–58.

17. A similar sentiment is expressed in *Lumen Gentium* 16; *Gaudium et Spes* 22; *Ad Gentes* 7 and 11.

18. Karl Rahner, 'Christianity and the Non-Christian Religions', p. 121.

19. For an appreciation of *Dialogue and Mission*, I am indebted to the excellent article by the late Redmond Fitzmaurice OP, 'The Roman Catholic Church and Interreligious Dialogue: Implications for Christian–Muslim Relations', *Islam and Christian–Muslim Relations (ICMR)* 3.1 (1992), pp. 83–107.

20. Jacques Dupuis SJ, 'Interreligious Dialogue', *Dictionary of Fundamental Theology*, Rene Latourelle and Rino Fisichella, eds. (New York: Crossroad, 2000), p. 522.

21. Francesco Gioia, ed., *Interreligious Dialogue: Official Teaching of the Catholic Church: 1963–1995*, Pontifical Council for Interreligious Dialogue (Boston: Pauline Books, 1997), p. 546.

22. Thomas P. Rausch, *Pope Benedict XVI: An Introduction to his Theological Vision* (Mahwah, NJ: Paulist Press, 2009), p. 61.

23. Cardinal Joseph Ratzinger, 'The Assisi Day of Prayer' (January 2002), *The Essential Pope Benedict: His Central Writings and Speeches*, John F. Thornton and Susan B. Varenne, eds. (New York: HarperCollins, 2008), p. 44. In the Assisi gathering entitled 'Pilgrims of Truth, Pilgrims of Peace' (27 October 2011), Benedict XVI is clearly reaffirming John Paul II's ecumenical and interreligious outlook as expressed in Assisi in 1986 and 2002. One notes the subtle modification that participants do not pray together, but will gather at the end of the day for a moment of silence and testimonials to peace. There is also the addition that five prominent non-believers have been invited. According to Cardinal Gianfranco Ravasi, president of the Pontifical Council for Culture, the Vatican makes a point of inviting them, because they are seen as actively engaged in a debate over ethics, metaphysics and truth. Such reflects the aim of the new 'Courtyard of the Gentiles' project, which seeks to promote discussions between Christians and non-believers around the world (see *Irish Catholic*, 20 October 2011).

24. James Corkery SJ, *Joseph Ratzinger's Theological Ideas: Wise Caution and Legitimate Hopes* (Dublin: Dominican Publications, 2009), p. 97.

25. Thomas P. Rausch, *Pope Benedict XVI*, p. 29.

26. Cardinal Joseph Ratzinger, 'Relativism: The Central Problem for Faith Today – Address to Presidents of the Doctrinal Commissions of the Bishops' Conferences of Latin America', J. F. Thornton and S. B. Varenne, eds., pp. 227–40. For a valuable discussion on relativism (to which I am indebted), see J. Corkery, chapter 7.

27. Cardinal Joseph Ratzinger, 'Interreligious Dialogue and Jewish–Christian Relations', *Communio* 25.1 (Spring 1998), pp. 38–9; also published in *Many Religions, One Covenant: Israel, the Church and the World* (San Francisco: Ignatius Press, 1999).

28. Cardinal Joseph Ratzinger, *Many Religions*, pp. 109–13.

29. Cardinal Joseph Ratzinger, *Truth and Tolerance: Christian Belief and the World Religions* (San Francisco: Ignatius Press, 2004), pp. 83f.

30. See Jürgen Habermas, Joseph Ratzinger, *The Dialectics of Secularization: On Reason and Religion* (San Francisco: Ignatius Press, 2006), pp. 79. With regard to the truth of who God is in Christ, Pope Benedict acknowledges the need to experience a purification from what is limiting in our Western and European culture. A freshness of thinking occurs here. I refer especially to a debate, which, as Cardinal, he held with the German philosopher and social critic Jürgen Habermas. Both were concerned from their own differing standpoints with articulating the role of religion and reason in determining the foundations of society. Benedict states that if we are to discuss the basic question of human existence today, an

awareness of the intercultural dimension of humankind is necessary. Broadly, he maps it out as (i) the West, with its two main poles of Christian faith and secular reason; (ii) Islamic belief and culture; and (iii) the cultures and beliefs of Hinduism-Buddhism. Referring to Christian faith and western secular rationality as the two main players who have had great influence on the establishment of social and cultural structures, he says we must now accept that they are not *de facto* universal. He warns of a 'pathology of reason' in this regard, such as when reason fails to see its cultural limitations. 'Reason,' he explains, 'must be warned to keep within its proper limits, and it must learn a willingness to listen to the great religious traditions of mankind.' *Ibid.*, pp. 73–80.

CHAPTER I

Judaism: The Way of Torah

He who is begotten in Judaism bears witness to his faith by continuing to engender the Jewish people. He does not believe in something. He is himself the belief.

FRANZ ROSENWEIG

Judaism fascinates and draws us in. Our world is indebted to the many Jewish people who have had a great impact on Western culture in science, philosophy and the arts. And yet the Hebrews were latecomers on the stage of history. A tiny band of nomads milling around the upper regions of the Arabian desert, they were unlikely to be compared with the great established powers of the Pharaohs and Phoenicians who surrounded them and took them into slavery. And the land to which they came, Canaan, was equally unimpressive: one hundred and twenty miles in length from Dan to Beersheba, and about thirty miles if one travels diagonally from the Mediterranean city of Tel Aviv to Jerusalem in the south east.

As Christians, we are indebted in a much deeper way than through cultural and other achievements. Through Jesus, we are inextricably linked with our Jewish brothers and sisters who are 'the good olive tree onto which have been grafted the wild olive branches of the Gentiles' (Rm 11:24). Our Jewish heritage is a truth we are reclaiming today for the greater enrichment of Christianity. *Nostra Aetate* dedicates its longest section to Judaism (NA 4–5). Here the Church is unambiguously stating that our relationship to the Jews is special; they are part of our salvation history. In renewing our spiritual bond with the Jewish people, we are indeed reclaiming our soul. But interestingly, the same document places Judaism in the context of the world faiths. And this also has a message: since our history together has been contentious to say the least, there is some value in approaching Judaism not only as ancestor and sibling but also as a world faith in itself. In doing so, we are freed to explore the religion and ask questions in open-ended and dispassionate ways. And a little knowledge of the singular beauty of Judaism will surely lead us on to a thirst for more.

Judaism has consistently reinvented itself over the centuries. A recounting of its story is not possible in a short chapter, and it would deflect us from focussing on the essence of Judaism by way of its major themes. Traditionally, those themes have been God, Torah and Israel. A popular axiom of the thirteenth century says that these themes are one, and as we read we will indeed find that they interweave. We will also see that 'Israel' means both *am Yisrael*, 'the People Israel', and *eretz Yisrael*, 'the Land'. 'The Land' will be discussed in the next chapter. Here, we will cover four main topics: the formation of the people (Israel); the meaning of Jewish revelation (Torah); the hallowing of time (practice of Torah); and by way of synthesis, the Jewish experience of God.

ISRAEL: A CHOSEN PEOPLE

The cornerstone of Judaism is the Hebrew Bible, that part of scripture commonly known as the Old Testament, and it is in this sense that the word 'Bible' is used in this chapter. Hebrew, the sacred language of the Jews, contains no word for 'Judaism'. Nor does it really have a word for religion. A more appropriate word, and one which is part of the ancient Hebrew vocabulary, is 'faith' (*emunah*). This does not mean 'belief' in the sense of creed or doctrine, it is the 'trust', the obedience and moral commitment of which Abraham was the exemplar (Gn 15:6). Two covenants in particular crystallise the story of Israel's relationship with God. They have also become the broad demarcations for two types of religious consciousness still claimed by Jews. They are the patriarchal covenant with Abraham (*Berit 'Abot*) of the early biblical period, and the later Sinai covenant with Moses (*Berit Sinai*), which was to become the basis for rabbinic Judaism as we know it today.

The Patriarchal Covenant with Abraham, who 'went as the Lord told him' (Gn 12:4)

The patriarch Abraham dominates the biblical account of the beginnings of Israelite religion. A shadowy though real figure, Abraham was the opposite of the pious Israelite, not to mention the Orthodox Jew. The texts of Genesis still show glimmers of his original strangeness. A Mesopotamian who migrated with his extended family to Canaan, Abraham most likely worshipped his own God, who is also called 'the God of Abraham' (Gn 24:27). Biblical scholars tell us that Abraham was no worshipper of the Yahweh god who manifests himself in revelation to Moses on Mount Sinai (though later biblical religion co-opts

Abraham as the true Israelite). Yahweh is not the god of the hill country and cultivated land in which the patriarchs lived; he is encountered in the wilderness. Exegetes have also concluded that the patriarchs – Abraham, Isaac and Jacob – took for granted the existence of several gods, but each group only worshipped their own God. Thus Abraham was a 'different' Israelite, not practising Torah piety. Indeed, the revelation of Yahweh's will in the Torah is something for later Israel. Abraham's religion has been summed up as simply consisting of one creedal element: belief in God, one ethical element: righteousness and justice; and one ritual element: circumcision.[1]

If Abraham, then, is so different and strange, why did he become so important for Jews over the centuries? Why, as Deuteronomy 26:5 states, claim this wandering Aramean as Father? Abraham is important to Jews and to all biblical believers because everything about him exemplifies the primal response of faith, the only response appropriate to the transcendent God in whom Israel later comes to believe. It is no coincidence that the Abraham story begins with the progressive word 'go':

> Go from your country and your kindred and your father's house to the land that I will show you. I will make of you a great nation, and I will bless you and make your name great, so that you will be a blessing. I will bless those who bless you, and the one who curses you I will curse; and in you all the families of the earth shall be blessed. (Gn 12:1-3)

And then there follows the bold words: 'So Abraham went, as the Lord had told him' (Gn 12:4), leaving the security of Sumerian culture where everything, the gods included, was civilised, predictable and dead compared with the living God by whom he was personally addressed. Abraham's faith is seen as a model for Israel's covenantal relationship with God. Covenant – an audacious idea in biblical Judaism and often not understood – signifies that between heaven and earth, between infinite power and finite human beings, there can be, and is, a relationship where law becomes love and love becomes law. Biblical covenant does not mean a two-sided treaty in the modern sense between two partners, where one of them can break it off at any time. It is a gracious choice in which God freely commits himself for the welfare of the people: 'I will establish my covenant between me and you and your offspring after you' (Gn 17:7). As a divine grace from which God never withdraws, covenant contains notions of fidelity and promises that provide consolation for the people in times of crisis.[2] Abraham's long life is a storehouse of all kinds of covenantal faith ingredients – doubt, cunning, expectation, canny haggling with God, risk taking and trustful obedience (as in the heartbreaking sacrifice of his only son, Isaac [Gn 22:1-19]). He is not just a distant shadowy figure to whom we might pay our respects as a memorial to faith. He stands for faith's movement *now*: its trust, its humility, its going forth into the unknown. As such, he is also claimed as father in faith by Christians and Muslims.

Abraham is important because, for the Jews, the patriarchal covenant is the divine guarantee of the continuance of Jewish identity. The birth of Isaac to the childless and elderly Abraham and Sarah demonstrates that Israel as a people continues to exist only because God wills it ('Isaac' literally means 'God laughs'). Furthermore, it is through Abraham that God gives Israel the Land. The unlikelihood of an utter stranger being chosen to have a homeland bestowed on him attests to the fact that the Land has always been seen as God's gift to Israel:

> I will establish my covenant between me and you and your offspring after you throughout their generations for an everlasting covenant, to be God to you and to your offspring after you. And I will give to you, and to your offspring after you, the land where you are now an alien, all the land of Canaan, for a perpetual holding, and I will be their God. (Gn 17:7-8)

The call to faith in an enigmatic and incalculable God, the divine promise of the flourishing of Israel as a people, the promise that through this people the Abrahamic faith would be a source of blessing for the multitudes, the sense of being 'chosen' or specially beloved of God, of being gifted as a people yet afflicted with a special destiny – these factors have shaped the singularity of Israel. In the covenant of Sinai, they are subsumed and given structural and practical expression.

Many Jews return to the early patriarchal covenant as the rock of their identity and their consolation in times of crisis as a people. Orthodox rabbi and eminent scholar, Joseph Soloveitchik, in discussing the patriarchal covenant has this to say:

> It seems to me that the content of the patriarchal covenant manifests itself in the sense of seclusion of the Jew; in his existential isolation; in the fact

that he must struggle against secular philosophies and political forces which the cultured non-Jew ignores; in the fact that the security of society does not ipso-facto provide security for the Jew. In other words, the Judaism of the patriarchal covenant is expressed in our identification with Abraham the Hebrew – 'All the world on one side and he on the other' [This quotation is a midrashic comment on the word 'Hebrew', *ibri*. The root *br* can mean 'on the other side'.] The patriarchal covenant is realised within Jewish consciousness because others point at him and say: 'He is a Jew!' In a word, the patriarchal covenant finds expression in … one's participation in the lot of all Jews, and in the consciousness of the fact that being Jewish is singular and unique. One who lacks this mentality and does not sense himself as bound to the strange, paradoxical Jewish fate, lacks the sanctity of the patriarchal covenant. One may observe the Torah and the commandments and be fully within the covenant of Sinai, yet at the same time profaning the patriarchal sanctity.[3]

The other identifying factors in the life of a Jew are social and ethnic. A Jew is one born of a Jewish mother or one who has converted to Judaism. A Jew who repudiates Judaism is not regarded as having severed all links with the Jewish community, although in some cases they may be excluded from religious rites in matters pertaining to the synagogue and burial. Therefore, a defining factor for Jews is belonging to a people, and someone might well assert 'I am Jewish' even when no belief is present.

The Sinai Covenant of Learning

This is the second great defining covenant of Jewish identity, which God made with Moses, to whom the Lord used to speak 'face to face as one speaks to a friend' (Ex 33:11). Not only is it the climactic revelation of Yahweh as the Transcendent One (Ex 3:13,14), but it is also the revelation of the 'commanding' and instructing God who reveals his will through the law. Moses, who had led the people from slavery in Egypt into freedom in the wilderness of Sinai, is the medium of the Sinai revelation. He speaks on the people's behalf to God and on God's behalf to the people. His is a far more difficult calling than that of Abraham, whom Thomas Cahill likens to a 'Sumerian Odysseus' – a man with a mission, all right, but a wily character who seemed up to any challenge.[4]

Moses is a man who does not think highly of himself, who never relies on his own talents, only on God's word. As 'very humble, more so than anyone else on the face of the earth' (Num 12:3), the Bible sees him as an authentic medium and true channel for God's word, and in the Jewish tradition he is revered as 'Our Teacher'. It is also in the context of the Sinai covenant that we find the fullest expression of Jewish identity as 'treasured people' (*am segulah*), connoting a relationship of special intimacy and destiny with God:

> Now therefore, if you will obey my voice and keep my covenant, you shall be my treasured possession out of all the peoples. Indeed, the whole earth is mine, but you shall be for me a priestly kingdom and a holy nation. (Ex 19:5-6)

> For you are a people holy to the Lord your God; the Lord your God has chosen you out of all the peoples on earth to be his people, his treasured possession. It was not because you were more numerous than any other people that the Lord set his heart on you and chose you – for you were the fewest of all peoples. It was because the Lord loved you, and kept the oath that he swore to your ancestors, that the Lord has brought you out with a mighty hand, and redeemed you from the house of slavery, from the hand of Pharaoh king of Egypt. (Deut 7:6-8)

To the divine injunction to obey God's voice and keep the covenant (as in Ex 19:5-6), all the people answered together and said, 'All the Lord has spoken we will do' (Ex 19:8). Here the people of Israel collectively assume a calling to bear witness to the one God through adherence to his laws, and to make God known to the world. In turn, the people are rewarded as God's 'treasured people', establishing them in a relationship of special intimacy and destiny with God. With the giving of Torah, identity with the land becomes somewhat relativised. Israel will also now become 'Israel of the portable Torah', so that its mission of being 'a light to the nations' (Is 42:6) may be accomplished anywhere in the world.

A Chosen People
There is a familiar quatrain which runs: 'How odd/Of God/To choose/The Jews!' The reply to which is: 'It is not odd, the Jews chose God.' An all-too-human response might be to resent what looks like favouritism on God's part, or conversely, to attribute religious arrogance to the Jews as a people. But we need to remember that the way God works in human history is through the concrete

and particular, through events and people. The concrete and historical become the sacrament of divine presence. The story of the Jews is unique in that their understanding of God was head and shoulders above that of their neighbours. It is possible that the above cited texts on 'election' simply reflect the dawning realisation on their part that among all the nations around them, they were the only monotheists and that this state of affairs was not of their own making. It was a gift and indeed miracle to which their scriptures bear testimony, but it was also a task and a mission in which they were enlisted as partners.

The doctrine of election has moved through various interpretations of being divine gift, fate even, or being summons to obedience to Torah, to service and to mission. A well-known *midrash*, a rabbinic and literary interpretation of scripture, tells a tale of how God offered the Torah to several nations. Edom and Ishmael rejected it because its moral requirements were alien to their cultures (in the Jewish tradition, Esau is the ancestor of Edom, the forerunner of Roman Catholicism, and Ishmael is the ancestor of the Arabs. The *midrash* implicitly asserts Israel's moral superiority over these two dominant cultures). Finally, God turned to Israel, who accepted the Torah with no questions asked. They said: 'We will do and hear' (Ex 24:7).[5] But then there is another more jaundiced *midrash* which evidences Jewish humour regarding the sheer weight of divine fate. In explaining the meaning of the word 'under' in the verse 'And they stood under the mountain' (Ex 19:17), this version implies that the Holy One overturned the mountain upon them, like an inverted casket, and said to them: 'If you accept the Torah, it is well; if not your grave will be right here.'[6] By accepting the Torah, then, Israel was committed to live as a nation apart, much as priests lived in a class, yet also to live in the world with the strong personal individuality of prophets. Like priests, they would serve God in the sanctuary of their lives; like prophets, they would speak God's Word to the people on his behalf, in order to make a home for God in the world.

It is a Jewish belief that election as a destiny involves the capacity to bear suffering and to learn from it. The eleventh-century Spanish mystical poet and philosopher, Judah Halevi, places Israel's capacity to suffer at the centre of his theodicy. Jews are the barometers of the pain of the world. Israel is a mystical community whose election and suffering are mysteriously and inextricably interwoven. It is the heart of humanity, healthier than all and at the same time more sick than all. Its long passion in history is the very mark of its election. Especially in periods of persecution, this more fateful and particularistic approach has sustained the Jews as a people, giving them a consoling sense of divine favour even when they felt the whole world was against them. Orthodox Jews, particularly of the Hasidic tradition of Eastern Europe, have interpreted persecution, even the Holocaust, as a punishment from God for their own unfaithfulness to Torah. Like the Suffering Servant of Isaiah 53:4, who mutely showed up the sins of those who led him to slaughter, the Jewish victims of the Holocaust did not fail in their divine calling. In their very suffering and death they alerted the world to the godlessness of Nazism. Perhaps the clearest expression of these goals is found in a letter written by a Jewish mother to her child living in the Warsaw ghetto in 1940, shortly before they were murdered by the Nazis:

> Judaism, my child, is the struggle to bring God down upon earth, a struggle for the sanctification of the human heart. This struggle your people wages not with physical force but with spirit and by constant striving for truth and justice. So, do you understand, my child, how we are distinct from others, and wherein lies the secret of our existence upon earth?[7]

A Light to the Nations

Because the belief that Israel is God's chosen people is laden with so many implications – not least the notions of superiority, and exclusiveness – Jews have found it necessary to constantly redefine what it means. Jewish interpretations today draw out the inherent universalism of Judaism. The election of Israel is by God for God, and for the fulfilment of God's plan for *all* humankind – for the 'multitudes' of whom Abraham is also father. This teaching is in line with the vision of the great biblical prophets, especially Isaiah, for whom Israel exists to be 'a light to the nations', and to bring God's salvation to the ends of the earth (Is 42:6).

Every generation of Jews has been imbued with the belief that the human person is in the image of God; that God is the hidden ideal to which we all aspire; that the Jews, as a people, are the 'priests of the ideal' and that this ideal can only be achieved in the world in which we live. Possibly the most potent name for Jews and Judaism is the biblical 'Israel', which means 'the one who has wrestled with God'. The name Israel comes from one of the most poignant and enigmatic stories in the Bible. Jacob is returning home after an absence of many years. He has been at war with his brother Esau, to whom he sends gifts in the hope of a reconciliation. If the gifts fail, prayer will help; if prayer fails, he is prepared for war. But an uneasiness still haunts him. As he is coming back, he meets a stranger:

And Jacob was left alone. And someone wrestled with him until daybreak, who seeing that he could not master him, struck him in the hip socket, and Jacob's hip was dislocated as he wrestled with him. He said, 'Let me go, for day is breaking.' Jacob replied, 'I will not let you go until you bless me.' The other said, 'What is your name?' 'Jacob,' he replied. He said, 'No longer are you to be called Jacob, but Israel since you have shown your strength against God and men and have prevailed.' Then Jacob asked, 'Please tell me your name.' He replied, 'Why do you ask my name?' With that he blessed him there. So Jacob named the place Peniel, 'Because I have seen God face to face,' he said, 'and I have survived.' The sun arose and he passed Peniel, limping because of his hip. (Gn 32:24-32, NJB)

The Bible clearly wishes us to understand that the encounter is somehow emblematic of the entire Jewish people. Like Jacob, Israel's faith is proactive in relation to God. It beseeches the heavens to bring down divine blessings. It is a faith that wrestles with God and is wounded in the process. The lesson for Jews is that just as Jacob and his family survived, so his descendants will live on in spite of the oppression of hostile powers. They attribute their survival to Torah, the divine mandate to hear the commanding God and make the world a place of God's blessing.

TORAH: GOD'S MERCY TO ISRAEL

One of the greatest difficulties Christians have in understanding Judaism is connected with the meaning of 'law'. For many people, the word has negative connotations. It is hard to see how someone can delight in the law with all his heart, even dance through the street in sheer joy with the books of the law in his arms, as Jews do on the day of Simchat Torah at the close of the Sukkot festival. Before the current developments in biblical studies, Judaism at the time of Jesus and Paul was depicted as fossilised and rigid. Such judgements were based exclusively on a reading of the New Testament, which isolated it from its Jewish context. Fortunately today, scholars are approaching the New Testament as a document coming out of Second Temple Judaism. The consequence of such reading is that we are learning for the first time that Jesus was a Jew, and that in his relation to the Holy One the observance of Torah played a big part in his life. We are also, hopefully, learning that an either/or mindset of Torah or gospel is fruitless. In fact, Christians are discovering that an appreciation of Judaism and Torah will illuminate their reading of the gospels.

An age-old contributory factor to this misunderstanding has been the fact that when the Hebrew Bible was translated into the Greek Septuagint, the Hebrew Torah was rendered as *nomos* – law. Any translation inevitably involves loss of content and, as a result of the association between the spiritual Greek culture and the more legalistic Roman culture, the word *nomos* took on a legalistic meaning. It is against this background that we must understand Paul's vigorous resistance to the law. But Paul was a Jew, and did not reject Torah as such: 'So the Law is holy, and the commandment is holy and just and good' (Rm 7:12). In the Letter to Romans he speaks as a Jew for whom Torah is revelation, instruction, teaching; not a treatise on the nature of God, but a revelation of God as the Holy One who is there for his people to instruct them in detail about his ways. In Romans 11, we find that Paul, the Jew, suffers in his love for his own people. It is fair to say that what he castigates is the fossilisation of Torah, the extrinsicism that can bedevil any religion when its laws become separated from its numinous source.

The Dual Torah

Torah has expanding meanings in Judaism. In the strict sense, it refers to the Pentateuch – the first five books of the Hebrew Bible. But it can also mean the whole Bible: the Pentateuch, the prophets and the writings. It may also include Oral Torah or commentary, as in the Talmud, which includes laws and teaching of the rabbis spanning a period of one thousand years. Finally, Torah may refer to the whole of Jewish life as observance of the *mitzvot*, or divine precepts for ethical living – 'Love your neighbour as yourself' (Lev 19:18) – and for worship: 'The Lord is our God, the Lord alone. You shall love the Lord your God with all your hearts, and with all your soul, and with all your might' (Deut 6:4-5).

However, it must be remembered that while the origins of Judaism – in terms of God, Torah, Israel – lie in biblical history, Judaism today, like Christianity, is not simply a religion of the Hebrew Bible. Its immediate origins lie in rabbinic Judaism which, as Norman Solomon reminds us, is actually younger than Christianity. Solomon is not discounting Pope John Paul II's spiritual designation of Jews as 'elder brothers' in the faith (something we will return to later), but he is reminding us that the major defining texts of rabbinic Judaism as we know it today were established in the post-New Testament period:

Strange as it may seem, the Talmud and other founding texts of rabbinic Judaism were actually written *later* than the gospels, which were the founding texts of Christianity. When the Pope recently referred to the Jews as the 'elder brother' of Christians he got it wrong; we are both, of course, 'children' of the Hebrew scriptures, but in terms of our defining texts (New Testament or Talmud), it is Christians who are the 'elder brother'.[8]

Because of the emphasis placed by Jews today on Oral Torah as commentary on and supplement to written Torah, rabbinic Judaism is often called the religion of the Dual Torah. Oral Torah, which attempts to build bridges from doctrine to life, is as comprehensive and varied as life itself. Through Oral Torah, God pokes his nose into Jewish affairs and has something to say about everything – the community of Israel, family and marital laws, commerce, crime, food, the life cycle, the Sabbath and festivals. Commenting on the text of Exodus 18:20, in which Moses is told by God to make known to the people 'the way they are to go', the rabbis of the Talmud taught that *Halakhah* (from *laleket* – 'to go') is 'something according to which Israel goes'.[9] It can be said that Halakhah as applied Torah is the umbrella word for Jewish law, while the individual prescriptions of Halakhah are the 613 *mitzvot*.

In modern times, non-Orthodox Jews have moved away from the traditional understanding of Torah and Halakhah. There has been a tendency to discount the divine origin of Oral Torah and even written Torah in some circles. Reform Judaism has, by and large, abandoned a commitment to Halakhah, leaving individuals to decide for themselves what observances are meaningful for their lives. Conservative Judaism maintains a halakhic commitment, but offers legal decisions and interpretations which attempt to adapt Jewish law to contemporary life. Orthodox Jews, however, maintain a strict observance of Halakhah.

'It's hard to be a Jew.' These were the words of an Orthodox Jew from the Terenure synagogue in Dublin during a lecture she gave to theology students. She displayed before them, with great reverence, the following objects used in Orthodox Jewish worship and lifestyle; the physical reminders to the Jew to live in the presence of the Holy One, and of Torah which is their 'way to go' as a 'holy people':

The *kippah* (skull-cap) is worn by men as a general expression of reverence. While the origins of it are unknown, many think it began to be used as a way of differentiating from the Christian practice where men uncover their heads at worship. Some Jewish men wear the *kippah* at all times; others only where the name of God is being spoken or at study and prayer.

The *tallit* ('shawl') is the garment most associated with prayer. Made of white wool, cotton or silk, though never a mixture (prohibited Lev 19:19), with either blue or black horizontal stripes at each end, it can be square or rectangular, and its central feature are the fringes (*tzitzit*) at each end of the four corners. The fringes are a reminder of the *mitzvot* of the covenant as we read in Numbers 15:38-41.

The same principle of physically preparing for prayer and purifying intention (*kavanah*) lies behind the wearing of *tefillin* (sometimes translated as 'phylacteries') for morning prayer in the synagogue and at home. In Orthodoxy, *tefillin* are bound to the body by a symbolic winding of two straps. The *tefillin*, black boxes made from the skin of kosher animals and containing the texts of Deuteronomy 6:4-9 and 11:13-21 (the first two portions of the *Schema*) and Exodus 13:1-10, 13:11-16, are placed with the aid of the straps, one on the arm opposite the heart and the other on the forehead. The *Schema* texts are also on a parchment (*mezuzah*) fixed to the front doorpost of a Jewish home. This tiny scroll is placed in a case and affixed to the right-hand doorpost. As with all religions, it is through reflection on orthodox beliefs and practices that one truly gets a sense of the religion's heart and its particular difference.

A Leap of Action

A leading figure in the Orthodox tradition and arguably ahead of his time in interreligious dialogue, was Rabbi Abraham Heschel (1907–72). Born in Warsaw, Heschel was the descendent, on both paternal and maternal sides of his family, of a long line of rabbis and scholars of the Jewish mystical movement of Hasidim. Forged in Eastern Europe during the eighteenth century in response to the teachings of Baal Shem Tov (c. 1690–1760), 'the Master of the Good Name', Hasidim emphasises the presence of God in daily life, and joy as the way of experiencing God. Heschel was also profoundly influenced by another Hasidic leader who challenged some of the Baal Shem Tov's teachings: Menachem Mendel of Kotzk (1787–1859), known as the Kotzker Rebbe (*rebbe* is a Hasidic leader whose position is based on heredity or charisma).

The Kotsker was the antithesis of Baal Shem Tov. From him, Heschel learned that while there could be a heaven on earth, there can also be hell; and that while God is found in song and joy, God is also found in absence and silence. In his study of the spirituality of Heschel, John C. Merkle tells us that it was the combination of two such divergent masters in Heschel's own spirit that largely accounts for the depth and breadth of his writings.[10] To read Judaism through Heschel's poetic prose is to disabuse oneself of any purely legalistic interpretation of Torah. He says Torah is more than law because it contains both Halakhah and Haggadah. *Haggadah* is the collection of Jewish lore, the inspirational narratives that recount the love story between God and the Jewish people. Without Haggadah, Halakhah degenerates into ritual fussiness. Performed in the spirit of Haggadah, all the observance of *mitzvot* becomes a training in love.[11] More properly understood, Torah, in its essential components of Halakhah and Haggadah, is not theology or theory, it is instruction in a path, and this path is 'the track of God in the wilderness of oblivion'.[12]

Heschel reminds us that Jewish identity lies primarily in being God's co-workers. The halakhic way of faith is a leap of action, a *doing* for God. By living as Jews they gain their faith as Jews. When Moses gave the people the law of the covenant, they answered: 'We will do and we will hear' (Ex 24:7). Which means that the orthodoxy of belief – the *hearing* of faith – is founded on action. Like the story of his father, Abraham, which began with the word 'go', a Jew is asked to take a leap of action rather than a leap of thought. He is asked to surpass his needs, to do more than he understands in order to understand more than he does. 'In carrying out the word of Torah he is ushered into the world of spiritual meaning. Through the ecstasy of deeds, he learns to be certain of the hereness of God.'[13]

The Task of Holiness

Holiness (*qedushah*) is the goal of Halakhah. Holiness is not a quality, it is a *mitzvah* – a command. It is expressed in a striking way in Lev 19:1, where Yahweh says: 'You must be holy as I the Lord am holy.' The *mitzvot* of holiness are numerous (the book of Leviticus is a biblical compendium of *mitzvot*): honouring father and mother, keeping the Sabbath, not exploiting the weaknesses of others, self-discipline as the use of creation, welcoming the stranger, being honest in trade. All of life is one piece. Thus the Jew is committed to holiness, whether during Sabbath or in the world of business. This means more than saying the Jew is committed to being and doing good. Heschel tells us that this was his discovery when he was a young student in a German university. His professors, who were formed in a Greek-German way of thinking, spoke of God from the point of view of the human. God was a postulate of reason. The problem for the human being was how to be good – humanly and rationally. But for Heschel, the Jew, the idea of the good was penultimate. What mattered was holiness – a likeness to God as God. For him, a Jew, being good meant striving to be holy; it is to order one's life in 'divine ways'; it is to live 'in the neighbourhood of God'.[14]

The *mitzvot* are the steps on the ladder of holiness. They are not simply to be ticked off as achievements, as the Pharisee does in the parable in the gospel of Luke (18:9-14). Neither are they an unnecessary ritual fussiness, as they sometimes appear to the non-Jew. There is a story told about Franz Rosenweig (d. 1929), a key figure among the German Jews in the 1920s. Rosenzweig grew up as a Christian, but returned to the spirituality of Judaism in his later years. Once, when asked whether he had observed a certain *mitzvat*, he tersely replied, 'Not yet,' indicating that coming to Judaism is a lifelong process of growth and understanding.[15] *Mitzvot* have to be performed from within. Like the Christian sacraments, they bring about the holiness of God. The Jew entrusts himself to the power for holiness of these commands in expectation and hope.

Yet Judaism is also a very this-worldly religion. The famous Orthodox Jewish philosopher and theologian Joseph Soloveitchik, in his pioneering attempt to write a philosophy of Halakhah, returns again and again to the concrete this-worldly personality of the Jew. As the basis for his thesis, he suggests that human beings fall into two great types: the *homo religiosus* and the *homo cogitans*. The first, the religious man, is intrigued by the mystery of existence. He thirsts for the living God, demolishes the bounds of this-worldliness, transforms himself into pure spirit and ascends on high. For him, the approach to God is a leap from the empirical and concrete into the mysterious. The second, the cognitive man, more secular and scientific, approaches reality systematically as something to be mastered with knowledge. Soloveitchik suggests that the Jew is both: he is religious, but is so in a primarily cognitive way, in that his religious disposition is shaped by Halakhah. The Jew does not wish to escape from the tumult of the world, from its sinfulness and betrayal, nor is he seduced by transcendence. When halakhic man approaches reality, he comes with his Torah from Sinai, in hand. He orients himself to the world by means of fixed statutes, firm principles. His approach begins with an ideal creation and concludes with a real one. He does not venture to rise to God, but strives to bring the Divine Presence into the midst of our concrete world. He believes God's true homeland is in the world. When God departs from the world, God is in exile. Indeed non-observance of Halakhah can cause the exile of God. Thus, the holiness of Halakhah is the *descent* of God into every aspect of life.[16] It is 'bringing God down' through the blessing (*berakah*) of certain foods and before attending events, such as a meeting with a wise person. Which means that when we respond with greater awareness to the gifts of life, we 'bring God down', we incarnate the Divine Presence in the world.

Furthermore, holiness means 'bringing God down' into the social world of human interaction in business and politics. In a memorable phrase, Heschel tells us: 'Judaism is the religion of the common deed.'[17] As mainly a prophetic faith, Judaism's concern is not with the mysteries of heaven but with the blights of society, the affairs of the marketplace. For the Jews nothing that has any bearing on good or evil or on 'repairing the world' is small or trite in God's eyes. Some time ago, I was part of a group listening to a rabbi, Dr Schindler, speak in his synagogue in Jerusalem. He was interrupted by the sound of hammering on the roof: 'The sweetest sound to Jewish ears,' he said, 'This is *tikkun olan*, our business, the "repairing of the world". God is our employer and we are his employees, his builders. Jewish faith is a task, an activity, and work is the key to it.'

TORAH AND THE HALLOWING OF TIME

Jews have not left to the world great architectural monuments. If their synagogues are remembered, and there are some famous synagogues, particularly in Europe, it is due to the greatness of the communities who have gathered in them, who have suffered, and even to the very fact that these buildings survived at all. The Jewish synagogue is more like a Muslim mosque than a church. It is a functional space, not only for worship but also for study and discussion. In fact, the holiness of the synagogue is that it provides the primary ambience for the holiness of the moments spent there by the community, for Judaism is a religion that aims at the sanctification of all time. The sanctification of time is the thesis of Heschel's marvellous little book, *The Sabbath*, from which the following text is worth citing in full:

Judaism teaches us to be attached to *holiness in time,* to be attached to sacred events, to learn how to consecrate sanctuaries that emerge from the magnificent stream of the year. The Sabbaths are our great cathedrals; and our Holy of Holies is a shrine that neither the Romans nor the Germans were able to burn ... Jewish ritual may be characterised as the art of significant forms in time, *as architecture of time.* Most of its observances ... depend on a certain hour of the day or season of the year ... The main themes of faith lie in the realm of time. We remember the day of the Exodus from Egypt, the day when Israel stood at Sinai; and our Messianic hope is the expectation of a day, of the end of days.[18]

Heschel is not saying here that the Jew finds human meaning only in time and not in space. To disparage space is to disparage the works of creation through which we contemplate the Creator. Rather, he is saying that living with greater consciousness is timeful living, because time is the medium in which we work out our inner freedom. Thus, it is primarily in the flow of time and history that Judaism paints its religious landscapes. Put simply, Jews find God more in the *when* than the *where*, which means that we learn quite a lot about Jewish identity from its history as a people and liturgical practices.

The Jewish liturgical calendar is primarily concerned with the hallowing of times and seasons. It operates on three levels: (i) The *hallowing of the human life-cycle*, in which, as in the Christian tradition, there are special ceremonies to mark birth, puberty, marriage and death. (ii) The *hallowing of the year* through the celebration of Holy Days and Festivals. The Jewish liturgical calendar has been the foundation for the Christian calendar, which is not too dissimilar in its structure. Jewish worship is congregational, and no doubt the weekly obligation of communal worship was passed on to Christianity and Islam. Moreover, many Jewish festivals are family festivals, in which there is plenty of scope for children and the child in everyone. The key to the Jewish calendar is nature. The days begin at sunset rather than midnight. Like Islam, the Jews follow a lunar calendar, though not strictly, in that they have adjusted to the Gregorian solar calendar by way of adding a sort of leap month seven times during every nineteen-year cycle. The most popular Bible-based festivals of the Jewish calendar are the three 'pilgrim' or 'foot' festivals – Passover, Weeks (or Pentecost) and Booths. In ancient times, to celebrate these festivals, people travelled to the Temple in Jerusalem. All festivals have in common the theme of rejoicing in the presence of God (Deut 16:14). The festive joy is expressed in feasting with good food and the wearing of fine clothes, and is only complete when families respond most generously at these times to the poor and needy. And (iii) the *hallowing of the week*, which operates in the celebration of Shabbat. Each of these Jewish ways of making time holy is outlined briefly below.

Rituals of the Life Cycle

The very first *mitzvah* in the Torah is: 'Be fruitful and multiply' (Gn 1:28). Here the need to perpetuate life for the survival of 'the eternal people' is clearly recognised. Children are regarded as a gift and the deprivation of them as a serious misfortune (Gn 16:1). The supreme expression of this belief is the practice of circumcision. The term *brit milah* means 'covenant of circumcision'. The *brit* referred to is the covenant between God and Abraham. Genesis 17:9-14 enjoins this covenant 'in the flesh' for all males on the eighth day after birth. The preferred place for circumcision is the family home where relatives and friends gather for the ritual, which is performed by an expert called a *mohel*. At this time, the child is also named. Circumcision for Jews is a wholly religious rite. But it has been estimated that one seventh of the world's population currently practice it, particularly Muslims, for whom it is a sign of submission to Allah. Alternatively, for the birth of a girl, the father of the family is called up for the reading of the Torah in the synagogue. Thanks are given for the new birth and the baby is given her name.

When the Jewish boy becomes thirteen, he is now a 'son of the commandments', a *Bar-mitzvah*. This is marked as a joyous occasion in the synagogue, where the boy reads a portion of the Torah. There is much variety within Jewish traditions. Reform Judaism, stressing equality between the sexes, from its earliest days considered that all the commandments were equally incumbent on girls, for whom the age of puberty is earlier at twelve years. Girls celebrate the *Bat-mitzvah*. Furthermore, in some liberal circles, due to concern that Jewish children at the ages of twelve or thirteen might abandon their studies, the formal marking of their adulthood is postponed to the later ages of fifteen or sixteen and marked by a ceremony of confirmation. This ceremony was often held on the festival of Shavuot, since what is being confirmed is their loyalty to the covenant of Sinai, which is the focus of that festival.

The Hebrew word for marriage, *kiddushin* ('sanctification'), expresses its special sanctity. Marriage is *the* sacred relationship. The Talmud says that a man cannot be fully a man without a wife, that a woman cannot be fully a woman without a husband, and that together they cannot fulfil themselves without God. God is the third partner in a Jewish marriage, just as he is present when a child is conceived. A Jewish wedding takes place under a canopy (*huppah*). At its simplest, the *huppah* can be a *tallit*, a prayer shawl held above the couple's heads by four friends of the groom. It may be a more elaborate and decorated construction on four poles, and can be in the open air or, more usually, in the synagogue. The *huppah* symbolises the sacred space of the marital home. There are some variations in the ceremony, but it generally takes the following form. First, the initial blessings are recited over wine, and both partners drink from a cup as a symbol of shared joy. Second, there is the giving of the ring by the groom, a crucial legal and religious moment where he says: 'Behold, thou art consecrated to me by this ring, according to the law of Moses and of Israel.' The third element is the *ketubah*, or marriage contract, which is the practical commitment of the husband to provide for his wife, assuring her financial protection from his estate in the event of divorce or his death. Sometimes, the *ketubah* is drawn up and signed during the marriage ceremony. Other features that often accompany a Jewish wedding include fasting beforehand and the breaking of a wine glass. In Orthodoxy, the breaking of the glass is a reminder of the destruction of the Temple, whilst in Reformed Judaism it is a more general reminder that even in joy there is always the fragility and sadness of life.

Divorce, while accepted in Judaism, is generally not encouraged. Every effort is made to save a marriage, but if a couple cannot get on, it is considered unhealthy to allow hatred to develop. Though marriages between Jews and non-Jews is a reality in today's pluralistic society, nevertheless an emotional charge remains when inter-marriage occurs. 'Out marriage' means marrying out of the Jewish faith, and since so much of Judaism is ethnic, cultural and home-based, it is perceived that in an 'out marriage' the Jewish faith and the very existence of Israel as a people is being diminished.

The realities of death, mourning and afterlife are inextricably linked in Judaism. The Jewish cemetery itself is called *Bet Olam* ('House of Eternity') or *Beit HaChaim* ('House of Life'). Though these names might have originally been euphemisms, they also express the belief that death is not the end. The same belief lies behind the common greeting to the recently bereaved: 'I wish you long life.' This is not to deny their grief but to assert that life, both of the deceased and the living, goes on. In Israel, Jews are buried directly in the earth. Elsewhere, they are buried in plain coffins. The body is washed according to established ritual and wrapped in a white shroud, the same kind of shroud is used for everyone who dies, irrespective of the person's status is the community. A man is also wrapped in his prayer shawl, the tassels of which are cut off as a sign that he is no longer obliged to fulfil the commandments. The most powerful prayer used at this time is the *Kaddish* (Aramaic for 'sanctification'). This exalted prayer of praise and thanks to God is part of synagogue worship, but in the thirteenth century it also became a forceful prayer for mourners. Children are obliged to say *kaddish* at the funeral of a parent and for eleven months after. The end of the funeral marks the beginning of a formal mourning period. The first seven days after death, the *shiva* (seven) period is one of great intensity. During this period, mourners sit on low stools quietly at home. They do not shave, cut their hair, use cosmetics or have marital relations. Friends and relatives come to care for their practical needs. Services are held and a candle burns continuously. Where possible, friends and neighbours join the mourners at home to form a *minyan*, the required ten people necessary to recite *kaddish*. Mourning is accepted and encouraged in Judaism. For the death of a parent, mourning continues for a year; the children return to work after seven days, but do not wear new clothes or visit places of entertainment. For the death of other relatives and friends, mourning lasts for a month. And yet for the most part, Judaism encourages a concentration on this life rather than on the next. The prospect of death is not one to be feared but to be kept in mind as an incentive to daily faithfulness. On the nature of the afterlife, there is a wide range of opinion among present-day Jews. But what matters is life as experienced; and life now and 'forever' is the will of the Living God, who takes no pleasure in the death of anyone (Ez 18:32).

Festival of Passover

Passover, a pilgrim festival, has layers of hidden meaning. It has roots in a springtime festival that was celebrated by nomadic shepherds before Israel came into existence. As the shepherds prepared to move their flocks from winter grazing to summer pastures, they sacrificed a young animal to win divine protection for themselves and their flocks. The Israelites adopted this festival and transformed it into a celebration of their liberation from Egypt. The fullest biblical account of Passover is found in Exodus 12:1-14. Celebrated in Nisan, which corresponds to the end of March and beginning of April, it is called 'the beginning of months' (Ez 12:2). The phrase, according to Michael Maher, means 'the most important month', coming from the fact that during it Israel's liberation from Egypt took place and Israel as a people was born. Maher also points out that verses 11-12 (also 26-27) which explain that the word 'passover' (*Pesach*) refers to the fact that the Lord 'passed over' the houses of Israel and struck the houses of the Egyptians with the tenth plague.[19]

The Passover sacrifice was originally celebrated by individual families. By the seventh century it ceased to be a domestic celebration and was permitted only in the Temple in Jerusalem (Deut 16:1-8). This explains why Jesus and his parents made a pilgrimage to Jerusalem for the festival to offer the sacrifice and eat the Passover meal (Lk 2:41), and why, as we find in Mark 14:12-14, he and his disciples had to find a place for their Passover meal in the city.[20] After the destruction of the Temple in 70 CE, when sacrifice could no longer be publicly offered, the Passover once again became a home-based celebration. It is the home Passover celebration we commonly associate with Judaism today.

Great time and effort are put into preparations for this celebration. The thorough spring-cleaning of the Jewish home is centred on the removal of every trace of leaven. This is in response to Exodus 12:17 which calls Passover 'the festival of unleavened bread'. *Matzah*, a bread in which the flour is kept especially dry by not giving it time to rise, is the central symbol in the Passover meal. The Haggadah ('order of telling'), the ritual book for the meal, calls it the 'bread of affliction' as it functions as a reminder that the escaping Israelites had no time to allow their dough to ferment. The removal of leaven (*hametz*) from the home has a ritual significance and involves varied procedures. Kitchen utensils, crockery and cutlery, used only for *Pesach*, are brought out. To enhance the ceremony, some pieces of *hametz* are hidden, and on the fourteenth of Nisan, the family members, especially children, enter upon a dramatic search for the last bits which, once found, are then ritually burnt. This removal of leaven also has a spiritual significance: leaven makes bread rise and it has come to symbolise the tendency in the human being toward pride and reliance on self rather than God.

The Passover meal is ordinarily known as *seder* ('order'), in that it progresses according to a sequence contained in the Haggadah. The most important Passover symbols are placed on the *seder* plate at the centre of the table. These include *matzah*, the central symbol; bitter herbs, usually represented by horseradish, providing a powerful reminder of slavery; green herbs (lettuce, parsley) dipped in salt water; *haroset*, a mixture of fruit, nuts, spices and wine to symbolise the mortar with which the slaves had to make bricks, and yet when eaten gives a sweet taste of freedom; a roasted shank bone, symbolic of the Passover lamb that was offered in the Temple (Ex 12:8); a hard-boiled or roasted egg, a symbol of fertility and new life but also a reminder of a special offering brought with the Passover lamb to the Temple, and eaten later at the Passover meal; wine, the symbol of joy, drunk four times during the *seder*; and the Cup of Elijah, a decorative goblet or glass, which is set for the prophet Elijah who, according to popular belief, was expected to return at Passover to announce the coming of the Messiah.

The *seder* is a participatory event. Everyone joins in discussions and singing. The future of the Jewish people lies with the children, so it is appropriate that the youngest child present utters the 'four questions' which ask why this night is different from others:

Why on this night do we eat unleavened bread?
Why on this night do we eat bitter herbs?
Why on this night do we dip our herbs?
Why on this night do we recline?

Norman Solomon tells us that 'Few Jews ever forget the words *ma nishtana ha-layla ha-ze* ... Why is this night different from all other nights?, which in so many cases brings back to them happy memories of a childhood nurtured in a loving family circle.'[21] Solomon also says that one of the joys of a well-run *seder* is the participation of all present in discussion, during which an attempt is made to apply the lessons of *Haggadah* to contemporary issues, such as who the marginalised groups in our society are, and by what means they might be liberated. But also remembering that there are still countries today where Jews experience oppression, the *seder* ends with the words:

The redemption is not yet complete ...
Peace, shalom ...
next year in Jerusalem,
Next year may all be free.

Festival of Weeks (Pentecost)

Seven weeks after the Passover festival of redemption, we come to a second pilgrim festival: Shavuot, the Jewish Pentecost. It is the festival of the giving of the law on Mount Sinai. While this is a more subdued celebration than Pesach, mainly consisting of the reading of Torah in the synagogue, it nevertheless has theological significance as the festival of revelation. It expresses the thought that freedom *from* slavery, the redemption, celebrated in Pesach, is not an end in itself but that it is also freedom *for* worship and service of God. In a way, Pentecost is the spiritual completion of the more historical physical redemption which the Jews commemorate at Passover. Confirmation ceremonies often take place in Reform and Conservative synagogues, since this time is considered to be appropriate for the Bar- and Bat-mitzvah rituals of commitment to Torah. These help to contribute to the celebratory significance of this festival, because lacking a ritual and a home base, it does not have the popularity of the other pilgrim festivals.

The High Holy Days

In late summer, the year dips to a low point as the community re-enacts the greatest tragedy of its history – the destruction of the Temple and the exile of the people. At the onset of the sixth month, *Ab* (in July–August), a new cycle begins, the reawakening of self-renewal and repentance (*teshuva*), individual and communal. This brings us to the thunderous climax of the High Holy Days of Rosh Hashanah (New Year) and Yom Kippur (The Day of Atonement). Because life and death hang in the balance during these ten days, they are also called the Days of Awe. The emphasis in both Holy Days is on the awesome demands of God on the Jew's relationship to his/her immediate family and people. They are serious days of reckoning and renewal, but not in any frightening sense. Lawrence Kushner tells us the spirit of *teshuva* pervades these ten days. Usually translated as 'repentance', it can also mean 'answer', 'apology' and, above all, 'return' – a going back to who you are meant to be:

> *Teshuva* is the possibility that even the most degenerate sinner can be reunited with God ... and that someone who has made *teshuva* is more beloved of God than someone who has never sinned.[22]

In contemporary Judaism the *shofar* (a ritual musical instrument made from an animal's horn) is sounded on the first day of the New Year, a day which is referred to in the Bible as 'a day for you to blow the trumpets' (Num 29:1). It is also sounded at the end of the Day of Atonement. Yom Kippur itself is also a major fast and is considered the most important festival of the Jewish year.

Festival of Booths

On the heels of the High Holy Days comes a third pilgrim festival, Sukkot, the Feast of Booths, the most joyous in the Jewish calendar. While Pesach and Shavuot centre on the great figure of Moses, Sukkot centres on the ordinary Jew. And whereas Pesach and Shavuot are festivals of high moments of faith – redemption and revelation – Sukkot is an eight-day festival of faithfulness. It is also known as the festival of creation, since it plays at re-enacting what it means to live as a redeemed people in the context of creation and creaturehood. Leviticus 23:39-43 gives us the *mitzvot* where Jews are commanded to live in booths or tabernacles (*sukkah*) for seven days. According to the tradition, Sukkot is also a harvest festival. Leviticus 23:39 refers to the 'ingathering' of the produce of the land in autumn, and it has been said that the sukkah could well represent the shelters the farmers lived in while harvesting the crops.

The Sukkot festival is a treasury of Jewish theology, and as with all festivals it is encapsulated in the halakhic details which surround it. Firstly, the sukkah is one of the few *mitzvat* into which one can throw oneself, body and soul. Building involves the whole family. The sukkah is a temporary fragile structure which may stand alone, or lean against the wall of the dwelling house. The most important part of the sukkah, halakhically, is the *s'chach* – materials of vegetable origin such as evergreen branches or rushes which form the roof. For support, these coverings may be laid across wooden slats or bamboo poles. No heavy boards are used to offer solid support, nor should any of the materials of the roof be nailed down permanently. Though completely covering the top, the materials should be loosely spread so as to be open to the heavens, with the stars visible.

There are some variations in practice as to how much time must be spent in the sukkah in order to fulfil the precepts of Torah. In Israel, many Jews sleep in the sukkah for seven days. In countries like Britain and America, where the climate in late September can be quite cold, many Jews simply dine in it. While some inconvenience must be experienced, sukkah living is meant to be joyful. For the children it is an adventure. For the whole family it is time for the breaking of boundaries, good food and sharing with guests.

Irving Greenberg, commenting on the sukkah, says it is an object lesson for postmodern religious life. The sukkah stands for an existential space that is universally human. It is constructed so as to recall the fragility and vulnerability of Jewish wanderings in the desert. Yet it is also a celebration of material wealth, signified by the abundance of harvest fruits.[23] The reading from Ecclesiastes with the warning 'vanity of vanities' might seem a bleak one for this festival of joy but, like the sukkah, it subtly hints at a dimension of life which reveals itself when the vanity of our attachments and human strivings is stripped away. Life, as it is, is of infinite value and joy in it cannot be postponed:

> I know there is nothing better for them than to be happy and enjoy themselves as long as they live; moreover, it is God's gift that all should eat and drink and take pleasure in all their toil. (Eccl [Qo] 3:12-13)

Furthermore, as the airy roof of the sukkah reminds us, this is a life that does not depend on the solid security of buildings and permanent structures. It is life that receives itself daily as gift from the sheltering Divine Presence. It is life that is rooted and yet not rooted. It is willing to move on. In history, the 'wandering' of the Jew has been deemed a curse, yet '*sukkah* consciousness' also means that Jews are always on an exodus journey. They are in society, yet not totally of the culture they inhabit. Their faith is portable.

As a festival of creation, nature features heavily in sukkah ritual. Central is the ritual of the 'four species'. The Torah commands Jews to take the fruit of a goodly tree (the *etrog* or *citron*), branches of palm trees (*lulav*), boughs of leafy trees (*hadassim*) and willows of the brook (*aravot*), and to rejoice before the Lord for seven days (Lev 23:40). These fruits of nature are bound together by the *lulav*, and Jews hold them in hand and wave them during services in the synagogue.

Of particular interest to Christians is the water drawing ceremony, which provides a context for our understanding of the words of Jesus when he went up to Jerusalem during the Festival of Tabernacles. On the last and greatest day of the festival, Jesus stood there and cried out:

> Let anyone who is thirsty come to me, and let the one who believes in me drink. As the scripture has said, 'Out of the believer's heart shall flow rivers of living water.' (Jn 7:37)

On the final day of the festival, a pitcher of water was drawn from Jerusalem's spring and poured upon the altar of the Temple. This was done in hope of a good rainy season. Israel depended upon good rains to prevent drought and starvation; the hilliness of the country made irrigation quite difficult. The water-drawing ceremony was the most joyous occasion in ancient Judaism. The precincts of the Temple were lit by huge *menorahs* (seven-branch candlesticks) and the usually dignified leaders of the Jewish people would perform acrobatic antics to amuse the people.

Sukkot is followed on the eighth day (or ninth in some traditions) by the feast of Simchat Torah (Rejoicing in the Torah). Simchat Torah is a post-Talmudic festival. It is based on a story about King Solomon celebrating when he finished reading the Torah. The final portion of the Torah, Deuteronomy 33:1–34-12, is read, and so that the cycle may not be broken, the first portion, Genesis 1:1–2:3, follows immediately. Anyone who has ever seen Simchat Torah in Jerusalem will never forget it. On the evening before, following the synagogue service, people dance down the streets carrying the Torah scrolls. In the morning, large groups from all the synagogues, singing and dancing, carry the scrolls while a prayer cloak (*tallith*) is held over them by four men. They are all on their way through the old city to the Wailing Wall. At the Wall, each in turn will take the scrolls in his hands while the others dance round them in circles. Jews welcome onlookers to join with them in the dance. They demonstrate the joy of a people who have received their law – 'the way they are to go' (Ex 18:20) – from God's hand, and for whom the law is not a burden but the Tree of Life.

Like the Jewish Sabbath, Sukkot is universal and eschatological in its vision. The perfect festival can only be anticipated. The liturgy tells us that, at the end of time, God will spread a *sukkah-shalom* – a Tabernacle of Peace – over the whole world, and that all the nations will come to shelter beneath it: 'Then everyone that survives of all the nations that have come up against Jerusalem shall go up year after year to worship the King, the Lord of Hosts and to keep the feast of booths' (Zec 14:16).

Minor Festivals

The year now takes on a normal rhythm with 'minor festivals' (ones which do not involve fasting or abstention from work) such as Hannukah and Purim. The spirit and purpose of Hannukah are summed up in its name, the Hebrew for 'dedication'. It celebrates the rededication of the Temple after it had been desecrated by opponents of the Jewish faith in the second century BCE. The festival recalls the time when Judea was part of the Seleucid (Syrian-Greek) kingdom ruled by Antiochus IV. In 175 BCE, he stepped up his attempts to force Greek religion on Jews. Having proclaimed himself a god, and taking the title Antiochus Epiphanes ('god manifest'), he issued decrees banning circumcision, study of Torah and Sabbath observance. Pagan altars were erected around Judea and unclean animals sacrificed on them. Finally, in the month of Kislev (December) 167 BCE, Antiochus set up an altar to the god Zeus in the Temple court and ordered that pigs be sacrificed. This sparked off a rebellion led by the elderly priest Mattathias and his five sons. After Mattathias's death, the loyalist Jews were led by his third son, Judah, nicknamed Maccabeus. The story of the rededication of the Temple, and of the Maccabean revolt which led to it, is told in 1 and 2 Maccabees, the main story coming in 1 Maccabees 1-4. By December 164 BCE, they had gained control of the Temple, and on the twenty-fifth of that month they built a new altar and relit the great menorah. After purification and rededication ceremonies, it was agreed (as in 1 Mac 4:59), that there should be an annual celebration of this event.

However, besides being a festival of dedication, Hannukah is also a festival of lights. This relates to a story in the Talmud that tells of a miracle: when Judah and his men entered the Temple, they found just one jar of oil that had not been defiled and with that they lit the menorah. This amount of oil would normally have lasted one day but, the story goes, it miraculously lasted eight days, giving time for fresh pure oil to be prepared. The Talmud recommends that to celebrate this miracle a lamp should be lit on each of the eight days. The symbol of this festival is the *hannukiyah* lamp. On it there are nine lamps or candles and a central one, the 'servant', is used to light the others. Over the eight days of the festival, the *hannukiyah*, with its lighted candles, is often placed at the windows of Jewish homes. Special songs, the giving of presents and the playing of games are part of the festival. It is not the 'Jewish Christmas', its central meaning is different. It celebrates the resistance of Judaism to the assimilation of ideas and practices contrary to its covenantal faith in the One God.

Purim also remembers a difficult period in Jewish history and urges hope and trust in God. Like Hannukah, this festival is not commanded by the Torah but stems from the decision of the rabbis to commemorate an historical event. It is based on a story told in the book of Esther – a book accepted in the canon of the Hebrew Bible only after much rabbinical dispute. The festival derives the name *Purim* from the word used in the book of Esther for 'lots'. These lots were drawn by the villain of the story, Haman, to decide on what day to slaughter the Jews. Esther had married the fifth-century BCE king of Persia, Ahasuerus, concealing her Jewish identity. Her only relative, Mordecai, who worked for the king, uncovered a plot by the king's prime minister, Haman, to kill the Jews. The plot seriously backfired when the king was informed of it by his wife. Impressed by Esther's risking of her own safety in admitting she was Jewish, he executed not the Jews but Haman himself.

The carnival atmosphere of this festival is captured by the children, who often dress up and enact humorous plays based on the story. They boo, stamp and wave rattles when Haman's name comes up in the reading in the synagogue. Reading of the whole of the book of Esther in public is one of the four *mitzvot* of Purim. The other three are festivity around a special meal, gifts to the poor and gifts to each other (cf. Esther 9:18-19). The most famous traditional foods associated with Purim are three-cornered pastries made with sweet dough, filled with a mixture of poppy seeds and honey. They represent Haman's hat, ears and pockets. The most light-hearted of feasts, it teaches the lesson repeatedly needed in Jewish history:

that oppressors will not have the last word against goodness and truth. In the light of the horrors of the Holocaust this commemoration has an added poignancy.

New Festivals

Two new non-biblical festivals are Yom ha-Shoah (Holocaust Remembrance Day), celebrated on 27 Nisan (between March–April), and Yom Ha-Atzma'ut (Independence Day), which occurs on 5 Iyar (between April–May). Whether in the past or the present, time and history are always the locus where Judaism, as a prophetic religion, carves its identity in partnership with the God of the covenant. These festivals are located in what Irving Greenberg calls the third great cycle in Jewish history. In the first cycle, the biblical period, God was unambiguously present as ruler and guide through the great kings and prophets. In the second cycle after the fall of the Temple, 70 CE, God becomes more hidden. This is the period of Judaism of the rabbis where Jews are called to be full partners in the covenant, bringing the Divine Presence into home and synagogue. In the present third cycle of Jewish history, marked even more by divine hiddeness, Jews must become God's executive partners. Halakhah, must become more secularised, Jews finding the hidden God everywhere – in the Holocaust, in business, in medicine, in political life, in the army, in social work, in learning.[24] This is a Judaism which appeals particularly to secular Jews. Jewish identity and difference are strengthened by bringing the 'sore surface of life' to consciousness. And thus potent words such as 'Holocaust', *'Kristallnacht'*, 'yellow star' and 'Hitler' feature in these more secular liturgical commemorations.

Shabbat (Sabbath) – The Palace in Time

'If you want a taste of Jewish theology, join a family for Shabbat,' says the English rabbi and popular writer, Lionel Blue. While a festival such as Passover is more ethnic in thrust – affirming Jewish identity tinged with emotion, and salted with not a little resentment against the Gentile 'other' – Shabbat is more universal, hence its fascination and challenge for non-Jews. Shabbat is addressed to the soul of the human being. It reminds us of God's primordial dream for the world and our place in it. It is a dream of Eden, where human beings exist in partnership and friendship with the divine and where justice and peace flourish. Traditional Jews believe that it is their prerogative to enact this dream once a week. They do it with great fidelity and believe it is their gift to the world. Jonathan Sacks, Chief Rabbi of the United Kingdom and the Commonwealth, writes:

> I am a Jew because of Shabbat, the world's greatest religious institution, a time in which there is no manipulation of nature or of our fellow human beings, in which we come in freedom and equality to create, every week, an anticipation of the messianic age.[25]

Three key biblical texts locate the *mitzvat* of *Shabbat*: God blessed the seventh day and hallowed it, because on it God rested from all the work that he had done in creation (cf. Gn 2:3).

It is from this text that we have the rabbinic saying that the first thing God made holy is not a place or thing but *time*. God makes time holy by withdrawing or resting (*shavat*). What is offered to our contemplation in Genesis 2:3 becomes a commandment in Exodus 20:8-11:

> Remember the Sabbath day and keep it holy. Six days you shall labour and do all your work. But the seventh day is Sabbath to the Lord your God; you shall not do any work – you, your son or your daughter, your male or female slave, your livestock, or the alien resident in your towns. For in six days the Lord made heaven and earth, the sea and all that is in them, but rested the seventh day; therefore, the Lord blessed the Sabbath day and consecrated it.

Finally in Deuteronomy 5:12-15 we read:

> Observe the Sabbath day and keep it holy, as the Lord your God commanded you. Six days you shall labour and do all your work. But the seventh day is a Sabbath to the Lord your God; you shall not do any work – you, or your son, or your daughter, or your male or female slave, or your ox or your donkey, or any of your livestock, or the resident alien in your towns, so that your male and female slave may rest as well as you. Remember that you were once a slave in the land of Egypt, and the Lord your God brought you out from there with a mighty hand and outstretched arm; therefore the Lord your God commanded you to keep the Sabbath day.

The stronger word 'observe' in the Deuteronomic version means that the Sabbath must be protected with care; it must be fenced around with prescriptions. Numerous *mitzvot* shape Shabbat, which begins on Friday at sunset and ends at sunset on Saturday. Anticipation reaches a climax toward the eve of the festival. The house is decorated. The previously cooked meal fills the home with the aroma of favourite foods. The table is set with the finest silver and china. An extra measure of cleanliness is created: rooms are tidied, linens changed, showers taken, fresh clothing worn. If we think Shabbat is but an orgy of food, dressing up and a clutter of prohibitions, we miss the point. As with any great drama meticulously prepared, the reward is in the doing. Paraphrasing the rabbis, Heschel writes: 'The Sabbath kept the Jews more than the Jews kept the Sabbath.' He goes on to interpret this saying to mean that Shabbat creates the human soul:

> Every seventh day a miracle comes to pass, the resurrection of the soul, the soul of man and soul of all things. A medieval sage declares: the world which was created in six days was a world without a soul. It was on the seventh day that the world was given a soul. That is why it is said: 'and on the seventh day he rested *vayinnafash*' (Ex 31:17); *nephesh* means a soul.[26]

One notices a constant dialectic in Jewish religion – a journey out into the sublime and back again into the domesticated and earthly. In this dialectic lies the shaping of the human soul. Judaism is wary of any understanding of the human as pure spirit only. The ultimate shaping or resurrection of soul means the saturation of the whole body, the resurrection of the flesh and blood people who live in families, and who are called to perfect the material world which is their home.

During Sabbath, this dialectic is played out as a tension between work and rest. Work refers to the productive creative activities Jews are mandated to carry out during the week. There are thirty-nine categories of work forbidden on the Sabbath. Thirty-nine, a symbolic figure, recalls the thirty-nine types of work which were performed in the building of the Temple.[27] The message is that constructive work in the world is holy work. The universe is destined to be the temple of the divine, and in perfecting the world, human beings are carrying out their calling to be co-workers with God in creation.

But one day a week, through the complex *mitzvat* of 'rest', the Jews are reminded that there is a limit to human striving. Ultimately, creation belongs to God. Shabbat is not just time off work. It is a shift in a mode of being, an entry into an end-of-time state which is a foretaste of the *shalom* of the Reign of God. 'It is not that one is forbidden to work,' writes Greenberg, 'it's that all is perfect, there is nothing left to do.'[28]

Shabbat, with its complex set of *mitzvot*, is 'a leap of action' in which one imaginatively lives for some time on 'the holy mountain' of the prophet Isaiah:

> There the wolf shall live with the lamb, and the leopard shall lie down with the kid, and the calf and lion and the fatling together, and a little child shall lead them ... They will not hurt or destroy on all my holy mountain; for the earth will be full of the knowledge of the Lord as the waters cover the sea. (Is 11:6-9)

As we have seen in the text of Deuteronomy 5:12-15, however, Shabbat also takes up the Exodus theme of liberation. To dwell in 'the knowledge of the Lord' means not only that one dwells in right relations with the Creator and all of creation; it also means that one tastes what it is like to be, for a time at least, free of the workaday world, with its enslavement to production, achievements and taskmasters. To experience this freedom is to live up to the ultimate promise of the Exodus experience.

Finally, the Jewish dialectic which tends to hold opposites together is played out in the poignant ending to Shabbat – the Havdalah ceremony. *Havdalah* means 'separation'. As the period of rest draws to a close on the Saturday evening, the mood becomes increasingly sad. People are sorry to see Queen Shabbat, lovely and beloved, departing. Something is lost: it is the coming home to oneself, 'the additional Jewish soul' which religious Jews believe they receive on Shabbat. But one cannot stay on 'the holy mountain' forever. Havdalah – like the Creator – makes distinctions, as the concluding prayer shows:

> Blessed art thou, O Lord our God and King of the universe, who makest a distinction between holy and profane, between light and darkness, between Israel and other nations, between the seventh day and the six working days.[29]

God divides the Sabbath from the days of the week to create a new dimension, 'a palace in time', an embodiment of divine presence which is a foretaste of the messianic age. There is a precedent for this, in that foremost among the names and epithets coined by the rabbis to symbolise the nearness of God is *Shekhinah* (meaning 'dwelling' or 'presence'). It is anticipated in the Bible in Exodus 2:58: 'And let them make me a sanctuary so that I can dwell in their midst,' and affirmed in the rabbinic Mishnah: 'If two men sit together occupying themselves with the words of Torah, the Shekhinah, God's presence is in their midst.'[30] The concept of the Shekhinah does not attempt to name the hidden essence of God, but attempts to name the effect of the divine essence as presence or immanence. While the Havdalah ceremony marks distinctions, it does not let the taste of the presence go. A small spice box is passed from hand to hand, a memory for the senses of the loveliness of Shabbat. And each person breathes as if it were once again the fragrance of the festival. Candles are lit, the father of the family sips from a cup of wine and then extinguishes the candle in the drop of wine which has overflowed from the cup. And thus the Sabbath ends. But it is not the end of the Shekhinah, whose dwelling in the community gives meaning to the working week.

GOD – THE HOLY ONE

Biblical language, as a whole, does not theorise about God. The language of the psalms is a language of the Shekhinah, of the divine immanence or presence. The language of biblical history describes God's actions in relation to Israel and the prophetic books speak the language of the commanding God, who is interested in all the details of the holiness of Israel's life. But even as far back as Abraham and the patriarchs, there were intimations of the transcendent essence of God. God is mysteriously more, ultimately unknown, yet personal and inviting. Someone to journey toward, and with, in faithfulness (*emunah*).

I Will Be There With You

On Mount Sinai we get a further glimpse of the unknown God. It is a revelation that sets the Jews apart as the caretakers of the purest monotheism. When Moses asks God to tell him his name, God's reply is 'I AM WHO I AM.' God also said to Moses, 'Thus you shall say to the Israelites, "I AM has sent me to you" … this my name forever, and this my title for all generations' (Ex 3:14, 15). In his persuasive retelling of the Hebrew Bible, *The Gift of the Jews*, Thomas Cahill writes:

> YHWH: What does it mean? Ancient Hebrew was written without vowels; and by the time vowel subscripts were added to the consonants in the Middle Ages, the name of God had become so sacred that it was never uttered. Even in classical times, as early as the Second Temple period, only the High Priest could pronounce the Name of God – and only once a year in the prayer of the day of atonement. Once the temple was destroyed in

70 AD, no Jew uttered the Name again. From that time to this, the devout have avoided this word of their Bible, reading 'Adonai' ('the Lord') when they come to the word YHWH. Many Orthodox go a step further, refusing even to say 'Adonai' and substituting Ha-Shem ('the Name').[31]

There have been many interpretations of this text of YHWH, but there remain, as Cahill points out, three outstanding possibilities, none of them mutually exclusive.

First, 'I am who I am' – this is the interpretation of the Septuagint, the Greek translation of the Hebrew Bible. It was this translation that St Thomas Aquinas used in the thirteenth century to undergird his theology of God as the only being whose essence *is* existence, all other beings being contingent and dependent for their existence on God. Such an interpretation also linked the biblical Creator with the philosophical First Cause. Second, 'I am who I am', in other words, 'None of your business, you cannot control me by invoking my name as if I were one of your household gods.' Third, the more contemporary interpretation favoured today by biblical scholars, 'I will be there with you' – emphasises the ongoing active presence of Yahweh, especially in the history of his chosen people, a presence which has all the drama of a great love story.[32] In the light of this interpretation, we will comment briefly on the classical Jewish tradition's understanding of God as Creator, Revealer and Redeemer, concepts which are also fundamental to the Christian tradition.

The Creator

Jewish belief in the Creator God is not a philosophical testimony to the First Cause. Firstly, it is a faith testimony that creation – in its beauty, its order and its sheer splendour – manifests the character of its Agent. Its ultimate purpose is the glory of God: 'The heavens are telling the glory of God, and the firmament proclaims his handiwork' (Ps 19:1–2). Psalms 95–100 exhort us again and again to praise the Creator. Just as God cares for the work of his hands, he will care for human beings:

These all look to you
to give them their food in due season;
when you give to them, they gather it up;
when you open your hand, they are filled with good things. (Ps 104:27)

Even though Job painfully learned that the ways of the Creator ultimately escape human comprehension, it is on the basis of this elemental bond with the Creator, that (with typical Jewish *chutzpah*) Job turns the tables on God with these words:

> Your hands fashioned and made me;
> And now you turn and destroy me! (Job 10:8-9)

Secondly, belief in a Creator God means that earthly existence is of unimpeachable worth. In the Genesis accounts of creation, Jews (as well as Christians and Muslims) find ground for their buoyant, affirmative attitude toward the world; their confidence in their human power and duty to work it for good; their belief that matter can participate in the condition of salvation itself (affirmed in the doctrine of the resurrection of the body); and that nature, particularly the promised land of Israel for Jews, can host the coming of God's kingdom on earth.

Thirdly, belief in a personal God. Since God's most important creation is the human being who is in his image (Gn 1:27), it follows that God too is personal. Made in the image of God, man and woman mirror the divine. Jonathan Sacks surmises that the greatest discovery of the Hebrew Bible is not that God is One (monotheism), but that the one divine being is a person:

> A different vision was born in ancient Israel, one that saw in the cosmos the face of the personal: God, who brought the universe into being as parents conceive a child, acting not blindly but out of love. We are not insignificant, nor are we alone. We are here because someone willed us into being, who wanted us to be, who knows our innermost thoughts, who values us in our uniqueness, whose breath we breathe and in whose arms we rest; someone in and through whom we are connected to all that is.[33]

It is the very radicality of this vision that protects the dignity of human life, for from it flows the moral universe of human rights, justice, the rule of law and the idea of human freedom. In light of this it is no accident that the Hebrew Bible takes the human covenant of marriage as a central metaphor for the relationship between humanity and God. There is nothing mysterious about Jewish religious faith, says Rabbi Sacks. It is not a leap into a void. It is analogous to relating to an-*other* human being through covenant – word given and word received and honoured in faithfulness.[34] God is husband and Israel is wife. So the prophet

Hosea puts it in a famous text which Jewish men recite every weekday as they don their *tefillin* for prayer:

> And I will take you for my wife forever;
> I will take you for my wife in righteousness and justice,
> in steadfast love and in mercy.
> I will take you for my wife in faithfulness;
> and you shall know the Lord. (Hos 2:19)[35]

The Revealer

Mount Sinai, in biblical history, is the place of revelation – not only of the divine Name but also of the Commandments. Even the very setting is significant. 'If God – the Real God, the One God,' says Thomas Cahill, 'was to speak to human beings and if there was any possibility of their hearing him, it could happen only in a place stripped of all cultural reference points … Only amid inhuman rock and dust could this fallible collection of human beings imagine becoming human in a new way.'[36]

This new way of becoming human means living in relationship with God in the here and now. Creator, Revealer and, as we shall see, Redeemer, are relational terms. The God of the Bible is a God-in-relation-to, a Revealer, an Utterer of his Word to believers, and to that extent differs from the self-enclosed God of the ancient religions and philosophers. With the revelation of Yahweh, the Israelites were launched into a new sense of time. The present moment was extricated from a storied past and auguries of the future. It was the moment where God was to be encountered, and it alone was real. It was where history was made. The Sinai commandments forbidding the adoration of false gods or forbidding murder, of their very nature, must be obeyed *now*. No wonder the rabbinical tradition and later Jewish theology spoke so forcefully of the Law Giver of the Bible as 'the Commanding God'. And yet the same tradition also stated that the Revealer of Torah is like 'an old man steeped in compassion'.[37] An 'old man' because he is wise to the human condition as imperfect and afflicted with the *yetser* (the evil inclination), and 'compassion' because, as a parent, he offers Torah as a remedy to his hapless children. 'Happy are Israel, for so long as they are engaged in Torah and charity, the *yetser* (evil inclination) is under their control.'[38]

As we know, the revelation of Torah is further developed in Oral Torah down through the ages. Even though some of these developments might appear bizarre to non-Jews, these laws remain testimony to the fact that the Jews were committed to developing an integrated view of human life and its obligations as coming from the Author of Life. The law was not seen as a burden imposed on Israel (as we are inclined to think due to a one-sided interpretation of the Pauline antithesis of law and grace). The law was the concrete shape of grace. It was the way to know God's will; to know one's self, one's destination. More profoundly, it was a call beyond moralising only, to entrust oneself to the mystery of holiness which is God's way: 'You shall be holy, for I the Lord your God am holy (Lev 19:2), and 'You shall be to me a kingdom of priests and a holy nation' (Ex 19:6).

The Redeemer

In Judaism, redemption usually denotes the saving of the Jewish people from exile and oppression. But as the Jewish theologian, Louis Jacob, points out, it is not quite correct to say that Judaism is totally unlike Christianity and that it knows nothing of the redemption of the individual soul from personal sin.[39] He notes that Psalm 130 speaks of the redeemer God in this way:

> O Israel, hope in the Lord!
> For with the Lord there is steadfast love,
> And with him is plenteous redemption.
> And he will redeem Israel from all its iniquities. (Ps 130:7-8)

Through sincere repentance and the power of Torah, 'the Jew is justified by deed'.[40] He experiences God alone as his Saviour. But there are earthly as well as spiritual aspects to redemption. As Lord of creation and human history, God as Redeemer is the guarantee that Israel's partnership with God will result in a new completeness for the people that will be physical as well as spiritual. What St Paul wrote in Romans 8:19-21, that 'the creation waits with eager longing for the revealing of the children of God' and that 'the creation itself will be set free from its bondage to decay ... to obtain the freedom of the children of God', is also the aspiration of Judaism. But whereas in Paul the transformation of earthly realities is imbued with the numinous qualities of Christian hope in God's gift, redemption in Judaism is more this-worldly, to the extent of having political and social implications. This ambivalence in the understanding of redemption also colours the related concept of Messiah.[41] This doctrine has gone through many fluctuations in Jewish history, but the emphasis on a personal Messiah and/or on the messianic age have all contributed to make this principle of Judaism one of the most fluid in its capacity for interpretation. Accordingly, Jacobs says that many Jewish thinkers are prepared to give up the doctrine completely. For others, Zionism and the establishment of the state of Israel are the more appropriate modern secular versions of messianism. But for some orthodox Jews, Jacobs rightly says that redemption and messianism ultimately mean

> that God will not allow his world to be surrendered to chaos and that the human drama will one day find its culmination on earth, and that believing more than this is opaque to humans and should be left to God.[42]

In this Torah-bound faith, the mysteries of redemption and messianism are best left to God because Jews do not predominantly see themselves as speculators on the mystery of God, but as priestly worshippers of the divine and as God's co-workers. A legend from the sixteenth-century Lurianic Kabbalah of the Jewish mystical tradition is often called upon to make this point. The legend is attributed to the Galilean rabbi Isaac Luria, and is his attempt to respond to the age-old questions of the existence of evil, what God's part in it is, and what humans must do. The legend tells us that, when first setting out to make the world, God planned to put a holy light into it to make it real. God prepared vessels to contain this light. But something went wrong; the light was so bright that the vessels burst, shattering into millions of broken pieces like dishes dropped on the floor. This was the 'breaking of the vessels'. It symbolised the reality of the world as we experience it, a world of broken fragments, which, says Luria, God cannot heal on his own. That is why God created us and gave us freedom of choice. We can allow things to remain broken, or we can work with God to 'repair the world' – *tikkun olam*.[43]

So whatever historical form redemption will take, it will always be 'a repairing of the world'. Orthodox Jews commit themselves to this, particularly through the sheer physicality of their worship, which Torah enjoins. The redemptive process is furthered when everyday activities, such as eating, drinking and working, are done in the service of God with a high degree of consciousness. In addition, there is also the immense moral energy which has always characterised Jewish people, that almost fanatical love for justice that connects Abraham, Moses and the prophets with the Jewish civil-rights and anti-apartheid activists, and the current aspiration of many Jews that the state of Israel might eventually become an example of a 'mended' portion of the world.

The Living God

Life (*hayyim*), as the Hebrew Bible understands it, is a pregnant term, expansive in meaning. It is more than biological; it is more than the mere duration of human existence. It is human existence, but with all that goes with it – health, good estate, happiness, peace, dwelling in the land. A man will give everything in exchange for life in order to avoid its stark opposite – death (Job 2:4).

Life in its fullness is possible only in relation to the Living God who is absolute Lord of Life and Death. Indeed, the felicitous image – the Living God – can be said to be the hold-all for all biblical images of God. The Living God takes no pleasure in the death of anyone (Ez 18:32) because he has not created human beings for death but for life (Wis 1:13f; 2:23). He is the source of the fullness of life. All yearnings for life in its varied forms are addressed to him. What is sought first and foremost is deliverance from physical and mortal danger, but closely associated with this is the renewal of inner life, through renewed obedience to the Torah, the 'tree of life to those who hold on to it' (Prov 3:18). In the great Psalm 119, dedicated to Torah, the psalmist prays for life:

> True to your faithful love give me life,
> And I shall keep the instructions you have laid down …
> I shall never forget your precepts,
> For by them you have given me life. (Ps 119:88, 93, NJB)

In Psalms 16:11, he yearns for life as living in a joyous friendship within the covenant:

> You will teach me the path of life,
> Unbounded joy in your presence,
> At your right hand delight forever. (Ps 16:11, NJB)

It is precisely this knowledge of God's plenitude of life that makes it possible for Israel to endure the tension of faith in the Name (*Ha-Shem*), the One they must not name, the transcendent God who is truly hidden. Living quality affirms the personality of the not-named God and attributes to him glory from the signs he has worked in the world (Num 14:21), attributes to him heart (Gn 6:6; 1 Sam 13:14), face (Ex 13:14f) and a consuming emotional warmth 'which neither tires nor wearies' (Is 40:28). Even the jealous zeal of God – 'For the Lord your God is a devouring fire, a jealous God (Deut 4:24) – is another aspect of intensity of the divine–human relationship. It is the passion God brings to all he does and touches. The Living God is real, someone to tangle with, someone to trust, someone from whom there is a response, and someone even to question and to call to account as does the psalmist: 'Why hold back your hand,/Keep your right hand hidden in the folds of your robe?' (Ps 74:11, NJB).

It is the same spirit of arguing with God that we find in the story of Jacob wrestling with the angel, in the prophet Jeremiah calling God to task, in the story of Job, and in contemporary Jews – such as Elie Wiesel – confronting God for allowing the Holocaust. We do not find this confrontational element in the prayer traditions of other faiths. Even in Christian liturgy it is played down, despite the fact that we pray the psalms, which invite us to bring all aspects of life to God.

Choose Life

The high estimate the Bible has shown for the God of Life is an indication of its regard for life in its total sense. Israel, in choosing life, mirrors the abundance of the Living God. The parting words of Moses to the people before they crossed over Jordan into the promised land were:

> Today I call heaven and earth to witness against you: I am offering you life or death, blessing or curse. Choose life, then, so that you and your descendants may live in the love of Yahweh your God, obeying his voice in holding fast to him; for in this your life consists ... (Deut 30:19-20, NJB)

Israel chose life and the Jews have done the same again and again throughout their history. Their survival against all odds on the world stage (currently about fourteen million in number, they are about two-tenths of 1 per cent of the world population), is not only because of their belief in the transcendent God; it is because as 'the eternal people', they themselves are that belief.

SUMMARY

This chapter has been an unfolding of Judaism in terms of its classic pillars: Israel (the people), Torah and God. Jewish belief in 'only one God' does not sound startling today, but it certainly was in the ancient world, where there were many gods and goddesses who pursued their own lives and interests. The monotheism of Judaism has been the foundation of Christianity and Islam, both religions acknowledging what they owe to this radical Jewish belief by understanding Abraham as their father in faith. But God, witnessed to in the Shema prayer (Deut 6:4), is also the Divine Presence through whom all the components of Judaism are understood – the people with whom the divine in freedom and love has entered into covenant relationship (initially with Abraham); and the Torah, which is given by the teaching and commanding God (of Moses) to be an instruction for Israel in how to live in fidelity to their calling.

The God of Abraham distinguishes himself strikingly from human beings, society and the cosmos. This Creator God, both personal and different from all the surrounding divinities of the ancient near East, is in no way consubstantial with the material world. This faithful and mysterious God opens himself towards the great biblical patriarchs who are called not only to believe but to trust. This open space is initiated by God. It is variously termed 'relationship', 'covenant' and 'revelation', all of which will dramatically unfold in the life of Israel as a history of salvation. Faith makes its appearance as the only way of responding to this God, since it is not human beings who go in search for God, but the divine being who goes in search for the human. The drama of this search is told in the Hebrew Bible and the Talmudic commentaries of Judaism today. It focuses on the call to imitate the holiness of God (Lev 19:2). But the 'imitation' of the divine holiness for a people who consciously saw themselves as partners and co-workers with God is not so much an ascent to God as the 'bringing down' of Divine Presence into the midst of their concrete world.

The Jews see themselves as a 'priestly people'. Their obedience to Torah prescriptions (traditional Judaism identifies 613 commandments in the Bible) is a consecration of every aspect of daily life. The rituals of the human lifecycle, the festivals and Holy Days celebrate faith in the divine election and, like sacraments, these rituals 'bring down' God's blessing into special times and seasons. The weekly Sabbath especially gives the flavour of Judaism. It is not a negative nit-picking about works to be avoided, it is about 'rest' from labour in order to experience the 'rest' of God in the work of creation. As mentioned before, there is a saying that 'the Sabbath keeps the Jews', which means that this weekly enactment of the theocratic social order acts as renewal for all of Jewish life. While, in its orthodox aspects, Judaism is a singularly God-centred religion, it is also quite practical and earthy. Jews consider themselves partners with God in the 'repair of the world'. As greatly concerned with justice, they can be said to foreshadow Christian Liberation theologies. Many of their liturgical festivals are home- and family-based, and are joyous and earthy celebrations. But salvation history for the Jews is also being constantly reinterpreted, and festivals such as Yom Ha Shoah and Independence Day are shaped by twentieth-century experiences.

A study of Judaism leads one to God as Creator, Revealer and Redeemer but, above all, it leads one to the Living God. Our Catholic heritage, shaped as it has been by high classical theology with little regard for the Old Testament, at least before Vatican II, has left us suspicious of so-called 'anthropomorphisms'. But in the psalms we learn that the Living God is real, is someone to tangle with. We can pray to God, 'the source of all life' (Ps 36:7), with joy and with tears. And it is salutary to remember that it was like this that Jesus prayed to his Father.

Further Reading

Ariel, David, *What Do Jews Believe? The Jewish Faith Examined* (London: Rider, 1995).

Blue, Lionel, *To Heaven With Scribes and Pharisees* (London: Darton, Longman & Todd,1990).

Braybrooke, Marcus, *How to Understand Judaism* (London: SCM, 1995)

Cahill, Thomas, *The Gift of the Jews* (Oxford: Lion Publishing, 1998).

Geffen, Rela, ed., *Celebration and Renewal: Rites of Passage in Judaism* (Philadelphia: Jewish Publication Society, 1993).

Greenberg, Irving, *The Jewish Way: Living the Holydays* (New Jersey: Jason Aaronson, 1988).

Maher, Michael, *Judaism: An Introduction to the Beliefs and Practices of the Jews* (Dublin: Columba Press, 2006).

Pilkington, C. M., *Judaism* (London: Hodder & Stoughton, 1995).

Potok, Chaim, *The Chosen* (New York: Fawcett Crest, 1967) [A novel which tells of the friendship between two boys from very different traditions of Judaism.]

Sacks, Jonathan, *Radical Then, Radical Now: The Legacy of the World's Oldest Religion* (London: Harper Collins, 2000).

Solomon, Norman, *Judaism: A Very Short Introduction* (Oxford: Oxford University Press, 1996).

Strassfeld, Michael, *The Jewish Holidays: A Guide and Commentary* (New York: Harper and Row, 1985).

Wittenberg, Jonathan, *Judaism: A Very Short Introduction* (London: SCM, 1996).

Wylen, Stephen, *Settings of Silver: An Introduction to Judaism* (New York: Paulist Press, 1989).

Zuidema, Willem, *God's Partner: An Encounter with Judaism* (London: SCM, 1987).

NOTES

1. Karl-Josef Kushel, *Abraham, Sign of Hope for Jews, Christians and Muslims* (New York: Continuum, 1995), p. 16.
2. *Ibid.*, p. 25. See Jonathan Sacks, *Radical Then, Radical Now*, p. 57.
3. Cited by Howard Joseph in 'Judaism: The Spirit of Judaism', *Dictionary of Fundamental Theology*, Rene Latourelle, ed. (Mahwah, NJ: Paulist Press, 1994), p. 534–5.
4. Thomas Cahill, *The Gift of the Jews*, p. 162.
5. David Ariel, *What Do Jews Believe?*, p. 115.
6. *Ibid.*, p. 16.
7. *Ibid.*, p. 251.
8. Norman Solomon, *Judaism: A Very Short Introduction*, p. 20.
9. Cf. 'Law, *Halakha*', *A Dictionary of Jewish–Christian Dialogue*, Leon Klenicki and Geoffrey Wigoder, eds. (Mahwah, NJ: Paulist Press, 1995), pp. 77f.
10. John C. Merkle, *Approaching God* (Collegeville, MN: Liturgical Press, 2009) p. 2.
11. *Ibid.*, pp. 49–54.
12. Samuel Dressner, ed., *I Asked for Wonder: A Spiritual Anthology – Abraham Joshua Heschel* (New York: Crossroad Publishing Company, 1998), p. 101.
13. *Ibid.*, p. 90.
14. Abraham Joshua Heschel, *Man's Quest for God: Studies in Prayer and Symbolism* (New York: Charles Scribner's Sons, 1954), p. 95.
15. David Ariel, *What Do Jews Believe?*, p. 183.
16. Joseph B. Soloveitchik, *Halakhic Man* (Philadelphia: Jewish Publication Society, 1983), pp. 9–19, p. 45.
17. Samuel Dressner, ed., pp. 88, 101–2.
18. Abraham Joshua Heschel, *The Sabbath: Its Meaning for Modern Man* (New York: Farrar, Straus and Giroux, 1951), p. 8.
19. Michael Maher, *Judaism*, p. 91.
20. *Ibid.*, p. 92. For a biblical understanding of Passover, I am particularly indebted to Michael Maher (pp. 91–9), and to C. M. Pilkington, *Judaism* (pp. 177–84).
21. Norman Solomon, *Judaism: A Very Short Introduction*, p. 58.
22. Lawrence Kushner, *Repairing the World: Introducing Jewish Spirituality* (London: Darton, Longman & Todd, 2001), pp. 87–8.
23. Irving Greenberg, *The Jewish Way*, p. 115.
24. *Ibid.*, p. 321.
25. Jonathan Sacks, *Radical Then*, p. 136.
26. Abraham Joshua Heschel, *The Sabbath*, p. 83.
27. Irving Greenberg, *The Jewish Way*, p. 136.
28. *Ibid.*, p. 131.
29. Cited in Willem Zuidema, *God's Partner*, p. 93.
30. Norman Solomon, 'Picturing God', *Themes and Issues in Judaism*, Seth D. Kunin, ed. (London: Cassell, 2000), p. 142.
31. Thomas Cahill, *The Gift of the Jews*, p. 109.
32. *Ibid.*, p. 108.
33. Jonathan Sacks, *Radical Then*, p. 183.
34. *Ibid.*, p. 69.
35. *Ibid.*, p. 86.
36. Thomas Cahill, *The Gift of the Jews*, p. 161.

37. Cited in Norman Solomon, 'Meditations on the Spirituality of *Halakha*', *Spirituality and Prayer: Jewish and Christian Understandings*, Leon Klenicki and Gabe Huck, eds. (Mahwah, NJ: Paulist Press, 1983), p. 70.
38. *Ibid.*
39. Louis Jacobs, *The Jewish Religion: A Companion* (Oxford: Oxford University Press, 1995), p. 414.
40. Michael Nutkiewicz, 'Jewish Spirituality', *The New Dictionary of Catholic Spirituality*, M. Downey, ed. (Collegeville, MN: Liturgical Press, 1993), p. 563.
41. Louis Jacobs, *The Jewish Religion*, p. 414, pp. 342–3.
42. *Ibid.*
43. Lawrence Kushner, *Repairing the World: Introducing Jewish Spirituality* (London: Darton, Longman & Todd, 2002), pp. 59–60.

CHAPTER 2

Jewish–Christian Relations

Judaism comprises two separate elements: a nation whose vocation is religious, a religion whose base is national.

MARCEL DUBOIS

Whoever meets Jesus meets Judaism.

POPE JOHN PAUL II

There is an asymmetry about Jewish–Christian dialogue. When reflecting upon Christianity, Christians necessarily encounter Judaism in biblical spirituality and theology. However, the Jew reflecting on his Jewishness does not necessarily need Christianity, and when dialogue does occur, the questions that come to the fore are usually political rather than religious. A Jew can be an authentic Jew without ever thinking about Jesus.

In a 1984 address to the International Council of Christians and Jews, Cardinal Martini likened the break between the Church and the synagogue to a schism.[1] It was the first great schism for Christianity, and like all those through history, it deprived the Church of contributions which could be very important for its health and vitality, thereby producing a lack of balance within the living equilibrium of the Christian community.

Unfortunately, the break with the Jews meant that parts of Christian theology developed as an anti-Jewish polemic, what the famous Jewish historian Jules Isaac called 'the teaching of contempt'.[2] For many years, as we know too well, Jews were portrayed as 'Christ-killers'. This Christian stereotype of the Jew was the primary cause of forced conversions, expulsions and pogroms. Eventually it was assumed that Jews would repent and return to Christ. Judaism also reciprocated the contempt; Christianity was dismissed as a religion practised by morally and culturally inferior Gentiles, based on an unintelligible claim that God had become a man. In such a scenario, truths and beliefs, divorced from history, took on an absolute and exclusive meaning and became batons with which to beat each other. In the opinion of many, it took the great moral and human issues raised by the Holocaust to motivate the Church to look again at 'the teaching of contempt' and face what was prejudicial in its theological assessment of Judaism.

Many concerns clamour for attention when we turn to Catholic–Jewish relations, the main three being the Holocaust and the anti-Judaism and anti-Semitism which contributed to it; the establishment of the state of Israel and its allied theology of the Land, which also calls for a response from the Christian world; and the ecclesial dimension of the dialogue through which the Church recognises that a deeper understanding of its essence will mean a retrieval of the lost and forgotten treasures bequeathed to it by biblical Judaism, among which is the recovery of the Jewishness of Jesus, and through which the Church will also come to appreciate the need to be in dialogue with the complementary voice that is living Judaism today.

THE HOLOCAUST

The Holocaust – *Shoah* in Hebrew, which means 'devastating or consuming wind' – is the event from 1933–45 wherein German Nazis and their collaborators killed more than three quarters of the Jews of Europe. To merely chronicle the rise of Hitler and the Nazis, and their swift success in eliminating the Jews of Eastern Europe, seems all too inadequate given the immensity of what they sought to accomplish. As a campaign of extermination it has been considered unique in the context of other genocidal events, because it was planned and implemented systematically. It was different also because of its 'religious' ideology. As Jewish philosopher Emil Fackenheim has observed, it was an attempt to wipe out the 'divine image' in history.

The roots of the Holocaust reach back into the process of social secularisation that was transforming Germany following on the First World War. Its philosophic parents included the Deists, the French Encyclopaedists, Feuerbach, the Young Hegelians, and evolutionists together with the new generation of scientists who, through their discoveries, left the impression that a triumphant materialistic civilisation was about to dawn in Europe. At its apex was the 'new man' of whom the philosopher Nietzsche had spoken so forcefully in the nineteenth century. The late Israeli historian Uriel Tal has captured the spirit in this way:

> God became man, but not in the theological New Testament sense of the incarnation of the word … or in Paul's understanding of the incarnation of God in Christ … In the new conception, God became man in a political sense as a member of the Aryan race whose highest representative on earth is the Fuhrer.[3]

In pursuit of their objective, the Nazis became convinced that all the 'dregs of humanity' had to be eliminated, or at least their influence on human development significantly curtailed. The Jews fell into this 'dregs' category. Hitler took advantage of the array of economic, social and religious stereotypes of the Jewish people provided by Christian and European history. He portrayed them as demonic to the core, even 'subhuman', 'vermin'; and the only antidote for vermin, he reasoned, was annihilation. So the Holocaust was conceived as the extermination of European Jewry.

The Shoah is an event which reduces all language to silence. Pope John Paul II, a towering figure in Catholic–Jewish relations, came to this question with an inside knowledge. During his historic visit to Yad Vashem in Jerusalem, March 2001, he said:

> In this place of memories, the mind and heart and soul feel an extreme need for silence. Silence in which to remember. Silence in which to make some sense of the memories which come flooding back ... We wish to remember. But we wish to remember for a purpose, namely to ensure that never again will evil prevail. As it did for the millions of innocent victims of Nazism.[4]

In order to draw some meaning from this 'orienting event', we ourselves also wish to remember because the Shoah represents a new era in human self-awareness and human possibility, over which hangs the spectre of either unprecedented destruction or unparalleled hope. For believers in God, it has altered the perception of the relationship between God and humanity: 'How can we speak of God after Auschwitz?' is the question post-Holocaust theologians ask today. Yet the common future of Jews and Christians demands that we remember. As Pope John Paul II said: 'There is no future without memory,' not only the silent pondering in the heart, but also the proactive enlightened remembering in which we non-defensively expose ourselves to facts and awkward questions. Such questions might include: how could the Holocaust have occurred in countries of longstanding Christianisation? And, was there a relationship between Nazi persecution and the anti-Judaism of the Christian tradition?

Anti-Judaism – Anti-Semitism

Edward Flannery, in his pioneering work *The Anguish of the Jews*, gives a working definition of anti-Semitism as constituted by three elements: hatred, contempt and stereotype of the Jew because he is a Jew. He says it should be distinguished from the indiscriminate hostility to which all peoples and groups have been prey, from anti-Judaism as a theological construct and from anti-Jewish manifestations that may lead to anti-Semitism but do not possess the attributes specified above.[5] But in his final chapter, he raises the question to another level and locates hatred of Jews as coming from the challenge that the inner forces of Judaism and the Jewish soul present to humankind. Put simply, Jews have always symbolically represented the demands of a divinely established morality. Historically, this stood in the way of Hitler's racial amoralism and his deification of the German state and *Volk* (the people). This view is supported by Hitler's remarks that conscience is a Jewish invention and that one needs to get the 'thou shalt' and the 'thou shalt not' out of Aryan blood. Flannery, citing Freud, makes a further disturbing observation for Christians: 'In its depths, anti-Judaism is anti-Christianity.' That is, hatred of the Jew is, on the part of rigid Christians, an unconscious hatred of Christ and the demands he makes on us – a hatred which has become displaced on Jews, the kinsman of the Founder.[6]

Another opinion that also probes the Christian conscience comes from the Dominican philosopher Marcel Dubois. Dubois lived and worked closely with Jews at the Hebrew University of Jerusalem. He affirms that our ability to understand the unique character of the Holocaust, and the anti-Judaism and anti-Semitism which contributed to it, is proportionate to the degree of our faith in God's special destiny for the Jews. In short, it was as an elected people that the Jews were rejected.[7]

And so we must ask how the Church, while taking over the Hebrew scriptures as part of revelation, could cut itself off from the people to whom the scriptures were first given. 'It is the ultimate scandal,' writes Edward Flannery, 'that in carrying the burden of God in history the Jewish people did not find in the Christian churches an ally and defender, but one of their most zealous detractors and oppressors.'[8] The reasons for this are theological in the sense that the anti-Judaism of the Church became virtually identical with its classic expression of its own self-understanding as replacing Judaism in the affections of the Holy One. This has been called by the daunting term 'supercessionism' (from the Latin *supersedere*, to sit upon, to preside over, to forebear). The main tenets of supercessionism as found in Christian theology are as follows:

God's revelation in Jesus Christ supersedes the revelation to Israel.
Therefore, the New Testament fulfils the Old Testament.
Christians replace the Jews as God's people.

Judaism is obsolete, its covenant abrogated.

Post-exilic Judaism is legalistic.

The Jews were Christ-killers.

Because they rejected the Christ, they must wander in exile though
they must not be killed.

We need only turn to the medieval artists of the Gothic cathedrals of Europe for
a graphic instance of supercessionism. Juxtaposed on either side of the portals
of many cathedrals are statues of the Synagogue in the physique of a woman,
head bowed, holding a broken staff of the law, with tablets of the commandments
slipping from her fingers, and of the Church – a woman, resplendent, erect and
triumphant. These pairings by medieval artists symbolised the passage of the
covenant from Judaism to Christianity.

While some scholars, such as Flannery, call this 'Christian anti-Semitism',
others use the more theological term 'anti-Judaism' to distinguish Christian
teaching and activities against Jews from more racial forms of prejudice.
Theological anti-Judaism's fundamental themes were first established during
the Patristic period. Examples of anti-Jewish rhetoric are found in the writings
of John Chrysostom (c. 347–407). Even in the context of the times in which he
was writing, his railing against Jews is breathtaking. A passage from his *Oration
Against the Jews* provides a sense of what was being said during that period:

It is because you killed Christ. It is because you stretched out your hand
against the Lord. It is because you shed the precious blood, that there is now
no restoration, no mercy anymore and no defence. Long ago your audacity
was directed against servants, against Moses, Isaiah and Jeremiah. If there
was wickedness then, as yet the worst of all crimes had not been dared. But
now you have eclipsed everything in the past and through your madness
against Christ, you have committed the ultimate transgression. This is why
you are being punished worse now than in the past … If this were not the
case God would not have turned his back on you completely. You who have
sinned against him and are in a state of dishonour and disgrace.[9]

Given his pre-eminence among the Western Fathers, the anti-Jewish polemic
of Augustine (354–430) is noteworthy. He taught that the role of Jews in the
world was to be a negative witness to Christianity. While warning against

Christian violence toward Jews, he did believe that Jews were to live in a state of condemnation and misery, and that Jewish existence was one of exile from God, the Messiah and the land:

> The Church admits and avows the Jewish people to be cursed because after killing Christ they continue to till the ground of the earthly circumcision, an earthly Passover ... In this way, the Jewish people, like Cain, continue tilling the ground, in the carnal observance of the Law, which does not yield to them its strength because they do not perceive in it the grace of Christ.[10]

Reference to the anti-Judaism of the Fathers must, however, be accompanied by two qualifications. First, these violent confrontational passages must be seen in context of the hostility of Jewish missionary activity in those years (Chrysostom especially was addressing himself to Jewish Christians who continued to participate in Jewish religious life). Second, one has to acknowledge that the rhetorical style of the day was passionate and heated by today's standards.

Yet, we also know from history that the Jewish people, through the centuries, have been marginalised and rendered socially miserable by the teaching, preaching and catechesis of the Church, and by the structures devised to protect unqualified supercessionist doctrines. The overriding themes of supercessionism have been triumphalism and the deicide charge. Triumphalism is endemic in all religions, and one has to give an affirmative response to the German political theologian Johannes B. Metz, who, reflecting on the Holocaust, puts this question to Christians today:

> Does there break through within Christianity again and again, a dangerous triumphalism connected with saving history, something the Jews above all had to suffer from in a special way?[11]

It is such triumphalism, born as it is of a sense of our possession of the Divine Mystery and of our sole right to protect it, that lead to the 'deicide charge' that, over time, was to assume demonic proportions and become an ideological stance in relation to the Jewish people. In Flannery's view, the deicide charge was 'the theological construct that provided the cornerstone of Christian anti-Semitism and laid the foundation upon which all subsequent anti-Semitisms would in one way or another build.'[12] However, in light of the Holocaust, a more modern sensibility that takes responsibility for the fact that our human sinfulness contributes to the death of Jesus will ask, 'Is not the Christ-God whom the Jews "killed" also the same Christ-God against whom we have all sinned?' Aided by a more subtle theology of God's redemptive relationship to sinful human beings, Christians have already been responding to this question. The Holocaust, having ruptured once and for all the literalness of our presumptions about the divine mystery and how we relate to God, has destroyed the foundations for religious triumphalism and exclusivism, and has forbidden us to continue speaking of God in ways that forget the other.

Suffering Unto God

There is a famous rabbinical tale in which a master asks his disciples if they love him. 'Of course,' they reply. 'Then what hurts me?' he asks. 'If you loved me,' the master concludes, 'you would know what hurts me.' What the master is saying is that we must not cloak our relationship with the other in ideology, such as a concern for power or status. Our relationship is real only if it is a moral relationship, addressing the other's need in a response of love.

A spectrum of Jewish thinkers have responded to the Holocaust. For some, the Shoah has buried any possibility of continued belief in a covenantal God and in the role of Torah observance. Jews must turn to a healthy paganism; they must live human existence as a totally earthly one, finding their security only in the possession of the Land of Israel. But for others, mainly the traditional, pious Orthodox who remain under the mantle of classical theism, the Holocaust is seen as divine punishment for sin. The problem with both these views, according to the centrist theologian Rabbi Irving Greenberg, is that in overtly attempting to explain the Holocaust, they are, without knowing it, prone to ideology.

To avoid ideology, any theological interpretation of the Holocaust cannot be handled at a purely theoretical level. 'No statement theological or otherwise,' writes Greenberg, 'should be made that would not be credible in the presence of burning children.'[13] Therefore the Shoah not only morally challenges our language about God; it also challenges faith. By this, Greenberg means faith becomes 'a moment faith'. It becomes a faith experienced intermittently, sometimes in moments of present redemption, and sometimes blotted out by the always-to-be-remembered possibility of the depths of irredemption, of which we are capable.[14]

Greenberg also reminds us that since the Holocaust we have entered into a period of theological silence about God, a silence that corresponds to the divine silence. In this silence, God is no longer the *deus ex machina* – the 'commanding', all-powerful intervening God of the Hebrew Bible – but rather a presence in hope. It is in the presence of this God that we learn to live in faith without answers to the many irreconcilables the historical experience of the Shoah has thrown up. Catholic theologian Johannes B. Metz argues for the same nescience and humility in our language about God. Our faith has to be in a real, though silent Presence/Absence. He uses the oft-cited text from the Holocaust survivor, writer and artist Elie Wiesel to explain his point. Wiesel describes the hanging of three prisoners in the camp at Auschwitz, one of them a child:

> The camp commanders refused to serve as hangmen. Three SS men took over the job. Three necks were put into three nooses within a short moment. 'Long live freedom,' shouted the grown-ups. But the child said nothing. 'Where is God? Where is he?' said someone behind me. The three chairs were tipping over … the child was lighter and was still living … Behind me I heard the same man ask: 'Where is God now?' And behind me I heard an answering voice: 'Where is he? Here he is – he hangs on the gallows.'[15]

Responding to the questions recounted by Wiesel – Who is God? Where is God? – Metz asks who, if anyone, has the right to answer these questions but the Jew, 'the Jew imprisoned together with his God in the abyss'.[16] Christians can no longer speak of God with their backs to Auschwitz. A language about God in line with the platonic and disengaged scheme of things that Christian theology can sometimes be has become inadequate. Since the Holocaust, the Jewish people have emerged in our lives as a 'dangerous memory'. They call into question our tightly sealed-up ways of linguistic identification in favour of a more subject-centred language that does not allow us to forget the other. In this we are returned to the moral language of biblical prophecy. Not a triumphalist language, because it is not shaped by victories, successes or superiorities, but rather by the negativities and irreconcilables of history. Like biblical language, it is eschatological and temporal. Eschatological, in that it knows no final explanations, only explanations that come at the end: 'God is the end that brings to an end.' Temporal, in that our base for 'naming' God is historical consciousness – the faith moments, the non-faith moments, the presence, the absence, our knowledge of God becoming an open journey, a remembering as well as a hope for the future.[17]

Out of the Jewish tradition, Abraham Heschel has been one voice for such a prophetic understanding of God. Moving to a teaching post in the United States in 1939, he escaped the horrors of Nazi Germany. Heschel referred to himself as 'a brand plucked from the fire of an altar of Satan'.[18] He bemoaned the immensity of what was consumed in that event: millions of human lives, the divine image of God in the human, faith in God's justice and compassion; in short, the obliteration of a whole God-consciousness. His core teaching on the *pathos* of God attempted to restore this God-consciousness. Heschel recovered this theology of divine *pathos* from the biblical prophetic tradition and from the Hasidic writings of his forebears. In the light of the Holocaust, an omnipotent dominant God no longer speaks, whether this God is the commanding God of the Bible who acts on behalf of Israel, or the Unmoved Mover of classical metaphysics and Christian theology. For Heschel, the idea of divine omnipotence is not a Jewish idea. The very fact that we human beings are historical creatures means that God's involvement with us must be historical, entailing a dynamic relationship of call and response on both sides. Not only is God involved in history, there is history in God. This does not mean that the divine essence changes but that God's mode of being in relation to the world changes. God takes risks. Heschel says if we could stop thinking of omnipotence as an attribute of God we would free ourselves to appreciate the true mark of divinity: infinite compassion, which he variously speaks of as divine *pathos* or the engaged concern of the Creator for his creatures. But while God's mercy in itself is too great to allow the innocent to suffer, there are forces in the world that can interfere with it. And God is at their mercy. In a striking phrase, he says God is waiting for us to redeem the world. His need is a self-imposed concern, a concern to make us partners with him in the divine enterprise.[19]

We find the same idea – that the vulnerability of divine presence makes space for us to 'stand up and be with God' – in the writings of the Lutheran pastor Dietrich Bonhoeffer. While in prison, before he was executed by the Nazi regime, Bonhoeffer probed such questions as our relationship to God and the realities of suffering and evil. His writings have inspired many. One of his main prison insights was that 'only a suffering God can help'. A 'suffering God' helps us to shed the *deus ex machina* God, helps us to wake up to a more ethical and responsible way of being with the Creator in the world, helps us to grieve with God.[20]

We Remember

The long-awaited response of the Catholic Church to the Holocaust, initiated by Pope John Paul II, was published in March 1998: *We Remember: A Reflection on the Shoah*.[21] More direct than previous Vatican statements, it brings the challenge of the Holocaust to the heart of Catholic theology. One notes that priority must be given to historical remembrance: 'The common future of Jews and Christians demands that we remember, "for there is no future without memory" (John Paul II). History itself is *memoria futuri*.' Firstly, the implication is that an authentic approach must grapple with the facts, for to know the facts is to be moved to change in our search for universal meanings. Secondly, there is acknowledgement of the particularly Jewish reality of the event. The document does this by use of the Hebrew Shoah, which in its Jewishness can never be expropriated for other tragic events. Thirdly, the document is forthright as a statement of repentance for the Church's part in a 'tormented' history of relations in which the different was penalised. And finally, there is a strong statement of resolve, of the need to take responsibility with regard to our relations with the Jewish people, in which the 'never again' of John Paul II is reiterated. We remember in order to care for the future. But we must also ground Shoah remembrance in the renewed memory of our special relation to the Jews, and in study and exchange that will dispel mutual ignorance of each other's traditions.

There have been lively responses to *We Remember*. One positive response from Jewish critics is that the document renders impossible the obscenity of Shoah denial among Catholics. However, for Jews also, *We Remember* does not sufficiently address the question of how the Holocaust could have occurred in European countries of long-standing Christianisation.[22] It is accepted by most critics that there is a distinction between theological anti-Judaism and the racial anti-Semitism of the Nazi regime, and that one is not the other. But in terms of their emergence in history, the distinction is not so clear cut. This has been the main critique of the Catholic Holocaust scholar John Pawlikowski, who insists that there is also an in-between reality – a Christian anti-Semitism – which, in its theology, catechesis and preaching, marginalised Jews:

> I like to speak of a classical Christian anti-Semitism providing an indispensable 'seedbed' for Nazism. And the Nazi ideologues themselves recognised the connection by utilising Catholic-based cultural entities such as the Oberammergau passion play in its earlier versions in promoting their ideology among the masses.[23]

Thus, accepting that Nazi ideology is a quantum leap and as such not a Christian phenomenon, Pawlikowski, who has been a significant presence in Catholic–

Jewish relations, considers that *We Remember* does a disservice to our relations with Jews in giving the impression that the Church's historical anti-Judaism played no role whatever in the success of Nazism.

Yet *We Remember* is offered as a true act of repentance (*teshuva*). Repentance is more than apology. Apology is directed to people whom we have harmed; it admits that we should have done otherwise in the past. Repentance is directed to the human conscience before God and includes a resolution and amendment for the future. Humanly we are reluctant to repent. When reminded of something like the Shoah, we say, 'I did not do it', 'I was not there', 'Why should I repent?' But repentance is about human sinfulness with which we are all in solidarity. It is this solidarity that the document articulates when it places emphasis on memory and the awareness of who we are in history. It is this awareness that we must allow into consciousness to shape our theology, so that the unspeakable iniquity of the Shoah will never happen again.

It is also heartening to learn that a significant number of Jewish scholars and rabbis have expressed trust in the Catholic declaration of repentance. One sees this in *Dabru Emet* ('Speak the Truth'), in which a group of 170 North American Jewish scholars stated in a full-page advertisement in *The New York Times* on 10 September 2000 that there has been an unprecedented shift for the better in Jewish–Catholic relations. The following is an extract from their statement:

Nazism was not a Christian phenomenon. Without the long history of Christian anti-Judaism and Christian violence against Jews, Nazi ideology could not have taken hold nor could it have been carried out. Too many Christians participated in, or were sympathetic to, Nazi atrocities against Jews. Other Christians did not protest sufficiently against these activities. But Nazism itself was not an inevitable outcome of Christianity. If the Nazi extermination of the Jews had been fully successful, it would have turned its murderous rage more directly to Christians. We recognise with gratitude those Christians who risked or sacrificed their lives to save Jews during the Nazi regime. With that in mind we encourage the recent efforts in Christian theology to repudiate unequivocally contempt of Judaism and the Jewish people. We applaud those people who reject this teaching of contempt, and we do not blame them for the sins committed by their ancestors.[24]

Dabru Emet warmly says 'yes' to the Catholic statement of repentance and the myriad expressions of it at local level in the life of the Church: 'We believe you mean it. There are more steps to be taken. Let us take them together.'[25]

THE LAND: *ERETZ YISRAEL*

For Jews, the land tradition and the state of Israel ranks as first priority in any interfaith discussion. While anti-Semitism continues to be uncomfortable for Jews, anti-Zionism is seen as a thrust against their very existence as a people. If we are to let the Jews define themselves, we will find that the question of the land, though secondary to redemptive peoplehood (*am yisrael*), is essential to their redemptive vocation. A Jewish scholar addressing a Christian audience several years ago said: 'For us Jews, Israel is our Jesus.' The issue of the land is complicated by many factors – the liberal Zionist movement, the militarism of the state of Israel and the merging of secularity and religion in the state's identity. Jewish faith has always held that its covenant with God was a landed one, and when Vatican II (1965) attested to the ongoing validity of this covenant, it also implicitly acknowledged the importance of the Land for the Jews.

Eretz Yisrael – the Land of Israel – has several formative moments: the original promise of the Land to Abraham and his seed through Isaac (Gn 17:7-8); the promise of the Land to the Jewish people as a whole (Deut 30:3-5); the conquest of the Holy Land by Joshua; then the conquest by King David; and, finally, the resettlement in the Land after the first exile under Ezra. It is important to note that while the promise is eternal, the actual boundaries vary through history.

Since 'peoplehood' is primary, Jewish faith can, and does, survive in diaspora. Yet, in diaspora existence it is considered that Judaism simply makes time or holds the fort in truncated fashion. Truncated, because in Jewish biblical faith *eretz* is a person, a female partner, a bride who plays a real role in the biblical drama alongside God, the people and the nations. *Eretz* is not earned. She is a gift from God to Israel. God gives the land but can also take it away at his pleasure. Exile is not without meaning. It is punishment for Jewish sins, and it is also atonement for the sins of others. Many of the Torah *mitzvot*, such as the commandment to let the land lie fallow every seventh year, are operable only within the land of Israel. Even for diaspora Jews, the festivals, prayers, laws and practices relate to the geography and climate of the country. In fact, the very existence of Israel keeps the diaspora community aware of its Jewish identity and prevents it from total assimilation into the non-Jewish world. And the Passover *seder* meal closes each year with the refrain: 'Next year in Jerusalem.

How Jews See the State of Israel

The question remains, however, of how Jews see the state of Israel today. Firstly, there is the extreme orthodox tradition imbued with longing for the coming of the ultimate Messiah-Redeemer. These Jews see the present 'secular' state of Israel as founded by human beings and not by God, and as an irrelevance and distraction from the true 'things of the end of time'.

Secondly, there is the secular stream (glibly referred to as the Jews of Tel Aviv), which in principle rejects the religious outlook and looks on Israel as on par with any other national state. This view is a flowering of an aspect of Zionism. Nineteenth-century Zionism, originating in Eastern Europe, believed that the Jews were primarily a nation. It promoted the return of Jews to Palestine (Zion – the poetic name for Jerusalem), in order to restore their status as a nation among the nations of the world. Zionism is a mixed blessing for Jewish living, and Jewish thinkers are ambivalent about it. It has been at the root of the longstanding Israeli–Palestinian conflict, which some say has created Arab resentment toward the West and fuels radical Islamic terrorism. Nevertheless, the philosopher Martin Buber has written that the establishment of the state of Israel has been a unique opportunity for the Jewish people to nurture and develop its own singular life and destiny:

> ... to simply leave the worldliness of politics to the Christians or to any other group of non-Jews ... is an invitation to be dominated and thus a threat to the very physical survival of the Jews themselves. The near destruction of all European Jewry in the middle of this century readily testifies to that.[26]

Thirdly, there is what is called 'the Judaism of Jerusalem', espoused and developed by Rabbi Abraham Kook (1865–1935), the first Chief Rabbi of Palestine in modern times. In this view, the present state of Israel may be deemed imperfect (though no more so than any other nation or state), but is yet a 'commencement of redemption', a God-given move in history to bring about universal peace for all people, a move in which Jews are privileged, indeed destined, to take part by working individually to ensure that the state is guided by the values and teachings of the Torah.

Fourthly, whether the state of Israel is viewed as totally secular or as a secular-religious entity, for many Jews today it exists because of the command to survive as a people. In the aftermath of the Holocaust, old ways of thinking were shattered for Jews. The idea of divine intervention in human history on behalf of those in danger, and on behalf of God's chosen people, was shattered by the Shoah. Human beings must take charge of their lives – politically as well as spiritually. Survival is the 614th *mitzvat*. The Land of Israel is a place of their own to go to in a world that can still seem hostile to Jews. For Christians to dismiss these fears as misplaced is to commit the worst mistake one can make in dialogue – to not take the concerns and fears of the other partner seriously.

The Church and the State of Israel

The establishment of the state of Israel is a call to Christians to stop seeing Jews from a theological perspective only. In the past, 'wandering' was seen as a divine punishment – the 'wandering Jew' a providential instrument of warning to educate humanity on the effects of unfaithfulness to God's covenant. While this 'perpetual wandering' theology has now been largely discredited, it is vital for Christians to know how influential it has been in shaping the Church's outlook. A telling episode occurred in 1904, when Theodor Herzl, father of modern Zionism, succeeded in obtaining an audience with Pope Pius X to explain to him the objectives of the new movement. According to Herzl's account, the Pope's reaction was unequivocal:

> The Jews have not recognised Our Lord, therefore we cannot recognise the Jewish people. It is not pleasant to see the Turks in possession of our Holy Places but we have to put up with it; but we could not possibly support the Jews in the acquisition of the Holy Places. If you come to Palestine and settle your people there, we shall have churches and priests ready to baptise all of you.[27]

Though definitely on the wane, this theology raised its head once again in 1948, in the Vatican's decision not to recognise the new state of Israel. The unofficial literary organ of the Vatican, *Osservatore Romano*, contained the following: 'Modern Zionism is not an authentic heir of biblical Israel, but constitutes a lay state. This is why the Holy Land and its sacred places belong to Christianity, the veritable Israel.'[28] It seems as if the loss of the land and the destruction of the Temple in 70 CE were seen as a divine judgement on the Jewish people. Having no validity in themselves, their continued existence was a witness to their own iniquity to the truth and flourishing of Christian faith.

Only in publications following the Vatican Council do we find truly positive attitudes to Israel. The very tone of the seminal 1965 document of the Council

– *Nostra Aetate*: The Declaration on the Relationship of the Church to Non-Christian Religions – constituted a breakthrough. But it made no reference to the land. However, it was followed by two texts concerned with application – *Guidelines* (1974) and *Notes* (1985) – and both documents acknowledge that the history of Israel as a people did not end in 70 CE.[29] *Notes* goes on to understand post-New Testament Jewish history to be an extension of biblical history, and acknowledges the integrity of Judaism as a 'saving witness in its own right in and for the world'. Here, the diaspora is interpreted in positive fashion as Israel's ongoing mission in the world, a mission which is a gift of the covenantal God to all peoples.

This sense of ongoing Jewish history as sacred history showed an openness to the reality of the return of the Jews to the state of Israel. And although official recognition of the state did not occur until 1993, when ambassadors were exchanged, the 1985 *Notes* did contribute to clarification of attitudes and policies. *Notes* distinguished between people, the land, and the state of Israel and respected the religious significance Israel had for the Jews as being a matter internal to the Jewish religion. It cautioned against a purely religious fundamentalist view which saw Israel as the literal this-worldly fulfilment of biblical promises. It recognised the validity of the state of Israel in international law – on moral, cultural and political grounds. But *Eretz Yisrael* was not seen as an issue to be treated in isolation. A passage from *Notes* deserves to be cited in full for the overall perspective it gave at that time on how *all* aspects of Catholic–Jewish relations must be considered to progress in necessary relationship to each other:

> The history of Israel did not end in 70 AD (cf. *Guidelines*, II). It continued, especially in a numerous diaspora which allowed Israel to carry to the whole world a witness – often heroic – of its fidelity to the one God and to 'exalt him in the presence of all the living' (Tobit 13:4), while preserving the memory of the land of their forefathers at the heart of their hope (Passover *seder*).
>
> Christians are invited to understand this religious attachment which finds its roots in biblical tradition, without however making their own any particular religious interpretation of this relationship ...
>
> The existence of the state of Israel and its political options should be envisaged not in a perspective which is in itself religious, but in their reference to the common principles of international law.
>
> The permanence of Israel (while so many ancient peoples have disappeared without trace) is an historic fact and a sign to be interpreted

within God's design. We must in any case rid ourselves of the traditional idea of a people punished, preserved as a living argument for Christian apologetic. It remains a chosen people, 'the pure olive on which were grafted the branches of the wild olive which are the Gentiles' … We must remember how much the balance of relations between Jews and Christians over two thousand years has been negative. We must remind ourselves how the permanence is accompanied by a continued spiritual fecundity, in the Rabbinical period, in the Middle Ages, and in modern times, taking its start from a patrimony which we long shared, so much so that 'the faith and religious life of the Jewish people, as they are professed and practised still today, can greatly help us to understand better certain aspects of the life of the Church' (John Paul II).[30]

A Religious Encounter

In conclusion then, it appears that the Church does not primarily relate to the Jewish people by way of political negotiation. It relates by way of religious encounter.[31] But since a religious or faith encounter between Christians and Jews is weighted with the promise and hope of their common biblical tradition, Christians need to be aware of a propensity, on the one hand, to expect too much from the state of Israel, and on the other, to consider its policies and actions beyond criticism. That said, it is by way of religious encounter that Christians relate to the distinctive difference of the importance of the land in Jewish faith. To the Christian no land is holier than another, and while it may be difficult to grasp the Jewish attachment to the land, one must nevertheless respect it. In a way, the concrete covenantal gift of the land may be said to parallel the 'scandalous' claim of Christians that the full and decisive revelation of God has occurred in the person of Jesus of Nazareth. Furthermore, to grasp the partly similar incarnational and earthly quality of Jewish faith is to go some way towards appreciating what return to Israel as a homeland means for the Jewish people. Many theologians, such as Marcel Dubois, see the return to the land as a manifestation of the concern of God for his chosen people and a renewal of their mission in the world. Speaking to Israeli friends in Jerusalem, Dubois had this to say:

Your return to Jerusalem has significance only if you understand and accept all its challenges. To come back to Jerusalem is not only for the Jewish people a matter of regaining the capital of a nation which has finally acquired its territory and independence. To come back to Jerusalem for the Jewish soul, means to assume the spiritual responsibility of a vocation which concerns the entire universe, its unity, its harmony and peace.[32]

In line with the biblical teaching on *Eretz*, many Jewish people aspire to being able to receive Jerusalem as a gift which they hold for the world. Despite the complexities of the Middle Eastern situation and the hostilities between different confessional groups, John Paul II has several times expressed the desire that Jerusalem would be the common hearth where the peoples of the Abrahamic faiths could model a way of living together in peace:

> Jerusalem, called to be a crossroads of peace, cannot continue to be the cause of discord and dispute. I fervently hope that someday circumstances will allow me to go as a pilgrim to that city which is unique in all the world, in order to issue again from there, together with Jewish, Christian and Muslim believers, [the] message of peace.[33]

Also, when John Paul speaks of the holy city becoming 'a sign and instrument of peace and reconciliation', his daring use of sacramental language conveys the Church's belief in the sacredness of the city in its concrete reality, and goes some way towards understanding the 'religious attachment' to the land and Jerusalem for the Jews.[34]

RENEWING THE SPIRITUAL BOND

The publication of *Nostra Aetate* in 1965 was the breakthrough for the Church in Jewish–Christian relations, and the longest tract in the document is on the Jews (par. 4). *Nostra Aetate* owes its genesis to Pope John XXIII; during World War II, Angelo Roncalli (later John XXIII) was the Apostolic Delegate to Turkey and Bulgaria. There he was privy to the terrible sufferings of Jews at the hands of the Nazis. These dramatic experiences moved him to work for Catholic–Jewish relations. Another significant factor was his meeting on 13 June 1960 with French-Jewish historian Jules Isaac. At the end of that meeting, Isaac enquired whether he, with the rest of the Jewish people, might hope for better relations with Catholics. Prophetically, the Pope is said to have replied: 'You have reason for more than a little hope.'[35]

As a declaration on the Jews, the document was originally intended for inclusion in either the *Dogmatic Constitution on the Church*, the *Decree on*

Ecumenism or the *Declaration on Religious Freedom*. But finally, after much political as well as theological discussion, it found its place as a totally new document on interreligious relations. *Nostra Aetate* became a starting place, a direction. Little is programmatically spelt out, but in it one observes a change of course that bears much fruit in subsequent documents, and especially in the addresses of John Paul II – all providing stimulus not only for Christian–Jewish relations but for progress in dialogue generally. The following considerations are the most important:

- In the context of the document as a whole, in which Islam, Hinduism and Buddhism are addressed, par. 4 on the Jews stands out as being the most ecclesial in tone. For it is in searching into her own inner mystery that the Church realises her need for a renewed relationship with the Jewish people.

- Central to *Nostra Aetate* is the notion of 'a spiritual bond' linking the Church with 'Abraham's stock'. The link is at once one of dependence and yet a call to action; and it is a living reality at this moment in time. We note the present tense: 'Nor can she forget that she draws sustenance from the root of that good olive tree onto which have been grafted the wild olive branches of the Gentiles (cf. Rm 11:17-24).' 'Spiritual bond' would become a major theme in John Paul II's addresses – and one he consistently tried to define.

- *Nostra Aetate* speaks positively of the Jewish people 'who have the adoption as sons, and the glory and the covenant and the legislation and the worship and the promises; who have the fathers, and from whom is Christ according to the flesh (Rm 9:4-5).' The Council is innovative here in interpreting St Paul and translating the ambiguous ruling verb *eisin* in the present tense as 'have'. The simple act of translating this verse of the letter to Romans according to the Apostle's evident intent contributes to overturning centuries of anti-Judaic polemic.

- The Church's relations to Jews takes a more subtle and ground-breaking path with the inclusion of the Pauline text, 'Even so the apostle Paul maintains that the Jews remain very dear to God, for the sake of the patriarchs, since God does not take back the gifts he bestowed or the choice he made (Rm 11:28).' The covenant endures today no less than in biblical times. Jews practising Judaism are to be honoured, revered and supported by Christians who need their witness. With this gesture, the Church transcends a theology of replacement; it commits itself to dialogue, to learning from the other as well as proclaiming its own truth.

- *Nostra Aetate* goes on to recommend that this mutuality of understanding and respect be supported also by biblical and theological studies. In this context, it is interesting to note that a reference to 'conversion' of Jews was removed from an earlier version as many Council Fathers felt it was not appropriate in a document striving to establish common goals and interests with Judaism.

It is obvious that the text identifies to an extent with a reference to Paul's struggles to understand the role of his own people Israel in God's saving plan (Rm 11:11-32). As in the Pauline text, there is also an eschatological note in the document:

Together with the prophets and the same apostle, the Church awaits the day, known to God alone, when all people will call on God with one voice and 'serve him shoulder to shoulder' (Soph 3:9; cf. Is 66:23; Ps 65:4; Rm 11:11-32).

In conclusion, while noting as a historical fact that 'certain authorities of the Jews and those who followed their lead pressed for the death of Christ (Jn 19:6)', the document denounces any imposition of collective guilt for the death of Christ on Jews then living or on Jews today. It then goes on to deplore anti-Semitism and all persecutions against all peoples.

One Covenant

Following on from the publication of *Nostra Aetate*, which includes the ground-breaking text of Romans 11:28 on 'the covenant that has not been revoked', much speculation has occurred on the meaning of covenant. Accepting that we no longer speak of 'new' covenant, in the sense of superseding the old, are we to say that God initiated two covenants – one to the Jewish people and the other, a totally new covenant, for Christians? If so, are we to accept that both faiths continue to exist side by side without dependence or relation as different religions? Or is it that, as is commonly held, there is but one revelatory covenant of God to the Jewish people and that Christianity is simply Judaism for the Gentiles? Pursuing the implications of these interpretations is beyond the scope of this book, but we will consider briefly a consensus emerging that more closely reflects the nature of biblical revelation and honours the interrelatedness of both faiths without reducing their differences. Richard Lux represents a Catholic perspective when he concludes: 'there is but one single covenant with two modalities'.[36] Jews and Christians are joined together in the covenant of Sinai which manifests itself in two different but related activities. For the Jews, this 'way' of covenant means walking the Way of Torah as lived and interpreted by the Talmud and the great rabbis through the centuries. For Christians, it means we are born into new life in Jesus, the Christ of the Gentiles; we take on Christ, who is Jesus-the-Jew, as the Way, the Truth and Life (Jn 14:6). Lux adds: 'Jesus-the-Jew's universal mission is to bring the Gentiles to the worship and life of the God of Israel by becoming part of the covenant of Sinai through him.'[37]

Reflecting on covenant in earlier writings, Pope Benedict XVI has this to say:

> There can be no question of setting the Old and New Testaments against each other as two different religions; there is only *one* will of God for men, only one historical activity of God with and for men, though this activity employs interventions that are diverse and even in part contradictory – yet in truth they belong together.[38]

And he goes on to develop more deeply the biblical 'covenant' of Sinai as 'witness' or 'testament' which distinguishes the divine in the Judeo-Christian tradition as *God-in-relationship* (as opposed to the self-enclosed God of philosophy) and as the wholly Other who initiates creative and free acts of love on our behalf.[39] In the light of this unifying dynamic of the divine-human love relation in biblical religion, Benedict implies there can be no separation of Judaism and Christianity. Both faiths are expressions of this dynamic of faith, hope and love in history. But neither can the relationship between them be one of replacement. From the earliest times – with the Fathers – there has been a sense that God's providence must be acknowledged as having given to Israel a particular mission in this 'time of the Gentiles'.[40] Therefore, with the holding together of 'one covenant' *and* 'the covenant never revoked', we have been launched into a 'both-and' way of thinking that characterises Christian–Jewish relations today, a way that has also been the hallmark of Pope John Paul II's writings and speeches.

Pope John Paul II

Catholic–Jewish relations was one of the most important themes of John Paul II's pontificate. He pursued the goals set by John XXIII and continued the process launched by Paul VI and Vatican documents of attempting to redefine ancient theological categories; but John Paul II stands out in that reconciliation with Jews was very much his *personal* agenda. Wherever he travelled, he sought out the

Jewish community and evoked their trust. His warmth and outreach was much appreciated, and in response to an audience with him, a rabbi, quoting a Jewish proverb – 'Words which come from the heart speak to the heart' – is recorded as saying that the Jews too, in response to this Pope, cannot but speak from the heart.[41]

Being Polish and having been a young man during the Second World War, the tragedy of the Shoah loomed large in John Paul's consciousness. He recalls that at least one fourth of the students in his elementary school in Wadowice were Jewish. After he became Pope, he commissioned one of these students, Jerzy Kluger, to bring a letter from him to the citizens of Wadowice for the unveiling of a commemorative plaque at the place where the synagogue had stood, honouring the Jews who had died in the Shoah, including all the members of Kluger's family who had remained in that town. Kluger was a life-long friend of the Pope and served as an unofficial go-between in the negotiations for the recognition of the state of Israel by the Holy See.[42]

In reading the papal addresses, one gets a sense of John Paul II's warmth and how he is in some way existentially and personally ahead of the letter of tradition. Both qualities feature in his tireless quest for reconciliation with Jews. There are certain themes in *Nostra Aetate* and the Vatican documents to which he returns again and again in addresses. They are staple fare for Christian–Jewish dialogue and are worth reiterating.

(i) The special quality of our relationship to Jews: in his historic visit – the first for a Pope – to the Rome synagogue, 13 April 1986, John Paul memorably referred to the Jews present as our 'elder brothers':

> The Jewish religion is not 'extrinsic' to us, but in a certain way is 'intrinsic' to our religion. With Judaism, therefore we have relationship which we do not share with any other religion. You are our dearly beloved brother and, in a certain way, it could be said that you are our elder brothers.[43]

(ii) That our relationship with Jews is a 'spiritual bond' (NA 4): this is something that John Paul probed again and again. In an earlier allocution to the Jewish community in Mainz (1980) he likened it to the relationship between the 'the first and second part' of the Bible.[44] Addressing the Anti-Defamation League of *B'nai B'rith* (1984), he said that the 'respect we speak of is based on the mysterious spiritual link which brings us close together, in Abraham and through Abraham, in God who chose Israel and brought forth the Church from Israel'.[45] Here, there is not the slightest hint of replacement theology, nor of Israel as having exhausted its role with the emergence of the Church. One can agree with the compiler of his speeches, Eugene Fisher's comment that 'the mystery in the Pope's profound vision lies much deeper than any such either/or theological dichotomies can reach' and that it resides in a both/and dialectic and is a way of thinking which he commends for Christian scholars and educators when they speak of Jewish–Christian relations.[46]

(iii) There is a legitimate diversity and yet convergence between the paths of Christians and Jews and, since we are diverse, there is great need for respect for each other's traditions. Recalling *Guidelines*, the Pope says Christians must 'strive to acquire a better knowledge of the basic components of the religious traditions of Judaism: they must strive to learn by what essential traits the Jews define themselves in the light of their own experience'.[47] This means accepting the reality of the doctrinal distinctions that divide us and the difficulties the Jewish soul experiences with the identity of Jesus. Yet deeper than the doctrinal distinctions is the reality of the eschatological convergence of both faiths. Rather than asking who is right, both Christian and Jews meet together 'in a comparable hope, founded on the same promise made to Abraham'. The larger context of their meeting is a both-and place; it lies within the accomplishment of the divine plan, when 'God will be all in all' (1 Cor 15:28). Living in comparable hope does not take from the particular value of being a Christian in the present, nor from the revelatory value of Torah and of Torah observance as an example to the world. In attesting to the eschatological emphasis of both faiths, the Pope, in a gentle and courteous way, is avoiding any triumphalism which might negate the identity of the other.

(iv) In light of this comparable hope, John Paul II calls Jews and Christians to joint action in implementing God's plan in history: such joint action is more than simple 'good neighbourliness'; it is the creation of a society where justice and peace reign, the *shalom* hoped for by the prophets and wise men of Israel. It is the commitment to being a people of faith, to standing 'shoulder to shoulder' in the work of sanctifying the divine name (*kiddush ha-Shem*) in the secularistic climate of our times.

Pope Benedict XVI

Benedict XVI's programme is, in many ways, in continuity with his predecessor's. All the themes are enunciated in his writings and meetings with Jewish representatives: the uniqueness of Judaism among the religions, 'the spiritual bond', the accepted 'divergences of beliefs', the 'eschatological convergence' with Christianity in which Jewish expectation is considered to be not in vain; and during an Auschwitz visit on 28 May 2006, he said, 'I can and must echo [John Paul II's] words: I could not fail to come here. I had to come.' However, he does diverge from the phrase 'elder brothers', opining that it might not be so welcome to Jews, since for them, the 'elder brother', Esau, was also the brother who was rejected. He speaks of the Jews as our 'fathers in the faith', proposing that this designation more clearly illustrates the character of our relationship to each other.[48]

As already referred to, Benedict brings to dialogue the mindset of the precise dogmatic theologian. He is concerned with enunciating and respecting difference, while also raising the question of truth. He models this robust type of dialogue in his book *Jesus of Nazareth,* in which he conducts an exchange with Rabbi Jacob Neusner.[49] Neusner, like Benedict, also places the question of truth unashamedly at the core of interreligious dialogue. Benedict tells us that he enters into Neusner's dialogue with Jesus in order to know Jesus, but also to understand our Jewish brothers better. Two things are happening here. First, he respects how the rabbi's Jewish faith and desire to remain with the 'eternal Israel' does not allow him to assent to the truth that Jesus is God's revelation in person. Second, from a reading of the text, one also sees how the rabbi's belief acts as a foil to the essence of Christian faith – the truth of who Jesus is. Indeed, this is always one of the gifts of interreligious dialogue. From this respectful exchange, one does not get a sense of two truths beside one another competing, or of one truth being superior to the other. It is more a sense of *different* theological truths being given recognition within the fraternal disposition of the partners in dialogue.

Judaism is Christianity's most important relationship theologically, and Benedict XVI honours this with special focus on and respect for the differences that are implied. But sensitivities from memories of past history always lurk near the surface, and these have been aggravated recently within his short pontificate. On 28 May 2006, the Pope visited Auschwitz-Birkenau. In his speech, he said he came as a son of the German people

> … a son of that people over which a ring of criminals rose to power by false promises of future greatness and the recovery of the nation's honour …
> The rulers of the Third Reich wanted to crush the entire Jewish people,

to cancel it from the register of the peoples of the earth ... By destroying Israel, by the Shoah, they ultimately wanted to tear up the taproot of the Christian faith and to replace it with a faith of their own invention ... [50]

Some Jewish representatives felt that Benedict's speech was not sufficiently upfront in acknowledging the overall responsibility of the German people and of the Christian churches for the Shoah, and resented the implied 'Christianisation of the Holocaust'.

The Church's traditional Good Friday prayer had already been reformulated to avoid communicating upfront a desire for the conversion of the Jewish people. However, in July 2008, Pope Benedict issued an edict permitting the re-use of the 1962 Latin Tridentine Mass, a version that included the controversial prayer in its original form. After protests from leaders of the Jewish community, the prayer was amended by Benedict.

There also occurred what is known as the Williamson Affair. On 28 January 2009, the Vatican revoked the excommunication of the Lefebrite Bishop Richard Williamson, seemingly unaware that he had publicly denied that Jews were gassed during the Holocaust. The outcry of Jews provoked the Chief Rabbinate of Israel to sever ties with the Holy See. Bowing to criticism, the Vatican, on 4 February, demanded that Williamson unequivocally distance himself from his remarks. When his subsequent apology was not sufficient, he was not restored to the clerical state. During the Pope's visit to Israel in that same year, his speech at Yad Vashem drew strident criticism from some Jewish commentators: it was felt that he had failed to condemn Christian anti-Semitism and had not sufficiently explained or apologised for the original lifting of the excommunication ban from Bishop Williamson. Some Jewish critics have commented that the Pope has a 'thin ear', and Walter Kasper, president of the council of the Vatican Commission for Religious Relations with Jews, has asked 'When is good good enough?'

Questioned about the Williamson Affair during a 2010 interview, the Pope admitted that from his side and that of his Vatican associates, the practicalities of the case had not been studied and carefully enough prepared, and that he was also very much aware that there exists a certain fragility about Jewish–Christian dialogue which means it can be easily damaged.[51] Yet when it comes to the issue of truth, we find that he does not qualify his statements. For example, in his 1997 interview as Cardinal with Peter Seewald, he had expressed the same opinion about the Holocaust as he did in 2006, that 'Hitler's annihilation of the Jews also had a consciously anti-Christian character', and 'must not be passed over in silence.'[52] As always, Ratzinger the theologian tends to express himself in a totalising and overarching manner in the interests of clarity and the fullness of truth. But it is one thing to do so in a published theological interview and another to use these words on the occasion of a public visit to the Auschwitz-Birkenau camp.

The well-known Vatican correspondent for the *National Catholic Reporter*, John Allen Jr, suggests that Benedict XVI has an agenda of his own in interreligious dialogue and that these gestures were simply those of Benedict and the Church doing what they had to do in our times. Allen sees a number of shifts in Catholic–Jewish relations.[53] Firstly, many of the European pioneers of Catholic–Jewish relations, for whom the living memory of the Holocaust was a powerful motivational force, are passing from the scene. Secondly, a demographic shift is occurring in Catholicism from Europe, and to an extent from North America, which means that Church leadership is coming from regions where pride of place is being given to dialogue with Islam and Asian religions. Thirdly, he suggests that Benedict's own preference for the intercultural dimension of interreligious dialogue, which places the accent on social and political cooperation for justice and peace, may drive Catholic–Jewish ties down the list of concerns. Furthermore, socially and culturally, in terms of population, Islam, Hinduism and Buddhism are now becoming the voices calling for a response.

The Homecoming of Jesus

'Jesus was and always remained a Jew.'[54] Recent collaboration between Jewish and Christian biblical scholars has introduced a new dimension to the quest for the historical Jesus – the Jewishness of Jesus. Not only does this serve to deepen Christian rootedness in 'the good olive tree', but it is a 'homecoming of Jesus', a replacing of the Aryan Christ with our Jewish brother, the rabbi of the gospels.

That he was born, lived and died in the land of Israel during the period that is now called Second Temple Judaism cannot be doubted. As a Palestinian Jew of the first century, we can surmise that, with his family, he would have observed the Torah, paid tithes, kept the Sabbath, attended the synagogue, kept the dietary code, spoke Hebrew and Aramaic – one could go on. Jeshua (his Jewish name) had a Jewish mother, which meant that he looked like other Jews, had dark hair and complexion and was possibly slight in stature. His family home would have been the first natural place in which he was nurtured in the tradition of Torah. Around the age of twelve or thirteen, he would have become 'a son of the commandments' – a coming of age that is marked today by the bar-mitzvah ceremony, in which the young boy is called up to read from the Torah before the assembled congregation in the synagogue. While the formal ceremony was established later than the time of Jesus, the episode of the boy Jesus in the Temple (Lk 2:41-52) raises interesting questions. Was he participating in Torah study with his elders or was there a hint of something like a bar-mitzvah here?

We can also surmise that the *Shema Yisrael,* the central confession of Jewish faith and a regular feature of Temple services (as it is in synagogues today), must have formed Jesus' mind and heart, indeed his physicality and lifestyle. It is worth reciting in full:

Hear, O Israel: The Lord is our God, the Lord alone. You shall love the Lord your God with all your heart, and with all your soul, and with all your might. Keep these words which I am commanding you today in your heart. Recite them to your children and talk about them when you are at home and when you are away, when you lie down and when you rise. Bind them as a sign in your hand, fix them as an emblem on your forehead, and write them on the doorposts of your house and on your gates. (Deut 6:4-9)

In response to the question of the scribe in Mark 12:28 – 'Which is the first of all the commandments?' – Jesus recites the Shema, aligning himself with the dual commitment of the religious Jew to worship the one God and to establish God's kingdom on earth through love of neighbour. We know from the gospels that both these concepts of the Hebrew Bible – the kingdom of God and loving obedience to the will of the Father – dominated his life. And they also find expression in the Lord's Prayer (Lk 11:1-4), which scholars consider today to be markedly Jewish. Jewish categories live on in this prayer – God as Father; the will of God; the hallowing of the name; the kingdom, earthly as well as heavenly; and forgiveness (*teshuva*).[55] As the prayer of the Jew Jesus, the Lord's Prayer is a 'bridge prayer', which every Jew without inner reservation can pray, as happens today in joint Jewish–Christian worship services.

Indeed, the reclamation of many of these ancient Jewish formulae enriches the imagination of Christians regarding the identity of Jesus. A number of famous Jewish scholars, to cite but a few, have contributed in no small way: Jesus was a 'a Jew among Jews' (Leo Baeck); 'a proto-rabbi' (Philip Sigal); 'a Galilean *hasid*

– holy man' (Geza Vermez); 'a good Jew of his time' (David Flusser); 'a Pharisee' (Harvey Falk); 'my elder brother' (Martin Buber); 'a Jew sharing the fate of his people' (Marc Chagall). This last reference is particularly poignant, because it raises the ambiguity of the image of the figure on the cross for Jews. For centuries, the crucifix was hated as an anti-Semitic weapon. But since the Holocaust, Jews, typified by the Russian artist Marc Chagall, have made a link to Jesus, some seeing him as another Jewish victim of oppression.

Christ in the Light of the Holocaust

Christian theologians are taking some of the above images on board in a step towards rethinking the central dogma of Christian faith – who Christ is. But they are also keeping in mind the question that will not go away – how can we speak of Christ after the Holocaust? It seems that two things are to be avoided: (i) a purely classical Christology, which displaces the Jewish people from an ongoing covenantal relation with God; and (ii) a spiritualising of the Holocaust, which sees the suffering of the Jews as somehow their destiny as God's redeeming people, even as Christ figures, in the world. With such statements we are forgetting that Christians were complicit in this suffering. We are also forgetting that, unlike the redemptive event initiated by God in the person of Jesus the Jew, the Holocaust was not a voluntary and free act for Jews, and that it is obscene to praise those who suffered for being passive victims in their tragedy. This 'passivity' and vulnerability is what post-Holocaust Jewish theologians distance themselves from when they advocate the judicious use of human power for the survival of their people. Therefore, a Christology after the Holocaust will destroy any simplistic notions of a commanding, all-powerful God. Through the cross, it will open up the reality of human evil and of divine vulnerability. It will bring to the fore a faith in Jesus that has discipleship at its very core. It will probe more deeply the death of Jesus as the form of God's presence in the world. It will not take refuge in the Figure on the Cross, as if *we* had no part in putting him there. And yet the Christian knows that it was not purely human decisions, whether of the Jewish or Roman authorities (though these gave body to the event), that put Jesus on the cross. The cross was one with his identity as the incarnate Son and revelation of the Father. On that belief, Jews and Christians continue to respectfully differ, and yet they may also find here some hope for communion.

Jesus, God and Incarnation

The Jews who own Jesus as brother have respect *for* his faith as prophet of the one God and as Suffering Servant of Israel and indeed as Rescuer/Redeemer. Christians, however, also have faith *in* Jesus. While accepting that his death was that of a Jewish martyr, Christians believe that in the Calvary event he was the Saviour of the world. In other words, the full significance of his death can only be understood because in him the divine presence was fully incarnate. That Jesus is the Son of God, that he is the divine presence incarnate in history, remains the classic Christian understanding, and it has been acknowledged eloquently by Jews such as Rabbi Samuel Sandmel:

> We [Jews] have not believed that Jesus was the Messiah; we have not been willing to call him Lord; we have not believed that the *Logos* became incarnate as Jesus; we have not believed that Jesus was, or is, the very Godness of God ... we believe that man must make his own atonement, not have atonement wrought for him.[56]

We have seen this difference being acknowledged in the dialogue between Benedict XVI and Rabbi Jacob Neusner. From the Middle Ages, the incarnation was seen as *shittuf* ('association'), the introducing of an element of mingling, by which something is associated with God and thus obscures the clear revelation of the one and only divine reality. (It is interesting to note in passing that Islam also teaches that nothing can be 'associated' with God.) And yet the idea of incarnation is not alien to Judaism. On this, the Orthodox Jewish philosopher, Michael Wyschogrod, says that Israel's God is a God

> who enters into the human world and who, by doing so does not shy away from the parameters of human existence. [God's transcendence always] remains in dialectic tension with the God who lives with Israel in its uncleanness (Lev 16:16), who is the Jew's intimate companion, whether in Solomon's Temple or in the thousands of small prayer rooms ... Thus, Judaism is incarnational – if by incarnational we mean that God enters into the human world, that he appears in specific places, and lives there so that thereby they become holy.[57]

In relation to Christian incarnation, Wyschogrod says there is no basis within the essence of the Jewish idea of God that *a priori* would exclude God's appearing in human form. But where Judaism and Christianity differ is that what Jews believe to be the incarnational destiny of an entire people – being called to serve as the place of God's dwelling – is, in Christianity, attributed to one son of the Jewish people: Yehsua.[58] What this difference is, the Christian can only humbly witness to and be grateful for as a free decision of God. It is not saying that Christian faith is better than Jewish faith, or that it results in greater hope or love – that will be seen only at the end of time. Recalling the salutary advice of the *Guidelines* (1975), we must 'strive to understand the difficulties that arise for the Jewish soul – rightly imbued with an extremely high notion of transcendence – when faced with the mystery of the Incarnate Word'.

Jesus, God and the Torah

And yet, this approximation to an understanding of 'incarnation' in Judaism is in a way a bridge, and an important datum for Christology. It has concrete implications for the humanity of Jesus as the place of revelation. Not only was Jesus physically Jewish, but he was Jewish in his human spirit and imagination, having been formed by the language of the Bible in the home and synagogue celebrations. He was Jewish in his very roots. To deprive him of this concreteness is to treat him like a meteor that falls by chance to earth, and rob him of any connection with a particular human history. The historical characteristics of Israel as a people so shape the identity of the Word made Flesh that to envisage him being born in a different race and culture would empty him of the destiny God had intended for him. That destiny was that in and through him, the gift of the Abrahamic faith would flower for the whole of humanity.

Our Christian faith *in* Jesus connects us to Jewish respect *for* the faith of Jesus. And the fact that Jesus is the one who invites discipleship is something we can share with our Jewish brothers and sisters. When we return Jesus to his 'home' in Judaism, it is amazing what new learnings will occur and how discipleship can be enriched. Coming to love Judaism as an 'elder brother' is to find one's carnal soul strengthened. It is to be exposed first hand to the *living* God of Israel, whose justice rolls like waters. This is important especially for Catholics, for whom the Incarnate Word has traditionally carried the weight of our religious affectivity and yearning. The Father Creator God has been somewhere there in the remote heavens *behind* the Christ, because the Hebrew scriptures' robust language about

God had come to be replaced by the more cerebral language of Greek and Latin culture. Returned to his biblical 'home' in Judaism, Jesus is rescued from being an 'Aryan Jesus'. The God whom he manifests in word and deed is not the God of philosophers only; he is the living God of the Hebrew scriptures. He is the God who in mercy has given Torah to Israel so that in observance of it, Israel would become light to the nations (Is 42:6). Jesus' stance on the Torah, as reconstructed with bits and pieces scattered throughout the gospels, appears rather straightforward. He was a practicing Jew, going to the synagogue on Sabbath (Mk 1:21; 4:16; 13:10) and to Jerusalem on the days of festivals (Lk 2:41f; Mk 11:1f); he wore the ritual fringes on his garment (Mk 6:56; Lk 8:44). But there were times when he broke the Law (as understood by some Pharisees), as in the instance of the dispute concerning the Sabbath (Mk 2:23-28).

In his discussion of this gospel pericope with Rabbi Jacob Neusner, Benedict XVI states that a conventional view of Jesus here as a liberal reformer critiquing an ossified legalism misses the point of the text.[59] Here Jesus speaks with the authority of God – 'I and the Father are one' – and lifts the understanding of Torah to an entirely new level. What he implies is that Torah is of God and identified with God, and that nobody can fully obey it, nor claim merit in any way for doing so (Lk 17:10). Indeed, one can only ask for forgiveness. Only Jesus can obey it fully, who in his oneness with the Father is 'the Torah – as the Word of God in person', 'God's living Torah'.[60] Benedict goes on to make the additional point that Jesus' substitution of himself for Torah, which implies that it is in the adherence to his person that God's will is truly obeyed, was not in any way an abolition of Jewish Law.[61] It was rather a bringing to the fore of the hidden universal intent of God for Israel to be a light to the nations 'that my salvation may reach to the end of the earth' (Is 49:6).

Yet when it comes to dialogue, neither Jew nor Christian should be pressed into affirming the teaching of the other community. As we have seen, one finds this foundational principle observed in the respectful exchange between Benedict XVI and Jacob Neusner. The aim of the conversation, Benedict reminds us, is 'to know Jesus and understand our Jewish brothers better'.[62] In doing so, we find our perspectives broadened and we come to learn yet another language with which we might name Jesus as the Son: 'God's living Torah' or 'Torah in person'. We are also reminded of the gospel truth that 'salvation comes from the Jews' (Jn 4:22) and that when we enter into dialogue with other religions, we will always carry with us this special relationship to Judaism.

SUMMARY

Many factors have contributed to development in the Church's relations with the Jewish people, but this chapter has focussed on three as especially significant:

- The Holocaust, which calls for an acknowledgement of and 'remembering' of the anti-Judaism of the Christian tradition (and to an extent the anti-Semitism spawned by it), and which always stands as a reminder of our human propensity for evil and of our ongoing need for *teshuva* or reconciliation.

- The establishment of the state of Israel with its allied theology of the land, a complex reality of 'a nation whose vocation is religious and a religion whose base is national' and which calls for a Christian response.

- Vatican II. *Nostra Aetate* (1965), *Guidelines* (1974), *Notes* (1985) and the pontificates of John Paul II and currently of Benedict XVI have all been concerned with the special relation of Judaism to the Church, and with retrieving the lost treasures of biblical Judaism. Emphasis has been placed on 'the spiritual bond' (NA 3) between Christians and Jews; on 'the Jewish religion as not extrinsic to us but in a certain way intrinsic to our religion' (John Paul II); on the fact that Jews 'are our elder brothers' (John Paul II) and 'our fathers in the faith' (Benedict XVI); and, above all, that God's covenant with the Jews has never been revoked (NA 3).

Areas of theology, particularly Christology and liturgy, have been enriched by a study of Judaism; and mandatory study is advocated for all Christians, if only to ground certain of our affirmations in relating to Jews today. These include:

- That God's covenant with the Jewish people remains forever.

- That Jesus of Nazareth lived and died as a faithful Jew.

- That the Bible both connects and separates Jews and Christians.

- That Judaism is a living faith, enriched by many centuries of development.

- That Christian worship which teaches contempt for Judaism dishonours God.

- That Christians should not target Jews for conversion.

- That the importance of the land of Israel for the Jewish people must be acknowledged.

- That Christians should work with Jews for the healing of the world.

FURTHER READING

Aitken, James K. and Edward Kessler, eds., *Challenges in Jewish–Christian Relations* (New York: Paulist Press, 2006).

Brooks, Roger, ed., *Unanswered Questions* (Notre Dame, IN: University of Notre Dame Press, 1995).

Catholic International, 13/22 (May 2002) [Special edition dedicated to Jewish–Catholic relations.]

Fisher, Eugene J. and Leon Klenicki, eds., *In Our Time: The Flowering of Jewish-Catholic Dialogue* (Mahwah, NJ: Paulist Press, 1990).

——————, eds., *Spiritual Pilgrimage: Texts on Jews and Judaism 1979–1995* (New York: Crossroad, 1995).

Flannery, Edward, *The Anguish of the Jews: Twenty-Three Centuries of Antisemitism* (Mahwah, NJ: Paulist Press, 1985).

Fleischner, Eva, ed., *Auschwitz: Beginning of a New Era? Reflections on the Holocaust* (Jersey City, NJ: KTAV Publishing, 1977).

Jacobs, Steven L., ed., *Contemporary Christian Responses to the Shoah* (Lanham, ML: University Press of America, 1993).

Klenicki, Leon and Geoffrey Wigoder, eds., *A Dictionary of Jewish–Christian Dialogue* (Mahwah, NJ: Paulist Press, 1984).

Lux, Richard C., *The Jewish People, The Holy Land and State of Israel* (New York: Paulist Press, Stimulus Books, 2010).

Merkle, John C., ed., *Faith Transformed: Christian Encounters with Jews and Judaism* (Collegeville, MN: Liturgical Press, 2003).

O'Hare, Padraic, *The Enduring Covenant* (Valley Forge: Trinity Press International, 1997).

Pawlikowski, John T., *What Are They Saying about Christian–Jewish Relations?* (Mahwah, NJ: Paulist Press, 1980).

Rittner, Carol, S. Smith and I. Steinfeldt, eds., *The Holocaust and the Christian World: Reflection on the Past Challenges for the Future* (London: Kuperard, 2000).

Wigoder, Geoffrey, *Jewish–Christian Relations Since the Second World War* (Manchester: Manchester University Press, 1988).

Willebrands, Cardinal J., *Church and the Jewish People: New Considerations* (Mahwah, NJ: Paulist Press, 1992).

Notes

1. Cited in John Pawlikowski, 'A Theology of Religious Pluralism', *Unanswered Questions*, pp. 155–6.

2. Jules Isaac, *The Teaching of Contempt: Christian Roots of Anti-Semitism*, Claire-Huchet Bishop, ed. (San Diego, CA: Holt, Rinehart and Winston, 1964).

3. Cited in J. Pawlikowski, 'Christian Theological Concerns After the Holocaust', *Visions of the Other: Jewish and Christian Theologians Assess the Dialogue*, Eugene J. Fisher, ed. (Mahwah, NJ: Paulist Press, 1994), pp. 29–30.

4. *Visit to Israel of His Holiness Pope John Paul II: Speeches and Addresses, March 2000* (Jerusalem: Israel Information Centre), p. 14.

5. Edward Flannery, *The Anguish of the Jews*, pp. 4–5. For much of the historical commentary that follows, I am also indebted to Rosemary Ruether, *Faith and Fratricide* (Minneapolis: Winston Press, 1985) and to Mary C. Boys, 'A More Faithful Portrait of Judaism: An Imperative for Christian Educators', *Within Context: Essays on Jews and Judaism in the New Testament*, David P. Efroymson, Eugene Fisher and Leon Klenicki, eds. (Minneapolis: Liturgical Press, 1993).

6. *Ibid.*, p. 287, pp. 292–3.

7. Marcel Dubois, 'Israel and Christian Self-Understanding', *Voices from Jerusalem: Jews and Christians Reflect on the Holy Land*, David Burrell and Yehezkel Landau, eds. (Mahwah, NJ: Paulist Press, 1992), p. 79.

8. Edward Flannery, *The Anguish of the Jews*, p. 295.

9. Rosemary Ruether, *Faith and Fratricide*, p. 146f.

10. Augustine, 'Reply to Faustus the Manichean', cited in Mary C. Boys, 'A More Faithful Portrait', p. 6.

11. Johannes B. Metz, *The Emergent Church* (New York: Crossroad, 1981), p. 24.

12. Edward Flannery, *The Anguish of the Jews*, p. 238.

13. Irving Greenberg, 'Cloud of Smoke, Pillar of Fire: Judaism, Christianity and Modernity after the Holocaust', *Auschwitz: Beginning of a New Era*, Eva Fleischner, ed., p. 23.

14. *Ibid.*, pp. 23–34.

15. Elie Wiesel, *Night: His Record of Childhood in the Deathcamps of Auschwitz and Buchenwald* (New York: Penguin, 1981), pp. 76–7.

16. Johannes-Baptist Metz, 'Facing the Jews: Christian Theology After the Holocaust', *Concilium* (1984), p. 29.

17. Ekkehard Schuster and Reinhold Boschert-Kimming, *Hope Against Hope: Johannes-Baptist Metz and Elie Wiesel Speak Out on the Holocaust* (Mahwah, NJ: Paulist Press, 1999), pp. 12, 42.

18. Cited in John C. Merkle, *Approaching God: The Way of Abraham Joshua Heschel* (Collegeville, MN: Liturgical Press, 2009), p. 7.

19. *Ibid.*, pp. 13–32.

20. Dietrich Bonhoeffer, *Letters and Papers from Prison* (London: SCM Press, 1971), pp. 360–1.

21. Published by Vatican Commission for the Religious Relations with Jews, March 1998.

22. Rabbi Leon Klenicki, cited in *The Holocaust, Never to be Forgotten: Reflections on the Holy See's Document, We Remember*, commentaries by Avery Cardinal Dulles, Rabbi Leon Klenicki (New York: Paulist Press, 2011), pp. 23–45.

23. John Pawlikowski, 'We Remember: Looking Back, Looking Ahead', *The Month* cclxi (Jan 2000), p. 5.

24. *Dabru Emet*, a Jewish statement on Christians and Christianity by more than 200 academic scholars and rabbis that appeared on 10 September 2000 in the *New York Times*. See *Catholic International* (May 2002), pp. 46–7. For commentary, see Edward Kessler, 'Jews Revisit Jesus', *The Tablet* (3 February 2001).

25. *Ibid.*

26. Cited in Robert A. Everett, 'The Land in Jewish-Christian Dialogue', *Introduction to Jewish Christian Relations*, M. Shermis and A. Zannoni, eds. (New York: Paulist Press, 1991), p. 102. Many attempts have been made to broker a two-state solution, involving the creation of an independent Palestinian state and state of Israel (after Israel's established borders in 1948). As recently as 2007 the majority of Israelis and Palestinians have been in favour of this. However significant areas of disagreement continue around borders, security, water rights, control of Jerusalem, Israeli settlements and the return of refugees, which mitigate against the level of trust each side has in the other. Many Jews distance themselves from what is happening in Israel. Some are critical of the treatment of Palestinians. Holocaust survivors ask whether Holocaust rage has still not been expurgated. Thus the conflict generates massive public debate, and there are relatively few forums that inherently maintain an impartial and non-partisan understanding of it (see israelipalestinian.procon.org).

27. From Herzl's diaries cited by Geoffrey Wigoder, *Jewish–Christian Relations Since The Second World War*, p. 75

28. Cited in John Pawlikowski, *What Are They Saying*, p. 120.

29. www.vatican.org. Both documents published in the appendix of Geoffrey Wigoder, pp. 144–59. *Guidelines* (1974) and *Notes* (1985): the publication of these documents is evidence that the decades following *Nostra Aetate* were creative ones in Catholic–Jewish relations. *Guidelines* is addressed to bishops and clergy, with a view to implementing dialogue at a local level. *Notes*, which is more extensively practical, recommends that even in areas where no Jewish communities exist, the exploration of Jewish–Christian relations be pursued, because the Church encounters her own mystery more deeply whenever she turns to reflect on the mystery of Israel. There is also an ecumenical aspect to the dialogue, because the very return of the Church to her origins in Judaism will also contribute to her search for unity in Christ with other Christian churches.

30. *Notes*, vi.25.

31. John Pawlikowski, *What Are They Saying*, p. 111f.

32. Marcel Dubois, 'Israel and Christian Self-Understanding', p. 81.

33. John Paul II, 6 March 1991, cited in *Spiritual Pilgrimage*, Eugene Fisher and Leon Klenicki, eds., p. 144.

34. *Ibid.*, p. xxxiv. Commentary by Eugene Fisher on Pope John Paul II's texts on Jews and Judaism.

35. Michael B. McGarry, '*Nostra Aetate*: The Church's Bond to the Jewish People: Context, Content, Promise', *Jewish–Christian Encounters Over the Centuries: Symbiosis, Prejudice, Holocaust, Dialogue*, Marvin Perry and Frederick M. Schweitzer, eds. (New York: Peter Lang, 1994), p. 391.

36. Richard Lux, *The Jewish People*, p. 39. For biblical commentary on single covenant theory, see Norbert Lofink SJ, *The Covenant Never Revoked: Biblical Reflections on Jewish Christian Dialogue* (New York: Paulist Press, 1991).

37. *Ibid.*, p. 40.

38. Joseph Cardinal Ratzinger, *Many Religions, One Covenant: Israel, The Church and The World* (San Francisco: Ignatius Press, 1998), p. 57.

39. *Ibid.*, p. 75.

40. *Ibid.*, p. 144.

41. Cited in Eugene Fisher and Leon Klenicki, eds., *Spiritual Pilgrimage*, p. 58 on the response of American Rabbi Mordecai Waxman to Pope John Paul II (28 October 1985).

42. John Paul II, *Crossing the Threshold of Hope* (London: Jonathan Cape, 1994), p. 97, p. 98. Cf. Tad Szulc, *Pope John Paul II: The Biography* (New York: Scribner, 1995), p. 69.

43. Eugene Fisher and Leon Klenicki, eds., *Spiritual Pilgrimage*, p. 63.

44. *Ibid.*, p. 15.

45. *Ibid.*, p. 32, p. 35. Commentary by Eugene Fisher.

46. *Ibid.*, p. xxxviii. Commentary by Eugene Fisher.

47. *Ibid.*, p. 5.
48. Benedict XVI, *Light of the World: The Pope, the Church and the Signs of the Times. A Conversation with Peter Seewald* (London: CTS, 2010), p. 82.
49. Joseph Ratzinger/Pope Benedict XVI, *Jesus of Nazareth*, trans. Adrian J. Walker (London: Bloomsbury, 2007), pp. 103–22.
50. www.jewishvirtuallibrary.org.
51. *The Light of the World*, pp. 120–30.
52. Joseph Cardinal Ratzinger, *Salt of the Earth: The Church at the End of the Millennium. Interview with Peter Seewald* (San Francisco: Ignatius Press, 1997), pp. 250–1. As Joseph Corkery points out so well in *Joseph Ratzinger's Theological Ideas: Wise Cautions, Legitimate Hopes* (Dublin: Dominican Publications, 2009), it is Benedict's style to set things clear first, take the fallout and then, in the cut and thrust of the fray, a more honest dialogue will hopefully ensue (p. 101).
53. John L. Allen Jr, *The Future of the Church: How Ten Trends are Revolutionizing the Catholic Church* (London: Doubleday, 2009), pp. 130–2.
54. *Notes*, 12.
55. An example is the *Kaddish* ('sanctification' in Aramaic), a prayer of praise and longing for the establishment of God's kingdom, and the coming of the messiah. Traditionally recited by Jews as a prayer of mourning for deceased parents for eleven months after death. See Michael Maher, *Judaism: An Introduction to the Beliefs and Practices of the Jews* (Dublin: Columba Press, 2006).
56. Cited in Daniel Harrington, 'The Jewishness of Jesus: Facing Some Problems', *Catholic Biblical Quarterly*, 49 (1987), p. 13. See the very readable biblical article by Mary Kelly, 'The Jewishness of Jesus' in *Priests and People*, 11.1 (January 1997), and the more theological issues raised by John Pawlikowski in 'Christology After the Holocaust', *Encounter* 59 (1998), pp. 345–68. See also James Charlesworth, ed., *Jesus' Jewishness: Exploring the Place of Jesus within Early Judaism* (New York: Crossroad, 1997) and Edward Kessler, 'Who is Jesus to the Jews?', *The Tablet* 18.25 (December 2010), pp. 24, 25.
57. Cited in Hans Hermann Henrix, 'Jesus Christ in Jewish–Christian Dialogue', *Theology Digest* 53:2 (Summer 2006), pp. 108–9.
58. *Ibid.*, pp. 109–10.
59. Pope Benedict XVI, *Jesus of Nazareth*, Vol. 1, Adrian Walker, trans. (London: Bloomsbury, 2007), p. 106. See pp. 106–12.
60. *Ibid.*, pp. 110, 169; *A Catholic Catechism* (Dublin: Veritas, 1994), nos. 5577–82. See Andre LaCocque, 'Law, *Halakha*: A Christian View', *A Dictionary of Jewish–Christian Dialogue*, Leon Klenicki and Geoffrey Wigoder, eds. (Mahwah, NJ: Paulist Press, 1995), pp. 120–2; Norbert Lofink, *The Covenant Never Revoked* (Mahwah, NJ: Paulist Press, 1991). More recent studies on this topic can be found in Philip A. Cunningham et al., eds., *Christ Jesus and Jewish People: New Explorations of Theological Relationships* (Michigan: W. B. Eerdmans, 2011).
61. Benedict XVI, *Jesus of Nazareth*, pp. 116–20.
62. *Ibid.*, p. 104.

CHAPTER 3

Islam: The Way of Equilibrium

Muslims consider there is a certain wilfulness and extravagant idealism about Christianity. Whereas Islam is a religion of equilibrium, a faith that is 'middle way' – a more realistic religion for 'forgetful' human beings.

FRITHJOF SCHUON

Religiously speaking, Islam is quite close to Christianity in that, like Judaism, it is related to the biblical faith of Abraham. Philosophically, it is close in that a study of Islam will show that it has absorbed elements of classic Greek thought, and Christians and Muslims today find themselves living and working together in a world which is gradually, if painfully, moving toward unity.

Yet for centuries, the Church has postponed relating to this difficult sibling. From the seventh to fifteenth centuries, the religion of Islam was not taken seriously by the Church. Seen only through Christian eyes and not for itself, it was dismissed as an heretical offshoot of Christianity, reducing the reality of Jesus and simplistically rejecting the Trinitarian mystery. From the sixteenth to the nineteenth centuries, during the Enlightenment and after, religious minority communities such as Jews and Muslims were brought in from the cold. The rational appeal of Islamic monotheism and its esoteric mysticism meant that the religion became an object of study for western scholars. Foremost among these orientalists was the great French Catholic scholar Louis Massignon (1883–1962). Massignon called Islam 'the sword of transcendence'. He believed that Abraham was the common father of Jews, Christians and Muslims, and that Muslims are validly connected to Abraham though Ishmael. A complex man, a man of prayer and action, a thinker and activist, an ordained priest yet exercising his priesthood in secret, a man of great intuitions which were not always well understood, Massignon felt called as a Christian to dedicate his life to the belief that Islam was within the economy of salvation and a place of grace for Muslims. As a result, Christian studies of Islam are greatly indebted to him.[1]

But the obstacles to dialogue are not just doctrinal. So much of the history of Christian–Muslim relations is bedevilled with conflict, and it is true to say that there has existed 'a culture of contempt' on both sides. *Nostra Aetate* shows awareness that reconciliation between Christians and Muslims is not easy. Its section on Islam urges both sides 'to forget the past and to strive sincerely for mutual understanding' (NA 3). It is interesting to note that the ideal of mutuality of relationship between Christians and Jews has, from the beginning, been an ideal for Muslims as part of Qur'anic teaching. The Qur'an calls on Jews and Christians, people of the book, to 'come to an agreement that we will worship none but God, that we will associate none with him and that none of us will set up mortals as gods beside him' (Q 3:64). Therefore, Christians are invited to move positively toward Islam. Some exposure to its beliefs and practice is necessary if we are to recognise the inner beauty of the faith experience which has sustained the House of Islam and continues to do so for 2.1 billion people today. Like all world faiths, Islam has its gifts to offer. As believers in the One God we have much in common with Muslims, and even a simple exposure to aspects of their faith can return us once again to untapped or neglected wells in our own tradition and enlarge our way of being Christian in the world.

In this chapter, we will ask 'What is Islam?' This question will be approached according to three themes, which Muslim thinkers often employ for similar teaching purposes. These themes are based on an authentic *hadith*, or story from the life of Muhammad. The story is, in effect, a summary of Islam. In the *hadith*, Muhammad responds to questions from a mysterious stranger who is the angel Jibril (Gabriel):

One day when we were with God's messenger, a man with very white clothing and very black hair came up to us. No mark of travel was visible on him, and none of us recognised him. Sitting down before the Prophet ... he said, 'Tell me, Muhammad, about submission (*islam*).'
He replied, 'Submission means that you should bear witness that there is no god but God and that Muhammad is God's messenger, that you should perform the ritual prayer, pay the alms tax, fast during Ramadan, and make the pilgrimage to the House if you are able to go there.'
The man said, 'You have spoken the truth ... Now tell me about faith (*iman*).'
He replied, 'Faith means that you have faith in God, his angels, his books, his messengers, and the Last Day, and that you have faith in the measuring

out, both its good and evil.' ...

'Now tell me about doing what is beautiful *(ishan).'*

He replied, 'Doing what is beautiful means that you should worship God as if you see him, for even if you do not see him, he sees you.'[2]

The *hadith* tells us that the three dimensions of Islam are *islam* (surrender), *iman* (faith) and *ishan* (holiness). *Islam* is derived from the root *'salama'* in Arabic and has two meanings, 'surrender' and 'peace'. He who surrenders himself to the 'divine will' gains peace. *Islam* as the first dimension of the religion is this daily surrender through the numerous helps which the religion offers – the Five Pillars and life guided by law *(shariah)* within the community. The very fact that the religion as a whole is also designated as Islam shows its practical thrust. One is a Muslim who acts like a Muslim.

Yet the second dimension, *iman*, or faith, is primary. Derivatives of *iman* occur five times more often in the Qur'an than derivatives of *islam* and often when Muslims speak about their faith, priority is not given to the popular Five Pillars, which non-Muslims usually expect, but to *iman* or creed.

Finally, there is *ishan*, the more subjective aspect of Islam, variously designated as 'beauty', 'righteousness', 'holiness' or simply 'devotion'. *Ishan* is the most attractive and fertile source for Christian–Muslim relations. Long before dialogue was established on a more formal basis between the Christian churches and Islam, there was an interest in the rich treasury of Islamic spiritual writers, the depths of whose search for God still continues to bridge differences between the religions.

Since *iman* is the heart from which everything in Islam springs, we will turn to it first in order to understand how its all-embracing logic governs the worldview of the Muslim.

IMAN: ARTICLES OF FAITH

There are six articles of Muslim faith: Belief in One God; Belief in Angels; Belief in the Prophets; Belief in Revelation; Belief in the Last things; Belief in the Measuring Out (that everything comes from God). These articles express the three foundational principles or 'roots' of Islam. Firstly, there is the great principle of Unity (*Tawhid*), which includes God, Angels and the Measuring Out. Secondly, there is the principle of Prophecy, which includes the line of prophets, including Jesus, leading to Muhammad and the revelation of the Qur'an. And thirdly, there is the principle of Return (to God), of which the doctrine of the Last Things is the manifestation.

As Christians, many articles of this creed may resonate with us, but we can also make a further comparison. As we know, Christianity is an historical religion, which also lays claim to an ahistorical or timeless essence. Jesus is an historical figure. But he is also the Christ, the *Logos*, the Divine Word, the Son who existed from all eternity. Or in current theological terms, we understand Jesus through a high and low Christology. Similarly, we can say there is a high and low Islam.

Islam claims not to be a new religion, but *the* primordial religion, the religion of 'pure faith' of which Abraham is the exemplar. For example, Muslims believe that the Qur'an – *Khitab* ('the Book') – was with God from the beginning. This is 'high Islam', and we will return to this later.

Yet, Islam was an historical and prophetic event which occurred in Arabia in the sixth century AD. The place of its revelation is the book, the Qur'an and its 'mouthpiece', through whom the revelation came about, is the prophet Muhammad. These two 'low' articles of the creed set the stage for the historical origins of Islam.

Belief in Muhammad the Last Prophet

Islam is the quintessential prophetic religion. It teaches that Allah has provided every nation with prophets to bring his message, for it would be unjust of God to require accountability of people if they did not know what was expected of them. Islam is the only biblical religion to affirm the message of *all* God's prophets. The Qur'an is clear on this:

> We believe in God and that which is revealed to us; in what was revealed to
> Abraham, Ishmael, Isaac, Jacob, and the tribes; to Moses and Jesus and the
> other prophets by their Lord. We make no distinction among any of them,
> and to God we have surrendered ourselves. (Q 2:136)

Over twenty-five prophets, Arabic and biblical, are mentioned in the Qur'an, and the six main biblical prophets generally agreed on by Muslim scholars are given honorary titles: Adam the Chosen of Allah, Noah the Preacher of Allah, Abraham the Friend of Allah, Moses the Speaker of Allah, Jesus the Word of Allah and Muhammad the Apostle (*Rasul*) of Allah.

Islam believes that prophets are sent only when there is need for them (such as when the Divine Oneness is challenged) or when previous revelations have become corrupted. 'A time of ignorance' is how the Qur'an describes Arabia before Muhammad's advent. The foremost religious shrine in Arabia, the Ka'aba, had become the centre for idolatry and corrupt trade, and the Bedouin tribes of the surrounding desert found refuge from the harshness of their lives in the placation of *jinns* (demons).

Therefore, sixth-century Arabia was in dire need of deliverance. The deliverance was the Qur'an; its messenger was Muhammad, whose name means 'the highly praised one'. Born around 570 CE, Muhammad was orphaned as a child and raised by his uncle, of whom the Qur'an states: 'Did he not find you an orphan and give you shelter? Did he not find you in error and guide you? Did he not find you poor and enrich you?' (Q 93:6-11).

Even though he was nurtured and protected by his extended family, one might ask if this early instability contributed to Muhammad's deep trust in the stabilising message he was later to receive from the angel Gabriel. It surely became a historical basis for his love for the poor, the orphan, the widow and other helpless victims. As a youth, Muhammad worked on his uncle's caravans, travelling to Northern Arabia and Syria. He was so earnest, dependable and sincere, he earned the nickname *al-Amin*, 'the one who is to be trusted'. Later, he married Khadija, a wealthy business woman for whom he worked. She was fifteen years his senior and his marriage to her lasted twenty-five years, until her death. Even though he travelled much and worked in service of people, Muhammad remained removed from the corrupt society of his time. He was given to solitude and reflection and Muslim scholars have suggested that he may have belonged to the *hanif* ('the pure ones'), a religious group independent of Jews and Christians, who witnessed to a monotheism of which Abraham's God was the prototype.

The record of Muhammad's life tells us that at the age of forty, in a cave on Mount Hira, he was visited by the angel Gabriel, and that with these words the angel chose him to be God's messenger to humankind:

Recite in the name of the Lord who created – created man from clots of blood. Recite! Your Lord is the Most Bountiful One, who by the pen taught man what he did not know. (Q 96:12)

Muhammad was overwhelmed: 'I cannot read or write. How can I do what you command?' was his response. He was to find enduring support in Khadija, who did not doubt for a moment the divine origin of the message entrusted to him. After some time the angel appeared more frequently, confirming for him that he was indeed the Messenger. The revelation which began on that Night of Power, which Muslims celebrate on the 27th of the month of Ramadan, continued over twenty-three years.

During the Meccan years, lasting until 622 CE, Muhammad emerged as a prophet and the mouthpiece of God. Disclaiming any divinity, he said he was only human (Q 41:5), not an innovation among the messengers, only a clear warner (Q 46:9). He did not present himself as a miracle worker, although miracles were attributed to him in later traditions, the Qur'an being the only miracle vouchsafed by God.

The uncompromising monotheism preached by Muhammad was a success, not only religiously, but also socially and politically, since it gave to the disparate tribes of the peninsula a dignity and equality before their powerful Persian and Byzantine neighbours – now they had their religion and their book. Yet this prophetic period of Muhammad was also a time of great suffering and rejection. A percentage of the Meccan community, particularly those led by the merchant Quraysh tribe, turned against him. Restricting worship to one god meant restricting revenues from the commerce in idols around the Ka'aba (see below). Muhammad's insistence on the equality of all persons before God and his call for social justice challenged their self-interest. And his insistence on shifting primary kinship from the tribe to the new community of faith invited ridicule.

The Ka'aba

The Ka'aba has a rich and venerable history. Tradition states that it was the first structure built by a monotheist for the worship of the One God. Some claim it was first built by Adam, but a stronger tradition has Abraham and Ishmael constructing the first Ka'aba circa 2000 BCE (Q 2:125). By Muhammad's time, sixth century CE, this structure had deteriorated into a place for the worship of idols.

The present Ka'aba is about forty feet long, thirty-three feet wide and fifty feet high. It is covered in black cloth with verses from the Qur'an embroidered on it in gold threads. Of particular interest is the black stone set in the eastern corner of the Ka'aba. This stone, about twelve inches in diameter, which a *hadith* explains was a meteorite from heaven, is a relic from the original Ka'aba. It is the focal point for pilgrims as they circumambulate the structure, kissing or acknowledging the stone as they pass. The area around the Ka'aba, including the city of Mecca, is a sacred precinct. It is *haram*; it is forbidden territory for non-Muslims.

Hijra: The flight to Medina

Partly due to ongoing persecution, but primarily because the new community needed to establish itself in a climate of peace where it could practice and legislate for its own needs, Muhammad and one hundred followers migrated in 622 CE to the northern town of Yathrib, later to become known as Medina, the city of the Prophet. The flight to Medina – the Hijra – is regarded by Muslims as the foundation of Islam, and for them 622 CE is year one of the Muslim calendar. The *Daral-Islam* (House of Islam), the Islamic state installed by Muhammad at Medina, inspired Muslims to visit on pilgrimage for centuries. Islam had its formative years, religiously, in that city – the first mosque was built and a rudimentary ritual life, later to become the Five Pillars of faith, was established there. The first call to prayer was heard in Medina. It was given by an offical of the mosque called the muezzin (Arabic *mu'adhdhin*, 'caller'), as still happens today. Under the Prophet's administration, a covenant of friendship was made with the Jews of the city. The doctrinal formulations of Muhammad were to be the basis on which Islamic states would respect the religious liberty of non-Muslims, and also determine the rights and duties of these people within the state.

Muhammad's mission in Arabia was completed when, after a number of battles, he peacefully took over Mecca and rededicated the Ka'aba to Allah. History tells us that in the tenth year of the Hijra, Muhammad undertook his own pilgrimage to Mecca. This symbolic pilgrimage has become the model for the annual *hajj* which Muslims make to that city. On the plain of Arafat, from the hill known as the Mount of Mercy, Muhammad delivered his farewell address: 'This day I have perfected my religion for you and have completed my favour for you. I have chosen Islam to be your faith.' After a few days, he returned to Medina in failing health. The record tells us that he died on 8 June 632 CE, and is buried in that city.

Of all the great religious figures throughout world history, no one has had as many detractors as the Prophet of Islam. Possibly the deepest resentment through the centuries has stemmed from the claim that he was the Seal of the Prophets and that, as the prophet of the Last Religion, he attempted to replace Christ. While this is a major theological difference, there are also minor prejudices that call for a sensitive response from Christians. Distinguished Shi'ite Muslim scholar Seyyed Hossein Nasr sees the problem as arising from the fact that Christians unfavourably compare the Prophet to Christ. The difficulty arises 'from the fact that the spiritual nature of the Prophet is veiled by his human nature, and that his obligations as guide and leader of the human community disguise his specifically spiritual function'.[3] Indeed, Nasr suggests that because of Muhammad's dual functions as Prophet and king, he should be more favourably compared to the prophet-kings of the Old Testament, David and Solomon, and especially to Abraham himself.[4] While the humanity and ordinariness of Muhammad is emphasised in the eyes of many pious Muslims and in the tradition of 'high' Islam, the Prophet is more than ordinary: he is the Primordial Man in the mind of God; he is 'the first of the Muslims' (Q 6:162); he is held to be free of moral fault and the repository of the virtues of all the previous prophets. Nonetheless, in one of the verses of the Qur'an he is told to ask forgiveness for sin (Q 47:21).

One of the most elaborate of these traditions of exaltation of 'high Islam' is based on the qur'anic chapter, the Night Journey:

> Glory be to Him who made His servant to go by night from the Sacred Temple to the farther Temple whose surroundings we have blessed that we might show him some of our signs. He alone hears all and observes. (Q 17:1).

The journey is from the Ka'ba to the Temple Mount in Jerusalem on a fabulous winged beast, and the ascent (al-miraj) to heaven, where he encountered the previous prophets, toured heaven and hell and was introduced into the presence of God. Many Muslims believe the journey involved locomotion but there is a strong non-literal interpretation which regards the Prophet's ascent as a mystical experience. As we have seen, Muslims do not say Muhammad was human and divine. Instead they say he was the perfection of the human and the spiritual, and that he can be profoundly understood only through the *hadith*, and of course the Qur'an, 'which bears the perfume of the soul of the person through whom it was revealed'.[5] Love and reverence for the Prophet is incumbent on Muslims, and mention of his name is always followed by the words 'Blessing and peace of God be on him'.

Belief in the Qur'an

> These are the signs (verses) of the clear Book. We have sent it down as an Arabic Qur'an, so that you might understand. (Q 12:1-2)
> There is no doubt in this Book. (Q 2:2)

The blending of admiration, respect and affection Muslims have felt for Muhammad throughout history is impressive, but they never mistake him for the earthly centre of their faith. This earthly centre is the book (*Khitab*), the Qur'an. *Qur'an* in Arabic means 'recital' and it comes from the first word of the revelation delivered by the Angel Gabriel to Muhammad around 610 CE. Over a period of twenty-three years, from that first moment (celebrated by Muslims as the Night of Power), until he died at Medina, the Prophet continued to receive words of revelation which were recorded by secretaries on whatever was at hand – dried-out palm leaves, pieces of broken pottery, ribs and shoulder bones of sheep, bits of leather and white stones. Within twenty years, under the Caliphate of Uthman (644–56), the Qur'an was canonically established in its present form, with numbering, titling and ordering of chapters added.

Four-fifths of the length of the New Testament, the Qur'an consists of 114 chapters or *surahs*. *Surah* means 'step' or 'gradation', by which the believer ascends closer to Allah. All except the ninth *surah* begin with the words: 'In the Name of Allah the Most Compassionate, the Most Merciful.' Each *surah* is composed of verses, and each verse of the Qur'an is a sign *(ayat)* of God to the Muslim. Islam teaches that the believer is supported by multiple communications or 'signs' from God. They are creation, the believing community, the signs 'within their very selves'. But the 'wondrous sign' is the Qur'an; like the Bible in Christianity, it helps the Muslim to read all other signs of divine presence. It functions as *Al-Dhikr*, 'the bringer-to-mind', educating the receptive human consciousness in the steady remembrance of God and in the imitation of the divine attributes.[6]

However the Qur'an's equation with the Bible needs some qualification. For Christians, the distinguishing object of faith is the person of Jesus Christ. The Bible as Word of God is about Jesus; but the Qur'an is not *about* God, it *is* God's presence in the form of written scripture. While Christians speak of incarnation, Muslims speak analogously of 'inlibration' ('becoming book'). Therefore we might better say that the parallel is between the Qur'an and Jesus. This is also evident in other important points. Both Christians and Muslims have their Holy Nights: Christmas celebrates the 'wonderful exchange' of incarnation, and the Night of Power celebrates the revelation of God in the Qur'an. Furthermore, there is a comparison to be drawn between the so-called illiteracy of Muhammad and the virginal conception of Christ. As a dogma, the virginal conception witnesses to the utter transcendence of the Divine Word, who was born of Mary the Virgin. And it is as a treasured teaching of Islam that the illiteracy of the Prophet witnesses to the transcendent gift of the Qur'an. In other words, the Qur'an is believed to be the earthly facsimile of the uncreated Qur'an, which is the Divine Reality itself. This is high theology and 'high Islam', but it helps us to appreciate why the Qur'an is central to Muslims' faith and can never be looked upon as just an ordinary text.

For this reason, the Qur'an is considered inimitable and untranslatable. The Arabic of the text is considered a divinely chosen language and is integral to revelation. As divinely chosen, it is also considered to be normative and without flaw. Muslims throughout the world must memorise the Arabic text, at least those parts of it that are used in worship. The consequences of this reverence of the text are manifold. For example, it is painful for Muslims to witness certain types of historical criticisms of the Qur'an, some of which plunder the text in order to show up its inferiority in comparison to the Judeo-Christian scriptures. Since these criticisms come from outside their faith, they perceive them as an attack on Muslim identity. While Muslim scholars concede that there is place for such scholarship both within and outside the tradition – and some do practise historical criticism – ultimately they would like the Qur'an to be appreciated as a document of faith and therefore as beyond analysis.

The Qur'an is the Muslim's primary means of encountering God. Its physical presence alone is a source of divine grace or *barakah* (blessing). Therefore, Muslims handle the text with great reverence and approach it only in a state of ritual purity. Since the Arabic language – with its sounds, music and rhythm – are part of revelation and play the same role in Muslim faith as the sacred humanity of Christ does for Christians, the experience of qur'anic recitation is a 'sacramental event'. By making the sounds in Arabic, even without understanding, a Muslim is participating in God's act of speech. God caused these sounds to be made, and reproducing them links the believer to that primal moment of revelation. In a sense, the information the sounds contain is less important than the sacramentality of the sound. A Muslim is someone who immerses themselves in the sound of the Qur'an, the sound of God's speaking. They taste the word; to pronounce the Qur'an devoutly is to have the word on one's tongue and receive it most profoundly. And they see the word, for Muslim artists have dignified the largest mosques, the humbles clay vessels, shrines and portals with verses of the Qur'an in ornate calligraphy, which remind us of the sculptures and iconographic stained glass of Gothic cathedrals like Chartres and Notre Dame.

There are many ritual uses of the Qur'an beyond recitation in prayer and devotion. It is often used as a protective device against evil spirits; for example, verses from it may be written on paper and enclosed in an amulet which is hung around the neck. In social relations, Muslims use phrases and expressions mined from the text. The most common are *insha' Allah* and *masha' Allah*: 'if God wills' and 'what God has willed'. The first refers to the future and expresses the human being's confidence in God's will and the realisation that nothing can be achieved without it. The second, said at the end of an act, reminds us that ultimately whatever occurs comes from God. When someone is asked how his or her health is, the answer is accompanied with *al-hamdu li-llah* – 'Praise be to God'. At the level of personal devotion, the most fundamental formula of the Qur'an is the first *shahadah*, the witness or testimony that God is One: *la ilaha ill' Allah*. It is the phrase first spoken into a child's ear at birth, sung as a refrain by children at school. It is constantly repeated by the Muslim throughout his or her life, because through repetition the Divine Unity centres the human soul; it is the last prayer uttered into the believer's ear at death.

After the *shahadah*, the most oft-used prayer is the *basmalah*, with which each *surah* of the Qur'an, except one, opens, and which translates as: 'In the Name of God the Compassionate and Merciful'. While the *shahadah* clarifies for the Muslim the truth of God's Oneness – 'There is nothing like unto Him' (Q 42:2) – the *basmalah* assures that the divine presence is caring and forgiving, touching individual lives and particular events. Thus the Shi'ite scholar Nasr speaks of the transforming power of the Qur'an: 'not only do the teachings of the Qur'an direct the life of a Muslim, but what is more, the soul of a Muslim is like a mosaic made up of formulae of the Qur'an in which he breathes and lives'.[7]

In response to the westerner's query as to why the Qur'an is so difficult to read, Nasr's response is holistic and experiential, a testimony to the Qur'an as sacrament of divine presence:

> The text of the Qur'an reveals human language crushed by the power of the Divine Word. It is as if human language were scattered into a thousand fragments like a wave scattered into drops against the rocks at sea. One feels through the shattering effect left upon the language ... the power of the Divine from whence it originated.[8]

An orthodox Muslim view such as this is necessary for interreligious dialogue, because it helps us to respect the faith with which the Muslim approaches the Qur'an. However, to the outsider and amateur the text can be daunting. It is broadly divided into two sections. The short Meccan *surahs* from the early part of Muhammad's life witness to his testimony to the One God. The longer Medinan *surahs* variously report on how God guided Muhammad in establishing Islam and on the rights and duties of the Islamic community. Interwoven are references to the Old and New Testaments as earlier revelations, which are not discounted, and in relation to which the Qur'an sees itself as culmination:

> We made a covenant with the Israelites ... and you will attain nothing until you observe the Torah and the gospel and that which is revealed to you from our Lord. (Q 5:70, 68)

> It is He [God] who sent down [revealed] to you the Book, confirming in truth all that preceded it; and before that He sent down the Torah and the gospel as guidance to humankind. (Q 3:3)

Here Jews and Christians are included with Muslims as 'People of the Book'. Nevertheless, for various reasons, Muslims regard the Old and New Testaments as limited in their recording of revelation, and the Qur'an, free from such limitations, is the final and infallible revelation of God's will. Its second chapter begins explicitly: 'This Book is not to be doubted' (Q 2:1). But for the believing Muslim, accepting the Qur'an does not imply a knowledge of all the finer points of the comparison of scriptures. Nor is the Qur'an important to him or her because it tells him everything he needs to know about God and the Path; this can be found in other sacred texts, such as the *hadith* from the life of Muhammad. What distinguishes the Qur'an for the Muslim is that it is the sacrament of the presence of God.

So far, we have explored two articles of the Islamic creed within the principle of 'prophecy' in Muhammad and the Qur'an. We now turn to the more basic governing principle of Unity (*Tawhid*), which includes God, Angels and the Measuring Out.

Belief in the One God

With the first half of the *shahada*, 'There is no deity but God', the testimony prayer-verse from the Qur'an, we are faced with as pure and unvarnished a statement of religious focus as one could imagine. In his telling of the following story from the Qur'an, John Renard, a specialist in Islamic studies, demonstrates that no one exemplifies this dedication better than the prophet Abraham:

One night, the scripture says, Abraham beheld a star and said, 'This is my Lord.' But when the star soon disappeared, he confessed, 'I love not things that set.' When the moon arose Abraham exclaimed, 'This must be my Lord.' But when it, too, set, he said, 'Were not my Lord guiding me, I would surely be among the lost.' And when he saw the sun come up, he said, 'This must indeed be my Lord for it is greater by far.' But when the sun went down, Abraham addressed his father's people: 'Far be it from me to set up partners with God as you do.'[9]

Renard goes on to tell us that in this simple turning to the One God lies the deepest meaning of the terms *islam* and *muslim*. The Arabic root S-L-M carries the connotation of being in that state of wholeness and balance that results from having all of one's relationships and priorities in order. The state is called *salam* (related to the Hebrew *shalom*, or 'peace'). When a person pursues that state in relation to God, it means attributing to God and to nothing else what belongs to God, and that is the root meaning of *islam*. One who achieves a state of propriety in relation to God is a *Muslim*: literally, 'one who brings about the state of *salam* in his or her own life and in the world'.[10]

The source of *salam* in the world is the Divine reality itself – which is God as the Divine Oneness or *Tawhid*. *Tawhid* holds a cluster of meanings, the main three being:

There Can Only be One God
This is what the prophet Muhammad proclaimed in sixth-century Arabia, that 'time of ignorance' before the advent of Islam. Pagan cults, polytheism and the influences of a distorted Judaism and Christianity are what Muhammad reacted to with singular passion and vigour. In fairness it must be said that Allah, which means 'the God' (from the Arabic *il illah*) was not an amalgam of an existing polytheism. Devotion to Allah existed alongside nature gods and goddesses. It was practised by the *hanif*, a tradition of believers independent of Jews and Christians who reflected the monotheism of the *hanif*, Abraham. Muhammad was considered a *hanif* and a follower of this high God of Abraham. To take this high God and proclaim that he was *the* God – *Allah* – the only all-powerful Creator to whom all people were subject, was not only a renewal of Abrahamic faith, it was also a social achievement because through the power of this belief the vast majority of Arabs of the peninsula became a people, a community of Muslims

transcending race and nation. This created a unity and energy which bore fruit after the death of the Prophet in the form of an Islamic civilisation that came to dominate the eastern Mediterranean, Iraq, Iran and India, and was powerfully present in black Africa and South East Asia. In this context, it is helpful to note that the term 'Allah', the Arabic word for the Divine Being, was also used by other Arabic-speaking believers, such as Iraqi Jews and Syrian Christians, and is still used today.

Nothing Can be 'Associated' with God

The sin of *shirk* is the 'association' of anything with God. According to the Qur'an it is the ultimate hardening of heart, the heinous sin which God will not forgive. God does not forgive the worship of others beside him, for whoever does this has gone far, far astray (Q 4:116). Such sin is unforgivable because it is not worthy of God who is without comparison (Q 42:11), nor worthy of the human person whose nature was created to know that 'there is no god but the God'.

The *surah* on Divine Oneness has just one verse: 'God is One, the eternal God. He begot none, nor was he begotten. None is equal to him' (Q 112:1-4). Verses such as the following have a decidedly anti-Christian bias: 'So believe in God and his messengers. And say not trinity. Desist from this. It is better for you. God is but one and only God, far above be he from having a son' (Q 4:171; 5:77). Because God is beyond comparison and nothing can be associated with God, it is a popular Muslim view that Christian prayer in the name of the Trinity and belief in the incarnation compromises beyond repair the Divine oneness.

In traditional Christian polemic against Islam it has usually been assumed that Muhammad's concept of God was formed only as a reaction to the two great biblical religions. But scholars today are telling a different story. The Dominican Islamic scholar, the late Redmond Fitzmaurice, wrote that the early Meccan verses of the Qur'an (e.g. 112:1-4 above) testify that Muhammad's experience and conviction of the utter oneness of God was totally original, overwhelming and personal, and that in the chronologically early sections of the Qur'an, the Prophet's experiences are expressed in striking, vivid images which are quite distinct from the images and language of the Bible. It was only later, with the growing assurance that the revelation he had received was identical with that formerly given to the Jewish and Christian communities, that the revelations began to be expressed in more familiar biblical language, speaking of the Hebrew patriarchs and Jesus as forerunners of the Prophet. Fitzmaurice surmises that

Muhammad must have been aware of the biblical stories of patriarchs and prophets circulating verbally in Arabia in pre-Islamic times (there was no Arabic translation for the Jewish and Christian scriptures before the coming of Islam). Encouraged by these stories, Muhammad approached Jews and Christians with the conviction that there was but one divine revelation and that the revelation given in the Qur'an was in harmony with the Torah and the gospel of Jesus. But later, when he discovered that the Jews and Christians did not accept him as a prophet sent by God to complete the work of revelation, we find the Qur'an reaching back behind both of these traditions to Abraham as preceding Moses and Jesus: 'No, Abraham in truth was not a Jew, neither a Christian, but he was a Muslim and one of pure faith [*hanif*], certainly he was not one of the idolaters' (Q 6:79). And in later *surahs* the critique of pre-Islamic polytheism takes the new form of being a rejection of any doctrine of sonship in God:

> Those who say: 'The Lord of Mercy has begotten a son,' preach a monstrous falsehood, at which the very heavens might crack, the earth break asunder, and the mountains crumble to dust. That they should ascribe a son to the Merciful, when it does not become the Lord of Mercy to beget one! (Q 19:88)[11]

Since one must never be distracted from God, who is at the heart of Islamic faith, no visible representations in places of worship of either Muhammad or 'Friends of God' (saints) are allowed. Although the Arabic word for mosque, *masjid,* means simply 'place of prostration', and that can be anywhere for a believer, Muslims have devoted enormous attention to creating an architecture which expresses this faith of 'non-association'. The Islamic mosque may appear empty to us, but the spaciousness within is not an emptiness to be filled. It is a witness in itself. It aims to evoke the infinite and limitless and places nothing between the believer and the Unseen. Islamic art is abstract, consisting entirely of calligraphic and geometric patterns. The colours used are refined and muted: green, the colour of life and paradise; blue, of the sea, sky and infinity; and gold, the colour of the sun and moon which represent the Divine Light and intellectual knowledge. And while the dome, which is Christian in origin, symbolises the divine plenitude of grace falling on believers and evokes peace and submission, the very Islamic minaret leaps audaciously to the sky and actively attests to the Divine Unity with which nothing can be associated.

Divine Unity is the thrust of the most well-known exclamation, *Allahu Akbar*, 'God is Greater'. Unfortunately, we associate it with being the rallying cry of militaristic groups, but its deeper religious meaning is that one does not even entertain a 'greater *than*'. Rather, one is moving into a space, the Unseen, the Unutterable in which all association stops. What has been considered the greatest praise of Muhammad – that 'he did not grudge the Unseen' – is the acknowledgement of his pure faith. But the Prophet also had a great knowledge of human nature. A story from his life tells us that the *shirk* – the sin of 'association' – he most feared for his followers was not the worship of false gods, but the caprice of the human heart which led people into attachments other than God.

Tawhid as Divine Oneness Overflows to Bring about Unity in All Things
Allah is 'Lord of the Worlds'. Through the divine will and law, Allah touches *all* aspects of creation, personal and family life, worship, government, the arts, architecture and politics. The divine will for the world is unity and peace, which God brings about through the cooperation of human beings. They are God's *caliphs* or vice-regents, and together with him they create the House of Islam which has been their destiny from the beginning of time.

Here we return briefly to 'high' Islam, the ahistorical, primordial and original religion given in the creation of Adam by God to humankind. Adam is considered to be the first prophet of Islam. Through him God made a covenant with human beings, inviting them to distinguish themselves from nature by witnessing that God is the Lord, and to come forward and be his vice-regents on earth:

> Your Lord brought forth descendents from the loins of Adam's children,
> and made them testify against themselves. He said: 'Am I not your Lord?'
> They replied: 'We bear witness that You are.' This He did lest you say on
> the day of Resurrection: 'We had no knowledge of that.' (Q 7:171)

In light of this text, we can agree with Nasr that all human beings are, by virtue of being created, called to a free surrender to God – to be *muslim*.[12] What distinguishes the Muslim community is that it is a particular historic expression of this call, guided by the Qur'an and the Prophet.

The Two Hands of God – Majestic and Near
Islam has Ninety-Nine Beautiful Names of God. They may be broadly divided into those which evoke majesty and awe-inspiring power and those which

express an awareness of God's beauty and approachability. Or alternatively, they symbolise the Godly characteristics of transcendence and immanence, which the tradition calls 'the two hands of God'.

While the more historical Judeo-Christian tradition in which God is both Creator and Redeemer focuses on the Creator's saving action in human history, in the Qur'an, God is Creator only, and divine communication is experienced, with the aid of the Qur'an, through the signs in creation and within human nature:

> In the creation of the heavens and earth, and in the alternation of night and day, there are signs for men of sense; those that remember God when standing, sitting, and lying down, and reflect on the creation of the heavens and earth, saying: 'Lord, You have not created this in vain. Glory be to You! Save us from the torment of the fire.' (Q 3:188-191)

All is given in what Muslims call the Trust (Q 7:171) between God and human beings at the beginning of creation. God and human beings are tightly bonded together in a din al-Fitr – a religion of nature. Islam teaches that we have been gifted with a theomorphic nature from the beginning – we are in the image of God – which enables us to act out the primordial trust and witness to God and respond to his call. Here we come up against a language of divine mystery which is very different from that of the Christian tradition. The mystery of God for the Muslim is witnessed through heartfelt utterances before the divine majesty, such as 'God is Greater', or 'Nothing is like him'. There is a sense that God does not need to reveal Godself to the Muslim, because God is 'clear', just as the Qur'an is the 'clear book' (Q 12:1-2). It is we who are in a state of unclarity. We are veiled from God because of the sin of forgetfulness (gaflah), a human weakness or distractedness in which we fail to remember who we are. Divine communication in revelation, therefore, is not a communication of the divine life as saving mystery in human history as it is in the Christian tradition. It is rather a merciful gift of instruction to 'forgetful' human beings. The Qur'an is the great reminder. Its purpose as revelation is to draw human beings into clarity and bring them back from forgetfulness to pure faith. Pure faith is a right and proper assent of the intelligence to the nature of things – that 'there is no God but God' – and to a standing in who one is from the beginning – a muslim before God.

As sourced in God the Creator, it is fair to say that Islam generally prefers abstract images and phrases to evoke divine transcendence – Allah's ineffable distance – over the divine as mystery, which is considered vague to Muslim ears. One highly instructive phrase, fascinating to westerners because it has such Middle Eastern flavour, is the Divine Ruse. The Qur'an refers to God as 'best of those who devise schemes' (Q 3:47, 8:30) to indicate that no human being can tell the mind of God and are better off not trying to second-guess the Creator as, ultimately, he will outwit them. In this context, John Renard records a story from the famous medieval Islamic pastoral theologian and Sufi, al-Ghazali. Once, when the angel Gabriel was with Muhammad, the two acknowledged that they felt stark terror in the presence of God. God then spoke to them to reassure them: they need not be afraid, for he had made them secure. Should they indeed be unafraid, Muhammad wondered? Had not God himself told them not to tremble? But Gabriel cautioned that they should not banish their fear too casually. They were after all in the presence of *God*. In that presence only a fool would know no dread. In short, the transcendent God is never boring or predictable.[13]

The Qur'an also emphasises divine sovereignty and power. Its best-known Throne Verse appears as an inscription around the interior of domes in major mosques around the world:

> God, there is no god but Him, the Living, the Eternal One. Neither slumber nor sleep overtakes Him. His is what the heavens and the earth contain. Who can intercede with Him except by His permission? He knows what is before and behind men. They can grasp only that part of His knowledge which He wills. His throne is as vast as the heavens and the earth, and the preservation of both does not weary Him. He is the Exalted, the Immense One. (Q 2:225)

The Throne Verse is the qur'anic way of saying that God is both the beginning and end of all things: the Creator, the Sustainer, the Provider, the Lord of Worlds. And yet the Qur'an also teaches that God has another 'hand': not that God *is* Father – Islam is uncomfortable with this – but that God is *like* a compassionate parent, very close, 'nearer than the jugular vein of your neck' (Q 50:16).

A first-time reader of the Qur'an is struck by the fact that, except for one, each *surah* begins with the words 'In the Name of God, the Merciful and the Compassionate' (*basmalah*). It is said that the 'merciful' (*al-Rahman*) describes God as he is in his eternal creative nature and that everything is brought into existence through the overflow of this innate 'mercy', while the 'compassionate' (*al-Rahmin*) refers to the blessings God pours out on forgetful creatures. Allah is the 'Ever-Forgiving' and the 'Effacer' (of sins). The tradition tells us that God spoke to Muhammad saying: 'My Mercy precedes my Wrath.' This means that Muslims believe that mercy is the very nature of God, whereas wrath comes into play with certain of his creatures.[14] As with the Judeo-Christian tradition, so in Islam, God's love is not sentimental like a river without banks. It has Two Hands, stringently demanding and yet mercifully all-inclusive. In a beautiful prayer that Muslims attribute to the Prophet, the believer negotiates their way between the Two Hands of God:

> I seek refuge in Thy goodness from Thy anger.
> I seek refuge in Thy pardon from Thy punishment.
> I seek refuge in Thee from Thee.

Belief in Angels

Belief in angels functions in Islamic faith much as it does in Judaism and Christianity. Sourced in the Divine Oneness (*Tahwid*), angels belong to 'the world of the Unseen'. They are assigned particular tasks by God and are endowed with the necessary spiritual powers to fulfil them. This means that they are not free, as human beings are; they are bound to do the will of God. In the qur'anic version of the Creation story, angels are asked to bow down before Adam and Eve because these first human beings had the courage to accept the burden of human free will, and because of this moral capacity humans have a higher status than angels. Several angels are mentioned in the Qur'an, but Gabriel is the most important. He is the bringer of revelation, announcing the Qur'an to Muhammad – just as he was the bringer of the good news of Christ's birth to Mary. The Archangel Michael's task is to supply sustenance to human bodies and knowledge to minds. Israfil will sound the final trumpet at judgement, and Azrael has the task of visiting each person when death draws near. There are also innumerable anonymous angels, but Islam teaches that God has assigned, at birth, two angels to each person. Just as Muhammad was helped by angels on his ascent to the unseen world, so every person has two guardian angels to help them discern the signs of their divine calling as they journey through life.

Belief in the Measuring Out

Just as Christians do, Muslims frequently use the expressions 'God willing' or 'If God wishes' as a linking of their actions to divine providence. There is an implication here that God oversees all creation and that nothing happens outside his will. This sort of language always raises the age-old questions and fears common to monotheistic religions – those of predestination and free will. As in Christian theology, there is no logical way out of this dilemma. We find verses of the Qur'an which say that 'God guides whom He wills', 'Allah does what pleases Him', 'Whom He permits will be able'; yet these are balanced by verses which speak of the responsibility of the human beings and their need to seek forgiveness, suggesting their responsibility for what they do and their freedom to change: 'God does not change a people's state until they change what is within themselves' (Q 8:53). John Renard sums up majority Muslim opinion as follows:

> With respect to freedom of action, God creates all potential deeds, including evil ones, but leaves human beings the option as to which they will 'appropriate' as their own. As for whether one's known choices render one unfit to be a Muslim, most would argue that the best position is to leave the ultimate judgement to God.[15]

And he concludes with the Muslim saying 'Trust in God but tie your camel' as not being unlike a saying attributed to Ignatius of Loyola: 'Work as if everything depended on you, and pray as if everything depended on God.' Both express something of the paradox of believing in the unfathomable mystery of divine omnipotence, while also acknowledging human responsibility. We now conclude this section on *iman* with reflection on the third principle of faith – eschatology.

Belief in the Return

'As he originated you, so you will return' (Q 7:29). Many features of Islamic eschatology will remind Christians of their own views on death, judgement, resurrection of the dead, and heaven and hell, although Islam is far more graphic. Because physical life and death are ultimately in the hands of God, Muslims, like Jews and Christians, are not under the control of impersonal 'Time' or 'Fate'. Life is not pure chance, they can use their freedom to attend to life as it happens because it is all part of the divine design. Yet we are accountable. Since Islam believes that earthly life is on loan from Allah, our actions have to prove us worthy of this divine loan. Apart from the One God, the Qur'an speaks more on the issue of the judgement of human actions than on any other topic. Judgement Day coincides with the Resurrection of the Dead at the end of time. It is described graphically by the Qur'an as a day of 'Cleaving Asunder'; of 'Cataclysm'; of natural disasters affecting stars, sky and oceans; a day when the graves will be opened and chaos will abound; when we will see our slightest good and evil actions in bold relief. Muslim scholar, Fazlur Rahman, gives an existential, though not watered-down, interpretation of the graphic text Qur'an 50:22:

> [Judgement Day is the] hour when every human will be shaken into an unique and unprecedented self-awareness of his deeds; he will squarely and starkly face his own doings, not-doings, and mis-doings and accept the judgement upon them ... [16]

The image of scales used in the Qur'an seems to be a direct reference to Meccan commercial life, in which scales were not always balanced. But Allah, the 'Weigher of Deeds' is always fair and just, merciful as well. However, in Islam there are no death-bed conversions. The belief is stark: if on balance our righteousness surfaces, we will dwell in the Garden; if not, we will spend the afterlife in the Fire.

The Garden of Bliss or Paradise and the Fire are described with vivid, concrete and sensual imagery. Paradise is a place of fountains, cool shades, carpets, cushions, goblets of gold, sumptuous food and drink. Hell is where souls are chained and yoked in burning fire. It is believed that the majority of Muslims, because of the power of the Qur'an in their education, take these images of Garden and Fire literally. For others, they are symbolic instructions on how to live, that is, not to wait until *the* death but to 'die before you die', as a *hadith* of the Prophet teaches.

Finally, an early tradition outside the Qur'an speaks of 'the punishment of the tomb', in which angelic interrogators question the deceased about their lives and deeds. It is possible that in this teaching, regarding a passageway between this life and the next, we may find a rough analogue for the Catholic doctrine of Purgatory.[17]

We have seen how *iman*, the Islamic creed, provides a protective house for believers in the One God. We now turn to the second dimension of the religion – *islam*, which is worship and practice. To the outsider, Islam may seem cluttered with regulations but for many Muslims this lifestyle frees them to experience a personal faith-life, characterised by great purity and directedness, and indeed a modesty and simplicity that is the hallmark of many practising Muslims.

Islam: Worship and Practice

> Righteousness does not consist in turning your faces to the East or West;
> but righteous is he that believes in God and the Last Day, and Angels and
> the Scripture, and the Prophets; and gives his wealth, for love of Him, to
> kinsfolk and orphans, and the needy and wayfarer, and to those who ask;
> and sets slaves free, and observes the Prayer and pays the Alms-tax.
> And those who keep their undertakings when they enter into them;
> And those who are patient in adversity, suffering and times of danger;
> Such are the sincere. Such are the God-fearing. (Q 11:117)

The doctrines we have engaged with so far comprise what is known as Islamic orthodoxy – 'right belief'. But in its detailed attention to practice and lifestyle, Islam is quite close to the spirit of Jewish *halacha* ('the way you are to go'). Like the Jews, Muslims view religion as a ritual patterning of life in the world under God's Lordship. Thus, the Five Pillars of Islam – the declaration of faith (*shahada*), prayer (*salat*), almsgiving (*zakat*), fasting in the month of Ramadan (*saum*) and the pilgrimage to Mecca (*hajj*) – and the striving of *jihad* which infuses all actions, are basically worshipful ways of living as God's vice-regents in the world.

Shahada: *'Witness' to Faith in the One God*

Brief, simple and explicit, the creed of Islam is: 'There is no God but God and Muhammad is his Prophet.' There is nothing more important than this testimony. It is sufficient for conversion and sincere recital before a designated representative of Islam makes a person a Muslim. These words of the *shahada* are said fourteen times a day if a Muslim says all his daily prayers. They are heard at every significant occasion from birth to death and countless times in between. The Muslim's goal is to be able to make this witness perfectly.

Salat: *Ritual Prayer*

Among the world faiths, the Muslim *salat* is significant in that it represents one of the few extant examples of the sacralisation of time and space recommended for ordinary people. In other religions, only Jews of the strict observance and monks and nuns of the Christian tradition have maintained this practice of prayer at specific hours throughout the day. The Muslim rites of prayer are five in number, prescribed for morning, midday, afternoon, evening and night. Each sequence contains the same pattern of bodily movements (*rakah*), including bowing and prostrating and beginning and ending with the erect posture. The final sequence of each prayer includes a salutation to the right and the left to include all the people of Islam.

Muslims are required to pray in the direction of Mecca. This is known as the *qibla* and it is marked in the mosque by a niche called the *mihrab*. Today, the *qibla* is a dramatic symbol of the unity of the Islamic community worldwide at prayer. But it is also rooted in an ancient belief that when one enters a sacred time, as in the five ritual prayers, one must also mark off and enter a sacred space. Commenting on 'prayer toward Mecca' (*Makka* in Arabic), John Renard sets it in context in this way:

> Traditional societies still reserve a strong sense of sacred geography, considering architectural siting and orientation at least as important as building materials. Christian churches were once always built facing the rising sun, synagogues facing Jerusalem. The exigencies of real estate availability, along with a broad range of distractions from the ancient sense of being rooted in the earth, have all but wiped out the vestiges of cosmic orientation in many religious communities. Islamic tradition has maintained a firmly grounded conviction of a spiritual centre, a symbolic *axis mundi*, a place in which heaven meets earth and from which all creation radiates. That place is Makka in the west-central Arabian peninsula.[18]

This turning to Mecca can generate a powerful implosion of religious energy and of intense common purpose in those praying.

The Friday *salat* is observed at noon prayer by a congregation in the mosque, yet *salat* can be observed anywhere. According to Islam there are no sacred places, no sacred persons, no mediators between the believer and God. Everywhere is a mosque or *masjid*, a 'place of prostration'. No walls, no ceremonies come between the believer and God. All that matters is that the place be clean – hence the prayer mat.

One comes with consciousness or intention (*niyya*) to prayer because *salat* is but the outer symbol of the inner prayer of the heart, which should be continuous and constant. In this, we are reminded of the *hadith* of Gabriel: 'Doing what is beautiful means that you should worship God as if you see Him, for even if you do not see Him, He sees you.' It is in this spirit that one understands the Muslim emphasis on ritual purity, the physical ablutions necessary before one enters *salat* or handles the Qur'an. In washing, the Muslim is symbolically, as well as physically, separated from the mundane world and restored to the original purity and balance required for standing in the presence of God. It is in this state that the Muslim recites the *Fatihah*, the opening *surah* of the Qur'an, at every *salat*. Like the 'Our Father', which expresses the essence of Christian prayer, the *Fatihah* (literally 'key' or 'opening') serves as the great prayer of Islam:

Praise be to God, Lord of the Universe,
The Compassionate, the Merciful,
Sovereign of the Day of Judgement!
You alone we worship, and to You alone we turn for help.
Guide us to the straight path,
The path of those whom you have favoured,
Not of those who have incurred Your wrath,
Nor of those who have gone astray. (Q 1:1-7)

It has only one petition, for guidance, and then it is simply a prayer that lets God be God. Following on from this prayer, the Muslim recites a portion of the Qur'an – it is believed that this text which wells up spontaneously in the heart of the believer is the expression of his or her invocation for guidance on the straight path.

Sawm: *Fasting*

A compulsory fast is prescribed for all adults who are capable of it during the lunar month of Ramadan. This month is the annual period of personal renewal in Islam, because it was during that month, on the Night of Power, that the Prophet first received the revelation of the Qur'an. Ramadan punctuates the year with a holy time in much the same way as *salat* sanctifies each day. From sunrise to sunset, one is to fast from food and drink, gambling, sexual activity and all sensual pleasures, including listening to music. One must also fast from evil thoughts and desires. 'Cultivate within oneself,' says the Prophet, 'the attributes of God.'

The Muslim fast is a time of intensified devotion and forgiveness. The hardships it imposes, especially in countries where Ramadan occurs in the heat and dryness of summer, are to be endured without flinching. Ramadan is a reminder that the duty of the flesh is to serve and never to engross the spirit.

For the individual, the ideal goal is to stand before God in one's original nature and, through abstinence, to remove the physical and mental accretions that veil one's relationship with Allah as Beloved. The rigours of the fast also remind one of human frailty and dependence as a creature before God. Experiencing hunger helps one to identify more easily with those who are in need – 'the barefooted ones' – and, in the Muslim tradition of the pious deed, the believer is expected to excel in good deeds during this month and to give generously to charitable causes.

Furthermore, the communal atmosphere of Ramadan powerfully reinforces the collective identity of Muslims all over the world. Research has shown that it is a time in which Islam attracts converts. Because of the scrupulosity of its practice, people who are spirituality searching tend to see Islam as a religion in which God is not treated with indifference.

Yet while Ramadan is a time of serious reflection, it is not sad or sombre. Ramadan nights, when the daily fast ends, are joyful times, when friends and extended family gather for food and simple entertainments. The local mosque is visited and some men even spend several nights there in spiritual retreat and vigil. The last ten nights, during one of which the Qur'an was revealed, are believed to be imbued with the spirit of the original Night of Power. No Muslim knows for certain which of the last ten nights is the Night of Power, but traditionally this night of the 'Descent of the Qur'an' is celebrated on 27 Ramadan. For the Muslim, this night is 'better that a thousand months, in it the angels and the Spirit descend, by the leave of their Lord, upon every command. Peace it is, until the rising of the dawn' (Q 97:3-5).

The very last day of Ramadan, Eid al-Fitr – the Feast of the Breaking of the Fast – is a celebration of release and a time for family unions and gift-giving. It is, to the Muslim, a taste of what paradise is like.

Zakat: *Almsgiving*
The Qur'an says:

> Give to kin, the poor and the traveller what they need; that is best for those who seek the face of God, and they will indeed fare well. What you give in the hope of profiting at the expense of people will gain you nothing in God's sight; what you give in the form of alms [*zakat*] as you seek the face of God – that will produce abundant return. (Q 30:38-39)

Fasting's dimension of social awareness connects it to this third pillar of Almsgiving, which like fasting is common to virtually all religious traditions. But Muslims have maintained a more systematic approach to the practice than have most branches of Judaism and Christianity. In Islam, one of the lessons of creation is that human beings do not own natural riches permanently; we merely borrow them. The root meaning of *zakat* is 'to purify'. The Qur'an says: 'Take of their wealth an offering to purify them and cleanse them thereby' (Q 9:103). *Zakat* is also linked with the efficacy of prayer, because if wealth is not purified, it becomes a burden and a veil between the believer and God. Furthermore, because Allah cares for 'the barefooted ones', the community, in its care for the needy, has a claim on the individual's wealth. Therefore, while *zakat* is a religious commitment, it is also an obligatory part of Islamic law (*shariah*), realised as a tax on two and a half per cent of one's savings. This is apart from what one might donate freely to charity and one's payment of the many state taxes imposed for the general welfare.

In this context, it is interesting to note that the prescription of almsgiving presupposes an approval of private ownership which takes precedence in Islam over any concept of communal ownership. An early Islamic spiritual writer observes how prayer, fasting and almsgiving were related in the following way: 'Prayer carries us halfway to God; fasting brings us to the door of his praises; almsgiving procures for us admission.'[19]

Hajj: *Pilgrimage*

This last pillar of Islam is the crowning experience of a Muslim's life and moves the heart as nothing else. It encompasses a complexity of meanings, but above all it is a 'return to the Centre', for the Ka'aba in Mecca – toward which all Muslim prayer is directed – is the *axis mundi*, the projection onto earth of the Absolute Centre who is God.

The *hajj* is required once in a Muslim's lifetime, but only if he or she is legally adult and physically and financially capable of making the pilgrimage. *Hajj* has the meaning 'to set out for a definite purpose' or 'to visit a revered place'. As with the *mitzvot* in Judaism, the commands in Islam, when literally obeyed, become the sacrament of spiritual gifts. Like all pilgrimages, the *hajj* is a moving to the edge, a liminal experience. The leave-taking of family and friends is solemn, even to the extent of making a will. Long ago, because of the dangers and hardships of travel, there was always the possibility that one may not return from the pilgrimage.

The Saudi government is responsible for providing all the physical necessities for over a million Muslims to make the pilgrimage at one time, and even with careful preparation there are still tragic deaths due to over-crowding and stampedes. The *hajj* opens with the *niyyah*, or intention, as they draw near to the city with the cry: 'Here I am, Lord, here am I.'

As male pilgrims approach *haram*, the sacred space surrounding the Ka'aba, they don the *ihram*, the white seamless cotton garment of ritual dedication; whereas women are permitted to wear their normal native garb. Distinctions of rank and hierarchy are removed and wealthy and poor stand before God in their common humanity. Then follows the circumambulation seven times around the Ka'aba, which stands cube-shaped in the centre of the mosque court. The climax of the pilgrimage is reached between the eighth and tenth day on the plain of Arafat, today an enormous tent city.

After a night's journey, the vast body of people stand from noon to near sunset recalling with the aid of sermons the 'standing' of Abraham against idolatry. This 'standing' ceremony is at the heart of the *hajj*, and if pilgrims fail to observe it the whole pilgrimage is rendered null and void. Pilgrims experience a special closeness to God, as well as to their Muslim brothers and sisters, during this long afternoon of repentance and prayer.

Near the plain of Arafat on the tenth day, animals are sacrificed in commemoration of Abraham, who, in his total obedience to God's command, prepared to immolate his son (in Islam, this was Ishmael not Isaac), for whom a ram was miraculously exchanged. The pilgrims celebrate this event by sacrificing thousands of sheep and distributing meat to the poor. In every other land where Muslims are to be found, the same rite is observed as the Feast of Sacrifice (Eid al-Adha), the greater of the two canonical feasts, the other being the Feast of Fast Breaking.

Other rites of the *hajj* take place in the immediate environment of Mecca. For example, at Mina, the pilgrims, in imitation of Abraham, perform a rite in which they renounce Satan. Abraham is a constant point of reference during the rites of the *hajj*, but it is important to realise that the sacred places of Islam are also linked with the memory of Adam. The tradition associates Arafat with the origins of the human race, with God's forgiveness of Adam and Eve after their expulsion from paradise, and with the first covenant or Trust in which the human being is called to witness that God is the Lord (Q 7:172). Having been regenerated at the wellsprings of the universal revelation to Adam, and having remembered

Abraham's faith, many Muslims conclude their pilgrimage with a journey to Medina to visit the grave of the Prophet.

Bearing henceforth the name of *hajji*, the pilgrims return home endowed with a new prestige. Their village or district celebrates their return, for they have come back saturated with *baraka* – the benign spiritual influence which emanated from the Centre, and by which the descendents of Abraham reconnect themselves with their timeless origin.[20]

Jihad: *The Sixth Pillar*

If, for the Buddhists, to live is to suffer, for the Muslims, to live is to struggle – to engage in *jihad* at all times and at various levels. Although not a 'pillar' in the usual sense, *jihad*, which Muslims nowadays prefer to translate as 'collective effort for the sake of Islam', is usually included among the canonical obligations. However, Muslims like to recall a saying of Muhammad when he returned from one of his last campaigns: 'We have now returned from the Lesser Holy War to the Greater Holy War.' The 'greater *jihad*', which has its parallels in Jewish *teshuva* ('repentance' or 'return') and Christian *metanoia* ('conversion' or 'turning'), is the inner struggle with what Muslims call the *nafs* or ego – 'what is between your ears' – which can lead one down alleyways of false attachments and forgetfulness of God.

This first level of inner *jihad* infuses all Muslim practice: *salat* means awakening from one's dream of forgetfulness to remember God; *sawm* means that one's passionate embodied self is reborn in purity; *zakat* implies spiritual generosity, nobility and a leaving aside of self; and in *hajj*, the pilgrim enacts the journey from the periphery to the centre of his being, the heart (*qalb*), which is one's own spiritual Ka'aba. This greater *jihad* is incumbent on all believers but, as we shall see later, the movement to the heart and pure love of God particularly characterise the Sufi mystical tradition.

A second level of *jihad* requires Muslims to strive to communicate the word of God, to build the House of Islam. The Qur'an commands that there be no compulsion in religion (Q 2:256) but, as the Last Religion, Islam is universal and missionary in thrust. The spread of the faith, however, must be done by peaceful means like preaching, travel, the establishment of educational institutions, and the personal witness of good example.

A third level of *jihad* – its outward sense – is popularly known in the west as Holy War. The classic text of the Qur'an is: 'Fight for the sake of Allah those that fight against you, but do not attack them first. Allah does not love aggressors' (Q 2:19). When one stays close to the religious sources of Islam, it becomes obvious that military *jihad* is defensive only, and the conditions for a Holy War are comparable with those for a Just War in the Catholic tradition. Muslims may defend themselves, family, country and religion (Q 4:75). They may defend fellow Muslims who are helpless and oppressed (Q 8:72), and they may fight to secure religious freedom. This does not mean that in Islam religion simply sanctions war. As the Shi'ite philosopher Nasr points out, *jihad* in the military sense must be understood as 'the attempt of a society to protect itself from being conquered by military and economic forces or by ideas of an alien nature'.[21]

However, Nasr does acknowledge with regret that religious sentiments have been misused by extremist Muslims to instigate and legitimise conflict. Yet must not Christians admit, since history is our witness, that Islam does not have the monopoly on this abuse? Muslim writers question whether western histories are fair to Islam in their accounts of its use of force and generally make the plea that the blots on the record of Muslim peoples should not be charged against their religion, whose presiding ideal is affirmed in their standard greeting: *as-salamu 'alaykum*, 'Peace be upon you'. In the present climate, in which the very word *jihad* conjures up terrorist attacks and suicide missions, it is becoming more urgent that both communities of faith – Christian and Muslim – move to repair the ignorance they have of each others' traditions.

UMMAH: THE COMMUNITY OF BELIEVERS

> We have fashioned unto you an *Ummah* in equilibrium so that you might
> be witnesses to humankind and the Messenger [Muhammad] might be a
> witness to you. (Q 2:143)

Islam, like Judaism and Christianity, is a community of faith. When Muhammad and his band of followers left Mecca for Medina, it was to establish a new identity, a faith community – the *Ummah* – transcending allegiance to particular tribes and places. But Islam is also submission to divine law as expressed in *shariah*. John Renard interestingly alerts us to the desert origins of the word *shariah*, telling us that it means 'oasis, source of water', which is derived from a rote meaning 'to set out for' the watering hole.[22] Like the Torah in orthodox Judaism, *shariah* legislates for the entire social unity of faith, government, ritual and moral behaviour, family, property, business and architecture. Sourced in the Qur'an and in the

Divine Unity (*Tawhid*), it repudiates any distinction between the religious and the secular. A *dar*, in Arabic, is simply a place where people circulate in their own habitat. Behind that territorial meaning lies a complete cultural concept which implies that Muslims are more at home under the protection of Islamic statehood, where they are legally, religiously and socially able to be themselves. Thus, Dar al-Islam (House of Islam) is an earthly place of equilibrium. Everything is in place in relation to the divine unity, both in the believer's soul and in society.

And yet the *Ummah* is not a given. Islam sees it as a stage of God's relations with human beings, and as a testing-ground. The Qur'an teaches that 'humankind was once a single community' (Q 2:213) but that disagreement grew rampant because of self-centred stubbornness and divisions multiplied. God could have kept that from happening, but he preferred to test humanity. In an interesting twist, the Qur'an turns disunity to advantage and issues a challenge to humankind:

> Therefore, vie with one another in good deeds, for God is the final goal for all of you, and it is he who will clarify for you those things about which you now argue. (Q 5:48)

Indeed Muslims also see a providential explanation for the multiplicity of religions in this text, and some Muslim groups who are not particularly eager to engage in interfaith relations would counsel that such matters are best left to God.

Four sources make up the *shariah*, which give the Islamic legal process its validity. The most important and most used are the Qur'an and the Sunna (the 'traditions' of the Prophet). The Sunna, which comprises the customs, words, deeds and habitual practices of Muhammad, is the ideal for Muslim behaviour. It is enshrined in a large body of literature called *hadith*. The *hadith* are similar to the gospels in that they preserve the words and deeds of the religious founder. Like the gospels, they are divinely revealed, but whereas Muslims consider the Qur'an the direct, literal word of God, the *hadith* represent the context of divine revelation as couched in the Prophet's own unique expression. In time, the *hadith* functioned as an interpretation and application of the Qur'an, which in general did not function as a legislative handbook. By the end of the ninth century, the words and deeds of Muhammad were institutionalised in a number of collections. Six of these have been especially considered authoritative – these are the Sunna, the second source of Islamic law. But Sunna also has an expansive meaning, in which it has come to include not only Muhammad's reported words and anecdotes of his deeds, but also the actual living practice of a given community of believers. That growing attitude, in turn, was based on a *hadith* that reports Muhammad as saying 'My community will not agree on an error.' In this expanding notion of Sunna we see the beginnings of a third source of religious law, *ijima* – the consensus of the community, not unlike the *sensus fidelium* in the Catholic tradition.

Finally there is Qiyas, which is reasoning or deduction on the part of experts with requisite qualification in cases not covered by the Qur'an and Sunna. Dissenting views are possible but majority opinion carries the day. Islam does not allow free examination of revelation or any amending of the law to conform to the tendencies of the age.[23]

Following these principles, Muslim law constitutes an imposing and highly elaborate science of how to arrive at and support moral decisions. Like Jews and Christians, Muslims hold that the basic thrust of their religion is the love of God and neighbour. But the qur'anic view is that the Jews narrowed revelation and restricted the Mosaic imperative of love of God and neighbour with their strong ethnic thrust. And Jesus, who is revered in Islam as the prophet of God's Spirit, left his gospel as inspiration only, which means that as an instruction for living, it is unfinished. Thus Muslims believe that it was reserved for the Last Religion, through the Qur'an and the Prophet, to systematise the teachings of the Hebrew scriptures and of Jesus, and to structure them in a way that showed understanding for the weakness and forgetfulness of human beings.

Yet the community of Islam is far from being monolithic. Like every religion, it has divisions. The main historical division is between the Sunnis ('traditionalists' from the Sunna tradition), who make up 87–90 per cent of the religion, and the Shi'ites (literally 'partisans'), who constitute the remaining 10–13 per cent and have large communities in Iraq and Iran.

The division between Sunni and Shi'ite Islam is a question of the form of authority in Islam, and can be loosely compared to the distinction between institutional and charismatic, such as we are aware of in the Catholic tradition. On Muhammad's death, a majority of his followers recognised his kinsman Abu Bakr as his successor. Abu Bakr, in turn, was followed by three successors, all four being known as 'the rightly guided Caliphs'. Muslims who recognise this authority are termed Sunni. In this tradition, the ultimate source of authority is the Muslim community as guided by the Sunna of the Prophet.

Some of the Prophet's followers, however, maintained that during his lifetime he had designated his son-in-law Ali as his successor, and they refused to recognise the authority of Abu Bakr. These were the party of Ali, the *shi'at Ali*. In the view of Shi'ite Islam, authority resides not in the community but in the divinely appointed leader, the successor of Ali, called the Imam. Shi'ites believe that God provides an Imam in every age, even though they are sometimes hidden. There are several different Shi'ite sects recognising different Imams.

While Sunnis and Shi'ites agree on the broad principles of Islam, Shi'ite Islam has a distinctive practice of its own, being more supportive of the mystical Sufi tradition and the cultivation of saints. The lands of Shi'ite Islam are dotted with shrines of holy persons, to which people make pilgrimage. The most celebrated of these is Husayn, the son of Ali, who was killed in a battle against other Muslims. Husayn's suffering quickly came to be interpreted as a voluntary self-sacrifice and is regarded by Shi'ites as redemptive and celebrated in a dramatic passion play in which the participants flagellate themselves with chains and smear themselves with blood, ritually sharing in Husayn's sacrifice.

Sunni–Shi'ite rivalries run deep in Muslim history. For this reason, as well as the existence of many lesser sub-groups in Islam and the absence of any one recognised religious authority, Christian–Muslim relations tend to be varied, becoming a form of contact with different 'groups' on specific issues. Without reducing contact with Sunnis, it is considered that Shi'ite Muslims are the natural partners for Catholic–Muslim dialogue, due to their many areas of mutuality: a profound contemplative and mystical tradition; veneration of saints, especially of Mary; a theology of sacrifice and atonement (for Shi'ites this comes through the death of Husayn); holy days and pilgrimages to healing shrines; intercessory prayer and strongly emotional forms of popular devotion; notions of infallibility and authority; and high emphasis on rational inquiry into matters of faith, praxis and theological study.

There is another division of more universal overtones: that between the generality of Islam and the more mystical Islam. But the generality of Islam, even though it is united under the rallying cry of 'God is greater' (*Allahu Akbar*), is still plural and diverse because, in the Muslim view, the mediations of divine will are multiple and varied as expressed in the social and personal, the political and the cultural:

> For masses of ordinary believers it means a framework of belief and behaviour, an encircling, demanding sense of God and obligation. For the sophisticated, it may mean simply a cultural identity, a setting of life inherited from history. For the mystical, it means 'the shade of the wing of Gabriel',

the passing away of the self in union with the divine. To the traditionalist, it is a sacred trust to be served and preserved, with a steadfast loyalty to what is given in the divine will and what is hidden in the divine knowledge. For the artists and architects and calligraphers, it is the inspiration of their creations, the cry from their minarets, the nurture of all their skills. Through all diversities, it is the invocation of the Name of the all Merciful.[24]

ISHAN: 'DOING THE BEAUTIFUL'

It remains to be said that Islam is more than an institutionalised mass religious culture. Islam is also *ishan*: it does the Beautiful. As the *hadith* says, 'Doing the Beautiful means that you should worship God as if you see Him, for if you do not see Him, He sees you.' Beauty is the name of Allah whose face is turned towards us, and *ishan* is the Muslim way of giving inner meaning to faith (*iman*) and to practice (*islam*). It is the experience of Islam at the heart level. The qur'anic verse, 'He is the first and the Last, the Outward and the Inward' (Q 57:3) refers not only to the Divine Nature as such, but to God's desire for close relationship with human beings. As 'Inward', God's primal resting place is in the hearts of believers. Some sacred *hadiths* are also quite moving, and have God saying: 'Heaven and earth cannot hold Me, but there is room for Me in the heart of the believer'; 'I was a hidden treasure and I wished to be known; so I created the world'; and 'I am in the midst of those whose hearts are broken for My sake.'[25]

Divine Oneness, Remembrance and Servanthood

Firstly, it must be said that Muslim spirituality is a spirituality of *Tawhid* – a centring on Divine Oneness as a presence. This presence is not as intimate or relational as that of God's presence in Jesus Christ. It is the presence of a beloved master to his servants, of a parent to his children. It is always a presence that never fails to bestow sustenance on those who turn to Allah. In fact Rizq, 'He who bestows Sustenance', is one of the Divine Names. Secondly, Muslim spirituality is about the remembrance of this presence through the outward observance of Shariah, through remembrance of the Divine Names and the qur'anic verses, through recitation of the prayers of the Prophet and personal prayer. Thirdly, Muslim spirituality shapes the believer to be a servant of Allah. And finally, in prayer as in so many dimensions of Islam, Abraham, the man of faith, sets the example. One must pray with great consciousness, with yearnings and sighs and no thought of self. It is said that when the patriarch prayed, his personal commitment and intensity was so great it caused his heart to bubble. One could hear Abraham praying for miles.

As we have seen, *salat* five times a day is the formal obligated prayer, but Islam also has a rich treasury of non-obligatory prayers, such as free prayers of supplication and petition for various human occasions. In one of the most famous sacred *hadiths*, Allah describes how supererogatory devotion establishes the most intimate relation between a servant and the Lord:

> My servant continues to come near to me by piety beyond what is required, so that I love him; and I show my love by becoming the eye with which my servant sees, the ear by which he hears, the hand with which he grasps. And if my servant approaches a hand's breadth, I go toward him an arm's length; and if he approaches an arm's length, I go forward the space of outstretched arms; and if he comes toward me walking, I go toward him running. And if my servant should bring me sins the size of the earth itself, my forgiveness will be more than equal to them.[26]

The most popular supererogatory prayer form is *dhikr* – the prayer of remembrance. A common *dhikr* practice is the recitation of the Divine Names on the *subha* (beads). Since the qur'anic Names for God are revelation and are one with God, to constantly remember a Divine Name is to be transformed into that attribute. We also know that the psalms, the gospels and letters of St Paul are full of allusions to the saving power of God's Name: 'Whoever calls on the name of the Lord will be saved.' And in Eastern Christianity, invocation of the Divine Name (the 'prayer without ceasing' enjoined by St Paul) takes the form of the 'Jesus Prayer', a practice made familiar by the widely read *Way of the Pilgrim*. As with the 'Jesus Prayer', the *dhikr* of the tongue moves to the *dhikr* of the heart. 'The remembrance of God makes the heart calm' says Qur'an 13:28 and 'Let your tongue stay moist with the remembrance of God' counsels Muhammad. But 'true *dhikr* is to forget *dhikr*'. This is a saying from the Sufi mystical branch of Islam where *dhikr* is practiced as a spiritual and ecstatic path.

The Throne Verse (Q 2:225) which we considered in relation to the hand of God as Creator, Provider, Sustainer and Lord of Worlds, provides a popular metaphor for the ultimate goal of mystics in Islam. John Renard refers us to the colourful character Bayazid al-Bistami (d. 874) who writes of his own spiritual journey in a way that opens us to the universal thrust of Islamic spirituality:

At the beginning I was mistaken in four respects. I concerned myself to remember God, to know him, to love him and to seek him. When I had come to the end I saw that he had remembered me before I remembered him, that his knowledge of me preceded my knowledge of him, that his love towards me had existed before my love towards him, and he had sought me before I had sought him. I thought I had arrived at the very throne of God and I said to it: 'O Throne, tell me that God rests upon thee.' 'O Bayazid' replied the Throne, 'we are told that he dwells in the humble heart.'[27]

The Sufi Tradition

In the Sufi tradition, the universal and mystical thrust of Islamic spirituality comes to the fore. It is particularly attractive to non-Muslims, in that it provides the most impressive evidence that within Islam there are men and women who have achieved profound religious insight and heights of sanctity. The current western interest in Sufism also illustrates the more general truth that the mystical enterprise is one of the more accessible paths for interreligious dialogue. But it must be remembered that Sufism is not a sect of Islam, it is rather a dimension –'Islam's living heart' – compatible with all dimensions of the religion, whether Sunni or Shi'ite, and with all states of life, intelligentsia or peasant, urban or rural. It is closely associated with popular religion, and yet it has produced the most elite and unforgettable expressions of Islamic spirituality.

A century or two after Muhammad's death, those within Islam, who were more directly concerned with its inner message, became known as Sufis. Alarmed by the worldliness they saw in Islam after its political conquests, they donned woollen garments (the root meaning of the word Sufi is wool, *suf*) to protest against the silks and satins of sultans and caliphs. Basically, they wanted to restore the more austere ideals of the beginning of Islam, which was marked by simplicity of life, poverty, prayers directed toward Mecca and nocturnal vigils. Also, they wanted to encounter God directly in this very lifetime, now. Over the next century or so, informal circles began to form around men and women known for their sanctity. Initially, the circles used the humble dwellings of their leaders as meeting places, but many groups soon grew to need larger facilities. By the twelfth century, a network of organisations dedicated to personal and communal piety were spread across the Middle East. These orders were called 'paths' (from the Arabic *tariqa*), each developing distinctive forms of ritual and devotional practice. For those who lived in community, there was a definite rule to be followed. In fact the 'brotherhoods' had much in common with the Christian religious orders – a three-year novitiate period, training in prayer, poverty and obedience, and a way of life which involved 'little food, little sleep and little talk'. A notable difference was that they were not cloistered celibates. They could marry and it was envisaged that they remain present in the world to give guidance and to nourish the worship and devotion of believers.

The Muslim spiritual writer, Annemarie Schimmel, tells us that *dhikr*, 'remembrance', is the hallmark of Sufi spirituality.[28] What is special about the practice of *dhikr* among the Sufis is that it is not just words said, it is also a path of transformation. Progress in *dhikr* is the barometer of the spiritual journey. Rules for the use of this or that Divine Name are laid down and personally assigned by a Sufi master or *Shayhk*, who knows the spiritual state of the aspirant. In the following classification of *dhikr*, we find a clearly defined theory and practice of mystical life, and the stages noted of beginner, proficient and 'perfect' (one who has arrived), are similar to those found in traditional Christian spirituality:

The Simple Remembrance of the Tongue

Certain qur'anic phrases are repeated in mantra-like fashion. This stage, which trains the Sufi to meditate on the 'signs' of God in the self and in creation, brings about a certainty and clarity of mind, withdraws the mind from trivia and the ways of the world, and confirms them in their vocation of seeking God.

Remembrance of the Heart

This is a movement away from the action, such as repeating words, to a resting in the eye of the heart as 'the source of certainty', and a confidence that *dhikr* fills all needs and is the source of salvation.

Remembrance of the Secret

The ongoing and an effortless thought of God. Here, 'the truth of *dhikr*' is the gift of heaven beyond the reach of the human will and effort that preceded it. In Islamic language, 'It is the supreme reality of *Tawhid* professed by one who attests the One after having himself been effaced.'[29] Again these divisions correspond rather closely with the traditional Christian understanding of progress in prayer as active meditation, active contemplation, infused contemplation. Although it must be noted that Islam does not speak of union with God, as we do in the Christian mystical tradition. In Islam, 'union with God', if we may use the phrase, is always a testimony of the effaced self before the One who is always greater.

Mystics of the Pure Love of God

Although the primary thrust of Muslim theology and spirituality is always surrender to *Tawhid* – divine oneness – the notion of the love of God does surface in some mystical literature. Generally in Islam, love refers to the merciful goodness (*rahma*) of the Divine Creator to his servants. But strict jurists say that human beings cannot love God in himself, they can only love his law, his service, his will. Perhaps unexpectedly, the mystic who largely moved away from this position was a woman, Rabi'a al-Adawiyya (c. 713–801).

Born in a poor home, Rabi'a was sold as a slave, but her holiness brought her freedom. She abandoned her career as a flute player and withdrew to a life of prayer and celibacy, living in the desert, south of Iraq near Basra, where a circle of disciples formed around her. Her choice of celibacy, novel for Islam, was not just asceticism but, to use a Christian expression, an act of renunciation for the pure love of God:

> The contract of marriage is for those who live in this world. I have no such existence; I have ceased to exist and have passed out of self. I exist in God and am altogether his – I live in the shadow of his command.[30]

One day, Rabi'a was seen walking in the streets of Basra carrying a lighted torch and a pitcher of water. 'Where are you going?' someone asked her. 'I am going to quench the fires of hell and set fire to paradise so that God may be adored and loved for himself and not for his rewards.' The theme of the call to the selfless love of God appears in many of her prayers and is treasured by the spiritual tradition:

> O God, if I worship Thee for fear of Hell, burn me in Hell, and if I worship Thee in hope of Paradise, exclude me from paradise; but if I worship thee for Thy own sake, grudge me not the everlasting beauty.

> O God, whatsoever Thou hast apportioned to me of worldly things do Thou give that to thy enemies; and whatever thou hast apportioned to me in the world to come, give that to Thy friends; for thou sufficest for me.[31]

The greatest and most profound of all Sufis, and one who brought out the full implications of the doctrine of divine love, was the Persian, Mansur al-Hallaj (d. 922). He refused to be prudent and hide the wonders of his experience of intimate union with God. Al-Hallaj took Jesus as the perfect example of the holy man in whom God was totally present. He was conscious of himself as the sacrament of God's presence and knew that this state of union was a gratuitous gift of God. He was accused by the authorities of Christian incarnationism, and when he expressed his experience of being possessed by God in the ecstatic utterance – 'I am the Truth' (i.e. God) – he was charged with departing from Islamic orthodoxy and with downplaying religious observance. He was scourged, mutilated and crucified in Baghdad. Al-Hallaj comes down in the Sufi tradition as a martyr of divine love, a Christ-like figure, who in his passionate and ecstatic way realised the ideal of the love of God, first introduced by Rabi'a. Another such notable of the thirteenth century, regarded as the golden age of Sufism, was the Persian Sufi, Jellalludin Rumi of Konya (1207–73). Like al-Hallaj, Rumi belonged to the tradition of 'intoxicated' Sufis, who claimed to speak out of a divinely inspired ecstasy. The greatest Persian mystical poet, his famous *Mathnawi*, 26,000 rhythmic couplets on mystical insight and experience, was considered by the Persians to be next to the Qur'an in holiness. Rumi founded a Sufi order, the Mevlevi, whose members combined music, poetry and dance in their rituals. Known in the West as the Whirling Dervishes, they sought a one-pointedness of communion with God through circular gyrations accompanied by music intended to represent the order of the heavenly spheres.[32]

Sober Sufis

Complementary to these are the 'sober' Sufis. Persian Sufi, al-Ghazali (1058–1111) is considered to be one of the greatest pastoral scholars in the history of Islam and someone with whom the ordinary person could identify. The story of his life is inspiring. After five years as a successful professor of theology in the university at Baghdad, al-Ghazali began to experience episodes of spiritual distress, which he called a 'disease' and 'unhealthy condition'. He knew *about* God but he did not *know* God. Thoroughly dissatisfied, he abandoned teaching, concluding that a teacher of religion must first become a religious person. The last step in his journey of honest doubt and spiritual crisis led him to live as a Sufi. What impressed him about the mystics was their capacity to circumvent theology and sense perception, and to experience God directly:

> I learnt with certainty that it is above all the mystics who walk on the road of God; their life is the best life, their method the soundest method, their character the purest character.[33]

There was an instinctive sense of balance in al-Ghazali. For the sake of ordinary believers, he would never make the claim, as some Sufis did, 'I am God'. This balance made him virtually unassailable to Islamic jurists. His writings combined theology and mysticism with such integrity that, ever since, Muslim philosophers and theologians have had to take Sufism seriously.

That does not mean, however, that Sufism is not without its aberrations. In its popular expressions it has been prone to degenerate into technique and superstition. In later years, its *shayks* were sometimes mere charlatans, who used their position to exploit the vulnerable. And there were, and are, those who call themselves Sufis who have nothing to do with Islam. Yet, as a movement, it has reached great heights and is still a source of deep piety for many Muslims. The universal spirit of the Sufi brotherhoods and the *dhikr* prayer practiced in groups with chanting, music and dance were the main reasons why Islam spread so successfully in Africa, India and further east.

Even a cursory glance at the rich devotional aspect of Islam can dispel the impression that it is a dry, anemic and self-contained tradition that speaks only to itself. There has always been a thrust toward truth in relation to the 'other' in Islam. We find it in the writings of Andalusian mystic Ibn al-Arabi (1165–1240), which are a product of the Spanish Golden Age, when Jewish, Christian and Muslim centres of learning collaborated in the search for truth. He died in Damascus in Syria, where he is buried. His words, arising from his collaboration with other religions, cross the centuries and still speak to the many today who are finding a way in the venture of interreligious dialogue:

> My heart has opened unto every form. It is a pasture for gazelles, a cloister for Christian monks, a temple for idols, the Ka'aba of the pilgrim, the tablets of the Torah and the book of the Koran. I practice the religion of Love; in whatsoever directions its caravans advance, the religion of love shall be my religion and faith.[34]

SUMMARY

Islam, a system of faith in the One God and a practice propagated as a finally revealed religion by Muhammad, entered history in Arabia in the seventh century CE. Christianity and Islam contain both common and opposing creedal elements, but our shared faith in one God is undoubtedly our foundational and fruitful base for dialogue with Muslims. Any study of Islam needs to begin with *iman* (faith), of which there are six creedal elements: belief in One God, belief in angels, belief in the prophets (Muhammad, Jesus and other biblical prophets), belief in revelation (Qur'an), belief in the Return (the Last Judgment), belief in the Measuring Out (nothing can happen against God's will, and everything that happens is with his permission).

Islam is not Trinitarian, and the Qur'an vehemently opposes the idea that God decided to become human in Jesus, and that through the person of Jesus Christ God is revealed in history as our redeemer. In the Islamic view, the human person has the capacity to come to know God adequately through the divine attributes and by experiencing Allah's power and greatness in the splendour of creation. Other more privileged signs of God are the words of the Qur'an, the teachings of the Prophet and the guidance of the Islamic creed and *shariah*. In some ways a less complex creed than Christianity, Islam still fascinates with the purity of its monotheism and the directness of the ways in which it channels believers to live in a house of divine presence.

From this flows the second dimension of Islam, which is *islam* – 'worship' or 'surrender'. The Five Pillars are the main support for living in the House of Islam. They are *shahada*, witness to faith; *salat*, ritual prayer; *sawm*, fasting; *zakat*, almsgiving; and *hajj*, pilgrimage. *Jihad* ('struggle'), which Muslims nowadays prefer to translate as 'collective effort for the sake of Islam', is usually included as a sixth pillar. *Jihad* is popularly known in the west as Holy War, and Muslims, drawing on the Qur'an, make justifications for it. Yet *jihad* is also *da'wah* ('mission'), the duty to spread the faith by word and example, always mindful of the injunction of the Qur'an (Q 2:256) that there be no compulsion in religion. The 'greater *jihad*' is the personal commitment of each Muslim to struggle with false attachments and forgetfulness of God.

Thirdly, Islam, like all religions, is more than an institutionalised mass; it has a rich inner dimension. It is *ishan* ('it does the beautiful'). *Ishan* is the experience of creed and practice at the heart level. It is Muslim spirituality, which is always a spirituality of *Tawhid* ('oneness') – a centring of the heart of the believer on Divine Oneness as Presence. The most important prayer-form for ordinary Muslims is the *dhikr*, the prayer of remembrance, in which the mind is centred by the repetition of the Divine Names on the beads, or by the recital of short verses from the Qur'an. In the Sufi mystical tradition, the *dhikr* is brought to a high level in the training of the mind and heart of practitioners. It is the way of union with God, but union with God for the Muslim is, above all, the effacing of the self as servant (*abd*) before the One Who is Greater (*Allahu Akbar*).

FURTHER READING

Abdulati, Hammudah, *Islam in Focus* (Maryland: Amana,1998).

Delcambre, Anne-Marie, *Inside Islam* (Milwaukee, WI: Marquette University Press, 2006).

Du Pasquier, Roger, *Unveiling Islam* (Cambridge: Islamic Texts Society, 1992).

Fitzmaurice, Redmond, 'The Sufis – Muslim Mystics', *Milltown Studies* 12 (1983), pp. 1–16.

Hossein Nasr, Seyyed, *Ideals and Realities of Islam* (London: Aquarian Press, 1994).

Jomier, Jacques, *How to Understand Islam* (London: SCM, 1989).

Mathewson Denny, Frederick, *An Introduction to Islam* (New York: Macmillan, 1994).

Murata, Sackito and William Chittick, *The Vision of Islam* (St Paul, MN: Paragon House, 1994).

Renard, John, *Seven Doors to Islam: Spirituality and the Religious Life of Muslims* (London: University of California Press, 1996).

———, *Responses to 101 Questions on Islam* (New York: Paulist Press, 1998).

———, *Understanding the Islamic Experience* [previously published as *In The Footsteps of Muhammad*] (New York: Paulist Press, 2002).

Stoddart, William, *Sufism: The Mystical Doctrines and Methods of Islam* (St Paul, MN: St Paul Pioneer Press, 1985).

Zepp, Ira, *A Muslim Primer: Beginner's Guide to Islam* (London: Sheed & Ward, 1992).

NOTES
1. Michael L. Fitzgerald and John Borelli, *Interfaith Dialogue: A Catholic View* (New York: Orbis Books, 2006), pp. 229–32. See also Anthony O'Mahony and Peter Bowe, eds., *Catholics in Interreligious Dialogue* (Leominster: Gracewing, 2006), Chapter 8.
2. In Sackito Murata and William Chittick, *The Vision of Islam*, p. xxv.
3. Seyyed Hossein Nasr, *Ideals and Realities*, p. 68.
4. *Ibid.*, p. 69.
5. *Ibid.*, p. 73.
6. Kenneth Cragg, *Readings in the Qur'an* (Sussex: Sussex Academic Press, 1999), p. 34.
7. Seyyed Hossein Nasr, *Op. Cit.*, p. 61.
8. *Ibid.*, p. 47.
9. John Renard, *Responses to 101 Questions*, p. 35.
10. *Ibid.*
11. Redmond Fitzmaurice, 'The Christian God and Allah', *The Christian Understanding of God*, James Byrne, ed. (Dublin: Columba Press, 1993), pp. 167f.
12. Seyyed Hossein Nasr, *Op. Cit.*, p. 28.
13. John Renard, *Understanding the Islamic Experience*, p. 22.

14. William Chittick, 'Eschatology', *Islamic Spirituality: Foundations*, Seyyed Hossein Nasr, ed. (London: SCM Press, 1989), p. 393.
15. John Renard, *Responses to 101 Questions*, p. 43.
16. Fazlur Rahman, *Major Themes of the Qur'an* (Minneapolis, MN: Bibliotheca Islamica, 1989), p. 106.
17. John Renard, *Responses to 101 Questions*, p. 41.
18. John Renard, *In the Footsteps*, p. 59.
19. Cited in Ira Zepp, *A Muslim Primer*, p. 123.
20. Roger du Pasquier, *Unveiling Islam*, p. 89.
21. Seyyed Hossein Nasr, *Traditional Islam in the Modern World* (London: Kegan Paul, 1987), p. 30.
22. John Renard, *In the Footsteps*, p. 47.
23. John Renard, *Response to 101 Questions*, pp. 50–2.
24. Kenneth Cragg and R. Marston Speight, *The House of Islam* (London: Wadsworth, 1988), p. 127.
25. John Renard, *Seven Doors to Islam Spirituality and the Religious Life of Muslims* (Berkeley, CA: University of California Press, 1996), p. 17.
26. *Ibid.*, pp. 16–17.
27. John Renard, *Understanding the Islamic Experience*, p. 151.
28. Annemarie Schimmel, *Mystical Dimensions of Islam* (Chapel Hill, NC: University of North Carolina Press, 1975), pp. 167f.
29. Jean Louis Michon, '*The Spiritual Practices of Sufism*', *Islamic Spirituality*, Seyyed Hossein Nasr, ed., p. 289.
30. Redmond Fitzmaurice, 'Sufis – Muslim Mystics', p. 5.
31. *Ibid.*
32. Cf. Annemarie Schimmel, *Rumi's World: The Life and Work of the Great Sufi Poet* (London: Shambala, 2001). See the comprehensive collection of poems, *The Essential Rumi*, Coleman Barks, trans. (San Francisco: Harper, 1996), which has contributed to the Western interest in Sufism and the poet.
33. Cited in Roger du Pasquier, *Unveiling Islam*, p. 156.
34. William Stoddart, *Sufism*, pp. 51–2.

CHAPTER 4

Christian–Muslim Dialogue

In Islam, the more something is of God the less the human is needed. In contrast, the biblical [Christian] view is that the more the divine is giving, the more the human is recruited.

KENNETH CRAGG

A major obstacle in Christian–Muslim encounter is the weight of history. Muslims still remember the atrocities committed during the Crusades in Palestine and the destruction of the great Islamic civilisation in Spain due to the draconian rule of Ferdinand and Isabella. Similarly, Christians still subconsciously hear the war drums of the Turkish army at the gates of Vienna. And today, many in the Christian West see the weakness of the present-day Muslim world as a danger. The Vatican Council acknowledges all this and urges both Christians and Muslims to move beyond the memories of historical conflict, 'to forget the past and strive sincerely for mutual understanding' (NA 3). But forgetting does not mean the denial of the past. Rather, it entails naming and owning some of the obstacles generated by our relationship, and moving forward from there.

NAMING THE OBSTACLES

A Christian Ignorance Regarding Islam

Even though the movement of dialogue has been largely initiated in the West by the Catholic and Christian churches, Christians, due to prejudice, hostility and misinformation, have remained largely ignorant of Muslim faith. By the Middle Ages it was widely accepted in the West that Islam was a treacherous offspring of the true faith. Legends abounded to denigrate its prophet and the Qur'an. In short, there was no need – theologically or spiritually – for Christians to relate to Islam.

Muslim Fear of Christian Mission

Muslim scholars speak of the deeply ingrained suspicion of Christian mission. Despite the great service given by missionaries in health and education, Christians have been seen as coming from the superior West and propagating their faith with the help of colonialism. From the Christian side, there is a certain diffidence in the face of Islam, an uncertainty about the motives of Muslims who come to dialogue: are they just strengthening the position of Muslim minorities in view of an eventual Islamic takeover? This is compounded by the fact that the religious freedom demanded by Muslims in western countries is not granted to Christians in certain Islamic countries.

Muslims Are Not Attracted to Dialogue

One reason for this is the strict finality of the qur'anic revelation and the ensuing theological consciousness it nurtures. While there is a small number of significant Muslim scholars who have worked in the area of Muslim–Christian dialogue, it is fair to say that the ordinary Muslim, espousing a very self-contained faith, feels no need to make such a move:

> By virtue of the simplicity of its presentation, its apologetic, the repetition of the same affirmations which have been understood since infancy and the atmosphere which it creates, Islam surrounds its faithful with a protective hedge. The sense of the sacred, the worship of the one God, the shoulder-to-shoulder solidarity, the basic values of the family and group support, the glories of past civilisation – all this is enough for those who experience it; why should they feel the need to look for anything else?[1]

Other reasons, and sobering ones at that, are differences of general social background and culture. All these have contributed to remove Muslims from the dialogue table. As one writer says, when they come to conferences and events, they are 'invited guests'. They are not the initiators. Indeed, they perceive dialogue as a Western invention.[2]

Fear of Secularisation

A number of Muslim scholars single out Western secularisation as a problem:

> We are not really facing for the most part the problem of dealing with Christianity, we are facing the problem of dealing with secularism in a particular guise – let us say, with a good leverage of Christian faith, but nonetheless by our standards … essentially a secular outlook … the modern

Christian often seems to be more a child of that tradition than the child of Christianity when Christianity was a solid, all-embracing, all-powerful faith.[3]

Obviously there is some truth in this view. Shi'ite philosopher Seyyed Hossein Nasr could see Islam speaking easily with Augustine, Bernard, Luther and John Wesley, but not with many western Christians today, though I surmise that in Rowan Williams, the Archbishop of Canterbury, and Pope Benedict XVI, he would find worthy dialogue partners. It is Nasr's view that between Islam and Christians of the West, there is, at present, the subtle presence of a 'third party'. The problem is that Christians have identified with this secular 'anti-religious spirit', and when they judge Islam in light of it, they make dialogue impossible.[4]

While appreciating Muslim fears, a distinction must be made between secularism and secularisation. Secularism is a way of life that is basically atheistic, though it may lack atheism's intellectual rigour. With a strong emphasis on the primacy of the individual, meaning and purpose are negotiated within the bounded autonomous self. The individual comes first and only then can we talk of freedom and belonging to community. Secularism poses as the defender of pluralism but yet can demand uniformity and conformity, France's ban on Muslim women wearing the *hijab* (face veil) being an example. Enforcing its ideas through the instrumentality of political correctness, but becoming uneasy and exclusivist when religion moves out of the church and on to the street. Religion is seen as a private affair and for some secularists is an irrational fundamentalism. However, Christianity has always engaged with the secular, because it recognises that there is no safe space for faith apart from the world and that it is in the world of open secularity that religion can best flourish. This is the main thrust of Vatican II's *Pastoral Constitution on the Church in the Modern World.* Using the language of mutuality in the proclamation of Christian faith, its spirit continued in the great social encyclicals that have vindicated human rights, respect for religious freedom, the values of democracy and primacy of justice, and the importance of human and social solidarity – in short, secularisation. This bringing to the fore in a modern way of the dialogue between reason and faith is also a concern of Benedict XVI, as we shall see in his challenge to Islam.

A Clash of Superiorities
This has been an obstacle to dialogue from the beginning. Both religions claim superiority as universal and final religions. Such claims are complex in nature,

for while Christianity claims its own theological superiority as being the final revelation of God in Jesus Christ, as a faith addressing modern and postmodern issues it has a certain cultural superiority. Islam, instead, claims a strict religious superiority which questions the purity of Christian commitment to monotheism. Strengthening the Muslim claim is the fact that while the raw total of Christians may be larger, the number of practising Muslims is greater (the World Christian Database in 2007 put the number of Muslims in the world at 1.6 billion, while Christians totalled 2.3 billion. This makes Christians 33 per cent of the global population and Muslims 21 per cent, meaning that together, Christians and Muslims represent well over half the human family).[5]

The Clash of Civilisations

This has to be mentioned because it is uppermost in our minds today. *The Coming Clash of Civilizations, Or, the West Against the Rest*, by Harvard political scientist Samuel Huntingdon (1993), has become an intellectual rallying cry for those who are convinced that Islam as a religious civilisation is fast filling the geopolitical power vacuum created by the breakdown of the Soviet union.[6] The Salman Rushdie affair, the ongoing terrorist attacks and barbarous actions by Middle Eastern Muslim extremists which culminated in the attack on the New York Twin Towers in September 2001 are seen as proof of Huntingdon's thesis. While this thesis as a largely political and secular document has some truth, the author does not moderate in any way his antipathy toward Islam. Relations with Muslims therefore become a question of realpolitik – how to save the West and, in particular, how to insulate the United States, as the core state of the West, from further incursions by what is seen as a violent civilisation.

The question now becomes, how does one relate to Islam when it appears that fanatical acts of violence perpetrated by Muslims are fuelled by religion? While this is a popular view of Islam in general, and one often communicated in the media, historian Bernard Lewis reminds us that some Muslim groups are in fact returning to a more fundamentalist outlook, in which all mankind is divided in two: the House of Islam, where Muslim law and faith prevail, and the House of Unbelief, or the House of War, which it is the duty of Muslims to bring into Islam. Lewis makes the interesting point that Islam, as a monotheism, has, at various stages, especially in Iran, been influenced by the dualism of cosmic religions. Evil was seen as a reality pitted against God: God had enemies and needed help to overcome them:

If the fighters in the war for Islam, the holy war 'in the path of God', are fighting for God, it follows that their opponents are fighting against God. The duty of God's soldiers is to dispatch God's enemies as quickly as possible to the place where God will chastise them – that is to say, the afterlife.[7]

When these more disoriented elements of contemporary Islam are put forward by the media as normative, moderate Islam is pushed aside, together with those who are interested in dialogue. In the face of realities such as these, pursuing the path of Christian–Muslim dialogue can appear singular and idealistic. Yet it is the patient commitment of individuals meeting across boundaries that is a very real factor in bringing about world peace. The thesis of Hans Küng has now become a slogan for work in interfaith :

No world peace without peace among the religions, no peace among the religions without dialogue among the religions and no dialogue among the religions without accurate knowledge of one another.[8]

While aware of 'the clash' that divides Muslims and Christians, the Church's way is not that of secular states; it is the way of dialogue. The Church is an intercivilisational pilgrim community; that is, the Church is no longer only Western European or North American, it is also Middle Eastern. And as such, members of the Church can find their experience of God positively shaped by Islam. It is in experiences such as these that boundaries are crossed. Mahmoud Ayoub tells us that we need to turn to Middle Eastern Muslims and Christians if we are to learn about dialogue in practice. He notes many instances where they live peaceably together in an Islamo-Christian culture, a culture nurtured by the Eastern piety and spiritual dynamism of the Holy Desert Fathers out of which Islam was born.[9] The implication here is that it is in returning to their roots that Christians and Muslims can move closer together.

Furthermore, with developments in dialogue today, the missionary thrust of Muslims and Christians need no longer be a threat to each other. In the past, the Muslim 'fear' of Christian mission has not been about mission as such, but about the ethics of mission, the use of genuine humanitarian needs for purposes of conversion. But even for the Muslim, mission or *da'wah* means that what matters to a person at a faith level is worth sharing. For many Muslims, *da'wah* is simply living by Islam and setting a good example for fellow believers and others. In this understanding, *da'wah* is a way of life and cannot be left out of dialogue.[10] Such practice is comparable with the vision of *Dialogue and Proclamation* (1991), which states that, in the mission of the Church, proclamation may be in words but may more often be simply the witness of Christian lives.

In this chapter, then, we will return to 'beginnings', to what essentially unites us – our brotherhood and sisterhood in the faith of Abraham, publicly affirmed by Pope John Paul II in his outreach to Muslims. We will then explore the differences that emerge in our understanding of faith in the One God. Moving beyond differences, we will briefly reflect on how we may come together in God's service, and finally ask what Benedict XVI's particular challenges are.

ONE IN THE FAITH OF ABRAHAM

From the seventh century, Christian polemicists accepted Islamic descent through Ishmael from the line of Abraham, but interpreted it in a wholly negative manner. Influenced by St Paul's letter to the Galatians 4:2-26, Muslims were called Ishmaelites or Hagarenes, descendants of Abraham's mistress, Hagar. Emphasis was placed on physical descent, with the object of excluding them from a spiritual link to the patriarch and the covenant. And yet it is also in the teaching of St Paul that Abraham is presented as the primal model of faith for *all* believers in the one God. The Qur'an attests to the spiritual meaning of this link with Abraham (16:120-123), and warns that physical descent is of no use if faith is lacking (2:124). While the Qur'an claims that the practice of Islam comes closest to the pure faith of the Patriarch (Q 3:68), it nowhere asserts that it is *only* Muslims who are Abraham's children. Of Christians, it goes so far as to say: 'You will find the nearest of all people in affection to the Believers [Muslims], those who say they are Christians' (Q 5:82) and it also advises:

> Dispute not with People of the Book save in the fairer manner, except for those of them that are wrong; and say: 'we believe in what has been sent down to us, and what has been down to you: our God and your God is one, and to Him we have surrendered.' (Q 29:46)

Since Vatican II, shared faith in the one God is being accepted as foundational in Catholic dialogue with Muslims. But it is interesting to note that support for this position can be traced back to a papal document written one thousand years ago.

In 1076, the Muslim ruler, al-Nasir of Bijaya (now in modern Algeria), wrote to Pope Gregory VII requesting that a local priest, Severandus, be ordained bishop to care for Christians in the ruler's domain. In his reply, the Pope, among other things, said: 'You and we owe this charity to ourselves especially because we believe in and confess one God, admittedly in a different way, and daily praise and venerate him.' The Pope concluded the letter with wishes for al-Nasir's health and with the prayer that 'after the long space of this life that same God will lead you into the bosom of blessedness of the most holy patriarch Abraham'. By acknowledging that a Muslim is a child of Abraham, this eleventh-century papal letter thereby implies that Christians and Muslims, through a common ancestor, form one family in monotheistic faith.[11]

The Vatican II document *Lumen Gentium* states that God's plan of salvation includes those who acknowledge the Creator. Of Muslims, *Lumen Gentium* says: 'In the first place, among them are the Muslims, who, professing to hold the faith of Abraham, along with us, adore the one and merciful God' (LG 16). Likewise, *Nostra Aetate* assures Muslims that the Church looks on them with esteem (NA 3). It goes on to highlight the common beliefs of the two religions, stating that Muslims, like Christians 'adore the one God, living and enduring, merciful and all-powerful, Maker of heaven and earth and Speaker to men'. There is a certain Muslim resonance here, in that 'living', 'enduring', 'merciful' and 'all-powerful' echo the Beautiful Names of God. The text goes on to say that while Muslims do not acknowledge Jesus as God, they revere him as a prophet, and honour Mary, his virgin mother, at times calling on her with devotion. It also alludes to the Islamic belief in final judgement and to the Muslim practices of prayer, fasting and almsgiving. *Nostra Aetate* opens up many avenues for dialogue but it does omit articles of the Islamic creed about which Muslims are sensitive. There is no mention of the prophet Muhammad nor of the Qur'an. Nor is there any discussion of the Muslim mystical tradition.

It has also been said that both *Lumen Gentium* and *Nostra Aetate* strike a note of caution regarding the relation of Muslims to the patriarch: the former saying that Muslims 'profess to hold' the faith of Abraham, and the latter claiming that they 'associate' themselves with the faith of Abraham. These are rather restrictive interpretations which seem to imply that while Muslims consider themselves in the line of the faith of Abraham, Christians do not feel this to be the case.[12] Archbishop Michael Fitzgerald, a scholar in Islamic and Arabic studies, alerts us to the fact that while there are ambiguities regarding the biological descent from

Abraham through Ishmael, and profound differences in the ways Jews, Christians and Muslims see Abraham, there is a spiritual unity, in that each religion finds in Abraham a model of faith. He considers that Muslim faith in the One God is recognised in *Nostra Aetate* as a faith that flows into daily living: '[Muslims] strive to submit themselves without reserve to the hidden decrees of God' (NA 3). Fitzgerald suggests that this basic attitude is by no means a fatalistic submission to a despotic divinity, but the response of an adoring servant to an 'ever Greater God'.[13]

Pope John Paul II moves beyond historical ambiguities and embraces Muslims as brothers and sisters in this faith in the One God. After his election as Pope, he lost little time in giving renewed impetus to the openness in relation to Islam. The encyclical *Redemptor Hominis* (1979) is one of the most important statements of his teaching office on the question of relations with the followers of other religions. Singling out Jews and Muslims specifically as worthy of our esteem, he urges Catholics to use a wide variety of human and spiritual means to come closer to other believers: 'dialogue, contacts, prayer in common, investigation of the treasures of human spirituality, in which, as we well know, the members of these religions also are not lacking'. In the same paragraph, John Paul acknowledges that the Spirit of truth is operative outside the Church in the many beliefs of the followers of non-Christian religions, concluding with the following life-giving words:

> It is a noble thing to have a predisposition to understanding every person, analysing every system and recognising what is right; this does not at all mean losing certitude about one's own faith or weakening the principles of morality. (RH 6)

One could say that this text was a charter for his pontificate, during which he made well over sixty trips to over 110 foreign countries, meeting with members of other faiths. John Paul was unambiguous about the spiritual bond that unites us in the faith of Abraham. In his message to the President of Pakistan (23 February 1981) he referred to Abraham as one 'to whose faith Christians, Muslims and Jews eagerly link their own'.[14] In Lisbon, on 3 May 1982, he spoke of how 'Abraham, our common forefather, teaches all – Christians, Jews and Muslims – to follow the path of mercy and love.'[15] And there was a special energy in his address to a great gathering of Muslim youths in Casablanca on 19 August 1985:

I often meet young people, usually Catholics. It is the first time that I find myself with young Muslims. Christians and Muslims. We have many things in common, as believers and human beings. We live in the same world, marked by many signs of hope, but also by multiple signs of anguish. For us Abraham is a model of faith in God, of submission to his will and confidence in his goodness. We believe in the same God, the one God, the living God, the God who created the world and brings his creatures to perfection. It is therefore towards this God that my thought goes and my heart rises: it is of God himself that, above all, I wish to speak with you; of him, because it is in him that we believe, you Muslims and we Catholics.[16]

When we are being returned to the faith of Abraham, we are not being asked to centre on an ancient figure, a religious giant from distant millennia. His importance to Jews, Christians and Muslims is that he is a symbol – and a critical one – of how to relate to the Transcendent. As symbol, he is *hanif*, a 'seeker'. He 'is not a man who possesses faith, but the movement of faith; he is not the security of faith, but the quest for faith; not the arrogance of faith but the humility of faith'.[17] This dynamic movement of faith is 'the spiritual body' in which Jews, Christians and Muslims are united, and as members of different communities, they are children of Abraham, each according to their own self-understanding. For Christians Abraham does not replace Jesus, since only faith in Jesus as the risen Lord makes Christians children of Abraham. As St Paul says, 'If you belong to Christ, you are all children of Abraham according to the promise' (Gal 3:29). For Jews, Abraham does not replace the Mosaic law, since it is through obedience to the Torah that they live the faith of Abraham. And for Muslims, Abraham does not replace the Qur'an and the Prophet, as they are both necessary for making the faith of Abraham concrete for the Muslim community.

The Witness of Muslim Faith

Many Christians living among Muslims have experienced the purifying effect of contact with Islam. It is as if their faith is being scoured of accretions and brought back to its essential content. Exposure to the greatness and 'purity' of divine transcendence in Islam can rebound for the Christian in a deeper appreciation of the divine love that became human in Jesus Christ, and so there is less of a tendency to take the incarnation for granted. Christians can also be challenged by

Muslims' firmness of faith and by their readiness to express that faith in public. Though he did not name Islam explicitly, John Paul II probably had Muslims in mind when he wrote that the firm belief of the followers of non-Christian religions – a belief that is also the effect of the Spirit of truth operating outside the visible confines of the mystical body – can make Christians ashamed at being often themselves disposed to doubt concerning the truths revealed to them by God (RH 6).

Engaging Our Differences
Jesus the Prophet and Servant of God

According to Islam, Jesus (who is *Isa* in Arabic) came, as the prophets before him, with a divine message. This message was the gospel (*Injil* – 'evangel'). The Qur'an recounts several events in the life of Jesus which appear in the gospels, and in addition one also finds echoes of stories from apocryphal scriptures. *Injil* in the Qur'an is not the life of Jesus, it is the message Jesus brought from Allah, namely a confirmation of Allah's monotheism and Moses's revelation of Torah. Furthermore, in confirming the revelation of Allah's Oneness, Jesus as prophet and servant is word of God *(kalimat* – Allah), and though he is spoken of as having been given the Spirit, it is not because he is a manifestation of the mystery of God but because he is at God's service and declares God's unalterable will.

Jesus is called many names: Apostle, Messenger, Messiah (Christ), Word, Prophet, Spirit and Servant. Incidentally, the word *abd* meaning 'servant' is best rendered theologically as 'creature', because in Islam the human being is the property of God. It is as creature that Jesus is servant.[18] The Qur'an does not draw neat distinctions between these titles, and that is why there is a good deal of overlap in their usage, but it is nevertheless helpful to be aware of their Islamic meaning. Jesus is born of the Virgin Mary but this is no proof of his divinity, simply a sign of God's omnipotence (Q 19:21). Jesus' miracles are explicitly acknowledged, but he works them not as God's Son but 'with God's permission' (Q 3:43). The Qur'an speaks variously of a 'Word of God' coming to Jesus or of Jesus being the Word, in that as prophet he speaks for God. Some Muslim commentators link this with the Virgin Birth and speak of Jesus as 'a Word which was cast on Mary'. The Qur'an also teaches that God 'strengthened Jesus with his Spirit' (Q 19:30-33). As Spirit-guided, indeed sometimes called Spirit, Jesus is accorded more honour and deference than all the prophets who preceded Muhammad, and as the Prophet's precursor complements the pragmatic legalism of the great warner.

For the average Muslim, Jesus is an example of sanctity, piety and the heartfelt experience of God, and as exemplar of *ishan* (holiness) he is especially loved by the Sufis.

The qur'anic summary on Jesus takes place between verses 5:67-72, and the following is a helpful commentary on the text:

> Prophet, Apostle of God, servant of God, these are titles which are applied in the Qur'an to so many other prophetic figures. But Christ is more than that. Everything in the Qur'an inclines us to represent him as being above the common condition of man ... An exceptional divine work, an exceptional messenger, favoured in all things by God, Christ witnesses to an exceptional divine concern. Through all that the Qur'an has to say about Jesus, we cannot fail to recognise an unquestionable convergence: everything it gives leads to the declaration of Christ's surpassing greatness.[19]

THE CRUCIFIXION

It is commonly held by Muslims that Jesus did not die on the cross, but was taken up into heaven by God before his death (see Q 4:157-159). The context of these verses is a strong polemic against the Jews for 'straying from the guidance of the Book' and in particular for falsely charging Mary with unchastity. The Jews go on to boast, as the Qur'an says: 'We killed Christ Jesus the Son of Mary, the Apostle of God.' Then a quick correction is added:

> But they killed him not, nor crucified him; but it was made to appear to them. For of a surety they killed him not. Nay. God raised him up to Himself.

These verses have been subjected to a great deal of interpretation and some first- and second-century interpreters speculate that a substitute was crucified instead of Jesus. Tradition has it that Jesus will return at the end of time to vanquish the anti-Christ and to usher in the age of justice. After forty years he will die and be buried in Medina with Muhammad and will rise in the general resurrection along with the rest of humankind.

Regarding the death of Jesus, the Islamic scholar, Hammudah Abdulati, presents the classic Islamic argument for its denial. Chief among his theses are: (i) Can the crucifixion be reconciled with the justice, mercy, power and wisdom of God? (ii) Is Jesus' death at the hands of his enemies consistent with the providence of God? (iii) Is it feasible to believe that the God who forgave Adam and Eve their sin would need a sacrifice of Jesus to forgive the human race?[20] This last thesis is the most compelling from an Islamic perspective. That there might be a significance in the death of Jesus is of little interest to Muslims. For Islam, unlike Christianity, does not attribute to the creator God a redemptive relation to humanity.

A Christian Response

One can have a number of responses to this short précis on Jesus in the Qur'an. The first might be a sense of disappointment that the reality of Jesus is short-changed. Christian readers may feel that they have nothing to learn from the qur'anic Jesus and that it leaves no room for them to communicate their faith in Jesus as Son of God and Redeemer.

The second is more complex. It asks us to look at truth more historically and to imagine the context in which Islam originated in sixth-century Arabia. In his campaign against ancient Arabic polytheism – according to which Allah had daughters and maybe also sons – Muhammad had no choice but to reject the term 'Son of God'. He also adopted the story of Jesus in a form then current among the Arabs and interpreted it to suit his own purposes. Here Jesus' greatness consisted of the fact that in and through him as the servant of God, God had been at work. Hans Küng speculates that Muhammad's 'Christology' (as well as his teaching on the Oneness of God, eschatology and judgement) was influenced by the sectarian Judeo-Christian communities who fled to the East after the fall of Jerusalem under Hadrian in 132 AD. Separated from the Jerusalem church, they gradually became removed from the more ontological ('two natures') understanding of Christ which was to become the orthodox teaching of the Church following the Councils of Nicea and Chalcedon. Küng offers the hypothesis that the Jewish-Christian movement, which came to grief in the early Church, has been preserved in Islam and to this day continues its influence in the world.[21] This more historical approach extends our imaginative sympathy and our patience with the development of religious doctrines. Through it, we realise how simplistic and exclusive formulations undermine the richness of the traditions around Jesus, who – no matter how we think about him – is not the exclusive property of one faith. And we begin to realise how close Jews, Christians and Muslims are when we see them in their origins.

A third response entrusts itself to the sharing of faith and mutual witness, which is also the aim of interreligious dialogue. It is true that our beliefs are different, yes, but stories of great religious figures and events are a free-floating possession of humanity and we have no right to make exclusive claims on them. That the Qur'an settles for an understanding of Jesus as prophet and servant of God does not mean that it has nothing to say to us. Rather than opposing it and saying it is false, we should open ourselves to the motivation that lead to this particular presentation of Jesus. Jesus, as 'servant of Allah', was and is revered as a pure witness to *Allahu Akbar* – 'God is greater'. While, as Christians, we believe that the Greater God has come close to humanity in the person of Jesus the Son, is it not also true, as the gospels remind us, that what is unique about Jesus is that his very humanity, his death and resurrection have meaning only in his relationship to the Greater God, who is also the Father?

Fourth, when we focus on the person of Jesus as a prophet yet 'more than a prophet' (Mt 11:9), there arises a 'more' not only of the incarnate presence of the ever Greater God, but the 'more' also of different divine revelation. Kenneth Cragg points out that the Qur'an is generous in that it commends: 'Let the people of the gospel decide [judge] by what God has sent down there' (Q 5:47).[22] Deciding by the gospel, Cragg says we have to ask whether warning, guidance, education and direction by law are sufficient for humanity's total need? He comments on the gospel parable 'The Wicked Husbandmen', in which a vineyard owner sends to the husbandmen, not a servant but his son: 'I will send my Son, the Beloved' (Lk 20:13). It is a strange logic, intuits Cragg, for if the owner was seeking only the obedience of his servants and a greater yield on the estate, why would he send his son, who was brutally killed: 'Clearly, in the parable, the sending of "the heir" is a lifting of the whole relationship.'[23] God is concerned with more than obedience; what matters is relationship to him. In the parable, the message of the gospel is that the reach of divine life toward us is costly. In the human need for a relationship with God beyond obedience there arises the mystery of redemption, which follows a different logic from the Qur'an. For Christians and Muslims the human being is in the image of God. But Islam differs in that it has no doctrine of original sin. In Islam, the theomorphism (bestowing of God-like attributes) of the human being is basically unsullied. Due to the distractions of daily life, the believer can be prone to forgetfulness of their divine calling (*gaflah*) and to egocentrism. But the human will is purified in obedience to the Qur'an and God's forgiveness is always available when one turns to him. Christian revelation takes on board both the greatness and wretchedness of the human, having long been illuminated by the teachings of the Judeo-Christian tradition and especially St Paul (Rm 7:15). And so at the heart of the gospel is the mystery of redemption – the descent of God into the reality of human iniquity and the lifting of the human to the new sphere of intimacy with God, in which we share in the divine life.

To conclude, it might then be said that Muslims believe that, at one level, Christians are too serious, pathological even, in their diagnosis of the human condition, but that at the existential and practical level, where it really matters, they are not serious enough. Here Islam is serious, supplying all the help and 'reminders' for 'forgetful' egocentric men and women to walk with integrity before the One God. This view has been expressed by Nasr, who contends that Christian revelation represents the inner, esoteric aspect of the Abrahamic tradition as spiritual *way* rather than *law* and that Christ did not bring a new law or *shariah* but a way (*tariqah*) based on the love of God. This particular function of Christ is expressed in the Qur'an's reference to his particular nature as 'Spirit of God' (*ruh Allah*) and to his 'supernatural birth', connected with the virginity of Mary. In supporting faith in the Divine Unity (*Tawhid*), in legislating for all aspects of the human and providing fences for its shortcomings and guidance for its political and economic realities, Islam, says Nasr, is a 'middle way'. It is necessary and providential. Its strength lies in the fact that *shariah* in its very practical delineations is *divine* law:

> Islam never gave to Caesar what was Caesar's. Rather, it tried to integrate the domain of Caesar itself, namely, political, social and economic life, into an encompassing religious worldview.[24]

As we have seen, the Qur'an is committed to the confidence that man is perfectible by divine revelation as merciful guidance. It is revelation as education, through its prophets as tutors. Its emphasis is on law, its pattern is habit, its goal is obedience. The world is its school. If Islam is to be true to the rational thrust of its faith, which charters humanity on behalf of God to God, it must succeed. Inevitably, one must ask if this desire for success breeds an instrumentalism in a religion. Historically, the Church has relied on Caesar to strengthen it as an institution, adapting Roman law as a base for canon law. Yet in its inner essence (although this is sometimes ignored), the Church is always under critique from the 'evangelical principle' which emphasises the priority of grace over law in the self-giving of God to human beings. This gospel prevents the Church from being transposed into a theocracy, or into a total religio-political system. Christians know that there is something costly about the relationship of the Ever Greater God to human beings; that the transcendence of God as Triune is the transcendence of a love that comes to meet us where we are; and that the drama of this love, in its costliness and grace, has to always be at the heart of whatever witness Christians offer to Islam.

Mary the Mother of Jesus

The Islamic tradition regards Mary and Jesus as the only two human beings born without 'the touch of Satan' – that which makes newborn infants cry. Since Islam does not consider Jesus divine, Mary is not considered to be the mother of God. Yet, as the mother of a prophet, she is worthy of high honour in keeping with the role God chose for her. Sura 19 is named after Mary. No other woman is mentioned in the Qur'an, and while Mary appears therein more often than in the New Testament, it is with interesting differences. In the Qur'an, her own birth is miraculous and Zachary looks after her in her youth. A 'spirit of God', identified in later tradition as Gabriel, visits Mary, 'breathes' the Word into her garment and she hastens to a remote place, ashamed of her unmarried pregnancy. There she gives birth while clinging to a palm tree for support. As she shakes the tree in labour, it showers her with fresh, ripe dates. Invited to eat her fill, she chooses to fast and keep silence for the day, a 'fast of silence' that later Muslim mystical poets interpret as her call to think of nothing but God. When relatives accuse her unjustly, the infant Jesus speaks up in her defence. Mainstream Islam has denied Mary and all other women in the tradition the status of prophecy, but it is worth noting that at least one historically important scholar, Ibn Hazm of Cordoba (d. 1064), held that Mary did receive the revealed message that makes one a prophet (*nabi*), even if it was not with the full status of 'messenger' (*rasul*).[25] Mary's spouse, Joseph, does not appear in the Qur'an, but traditional lore includes him in Quranic New Testament scenes.

Muhammad, a Prophet

Tunisian Muslim scholar Mohammed Talbi, who has contributed much to Christian–Muslim dialogue, sums up the feelings of Muslims when he says:

> The Qura'nic veneration for Jesus prevented Muslims from letting any of their indignation extend to the founder of Christianity. The reverse is not always the case … concerning the Messenger of Islam.[26]

Nasr, who shows a deep appreciation for Christian theology, speaks with feeling when he says that the heart of Islamic–Christian misunderstanding is not the doctrines – these can by explained theologically, metaphysically – but the continual denigration of the Prophet with platitudes, diplomacy, humanitarian gestures towards Islam, and omission from Vatican declarations, as in *Nostra Aetate* 3, where he is just left aside.[27] As Christians become increasingly aware of Muslims' particular sensitivities, they will wish to acquaint themselves more with the authentic life and work of the Prophet. They will take into consideration the time and environment in which he lived in order to understand how, in his teaching and behaviour, he became the supreme model of the Islamic ideal. Also they will disassociate themselves from the negative judgements that came from our former concern for polemics and apologetics, and the question they will be addressing is: is Muhammad a prophet?

However, this question has to take into consideration our different definitions of prophethood in the fullest sense. In the Christian economy, prophecy in salvation history points to and reaches its fulfilment in the event of the Incarnate Word who is 'more than a prophet' (Mt 11:9). Neither Muhammad nor his status has been mentioned in official Church teaching. But in the context of religion in general, the most common interpretation would be that a number of factors conspired to shape him and make him a great religious reformer: 'the time of ignorance' in sixth-century Arabia, the Prophet's personality ('he was of a tremendous nature' [Q 68:4]), and his deep conviction that he was the recipient of a God-given message ('Make known that which hath been revealed to thee from the Lord' [Q 5:67]). The Dominican Islamic scholar, Jacques Jomier, likens the rise of Islam to the Protestant Reformation. A saint could achieve genuine reform without betraying the essentials of the message but the great reformers who are not saints can reread the biblical message in their own terms, in their own cultural context, and can leave us with a partial truth, but a truth nevertheless.[28]

The truth of Islam that Muhammad left us with is the truth of the Lordship of God and a call for justice and human dignity that cannot be silenced. The historical embodiment of this truth is the religious community that began in the Prophet's lifetime. Its continuation today, with over two billion members, evidences a quality of life that is on the whole satisfactory, and over the centuries it has produced many upright and saintly persons. Therefore, when asked if Mohammed was a prophet, we can repeat what was uttered long ago by Patriarch Timothy of Baghdad (d. 823) to the Caliph of his time: that Muhammad 'followed the way of the prophets'.[29] Through his proclamation of faith in the One God, he was *like* the biblical prophets. Yet in 'deciding by the gospel', or theologically, Muhammad is not to be identified with them, because the hallmark of their teaching and lifestyle was their correspondence with the One they foretold, who manifested in his flesh the coming of God himself among us as suffering Redeemer. But if in 'deciding by the gospel' we regret what has been termed 'the Caesar' in Muhammad, it has to be, as Cragg points out, for the sake of the many 'things of God' (Mt 22:21; Mk 12: 17; Lk 20:25) that move us to acknowledge him, and for which he is revered as the Prophet of Islam.[30]

The Qur'an and Revelation

As we have seen, the Qur'an constitutes the primary nourishment for the faith of Muslims, as they learn it by heart in childhood and have it constantly brought to mind through the many channels of Arab-Islamic culture. Muslims do not expect that Christians will hold to the convictions of Islam, so they will be content if we say, 'The Qur'an declares that ...' or 'as it is written in the Qur'an ...' Such expressions show respect for both Christian and Muslim feelings. Nevertheless, believers of both faiths consider themselves to be the fortunate beneficiaries of 'the gift of the Word', and it would be fitting, then, that both parties dedicate some time to clarifying the ways in which their religions receive and understand God's Word.

We know that for Christians, divine revelation culminates in Jesus Christ, the Word made flesh, and every book that claims to be the Word of God must be appreciated in terms of this regulating principle. Yet theologians of interreligious dialogue today are moving beyond the position that the Qur'an has no relationship to the Judeo-Christian stream of salvation history. The revelation of God in Christ is not monolithic. We must, writes the Dominican theologian, Claude Geffré, entertain the possibility that, in the gracious providence of God, the unique revelation of God may take 'differentiated' forms.[31] Just as Muhammad is being recognised as a genuine prophet for Muslims, so the Qur'an must be recognised as a revelation of God appropriate for Arabs in its original context and still appropriate for Muslims all over the world today. And as a 'differentiation' of God's revealing Word, it is a 'reminder' (*dhikr*) for Christians, as it is for Muslims, that whatever the differentiation 'God is our adequacy' (Q 3:173).

COMPETING IN HOLINESS

For each of you we have appointed a law and a way of conduct. If God had so willed He would have made you all one community. But it is His will to test you in what He has given you; so compete in goodness. To God shall you all return and He will tell you about what you have been disputing. (Q 5:48)

Our differences give us our identities. The more we understand the other as he or she is and wishes to be, the more each of us, Christian and Muslim, paradoxically, is freed to 'give an account of the hope that is in us, and to do it with courtesy and a clear conscience' (1 Pt 3:15). We have also engaged in some small way in what Pope John Paul II referred to as 'the noble' engagement of learning about the other (RH 6). Such learning is an adventure. We may not in the end know what to do with it, but the coming together of the religions is ultimately about 'competing in holiness' (John Paul II), or, as the Qur'an says: 'competing in goodness'(Q 5:48). Thus there arises the possibility of so many other levels of meeting between Christians and Muslims, such as the dialogue of life, the dialogue of service and the dialogue of religious experience.

The Dialogue of Life

For most people, dialogue is carried out by what has come to be called the 'dialogue of life'. Here we do not choose our dialogue partners: we live together in neighbourhoods, we meet socially and we work together. As Christians and Muslims, we bear daily witness to the values derived from our respective faiths, announcing what we profess in deed more so than words. The particular challenge for Muslims living in the West is that they have lost the shelter of the Islamic state and culture. Yet, as Kenneth Cragg points out, while this can be a source of suffering, it can also be a challenge to Muslims to recover Islam in its pre-Hijra phase (before Muhammad's flight to Medina); a recovery of the call to Islam before it became a culture – and how this can be purifying:

As Islam recognises its vocation to be just a religion in situations where it is a minority faith, the quality of Islamic faith in its cohesion and understanding of compassion can contribute to the common good of other faiths as well.[32]

It is this kind of faith that Pope John Paul II welcomed and encouraged when he addressed ex-patriot Muslim guest workers in Mainz in Germany in 1980:

> With upright hearts you have carried your faith from your homeland into another land. If you pray here now to God as your Creator and Lord, then you too belong to that immense band of pilgrims who from the days of Abraham onwards, again and again have set out from home in order to search for the true God and find Him. When you are not afraid to pray in public, you give an example to Christians which deserves our respect. Practise your faith in foreign lands, too, and do not allow it to be misused by any human or political interest.[33]

A God-Centred Ethic

Muslims scholars who have been exposed to Western thought acknowledge that the adventure of dialogue with Christians is less perilous than staying within rigid boundaries of faith and defending frontiers that have now become an anachronism. Tunisian Muslim, Mohammed Talbi claims:

> The dividing lines between different faiths is no longer run in the same direction as before. The opposition is not so much between different concepts of God and the way in which to serve him. A far deeper division has taken place between those who are striving to attain man's destiny without God, and those who can conceive of man's future in and through God.[34]

The threat of secularism has led Muslim and Christian scholars to press for the joint development of a God-centred ethic as one of the most fertile grounds for collaboration and service to humanity. The Qur'an is quite prescriptive on shared ethical issues with Christians: 'Help one another in righteousness and piety, but help not one another in sin and rancour' (Q 5:2). More fundamental is the famous text of The Trust (Q 7:171), wherein God calls all human beings to stand forth and be his witnesses. Here we stand with Muslims in a common allegiance to God the Creator. This principle enjoins people of all faiths to develop a global ethic with a view to creating a climate conducive to the survival of humankind, the attainment of peace and harmony and the enrichment of life for all.

In this God-centred ethic, the Christian emphasis on love must be integrated with the qur'anic focus on justice. The text of Matthew, 'Not everyone who says to me, "Lord, Lord", will enter the kingdom of heaven, but only the one who does the will of my Father in heaven' (Mt 7:21), concurs with the Qur'an: 'Do justice, it is nearer to piety' (Q 5:8) and 'God loves those who act in justice' (Q 49:9). A God-centred ethic has also to find a solution to the contentious issues of human rights for all peoples, regardless of religion. In this connection, Western Christians need to remind themselves that Muslims live among them as minorities. Their challenge is to practise Islam as simply one faith in a more plural society. While they may have equality with all citizens of the state, they may feel marginalised at a religious level. For example, the Muslim religious holidays are not always recognised, dietary restrictions and dress codes can pose difficulties in public schools and workplaces, and prisons, hospitals and homes for the elderly do not always ensure that the religious services and dietary provisions are suitable to Muslim residents' needs. Such behaviour undermines the cherished principle of collaboration and does not model the ideal of religious freedom which Christians often expect to be observed where they live as minorities in Islamic states.

Communicatio in Sacris: A Note on Interreligious Prayer

A dialogue centred on the sharing of ideals and values will not be enough for believers who know that the most fundamental dialogue is the one which God himself initiates and develops in the hearts of people. This dialogue comes to fruition in the *communicatio in sacris* – the sharing of sacred things, especially in prayer. It is this conviction that led John Paul II to invite representatives of different religions to Assisi on 17 October 1986, to pray for peace. The Assisi event has been the stimulus for engagement in multi-religious prayer and worship, whether formally or informally. But responses to these developments have also shown that multi-religious prayer and worship is a delicate issue, doctrinally and pastorally, and must be approached with thought and care. 'Prayer is the banquet of monotheists,' a Muslim Imam once said in a lecture, and Muslims do give great witness to prayer.

As Christians we share a common faith with Muslims in the Creator God who is Sustainer and Judge. It is our fundamental belief in the One God that binds us together. Like *hanifs* (seekers of the One), we entrust ourselves to the movement of faith as Abraham did and so, whatever our differences, 'we stand together before God'. Such will be the basis for our coming together in prayer, and indeed of our service to humanity.

But Christians and Muslims stand together differently. When it comes to situations of public and formal prayer, the old Latin saying, *lex orandi, lex credendi* (our prayer arises from and ratifies our belief) comes into play. At the heart of Muslim faith is the resolute witness to the divine greatness (*Allahu Akbar*). Before God, the Muslim considers himself *abd* in the dual sense of slave and adorer. Based on God's absolute right to praise, the preference is for non-personal prayer. Christians may be tempted to see the repetitious structure of *salat* as a ritual formalism, but for the Muslim it expresses a negation of self before the inscrutable will of God. In a sense, it is God who is praising God through the gestures of the believer. Another aspect, though secondary, is that when Muslims pray they act as witnesses. They publicly affirm membership of the *Umma*, the community of those who submit and bear witness to the One God. Even when prayer is carried out in private, the communal dimension is there, if only because the person praying turns towards Mecca, the centre of the *Umma*.

These characteristics of praise, of adoration, of being members of a greater whole are also true for Christians at prayer. We are members of the Body of Christ who himself prays in and for his people in our prayer, whether public or private. But there is a major difference, in that Christian prayer is incarnational. It finds expression in words, signs, symbols and gestures that witness not only to divine transcendence but also to divine immanence, to the mystery of a divine love present in the person of Jesus and indeed in the communion of saints. This, to the majority of Muslims, can appear to be an invasion of 'the space of God'. It has been said that the heart of Muslim prayer is the witness to divine greatness of the Absolute, and that at the heart of Christian prayer is the witness to the absoluteness of Divine Love.

The Teaching Document of the Bishops' Conference of England and Wales (2010) advises how multi-religious prayer must be conducted in a way that is respectful of where we stand with others in faith:

> The guiding principle of Assisi, and guide for us, is 'We don't come to pray together, but we come together to *pray*.' As each religion prays, thus expressing its own faith, the others do not join in: they respect and silently give encouragement to those who are praying, and are in quiet solidarity with them on the basis of their own belief, and of the inner prayer that flows from it.[35]

It goes without saying that multi-religious prayer requires maturity in faith. It also requires preparation, especially when it comes to children. There is always the danger of confusing those with little experience or catechetical formation, and in the effort to be inclusive there is the risk that prayer across the faiths will be reduced to the lowest common denominator.

If, for formal and public occasions, we come together to stand individually in prayer, it is also possible, following the examples of the mystics and saints, to develop forms of praise and intercession which allow for a common experience of prayer. Such prayer is possible for people who are already friends. In this more simple coming together, they understand each other as *hanifs* – 'seekers of God' in the original Abrahamic sense. They can work with readings and prayers taken from their respective traditions. For both Muslims and Christians, to read is to 'remember' – to practise *dhikr* or to ruminate on the Word as a *lectio divina*. This may be done with the *Fatiha* or with the Lord's prayer, with the Beautiful Names of God or with key Qura'nic verses and verses of the Psalms.

By participating in this sharing, Christians and Muslims can find themselves oriented toward a spiritual emulation which can only draw them closer together. It is in the boldness of such meetings that they are enabled to move beyond clinging to the particularities of their faith as inheritances that keep them apart. Here interreligious dialogue reaches a much deeper level, that of the Spirit, where its validity lies in the deeper conversion of all towards God (DP 40-1).

THE CHALLENGE OF BENEDICT XVI

The relationship to Islam is one of the few areas where one notices a substantive difference between John Paul II and Benedict XVI. In a 1996 book-length interview with journalist Peter Seewald, the then Cardinal Ratzinger's view of Islam appears to range more widely than questions of religious difference. Here he expresses doubts about including Islam in Western-style pluralistic democracy in a similar way to the various Christian denominations, implying that Islam is more complicated, being the interplay of society, politics and religion, and indeed acknowledging that it must be addressed today because of its enhanced identity and renewed self-consciousness.[36]

Benedict has also irritated some Muslims owing to his opposition to Turkey's candidature for the European Union. In a preface to a 2008 book by an Italian philosopher and politician, Marcello Pera, he contends that interreligious dialogue is 'strictly speaking not possible', since it entails putting one's faith in parenthesis. Following this, Vatican spokesman Fr Frederico Lombardi explained that Benedict is not opposed to dialogue and to opening Christian faith to the challenge of the other, but that dialogue, as the Pope embraces it, is also an intercultural activity and must also address the human consequences of fundamentally different religious choices.[37]

The greatest crisis of Benedict's pontificate to date has been the fallout from his address on 12 September 2006 at Regensburg University, where he had taught for a number of years. The address, 'Faith, Reason and the University', was not about Islam at all but on a topic of great concern to him – that the intellectual traditions of Europeans from the late Middle Ages onwards have been chipping away at the fusion of faith and reason, placing them in completely separate spheres. By way of an example, Benedict ill-advisedly, or maybe on purpose, referred to the concept of divine transcendence in Islam, where the divine will is beyond all human categories, even that of rationality. He illustrated his point with an exchange, thought to have taken place in 1391, between a Persian scholar and the Byzantine Emperor, Manuel II Palaeologus. Manuel, the leader of the last Christian state in the East, belonged to a world in which Islam was the real superpower. Aware that the Qur'an states that 'There is no compulsion in religion', he knew from experience that it also speaks of holy war. During his address, Benedict described how Manuel turned to his interlocutor somewhat brusquely with these words:

> Show me just what Muhammad brought that was new, and there you will find things only evil and inhuman, such as his command to spread by the sword the faith he preached.

The emperor, having expressed himself so forcefully, then goes on to explain in detail why spreading the faith through violence is unreasonable.[38]

The question of reason and faith, and the related one of coercion in religion, were not inappropriate for a university lecture but it was the choice of the six-hundred-year-old text in particular that enraged Muslims worldwide. The Pope referred to his address four times afterwards in an attempt to dissociate himself from the text's comments. Passions cooled, however, after his successful visit to Turkey. In the Blue Mosque, the Grand Mufti paused abruptly to say: 'I am going to pray.' Facing Mecca, Benedict bowed his head, and silently, his lips moving, prayed beside the Muslim cleric, a gesture that was widely accepted as manifesting respect for Islam.

It has been said that John Paul II built bridges of humanism and brotherhood between the religions. Their base was the common belief in the One God. Benedict's approach is that it is now time to walk across those bridges and engage more truthfully with what is found at the other side. God is truth and acting unreasonably is against God's nature. In our dialogue with other religions, the critical issues of truth and reason – with their practical and cultural implications – can never be laid aside. Therefore with Islam, Benedict is concerned with social and cultural issues such as religious freedom and freedom of worship, the separation of the religious and political, and the rights of minority Christian groups to be accepted as citizens in theocratic states. While there is a mosque in Rome, there is no church in Saudi Arabia – this is not simply a question of different doctrines, or even of reciprocal give and take between religions, it is a question of human rights. Taking seriously the cultural impact of Islam and the propensity of certain groups towards violence in the name of God, Benedict is not afraid to ask the hard questions. Rather than focussing in an irenic way on Islamic monotheism, he turns to its cultural and social effects, thereby elevating Islam, along with its 2.6 billion believers, to a position of undeniable consequence in the Church's dialogue.[39]

Furthermore, as Thomas Rausch points out, during a moment in history when most Muslims perceive Europe as completely secular, if not irreligious, Pope Benedict is perhaps the one leader who can command their respect, because he speaks as a believer.[40] The positive Muslim response to his Regensberg lecture, which took place on 20 August 2005, supports this view. Thirty-eight leading Muslim intellectuals and religious leaders wrote a first *Open Letter to His Holiness Pope Benedict* on 12 October 2006. The signitaries endorsed Pope Benedict's statement in Cologne that

Interreligious and inter-cultural dialogue between Christian and Muslims cannot be reduced to an optional extra. It is, in fact, a vital necessity, on which in large measure our future depends.

While applauding his efforts to oppose the dominance of positivism and materialism in human life, they were concerned about perceived errors in his speech. The most basic issue raised was that the dichotomy between faith and reason, a Christian theological position, does not apply in the same way in Islam. But this does not mean that reason and intelligence are devalued, because as 'signs' of God they are in consonance with the Quranic truth of revelation. The signatories clarify the meaning of *jihad* specifically as 'struggle' on the way to God and say that for a religion to regulate rules for war, or outline circumstances in which war is necessary, does not make the religion warlike.

They also considered Pope Benedict's statement that 'for Muslim teaching, God is absolutely transcendent', to be simplistic and misleading. This is in light of Quranic texts which state that 'God is closer than the jugular vein' and 'wheresoever you turn, there is the Face of God', and the frequently used Name, the Merciful One, which expresses God's concern for human affairs. Yet they expressed willingness to work with the Pope in building peaceful and friendly relations based on mutual respect, justice and on 'what is common in essence in our shared Abrahamic tradition, particularly the two greatest commandments' in Mk 12:29-31 – love of God and neighbour.[41]

A year later, in October 2007, a second longer letter, *A Common Word Between Us and You*, addressed to the Pope and leaders of all the major Christian denominations, was published. The 138 signatories were representative Muslim scholars and religious leaders from forty-three nations and from all major Islamic traditions. The aim of the letter was to once again press for a harmonious dialogue between Muslims and Christians and to establish a 'common word' on which they may come together. As in the first letter, this 'common word' is the call to adhere to the oneness of God and to the two-fold commandment of love of God and neighbour – supported by both the Qur'an and the gospels.

It may be said these letters set a precedent, in that they brought together so many leading authorities and schools of Islam and united them in a positive affirmation. A precedent also in that Muslims were associating themselves affirmatively with the gospel in the face of traditional claims that the Christian Scriptures have been corrupted in transmission and are unreliable. And a precedent in that they challenged Muslims and Christians to live up to their own sacred teachings, implying that the basis for dialogue between the religions is not simply culture or politics, but is theologically sourced in the respective (though differing) Christian and Muslim identities in relation to God.[42]

Both letters show that representative Muslims do not see Benedict XVI as a crusader from the outside. Nor does Benedict see himself in that way. They focus on what both religions have in common – 'We both defend major religious beliefs – faith in God and obedience to God – and we both need to situate ourselves correctly in modernity' – which means facing issues such as how truth and tolerance are related.[43] Benedict comes to dialogue with a strategic purpose: he intends to create a conversation that supports the work of Islamic lawyers, scholars, religious leaders and reformers who claim that there are sources within their own authoritative texts and history on which modern societies can be built, based on the conviction that it is God's will that we be tolerant of those who see God differently. And that into the future, Islam may also find, within itself, the theological resources to make a distinction between 'God and Caesar'.[44] As their collaborator in faith, Benedict invites Muslims to enter into partnership with him in crossing the divide between those who conceive of humanity's future in and through God and those who envision human destiny without God.

SUMMARY

Islam has always been a challenge to Christianity in that both present themselves as final and true religions. But an added dimension to the challenge today is the rise of Islam as a culturally dominant power. For centuries, the Church persisted in responding disparagingly to its theological content, while Islam had an innate fear of mission and viewed the legitimate secularisation of Western Christian faith as being a capitulation to the secularism of Western society. Both were deep-seated outlooks that allowed little room for dialogue. *Nostra Aetate*'s statement that 'the Church has a high regard for Muslims' (NA 3) might seem, to our ears, outworn, but the openness it implied at that time was truly a new beginning. Pope John Paul II was to take this further by emphasising the common generic faith in the One God of Abraham that binds together Christians and Muslims as brothers and sisters. And, since the Spirit of truth is present is all religions, he praised and welcomed the disposition to study and engage with beliefs other than Christian (RH 6).

However, Christians and Muslims specify their faith in the One God differently and dialogue must honour this. Muslims witness to the Divine Oneness (*Tawhid*) of God, who is 'ever greater'; Christians witness to the Triune God of communion, who crosses the chasm between the divine and the human to the extent of being willing to suffer and die on the Cross, without ceasing to be God. Muslim witness to the greatness of God is a witness to Truth beyond our capacities; Christian witness to the ever greater God is a witness to the truth of the greatness of divine love. The Qur'an is logically consistent when it strictly rejects any statement about Jesus being anything more than the servant (*abd*) of God and a prophet. Other major points of difference are Muhammad and the Qur'an itself, and, according to Muslims, by not mentioning them, *Nostra Aetate* fails to give them status. Once again there is a clash of perspectives on how God relates to us: Christian revelation reaches its fullness in Jesus Christ who is the word made flesh, and in this perspective prophecy refers to the biblical prophets whose lives and teaching were a witness to the One they foretold, Christ. Muhammad is not a biblical prophet in this sense, nor is the Qur'an revelation in the sense of being part of the Judeo-Christian scriptures. Yet we must acknowledge that Muhammad and the Qur'an's unambiguous proclamation of the one transcendent God, which have undoubtedly been *the* source of God's word for the community of Islam, can also be word of God's grace in the world for Christians.

Doctrinal Christian dialogue with Islam tends to be static, due to these sharply defined differences. More dynamic is the dialogue of action, advocated by *Nostra Aetate* as 'the preservation and promotion of peace, liberty, social justice and moral values' (NA 3). In short, a God-centred ethic. Yet it is interesting to note that with Pope Benedict XVI, the dialogue is taking a new turn: he takes Islam seriously as a creed, but also implies that we have a prophetic responsibility to question our creeds if they in any way endorse violence or curtail religious freedom and human rights. And so, by inviting Muslims to the dialogue table he positively desires partnership in witnessing to faith in the transcendent God in our secularised culture.

FURTHER READING

Borrmans, Maurice, ed., *Guidelines for Dialogue Between Christians and Muslims* (Mahwah, NJ: Paulist Press, 1981).

Catholic International, 13:1 (2002) [special edition dedicated to Christian–Muslim relations].

Cragg, Kenneth, *Muhammad and the Christian: A Question of Response* (Oxford: Oneworld, 1999).

_____, *The Call of the Minaret* (London: Collins, 1986).

Fitzgerald, Michael L. and John Borelli, *Interfaith Dialogue: A Catholic View* (Maryknoll, NY: Orbis Books, 2006).

Kimball, Charles, *Striving Together: Way Forward in Christian–Muslim Relations* (Maryknoll, NY: Orbis Books, 1991).

Mohammed, Ovey SJ, *Muslim–Christian Relations: Past, Present, Future* (Maryknoll, NY: Orbis Books, 1999).

Recognize the Spiritual Bonds which Unite Us: 16 Years of Christian–Muslim Dialogue (Vatican City: PCID, 1994).

Siddiqui, Attaullah, *Christian–Muslim Dialogue in the Twentieth Century* (London: Palgrave Macmillan, 1997).

Swidler, Leonard, ed., *Muslims in Dialogue: The Evolution of a Dialogue* (Lampeter: Edwin Mellen Press, 1992).

Troll, Christian, *Dialogue and Difference: Clarity in Muslim–Christian Relations* (Maryknoll, NY: Orbis Books, 2010).

NOTES

1. Jacques Jomier, *How To Understand Islam* (London: SCM Press, 1989), p. 134.
2. Ataullah Siddiqui, *Christian–Muslim Dialogue in the Twentieth Century*, p. 169.
3. *Ibid.* p. 51, interview with Gai Eaton, Islamic Centre, London.
4. Seyyed Hossein Nasr, 'Comments On A Few Theological Issues in the Islamic–Christian Dialogue,' *Christian–Muslim Encounters*, eds., Yvonne Haddad and W. Haddad (Florida: University Press of Florida, 1995), p. 465.
5. John Allen, Jr., *The Future of the Church: How Ten Trends are Revolutionizing the Church* (London: Doubleday, 2009), p. 98.
6. For a critique of Huntington's article see Scott Alexander, 'The "Clash of Civilizations" and the Dialogic Imperative: A Self-Fulfilling Prediction?', *Chicago Studies*, 14 (2002), pp. 192–208.
7. Bernard Lewis, 'The Roots of Muslim Rage', *Catholic International*, pp. 50–2.
8. Hans Küng, 'Christianity and World Religions: Dialogue with Islam', L. Swidler ed., p. 251.
9. Mahmoud Ayoub, 'A Muslim Appreciation of Christian Holiness' in *Islamochristiana* 11 (1985), p. 96. See Ayoub in 'Christian–Muslim Relations in the Twenty-First Century, A Roundtable Discussion', *Islam and Christian Muslim Relations*, 3 (June 1992), pp. 25–6.
10. Ataullah Siddhiqui, pp. 70–8.
11. Thomas Michel, 'Christian–Muslim Dialogue in a Changing World', *Theology Digest* 39 (1992), p. 305.
12. Thomas Michel, 'Islamo-Christian Dialogue: Reflections on the Recent Teachings of the Church', *Secretariat for Non-Christians Bulletin*, 20 (1985), p. 183.
13. Michael Fitzgerald and John Borelli, pp. 116–19.
14. *Origins*, 10:37 (1981), p. 592.
15. Cf. Thomas Michel, 'Islamo-Christian Dialogue', p. 184.
16. *Origins*, 15:11 (August 1985), p. 174.
17. Karl Joseph Kuschel, *Abraham: Sign of Hope for Jews, Christians and Muslims* (New York: Continuum, 1995), p. 204.
18. Geoffrey Parrinder, *Jesus in the Qur'an* (Oxford: Oneworld, 1996), p. 34.
19. Colin Chapman, *Cross and Crescent: Responding to the Challenge of Islam* (Westmount, IL: InterVarsity Press, 1995), p. 240.
20. Hammudah Abdulati, *Islam in Focus* (Maryland: Amana, 1998), pp. 160–2.
21. Hans Küng, 'Christianity and World Religions: Dialogue with Islam', Leonard Swidler, ed., pp. 266f.
22. Kenneth Cragg, *Muhammad and the Christian*, p. 120. See Chapter 8.
23. *Ibid.*, p. 129.
24. Seyyed Hossein Nasr, *Christian–Muslim Dialogue in the Twentieth Century*, Ataullah Siddiqui, ed., p. 154.
25. John Renard, *Responses to 101 Questions on Islam* (New York: Paulist Press, 1998), pp. 108–9.

26. Muhammad Talbi, 'Islam and the West: Beyond Confrontations, Ambiguities, Complexes', *Encounter* 108 (1984), p. 4.
27. Seyyed Hossein Nasr, *Christian–Muslim Dialogue*, Ataullah Siddiqui, ed., p. 161.
28. Jacques Jomier, *How to Understand Islam*, pp. 146–8. See Christian Troll, 'Muhammad: Prophet also for Christians?', *Theology Digest* 54:1 (Spring 2010).
29. *Guidelines for Dialogue Between Christians and Muslims*, p.58.
30. Kenneth Cragg, *Muhammad and the Christian*, p. 159.
31. Claude Geffré, 'Le Coran, une parole de dieu differente', *Lumiere et Vie* 3 (1983), p. 31. That divine revelation may take differentiated forms is a hypothesis of a number of theologians and something we will return to in the final chapter.
32. 'Cross Meets Crescent: Interview with Kenneth Cragg', *The Christian Century* 115:5 (1999), p. 183.
33. *Recognize the Spiritual Bonds*, p. 30.
34. Muhammad Talbi, 'Islam and Dialogue – Some Reflections on a Current Topic', *Christianity and Islam – the Struggling Dialogue*, ed. Richard Rousseau (Montrose, PA: Ridge Row Press, 1985), p. 62. For Muslim scholarship on a 'God-centred ethic', see Ovey Mohammad, SJ, *Muslim–Christian Relations*, Chapter 4.
35. Catholic Bishops' Conference of England and Wales, *Meeting God in Friend and Stranger: Fostering Respect and Mutual Understanding between the Religions* (London: CTS, 2010), p. 59. See Joseph Stamer, 'Can Christians and Muslims Pray Together?', *Theology Digest*, 46:3 (1999), pp. 209–15; Christian Troll, 'Common Prayer of Christians and Muslims, *Theology Digest*, 5:4 (2006), pp. 321–30; Joseph Cardinal Ratzinger, *Truth and Tolerance: Christian Belief and World Religions* (San Francisco: Ignatius Press, 2004), p. 106f. on multireligious and interreligious prayer.
36. Joseph Cardinal Ratzinger, *Salt of the Earth: Christianity and the Catholic Church at the End of the Millennium*. Interview with Peter Seewald (San Francisco: Ignatius Press, 1997), pp. 245–6.
37. Cf. www.vatican.org. Benedict and *New York Times* report, 23 November, 2008. Also reported in John Allen Jr., *op. cit.*, pp. 117–20. For dialogue between the then Cardinal Ratzinger and Marcello Pera, see *Without Roots: The West, Relativism and Christianity* (New York: Basic Books, 2007).
38. Text of 'Faith, Reason and the University', *Irish Times*, 18 September 2006 or www.vatican.org.
39. John Allen, Jr., *op.cit.*, p. 119.
40. Thomas P. Rausch, SJ, *Pope Benedict XVI: An Introduction to His Theological Vision* (New York: Paulist Press, 2009), p. 39.
41. www. catholicculture.org/culture/library/view.cmfm?id=7910
42. Miroslav Volf et al., *A Common Word: Muslims and Christians on Loving God and Neighbour* (Grand Rapids/Cambridge: Eerdmans, 2010), pp. 30–50. For further discussion of the letter, see Martin McGee, OSB, 'Surprised by Love – the Heart of Christian–Muslim Dialogue', *The Furrow* (December 2011), pp. 681–8.
43. Benedict XVI, *Light of the World: The Pope, the Church, and Signs of the Times* (London: CTS, 2010) , pp. 97–101.
44. See George Weigel, *God's Choice: Pope Benedict XVI and the Future of the Catholic Church* (London: HarperCollins, 2005), pp. 238–40.

CHAPTER 5

Hinduism: The Way of Experience

From the unreal lead me to the Real
From darkness lead me to Light.
From death lead me to Immortality.

BRIHADARANYAKA UPANISHAD

To pass from Islam to Hinduism is not to merely go from Arabia to India, but to enter a new spiritual climate. It has been likened to passing from the purity and austerity of the mosque to the shade of a huge and ancient banyan tree, under which myriads of unrelated creatures seek a fixed or temporary home. The presence of deity is everywhere and, to western eyes, in unexpected and even trivialising ways. Wandering through Varanasi, one passes a Krishna café, the Shiva Cement Company, Lacksmi Footwear and a Saraswati bookstore. The Punjabi driver has a Kali image on the dashboard of his car. Beside it are incense sticks for his morning prayer. Meeting with a family, there are more signs and symbols of devotion. The mother, a widow, is a devout worshipper of Shiva; her sister, equally devout, follows the teachings of Ramakrishna; the eldest son, an accountant educated in London, is a worshipper of Shiva (but not as dedicated as his mother); his wife and her family worship Krishna in the home, yet they go to the temple of the goddess Durga for special occasions and visit a teaching centre dedicated to Vishnu, where they sing devotional songs to Krishna. Another family would have a different pattern. A third probably another. The way in which the Hindu rubs shoulders with divinity in every field, in every street is the particular challenge of Hinduism. Herein also lies its inscrutability, for we must try to understand this very different way in which the Hindu sees God.

Hindus are the third largest religious group after Christians and Muslims, and make up about 15 per cent of the world's population. A serious appreciation of other eastern religions, such as Buddhism, Jainism and Sikhism, requires at least a general familiarity with Hindu theology. In recent times, various Hindu mission-type movements, such as the Ramakrishna Mission founded by Vivekananda

(1863–1902), Transcendental Meditation and ISKCON (the International Society for Krishna Consciousness) have contributed to its slow and steady growth in the West. It has also come to us in the writings of spiritual seekers such as the English Benedictine, Bede Griffiths, and the French Benedictine, Henri Le Saux. And now, in a globalised world, Hinduism has come to us in the family who live next door.

This chapter takes its cue from the main sacred texts of the religion, beginning with the more ancient and obscure Vedas, followed by the Upanishads and Bhagavad Gita of classical Hinduism. The approach will be partly historical, appropriate for a religion that is essentially fluid and developmental. Like all religions, Hinduism is a way of salvation, but for many Hindus, that salvation is not necessarily through belief in God (or gods) or in public worship, but in ethical observances and in the practice of the special sacraments (*samskara*) or rites of passage which govern their lives. Hinduism is a vast cultural container that allows for a diversity of religious beliefs.[1]

The Eternal *Dharma*

No word is more omnipresent in the sacred texts than *dharma*, meaning 'subtle' and 'very difficult to know'. Etymologically, it derives from *dhr*, meaning 'to hold', 'have', or 'maintain' – the same root from which are derived the Latin *firmus* (firm) and *forma* (form): '*Dharma* is, then, the form of things as they are, and the power that keeps them as they are and not otherwise.'[2] Sometimes compared to righteousness in the Jewish tradition or to natural law in Catholicism, *dharma* is never personified, yet it operates at many levels. As cosmic, it determines and governs the way the universe operates; as moral, guides the human being individually (if he is attuned to it) as to the path he should take to liberate his spirit. And as with all religions, a tension often occurs between the *dharma* written in sacred texts and the individual *dharma* of the human person. While there is but one *dharma*, there can be multiple *sadhanas*, or ways of realisation.

Dharma is one of the Sanskrit words which defy meaning. Loosely, for the Hindu it means 'religion'. But religion also embraces one's particular way of realising one's *sadhana*. Furthermore, it can also embrace the sect to which one belongs, the main ones being Vaisnavism, Saivism and Shaktism. *Dharma* may also mean the *marga*, or the path, one follows in society due to the caste into which one is born. But generally speaking, *dharma* is religion as it is expressed in the Hindu way of life.

All aspects of Hinduism – the sacred writings, the worship of gods, the teaching of Brahmins (priests) and gurus, the traditions of the caste system – provide a resource for the Hindu to live out his dharmic calling. He is free to choose from one or another source. Not all Hindus believe in God or gods, but they consider themselves ethnically Hindu because of their way of life. Yet for the majority, it is through reliance on a Supreme Divine Being that one can live out one's dharmic calling and see the light. That is why Hinduism itself is often called the *sanatama dharma* – the eternal religion – which, as law and duty, is considered to have supra-human origins. The Divine Being is Creator, but he is so as illuminator of minds. Hinduism is a religion of light, of illumination. One of its most sacred prayers, equivalent to the Christian 'Our Father' or the Muslim *Fatiha*, is the Gayatri Mantra that appears for the first time in the Rig-Veda (III 62:10). The Gayatri Mantra is repeated several times by Hindus during morning prayer: 'We meditate upon the glorious splendour of the Vivifier Divine. May he illumine our minds.'[3]

LIGHT UNFOLDING, THE VEDAS AND WORLDVIEW

'Hindu' derives from the Persian word *hind*, the name given to the Indus river in North India. Archaeological excavations which took place in 1922 have revealed that an ancient culture flourished in the Indus valley dating from about 2500–1500 BCE. Cities with great brick walls, shops, granaries, houses, graves and sanitation have been excavated. The small stone seals that were unearthed are engraved with pictures of animals such as tigers, bulls, elephants and eagles. A swastika also appears, an ancient religious symbol perhaps representing the sun. Other religious objects are female images suggesting worship of the mother goddess.

From about 2000 BCE, the valley was invaded by central Asian tribes who referred to themselves as 'Aryan', 'noble' and 'lordly'. They despised the more cultivated dark-skinned native inhabitants, characterising them in their literature as black-faced, snub-nosed, unintelligible and irreligious, despite the fact the Aryans themselves were less civilised than these people. With their horses, recently domesticated, and with powerful armed bands, they besieged and destroyed cities, broke down dams and irrigation works and enslaved the local people. The Aryans eventually substituted the older religion with their own, or at least with the form of their religion, for which we have ancient texts. Hindu scholarship is now showing, however, that the earlier religion never died. Its resurgence is a valuable enrichment and 'indianisation' of classic Hindu religion.

From this ancient tradition come high gods such as Krishna and Kali (the Mother Goddess), both of whom are black, like the people of the Indus.

The majority of Hindus reside in India, where they constitute four fifths of the country's entire population. To understand Hinduism, we must bear in mind that the very land itself has been, for thousands of years, the fountainhead for religious mythology, pilgrimages, and the sense of God imbued with fear and terror or as source of stability and peace. Governed by the mighty Himalayas – its peaks – clad in eternal snow, irrigated by powerful rivers which both nourish and ravage the landscape, and suppressed by murderous summer heat and cloud-heavy monsoons – the land is a dramatic cosmic partner in living out *dharma*.

Hinduism is particularly tied to specific places and local traditions. Districts associated with *avatars* – incarnations of the divine – are holy and are places of pilgrimage for people of certain sects. The great Ganges river is a source of purification from sin and some mountains and hills, such as Arunachala in south India, are considered to be sacred from time immemorial. Cows, snakes, rats and vultures are sacred. In ancient times, it was even believed that beyond India's boundaries salvation could not be gained. So, just as the study of Judaism is inextricably bound with the land of Israel, so too is Hinduism, and to understand it we must honour the elements of the sacred land that enters into its myths and practices. In his comprehensive survey, Klaus Klostermaier warns against being seduced by attempted universalisations of Hinduism that abstract it from its geographical context, such as we find in influential reformers like Swami Vivekananda or Sarvepalli Radhakrishnan, for such interpretations are largely a result of their Western and Christian training.[4]

The Vedas and Sacrifice

The Vedic scriptures are important because they are fundamental to understanding the Hindu concept of God. *Veda* means 'knowledge' (akin to the Latin *videre*, to discern). Considered to be the earliest documents of the human mind, scholars place them roughly contemporary with the oldest parts of the Hebrew Bible, around 1000 BCE. Even though tradition acknowledges human involvement in their composition, they are ultimately believed to be inerrant and of divine origin, a revelation, a *sruti* – 'that which was heard', or 'given' to the seers (*rishis*). They are not a single unified text but, like the Bible, the outcome of a long process of composition. There are four Vedas, of which the most sacred is the Rig-Veda: a collection of hymns addressed to a variety of gods who represent dominant aspects of the natural universe. The Sam-Veda is largely a collection of verses arranged for liturgical use by the priests; the Yajur-Veda is also related to ritual observances for sacrifice; and the Atharva-Veda, probably intended for worship in the home, contains spells and chants designed to ward off evil and ensure well-being. Perhaps the single most obvious genuine parallel with Vedic literature are the Hebrew psalms. In both cases, the texts seem primarily intended for liturgical use; both include various genres of poetry, both praise divine powers, call on them for help, lament the triumph of evil and pervasiveness of suffering and ask probing questions about the destiny of humanity and the cosmos.

The Vedas have a permanent influence in the shaping of Hinduism. Firstly, as ancient texts they remain fundamental for understanding theism in India. Though they belong to the early polytheistic stage of religiousness, theirs was not a simple or naïve polytheism, in that in them one finds a strong tendency to see the individual gods as aspects of the Supreme God or divinity itself.[5] Elements of Vedic belief are still alive in orthodox Hinduism. Though many of the more important deities – such as Indra and Agni – are now forgotten, two comparatively insignificant gods of the Rig-Veda – Vishnu, connected with sun and sacrifice, and Shiva, 'the auspicious', a fierce mountain god – have today become the chief Hindu deities. Unlike the three monotheistic religions, which exclude all other gods but One, Hinduism assimilates and includes. The gods of the Vedas are names/forms (*nama rupa*) of the One Being – Brahman – who is beyond name and form. The gods are *devas,* in Sanskrit 'shining ones' or supranatural beings, who may be compared to the cosmic powers of nature in St Paul. But they are also functional beings, in that they serve particular human needs. In this way, they are not unlike the saints of the Catholic tradition.

The Hindu attitude of sacrifice before deity is also the bequest of the Vedas. This is spelt out in their prose commentaries, the Brahmanas. These texts go into great detail on *how* to offer sacrifice, since it is in the correct performance of the ritual that human welfare is ensured. Vedic sacrifice, touching the universe at its very centre, restores order (*rta*) and truth (*sat*). The properly performed ritual is considered to be more ultimate in power than the deities themselves. Its model is the cosmogenic myth 'The Hymn of the Primeval Man', which records the world being formed as a result of a great sacrifice performed at the beginning of time: a mighty primeval male person (*purusha*) was sacrificed to the lesser gods and mystically survived his own dismemberment, producing from the different parts of his body all the various features of the universe, including the four great classes of society. Thus the Vedic sacrifice of slain animals was a repetition of this primeval creative sacrifice. It meant aligning oneself in partnership with the gods in sustaining the 'order' of the universe as coming from God and returning to God. Vedic sacrifice, in its original sense, is not widely practised in India today, but it remains significant in that it is from the divinisation of sacrifice that the sacred word Brahman arises, designating the Absolute Reality beyond the entire phenomenal world. Thomas Berry tells us that in the Vedas

> transition from sacrificial act to ontological absolute was possible because the sacrifice was considered the dynamic whereby the entire cosmic-human order was sustained in existence.[6]

The spiritual ideal of sacrifice continues to pervade Hindu ascetical practices, and its profound interpretation as 'consecrated action' in the Bhagavad Gita was exemplified in the life of Mahatma Gandhi.

Hinduism is a cosmic religion, and belief in an absolute cosmic power as being the one and impersonal Brahman comes from the Vedas. Bede Griffiths tells us that the word originates as a sacrificial utterance. Brahman comes from the root *bhr*, which means 'to grow or to swell'. He reminds us that words have not only a literal meaning in Hinduism, but also a psycho-spiritual active meaning.[7] The 'swelling' expresses the rising up of the awareness of God in the heart of the one making the offering. Brahman is the sacred word, the mantra, that ensures the sacrifice communicates and is accepted.

A corollary to the emphasis on sacrifice in the late Vedic period (900–500 BCE) is the growth in the power and prestige of the Brahmin priests. Only the priests with the knowledge of Sanskrit could perform the sacrifice properly. This period was certainly one in which the priests began to exert an immense influence on Indian society, an influence they have by no means lost.

A further legacy of Vedic religion is the caste system, for which there are many explanations: that it was a measure taken by the Indo-Aryan invaders to protect the purity of their race, and, therefore, it was not a coincidence that the Sanskrit word *varna* means 'caste' and at the same time 'colour'. That it was an expression of the principle of order and service in the original tribal and clannish Indo-Aryan society – warrior nobles, the Kshatriya, once protected the people and maintained contact with deities and offered sacrifice, but with the crystallisation over time of the notion that members of society assumed defined duties in keeping with their abilities and situation, the conviction arose that the area of worship, with its inerrant selection of and recitation of sacrificial texts, needed a specialist group. Thus the caste of the Brahmins came into being. Trained in the Sanskrit texts, they controlled all the rites and handed down this knowledge to their sons. It is not surprising that this 'elite' caste, due to the prestige of their secret knowledge and powers, gradually replaced the Kshatriya at the uppermost level of society. Compared to the ruling class and business people, many Brahmins are poor, but they still have pre-eminence in present-day India.

The more influential explanation of caste, however, is the mythical-religious one from the 'Hymn of the Primeval Man' in the Rig-Veda:

When they divided (primal) Man
Into how many parts did they divide him?
What was his mouth? What his arms?
What are his thighs called? What his feet?

The Brahman was his mouth,
The arms were made the prince,
His thighs the common people,
And from his feet the serf was born. (10,12)

The implication of the hymn is that to be born into a caste is to have an inescapable dharmic duty to fulfil, and that in doing the work that is proper to them, persons fulfil their destiny.

Members of the higher castes are the Brahmins, Kshatriyas and the Vaishyas, the latter of whom are the business people. These three are called 'twice-born', since their children, usually at the age of twelve, are solemnly accepted into their caste as full members and are thus 'born' a second time. The Shudras are the largest caste: their *dharma* obliges them to serve the members of the castes above them as auxiliary workers, servants, shepherds and sometimes craftsmen. The work of the Shudras can also be carried out by other castes. However, even a Shudra will not undertake particular activities – slaughtering, tanning and laying out the dead. These tasks are left to the Pariahs, the 'Untouchables'.

These poorest of the poor are without caste. Mere contact with such a person is said to make a person of higher caste unclean. Considered incapable of understanding the Vedas and sacred writings, they are forbidden to enter temples and take part in worship. They live outside the law and are obligated only by the regulations for 'Untouchables'. However, there were and are exceptions in the history of India to the contempt for such people. Some of the greats saints who are venerated in India today were pariahs and it should be noted that Sadhus and Sannyasins, the 'renunciants' or Hindu monks whom one meets around India, stand by choice outside the caste system. The great statesman Mahatma Gandhi concerned himself with bettering the condition of 'Untouchables' and achieved some success; the term *Harijan* – 'angels of the deity' – comes from him. He ensured that these Harijans could at least enter some of the great temples.

Class and caste are terms which are used interchangeably, but for the sake of completeness, it must be mentioned that recent commentators distinguish between them. Of the four classes or action groups, the Vaishyas and Sudras particularly are subdivided into numerous castes (*jati*). These were formed through the mutual contact of endogamous tribal groups with an exclusive right to certain occupations, crafts and traditions. They also have their hierarchies and stipulations about whom to relate to and who not to marry. Although the class/ caste system was officially banned by the Indian Constitution in 1947, it has in no way disappeared from the hearts and minds of the country's people. Whereas in many countries loyalty is to the nation or state, in India, loyalty is primarily for one's caste, because it is the local caste council that more immediately cares for people. In fact, in the orthodox view, there are two canons for being a Hindu – to accept the Vedas as revelation and to obey the *dharma* of one's caste. And for an outsider to become a Hindu, he/she must be reborn into a caste.

THE UPANISHADS AND REALISATION

The Upanishads are later additions to the Vedas. Usually classed in Hindu literature as Vedanta – 'the end of the Vedas' they represent a corrective to, rather than an affirmation of, the Vedic way and are an 'end' in that they are the quintessence of Vedic religion. Scholars have chosen to refer to this period between 800–500 BCE as an 'axial period', a time characterised by dramatic advances in thought around interiority of awareness and autonomy of the human person. This period witnessed the rise of the questioning Buddhist and Jain movements in India, of Confucius and Lao Tsu in China, of the great prophets in Israel and the beginnings of Greek philosophy. It was also the period in which these Hindu texts were created.

Upanishad variously means 'sitting down near', 'session of sweet silent thought' and 'secret teachers'. To 'sit down near' and read is to be filled with wonder and gratitude for these ancient texts, which, without doubt, speak a word of God from a different tradition. These mystical writings are often referred to as 'the Himalayas of the soul'. Like the Vedas, they are also canonical literature, *sruti* ('heard') or revealed divine wisdom. Even to this day, all theological discussion within orthodox Hinduism must be settled directly or indirectly from the *sruti*, the highest communication to human beings from the realm of Absolute Truth.[8]

Brahman

Like the Bible, the Upanishads speak of the beginnings of things. In the beginning, there was nothing: death, soul, Brahman. When Brahman occurs in the Rig-Veda it means the magical inner power or mantra of sacrifice which can move gods and the universe to grant what humans desire. The Upanishads reduce the many gods of the Vedas (3,306) to a revelation of an inner divine essence, which is an impersonal divine power – a holy energy – and is ultimately akin to a world soul. The supreme mantra which invokes the presence of Brahman is OM (pronounced *aum*). Considered to embrace all sounds, it has tremendous sanctity in India. Commenting on a text from the Maitri Upanishad – 'There is an OM which is silent and an OM which is sound; and sound comes out of the silence' – Bede Griffiths writes:

> Brahman was seen as the silence, and out of that silence comes this word, this OM, and then it returns to him. When we utter OM we are invoking a divine presence and surrendering ourselves to it.[9]

In this divine presence, the many gods of the Vedas are reduced to the one divine essence, the unchanging world soul, 'the Real of the real'. The oft-cited priestly prayer of the Brihad-aranyaka Upanishad gives Vedic sacrifice its true meaning, which is the inner sacrifice of the self:

> From the unreal lead me to the Real.
> From darkness lead me to Light.
> From death lead me to Immortality. (Brihad-aranyaka Up. 1.3.28)

The simplest and most reduced word for Brahman is *tat* ('that'): 'That from which all words turn back together with the mind.' The Upanishads often make their point in the form of stories. In the early Vedic period, women were on equal footing with men and great intellectual ideas were often discussed between husband and wife. Gargi, the wife of a Vedic seer, tried to discern the source of everything and pressed him with a series of questions. She moved through all the elements of creation to ask:

'What is the world of heaven woven from?'
'It is woven in the Creator.'
'In what are the worlds of the Creator woven?'
'They are woven in the world of Brahman.'
'In what are the worlds of Brahman woven like warp and woof?'
'Oh, Gargi, do not ask too much, lest thy head fall off!' (Katha Up. 5)

Brahman is the end of questioning: 'All the worlds rest in that Spirit and beyond him no one can go. This in truth is That' (Katha Up. 5). In Vedanta, Brahman is 'the true of the true', 'the Real of the real', the ineffable. Described only through negatives, as the One 'without a second', Brahman is *neti, neti,* 'not this, not that':

Known by him who knows it not. He by whom it is known knows it not.
Nor understood by those who understand it, it is understood by those who
do not understand it. (Kena Up. 11,3)

And yet Brahman is immanent – *iti iti* – which means that it is in this world and particularly in human experience that we touch the Absolute Reality. As we shall see, divine immanence rather than transcendence predominates in Hindu theology. Undergirding this is the Hindu understanding of creation which differs fundamentally from the Judeo-Christian. From Genesis and the *creatio ex nihilo* doctrine we learn that creation is freely initiated by God's word; it has a beginning, a history and it will end. In the Upanishads, the world has always existed as a divine emanation. 'As airy threads from a spider, or small sparks from a fire' which has no end (Brihad-aranyaka Up. 2.1), Brahman endlessly emanates all created realities, for the world is eternal like its divine source. In Genesis, the created world is given to the human being. Adam and Eve are its stewards. In Hindu cosmology, the human beings are part of the warp and woof of the cosmic drama. They are destined to play out and endure in their personal histories the cyclic patterns of cosmic death and rebirth.

Maya, Samsara, Advidya, Karma, Moksha

Focussing on creation leads to a cluster of important Hindu concepts – *maya, samsara, advidya, karma* and *moksha* – the latter raising the question of salvation in Hinduism. Hindu writings distinguish the world from Brahman by saying that compared with Brahman, who alone is Real, the world is unreal. It is said that a mysterious creative divine power, *maya* (from the root meaning 'to measure') playfully and magically intervenes to create the world. Some later commentators on Vedanta, such as the eighth-century philosopher Shankara, speak of *maya* as the doctrine which preserves the appropriate relation between the Absolute Creator and the transient creature, an interpretation which may be compared to Aquinas's doctrine of the dependent contingency of all created things.[10] Thus the intention of *maya* is to discourage any innate tendency to impose on the Creator the attributes of creation.

However, there is also something fearful about *maya*. In a religion where feeling and experience predominate at the popular level, *maya* is experienced as being at the mercy of Brahman's playful, if not sinister, relation to the world. It is that bewitching state of affairs that destines us to live in ignorance of our true identity, as being one with the divine. A well-known parable runs as follows: suppose you are walking in a forest and you become terrified at the sight of what you think is a serpent. You go out of your way to avoid the danger, only later to discover that it was a coiled rope. *Maya* is the illusory serpent that plays tricks with our minds, or a human mental condition which attributes more reality to the phenomenal world than that world possesses. In this mental confusion, Brahman playfully tests the human being and waits patiently until he/she comes to her senses. Due to ignorance (*advidya*), we fail to realise our true place in the order of things; we get trapped in the illusory material world of *maya*, and this entrapment involves, *samsara*, or the endless cycle of birth and rebirth to which the soul becomes subject. *Samsara* is the place from which the human being makes a desperate bid for salvation.

Hinduism understands salvation as an ongoing process of improvement in the conditions of rebirth and ultimately as surpassing entirely the need for rebirth. The idea of rebirth is strange to the West, although Plato taught it at the end of the *Republic*. It is a widespread Indian belief, supposedly coming from the ancient pre-Aryan peoples of the Indus. But in the Upanishads, as in Plato, it has a moral dimension, called *karma*. *Karma* means 'deed', or the fruit of one's actions. It is the law of cause and effect. A good or bad rebirth depends on one's previous actions. R. C. Zaehner expresses the effects of *karma* with full realism:

> Those whose conduct had been good, will quickly attain some good birth, the birth of a Brahmin, or a ruler or a merchant. But those whose conduct has been evil, will quickly attain an evil rebirth, the birth of a dog, or a hog or an outcaste.[11]

While *karma* and *samsara* attempt to give explanation to the ills and inequalities of life, the overall thrust of Hinduism and *dharma* is *moksha* – salvation. Hindus desire to be delivered from illusion, to shed the knots of karmic rebirth, to get off the endless wheel of *samsara*. This deliverance is *moksha*. The law of *karma* means the Hindu is patient with the human condition. Not to accept one's earthly condition would be to worsen it, that is, lengthen the time prior to salvation. As we shall see, *karma* is one of the pervading elements in Indian spiritual life (including Buddhism and Jainism) and while it is true that we reap what we sow, it is also true that being totally governed by *karma* can lead to fatalism or to a severe spiritual individualism and self-preoccupation.

Furthermore, in the Upanishads, Hindu salvation is not a place nor a 'heaven', but a condition in the sphere of the Absolute, beyond the polarities of suffering. In this high period of Hindu thought, salvation is a shedding of all the fetters of *samsara*, an 'extinction' (as in Buddhist *nirvana*) of all the layers that hinder us from finding the true self, which is God within. And because the deep problem is that of *avidya*, trapping us in samsaric existence, the desire for salvation is variously spoken of as desire for knowledge, for truth, for light, for the mind and for immortality. The Upanishads also use the same language in describing Brahman as Truth, Light and Immortal One (Svetasvatara Up. 2).

Finally, in the Upanishads, salvation is primarily individual; even social and family bonds are seen as fetters to break through, if one desires to attain this higher liberation. One sees many wandering ascetics in India. These are the *sannyasi*, 'renunciants' or monks, who have renounced family, home and wealth. Scantily dressed, sometimes living in remote forest and mountain regions, or attached to shrines near Hindu temples, they depend on the local people for food and drink. Their desire is to know one's own soul and God, or in true Hindu fashion, 'to see

God'. Later, we will find in the theistic cults inspired by the Bhagavad Gita that generous service to the community is also part of the way of salvation. We see this lived out in saintly people of later Hinduism, such as Ramakrishna and Gandhi. And yet Gandhi, the pragmatic untiring servant in the world of politics to which the mystical might seem marginal, once said that in all his work his goal was 'to see God' as Truth.

Atman-Brahman

If all creation is sourced in Brahman and is its manifestation, what then is the human person? The human person, in depth, is 'soul' or *atman* (from the root meaning of 'breath'). That *atman* and Brahman are one is the high point of the teaching of the Upanishads. In a famous series of questions in the Chandogya Upanishad, we are told how a sage reveals the implications of this special knowledge to his son. The boy, Svetaketu, had been away to study the *dharma* with a master for twelve years. He returned home proud and conceited. His father, seeing that he had not really understood the inner nature of the soul, proceeded to teach him through a series of acted parables, such as the following:

'Bring me a fruit from this banyan tree.'
'Here it is, Father.'
'Break it.'
'It is broken, Sir.'
'What do you see in it?'
'Very small seeds, Sir.'
'Break one of them, my son.'
'It is broken, Sir.'
'What do you see in it?'
'Nothing at all, Sir.'
Then his father spoke to him: 'My son, from the very essence of the seed which you cannot see comes in truth this vast banyan tree.
Believe me, my son, an invisible and subtle essence is the Spirit of the whole universe. That is Reality. That is *atman*. Thou art That.'
(Chandogya Up. 6, 12-14).

This last phrase: 'Thou art That' (*tat twam asi*), meaning 'you yourself are that very soul divine', is the outstanding thesis of the Upanishads. From it flow other mysterious sayings, which can sound like blasphemy to Western Christians. They are: 'I am Brahman' and 'All this world is Brahman'. Intuitions such as these are the basis for *advaita* theology, the 'non-dual' relationship of God to the self, developed by Sankara in the eighth century and partly espoused by Christian monastics such as Henri Le Saux and Bede Griffiths.[12] According to Griffiths, to characterise the statement 'I am Brahman' as pantheism (a literal identification of the world with God) or as monism (a denial of the reality of the world in favour of divine oneness) is to come at Hinduism from the outside. It is to apply alien categories of western, rationalistic Greek philosophy to religious intuitions which are primarily attained with 'the mind in the heart'.[13] What the Upanishads speak of is 'That (*tat*) from which all words turn back, together with the mind.' The rational mind must also turn back from a reality that cannot be treated as an object, but can only be known in the deeper reaches of the human spirit. There is a true expression of this in the Chandogya:

> In the centre of the castle of Brahman, our own body, there is a small shrine in the form of a lotus flower, and within can be found a small space. We should find who dwells there, and we should want to know him …
> The little space within the heart is as great as this vast universe.
> The heavens and the earth are there.
> And the sun and the moon and the stars;
> Fire and lightning and winds are there;
> And all that now is and all that is not:
> For the one universe is in Him and He dwells within your heart.
> (Chandogya Up. 8, 1).

Bede Griffiths tells us that this is the great gift of the Upanishads – the evocation of the inner shrine or *guha,* the cave of the heart, where the meaning of life and of all human existence is to be found.[14]

To say *atman* is Brahman is to radically believe that it is through the self that one comes to know God. 'The self is the foot-trace of everything, for by it one knows everything, just as one can find again by footprints what was lost.'[15] But self as *atman* is the True Self; it is a deeper tracing than the everyday self, more subtle, more original, the most important thing that can be known. In this awareness of self, God is known, not as an object 'out there', but as realised subjectively in our experience. Yet it is a difficult path to tread, as the Chandogya says:

The wise should surrender speech in mind, mind in the knowing self, the knowing self in the Spirit of the universe, and the Spirit of the universe in the Spirit of peace. Awake, arise! Strive for the Highest, and be in the Light! Sages say the path is narrow and difficult to tread, narrow as the edge of a razor. (Chandogya Up. 3)

As with all Oriental teaching, it is not just a theoretical belief, it is a practice, a discipline. It is a journeying toward the divine by way of a reining in of the psycho-physical aspects of one's nature. Hence the importance of the accompanying yogic traditions in Hindu religion and of the role of the master or guru in the individual guidance of the seeker, 'For the way to Him is through a Teacher who has seen Him' (Katha Up. 2). The great message of the Upanishads then, is that Brahman – the Supreme Spirit of the universe, is one with the human spirit. We are caught up in the being of God. Priority is given to divine immanence, in that we come to know God through the 'foot-traces' of the self, 'not through learning, or through the intellect or sacred teaching' (Katha Up. 3), and not by way of revelation, which is the address of another as in the Judeo-Christian and Islamic traditions. And yet the Upanishads do witness to divine transcendence:

He comes to the thought of those who know him beyond thought, not to those who imagine he can be attained by thought: he is unknown to the learned and known to the simple. (Kena Up. 2)

The Upanishadic worldview is often called Brahmanism. There is much in this thinking that Christians can marvel at – above all there is the ineffability of the divine mystery. But there is also much to question. Brahman-Atman is an impersonal reality. There is no emphasis on the survival of the personal self in a relationship with Brahman.

Hinduism, developmentally, may be said to be a conflation of multiple religious insights, but toward the end of the Upanishadic period, in the Svetasvatara Upanishad (third century BCE) we find the awareness that the supreme way of salvation is founded on a personal God. This Upanishad is considered to be a bridge to the personal theism of the Bhagavad Gita. A distinction is made between Brahman, who inhabits all things as Spirit, and the nearer divine being with personal form, who takes initiative in the affairs of human beings. This God is Rudra (Aryan god from the Rig-Veda, and antecedent of Shiva), of whom there is no second. We find God in this sense appealed to, in words reminiscent of the Hebrew prophets, as the supreme great Lord of lords, the supreme God of gods, the supreme Ruler of rulers, the adorable, the transcendent, the Lord of the universe, to whom all go for refuge:

> I go for refuge to God who is one in the silence of eternity, pure radiance of beauty and perfection, in whom we find peace. He is the bridge supreme which leads to immortality, and the Spirit of fire which burns the dross of lower life. (Svetasvatara Up. 6)

THE GREAT EPICS AND A PERSONAL GOD

Following on from the Upanishads from 400 BCE, we enter into a period of extensive religious writing which includes the Great Epics. Though not canonical revelation, they are known as 'remembrances' (*smriti*). Akin to tradition in Catholicism, they have an authority which shapes the religious imagination and piety of ordinary Hindus. They are accessible to everybody, including women, whose status in Hinduism is still lower than that of men, and to the lowest members of society. The most popular are the epics, the *Ramanayana* and the *Mahabharata*, composed between 200 BCE and 200 CE. The Sanskrit *Ramayana*, 'The Career of Rama', tells the story of Prince Rama, who was cheated of his inheritance and went into exile in a forest with his wife, Sita. Sita was stolen by Ravana, the demon king of Lanka (Sri Lanka). Rama and his brother, together with the monkey god, Hanumman, crossed to Ceylon, defeated Ravana and brought Sita back. Rama then had his throne restored and reigned happily with Sita. This simple story gained religious importance because Rama is believed to be a 'descent', an *avatar*, of the high god Vishnu. He and Sita, who is known for wifely dedication, constitute the Ramaraja, 'the Kingdom of Rama', and represent the ideal state of family life and community to which Hindus aspire.

The *Mahabharata*, the 'great *Bharata*' or war epic, the longest poem in the world, is a narrative of legend, myth, morality and religion, and mainly revolves around the struggle between two related families, the Pandyas and the Kauravas. The Pandyas are five brothers who have a right to the throne which has been usurped by King Dhritarashtra and his hundred sons. The Bhagavad Gita – 'The Song of the Lord' – is inserted into the poem at the point where the two armies meet to join battle. The Gita, called the New Testament of India, is about the length of the Fourth Gospel.

The context for its teachings is a discussion between Krishna – an *avatar* of the high god Vishnu – and the warrior Arjuna, who leads the Pandyas. This small book is a pocket synthesis of Hinduism – in it we find Hindu beliefs and guidance for the observance of *dharma*. These beliefs include the best of the Vedas, such as the notion of sacrifice; the Truth of God within from the Upanishads; and new developments of devotion to a personal God in his *avatara* manifestations. Grounding all this are the three classic Hindu *margas*, or paths to the divine.

THE BHAGAVAD GITA AND THE HINDU PATHS TO THE DIVINE

In the Bhagavad Gita, the three paths of life – work/duty (*karma yoga*), meditation (*jnana yoga*) and devotion (*bhakti yoga*) – are all forms of service to and worship of a loving God. Religious practice in Hinduism expresses itself in a way of life which has been laid down by ancient texts such as the *Laws of Manu*, which still shapes practice today.[16] As a religion, Hinduism is open-ended and non-dogmatic regarding beliefs, but it is quite detailed and prescriptive regarding lifestyle, whether socially as a caste member, or individually, in that every Hindu is bound to practices which, at least in their original meaning, tend toward the gradual spiritualisation of life. As well as the Three Paths, which we will consider later, there are also the Four Ends of Life and the Four Stages.

The Four Ends of Life

Human pursuits can be guided by four different kinds of motives. We may act out of duty (*dharma*), or simply for material gain or prestige (*artha*), or solely to obtain pleasure (*kama*) or, finally, we can act to achieve our spiritual liberation (*moksha*). *Dharma* is the most fundamental of the Four Ends, as it implies not only fulfilling one's general moral obligation towards others, but also observing the duties of one's caste or sub-caste. In the Hindu law books there is nothing wrong with the second and third ends, but they must be also guided by duty. Hinduism says you can have what you want, but pleasure and wealth must be sought intelligently: 'The guiding principle is not to turn from desire until desire turns from you.'[17] In time, however, life will teach you that these are but toys compared with true spiritual liberation.

The Four Stages (*Ashramas*)

Duties of *dharma* are also appropriate to one's stage in life. On being invested with the sacred thread, some Brahmin boys enter the first stage: *brahmacarin*, the celibate student whose chief duty is to study the Vedas, live in the house of his teacher and minister to him. When his education is complete, he returns home, marries and becomes a householder: *grihasta*. As *grihasta* he must firstly provide in his home a suitable space for the deity his family worships, and secondly he may rightfully build up material wealth to provide a comfortable home for the family and to be of service to his caste. When his hair turns grey and he sees his children's children, ideally he should abandon his home and, accompanied by his wife, live a more simple life, engaging in prayer and meditation. This stage is *vanaprastha*, 'the forest-dweller'. Beyond this is the final stage of the homeless religious beggar, the *sannyasin*, who wanders the length and breadth of the land, owning nothing and attached to nothing. No more than a small proportion of Hindus at any time have strictly followed this progression, but it stands as a framework of ideals within which the people have lived their lives for millennia.

Hinduism is not an eschatological religion; there is no invitation to embrace the values of the end of time now – there is no end of time. In Christianity, we have the religious orders, where it is appropriate for young people to renounce marriage and the acquisition of wealth and to live the ideals of the end, as it were, from the very beginning. The Hindu stages honour psychophysical growth: one seeks and finds God depending on where one is in life. Duties within the community are linked with age, and yet there is always an inner dynamic toward overcoming ignorance and relinquishing selfish illusions.

The Three Paths (in the Gita)

As previously noted, the Gita is inserted into the *Mahabharata* at the point where two armies are about to go into battle. Arjuna, the hero of the Pandavas, is seated in his chariot facing the enemy. He sees opposite him the Kauravas who are his own relations, friends and teachers. He is unable to go to battle. He lays down his arms in despair. From this gesture, commentators surmise that the problem the Gita addresses is the human being faced with the battle of life. The blind king Dhritarashtra is also a symbol of the ego, the false self. His hundred sons are symbols of the confusing passions and desires that flow from the sightless ego. The chariot is a symbol of the human body; the seated Arjuna is the confused soul. The charioteer is Krishna, the Lord who has come to instruct him. The whole text consists of Krishna's discourse with Arjuna – the Spirit of God speaking to the spirit of man and teaching him how to conduct his life.

It is helpful to split the text into three paths which refer to *karma yoga, bhakti yoga* and *jnana yoga* – although we do find that the *bhakti* teaching of devotion to a personal God presides over the whole text.

KARMA YOGA

In these early chapters, we find guidance on how to reach union with God while engaged in the battle of life. It is a basic Hindu teaching that all *karma* (action) is a fetter and can result in suffering of some kind: even the desire for good works can confuse the mind and excite greed. In helping Arjuna to solve his dilemma about carrying out his duty as a Kshatriya, Krishna offers four principles of spiritual guidance:

(i) All work is to be done without seeking a reward:

> Set thy heart upon thy work, but never on its reward.
> Work not for a reward, but never cease to do thy work. (Gita 2:47)

> This is not a question of indifference or of not working, as we are born to work, Krishna says; it is a question of working with 'evenness of mind' (Gita 2:48-50)

(ii) Everything you do is to be offered in sacrifice. We exist within a cosmic order which is sourced in a primal divine sacrifice. Sacrifice sustains the order of the universe, and you do this by returning actions to their source. In a spirit of *bhakti*, Krishna tells Arjuna:

> Offer all thy works to God, throw off selfish bonds
> And do thy work.
> No sin can then stain thee, even as waters do not stain the leaves of the lotus. (Gita 5:10)

> Whatever you do, or eat, or give, or offer in adoration,
> Let it be an offering to Me; and whatever you suffer, suffer it for Me. (Gita 4:25)

The Gita calls this the path of 'consecrated action' (Gita 3:7). In a sense, it is the imitation of Krishna himself, who, as God, does not work and yet works. We find here a reinterpretation of Vedic religion. In a pluralistic world of gods, selves, castes, the Vedas were concerned with the restoration of cosmic order through righteous action and ritual sacrifice to the gods. Vedic sacrifice now becomes 'consecrated action', the offering of the personal self in righteous action to God:

> There are yogis whose sacrifice is an offering to the gods;
> But others offer as a sacrifice their own souls in the fire of God. (Gita 4:25)

(iii) There is the mysterious and beautiful teaching that when we try to do our work in a spirit of detachment, or offer it in sacrifice, we are in union with divine action; it is God himself who will be acting in us:

> Who in all his work sees God, he in truth goes with God.
> God is his worship, God is his offering, offered by God in the fire of God.
> (Gita 4:24)

(iv) The Upanishads' teaching on Brahmavidya–Atmanvidya, 'knowledge of Brahman' as 'knowledge of the self', is given further meaning in the Gita, a meaning that centuries later we find voiced in the teachings of St Ignatius Loyola: the detached *karmayogi* in lifting all things up to God, 'finds God in all things':

> And when he sees me in all and sees all in me, then I
> Never leave him and he never leaves me.
> He who in this oneness of love, loves me in whatever he sees, wherever this
> man may live, in truth this man lives in me. (Gita 6:30-31)

In conclusion, then, *karma yoga*, the path of selfless action, aims to resolve the age-old problem of suffering in the sense of dissipation and waste of life. Action detached from its fruits is a true sacrifice to God. As 'consecrated action' it purifies the traces of greed and samsaric existence and leads to an eternal personal relationship with God. It also issues in a more fruitful service of others.

BHAKTI YOGA

Bhakti yoga, or the path of love, is 'the more excellent way', the Gita's core teaching of devotion to a personal *Bhagavan* or Lord. Christians, Jews and Muslims have difficulty with the seeming indistinction of Hinduism between divine transcendence and the created universe, yet there are many teachings in the Gita with which one can resonate:

By Me, Unmanifest in form,
This whole universe was spun;
In Me subsist all beings,
I do not subsist in them.

And (yet) contingent beings do not subsist in Me –
Behold my sovereign power (*yoga*)!
My self sustains (all) beings, it does not subsist in them;
It causes them to be. (Gita 9:4,5. Zaehner trans.)

In the person of Krishna, the form of the unmanifest Brahman expresses itself with will and freedom in creation. 'I do not subsist in them' means that the divine existence is not at the level of material and created things: God does not need them in any way. Mascaro translates it: 'All beings have their rest in me, but I have not my rest in them' (Gita 9:4) In the mysterious phrase 'They do not subsist in me', Krishna is, according to Zaehner, speaking about the Divine Self in essence, which does not contain created things like water in a pot but maintains them in existence by his 'sovereign power'.[18]

While the truth of the transcendent God is known in creation, the truth is also known in the heart: 'God dwells in the heart of all beings, Arjuna' (Gita 18:61). As we shall see when we come to look at Gandhi, the knowledge of God is the truth of love:

By love (*bhakti*) he knows me in truth,
Who I am and what I am.
And when he knows me in truth,
He enters into my being. (Gita 18:55)

In the light of this teaching, Arjuna, the man of action, is urged to go to God in *bhakti* devotion with all his soul:

Give me thy mind and give me thy heart,
Give me thy offerings and thy adoration;

And thus with thy soul in harmony,
And making me thy goal supreme,
Thou shalt in truth come to me. (Gita 9:34)

The Gita concludes the eighteenth chapter with its secret doctrine – that we are loved by God:

Hear again my Word supreme,
The deepest secret of silence.
Because I love thee well,
I will speak to thee words of salvation.

Give thy mind to me, give me thy heart,
And thy sacrifice and thy adoration.
This is my word of promise:
Thou shalt in truth come to me,
For thou art dear to me. (Gita 18:64-5)

Hindu spiritual practice has led Bede Griffiths to call the Gita the Indian gospel of salvation and love.[19] 'Come to me for thy salvation,' Krishna says to Arjuna, 'I will make thee free from the bondage of sins. Fear no more' (Gita 18:66). He whose grace releases from the bondage of *karma* brings light to the deluded mind of the Kshatriya, and brings salvation and personal immortality to Hindu and non-Hindu alike. The final response of Arjuna is one of personal communion in which he hands over his will to this loving God:

By thy grace I remember my Light,
And now, gone is my delusion.
My doubts are no more, my faith is firm,
And now I can say 'Thy will be done' (Gita 18:73).

JNANA YOGA

We find the Upanishadic teaching on *jnana yoga* – the path of knowledge – presented by Krishna in the Gita:

But some there are whose ignorance of self
By wisdom is destroyed:
Their wisdom like the sun,
Sheds (a ray of) light on that All-Highest.

Souls ... bent on That, selves bent on That,
With That their aim and That their aspiration,
They stride (along the path) from which there is no return,
(All) taints by wisdom washed away. (Gita 5:16,7. Zaehner trans.)

More psychological and mystical than *karma yoga*, *jnana* addresses the basis of all human suffering, which is ignorance – *avidya*. The seers of the Upanishads taught that the ignorance of the True Self (that *atman* is Brahman) is even more fundamentally alienating than the greed which distorts action. That *atman* is Brahman is an intuitive knowledge and a mystical way of being, attained primarily through the higher levels of meditation. For the *jnanayogi* it is *the* way of liberation from *samsara*. One with *That*, he is beyond the clutches of good and bad *karma*. His goal is not a personal heaven but absorption in Brahman.

In this context, the Gita also speaks of *dhyana yoga*. Complementary to *jnana*, and more of a preparatory training ground for communion with the divine, *dhyana* is meditation with certain mental and physical elements. In Hinduism, it is considered a way of liberation (*moksha*), but it is also a good psychological discipline for calming the mind and in helping arrange one's life more appropriately. It is this meditational yoga that is practiced worldwide today, particularly as a help for Christian prayer. In an oft-cited passage, the Gita describes *dhyana yoga* in a remarkably clear way, linking it with personal devotion to Krishna:

Let the yogin ever integrate (him)self
Standing in a place apart,
Alone, his thoughts and self restrained,
Devoid of (earthly) hope, nothing possessing.

Let him for himself set up
A steady seat in a clean place,

Neither too high nor yet too low,
With cloth or hides or grass bestrewn.

There let him sit and make his mind a single point:
Let him restrain the motions of his thought and senses,
And engage in spiritual exercise (*yoga*)
To purify the self.

Remaining still, let him keep body, head and neck
In a straight line unmoving;
Let him fix his gaze on the tip of his nose,
Not looking round about him.

(There) let his sit, his self all stilled,
His fear all gone, firm in his vow of chastity,
His mind controlled, his thoughts on Me,
Integrated, (yet) intent on Me.

Thus let the yogin ever integrate (him)self,
His mind restrained;
Then will he approach that peace
Which has *nirvana* as its end
And which subsists in me. (Gita 6:10-14. Zaehner trans.)

This particular path of Hindu knowledge, though exalted, is limited in appeal. It is more suitable for people with certain gifts and education, and who have freedom from social responsibilities. It does not provide a way of liberation for the low caste *sudra*, the 'Untouchables', the *candelas* (corpse carriers), nor even for Arjuna. It is interesting to note that Krishna recommends the more worldly and engaged *karma yoga* (aligned with *bhakti* devotion to God) for this *Kshatriya* with his warrior personality. Hinduism is deeply immersed in the analysis of human nature, in the so-called *gunas*, the psychological propensities which can be indicators as to the path of salvation appropriate for an individual person. Since they provide a holistic view of the person, these insights can be valuable and should not be disclaimed. Yet for the Christian, they can be limiting unless placed in the wider context of God's grace. This is due to the predominance given to the power of *karma*, both in the *jnana* and *karma yogas*, wherein the ultimate principle of liberation is the law of *karma* itself, which guarantees that actions produce results and that no effort, however small, will be in vain. In effect, this means that if one stays with the discipline of sacrificial action and/or with silent absorption in Brahman, one will reach liberation and self-realisation.

But in the Gita, we also find a radical departure from this reliance on the self. Krishna's instruction to Arjuna to focus his attention 'on Me' invites a faith in a transcendent and personal God in whose loving hands lies the liberation of the human being.

Exemplars of the Paths

Though the three great Hindu paths of life appear to converge and are considered to reach their fulfilment in *bhakti* devotion, as always with Hinduism, the whole never suppresses the gifts of the parts. There are Hindus of great influence and holiness whose *dharma* calling has led them to exemplify one path more than another, and the study of their lives becomes a concrete sampling of the variousness of Hindu wisdom. Differing in philosophies and spirituality, they appear strongly opposed to one another, and yet they are Hindus. The three exemplars with which we will concern ourselves here addressed the problem of human suffering in different ways and, above all, they desired to 'see God':

- Mohandas Gandhi (1869–1948) was predominantly a *karmayogi*. His Hindu background was Vedic Brahminism. He was a worshipper of the personal God, Rama. In a life of self-sacrificing action, he addressed the greed and injustice of Hindu society. We will return to Gandhi in the context of Hindu–Christian dialogue in Chapter 6.

- Ramana Maharshi (1879–1950) was a practitioner of the *jnana* of the Upanishads or Brahmanism. His solution to human suffering was radically other-worldly and inner-directed. From his cave in Arunacala in south India, where he meditated, the Maharshi taught that the search for inner liberation must never be put aside for the sake of social action. Asked 'Would it not be better if the Saints mixed with others?,' he replied: 'There are no "others" to mix with.' The Self is the only Reality. To a further question, he responded:

The Power that created you has created the world as well. If it can take care of you, it can similarly take care of the world also … If God has created the world, it is his business to look after it, not yours.[20]

The Maharishi's *advaita* path of mystical contemplation has always appealed to the monastic traditions of all religions, and is now being more widely appreciated as one of India's gifts to Western Christians.

• A. C. Bhaktivedanta (1896–1977). The path of *bhakti* yoga is best represented in the life and writings of Swami A. C. Bhaktivedanta, the most well-known missionary of devotional Hinduism in the twentieth century. He grew up in Calcutta in a very religious home, his father a devout Vaisnava (worshiper of Lord Krishna). As a young man, he was deeply influenced by the great Vaisnava sannyasi, Sarasvati, who had renounced the world to dedicate his life to Krishna as a wandering missionary. He was persecuted and rejected because of his attitude to the caste system, believing that belonging to a caste was a state of one's heart or a personal vocation. It was Sarasvati's practice to initiate non-Brahmin followers into the Brahmin priesthood, and in 1932 Bhaktivedanta received his initiation.

After the death of his master, Bhaktivedanta finally withdrew from his family business in order to give all his energies to what Sarasvati had commissioned him to do – to preach the message of Lord Krishna in English. In 1959, he became a wandering 'renunciant' and preacher. This was the prelude to the journey he made to the US in 1956, where, in the Bowery in New York, now aged seventy, he set up a mission for Krishna consciousness for the downtrodden, the hippies, drug users and rejected of society. From that same centre, he began to train an order of monks and nuns who, like himself, were vegetarian and rejected intoxicants, illicit sex and gambling. From there, he also founded ISKCON, the International Society for Krishna Consciousness, well known from the authoritative chant which his followers still use today: 'Hare Krishna, Hare Krishna, Krishna, Krishna, Hare, Hare.' Bhaktivedanta's appropriation of Hindu Bhakti devotion and interpretation of the Gita is highly personal and non-dialogical. Today, ISKCON may be said to be guided by the following three rather fundamentalist principles:

(i) That Krishna is the only Supreme and personal Lord of the universe. There is no other.

(ii) That the Vedas, Upanishads and Gita are all literally true. That the lives of Krishna are to be taken as historically accurate.

(iii) That only devotional ecstasy directed to Krishna leads to salvation and destroys *karma* and that the *bhakti* path is superior to all other paths.[21]

Another Indian *bhakti* mystic and teacher, possibly with more ecumenical outreach and appeal to westerners, is the Bengali poet, Rabindranath Tagore (1861–1941). Tagore brought India and its spirituality into the realm of world literature, especially though his collection of English poems, *Gitanjali: Song Offerings* (1912) and he was awarded the Nobel Prize for Literature in 1917. Tagore's poems evoke the conditions for relating to the divine across all the religions – the desire for 'the glance of God' (Krishna in the poem below), and the spiritual poverty necessary for communing with the divine:

I had gone a-begging from door to door in the village path, when thy golden chariot appeared in the distance like a gorgeous dream and I wondered who was this King of kings!

My hopes rose high and methought my evil days were at an end, and I stood waiting for alms to be given unasked and for wealth scattered on all sides in the dust.

The chariot stopped where I stood. Thy glance fell on me and thou camest down with a smile. I felt that the luck of my life had come at last. Then of a sudden thou didst hold out thy right hand and say 'What hast thou to give to me?'

Ah, what a kingly jest it was to open thy palm to a beggar to beg! I was confused and stood undecided, and then from my wallet I took the least little grain of corn and gave it to thee.

But how great my surprise when at the day's end I emptied the bag on the floor to find a least little grain of gold among the poor heap. I bitterly wept and wished that I had had the heart to give thee my all.[22]

Bhaktism also pervades the later devotional scriptures of India. Here God is personal *Bhagavan* or Lord. Here the worldview is, in some elements, closer to the Christian. It holds that the Bhagavan, such as Krishna, is ultimate and absolutely real, and that his disciples may share in that reality through loving devotion to him. Above all, the Bhagavan is gracious, capable of acting as a forgiving parent, of removing the burden of *karma*, of liberating from cosmic forces and ensuring that his devotees will have eternal life with him in heaven. In Bhakti, God is available to everyone – the householder and serf, as well as the Brahmin.

In the opening centuries of the Christian era, there emerged what Thomas Berry calls 'the new Hinduism' in which divine personality permeates the whole range of Hindu consciousness.[23] It is the Hinduism of *puja* (image worship) and *bhakti* (devotion). Along with *puja* came the need for the building of temples. Prior to this, all that was needed were altars. From the fifth century CE onwards, hymnody used was in the vernacular, spoken and sung by the people and providing the immediacy of devotional expression. Yet the worship continued to retain its roots in the sublime intuitionism of the Upanishads and the Gita. Indeed, one of Hinduism's amazing characteristics seems to be its capacity to communicate lofty religious insights throughout the whole of society, combined with an extreme tolerance for a variety of interpretations by its devotees.

GOD – ALL AND EVERYTHING

Ancient tradition has it that there are 330 million gods in India – as many as there are believers. For truth is *realised* truth, and the truth of who God is is truth as experienced. As we have seen, the peak of realised truth is the realisation of Atman-Brahman in Upanishadic Hinduism. But equally bent on realisation is the popular theism of Bhakti Hinduism, with its cast of colourful divine personalities – both infinitely attractive and unimaginably fearsome – attending to the needs and fears of their devotees and providing a narrative language of interpretation that is both comfort and challenge.

Brahman as Absolute Divine Being is not a personal object of worship. Beyond the polarities of the one and the many, form and formlessness, male and female, immanent and transcendent, Brahman exists. Yet Brahman is more than a functional substratum of the universe. The seers give us these beautiful words for the unnameable divine essence: *Sat-Cit-Ananda* – Truth, Consciousness, Bliss, which, when desired above all things, communicates with the human self as 'That which you are' – *tam twam asi*. While the Absolute, in its transcendent aspect, is far removed from the experience of the majority of people, the Absolute as immanent presence is within the reach of all. Here the Hindu rubs shoulders with aspects of and different levels of Godhead in every field, on every street.

For Jews, Christians and Muslims – for whom belief in God excludes all gods but One – this can be mystifying, but Hindu monotheism is a cosmic monotheism of assimilation which honours the multifarious levels of experience of the divine by way of inclusion rather than exclusion. At the popular level of devotion, one can say that the Hindu God is All *and* Everything.

What then is the unifying factor in such a multifarious belief system? What personalises it, brings it close? John Renard suggests it is the *istha devata* – 'the chosen deity' – which, like creed and doctrine in Christianity and Islam, provides the basic stabilising element.[24]

What generally guides the choice of deity is geography, caste and the religious narrative tradition of a family. The chosen deity fulfils the deep Hindu desire to see God, to have a 'sight' (*darshan*) of the deity. An additional unifying factor, at the theological level, is the *Trimurti*, the teaching from the epics that Brahman has three different but complementary aspects: Brahma, the Creator; Vishnu, who preserves and restores order; and Shiva, who is both creator and destroyer. The cult of Brahma is much less represented than those of Vishnu and Shiva, who are the most popular *istha devatas* in India – the Vishnuites making up 70 per cent, and the Shivaites 25 per cent of practitioners of the Hindu religion. Vishnu and Shiva have presided over the religious life of India for the past 1,500 years, along with their *shakti* (goddess) consorts. Neither must one forget the innumerable village deities.

Many Western Christians and strict monotheists, such as Jews and Muslims, may look aghast at the pantheon of Hindu deities and ask how we relate to them. Hindu scholar, Francis X. Clooney SJ, recommends that we must not let ourselves be put off by the multiplicity of personages and their appearances, but must delve deeper to appreciate the Hindu way of spiritual engagement, which can be lavishly graphic and filled with cosmic imagery – at once frequently consoling and shattering to the human sensibility. In *Hindu Wisdom for All God's Children*, Clooney invites us into a kind of *lectio divina*-type reflection on the most popular Hindu deities. Gently but firmly, he encourages us to engage with alternative mediations of transcendence and immanence and to trust ourselves to them.

Vishnu and Krishna

Vishnu is generally worshipped in the forms of his incarnations. He is believed to be the guardian of *dharma*, and whenever the law is in danger of being diluted, he appears as an *avatar*. The incarnations of Vishnu are full or partial. Partial avatars are quite common, in that any great and good person may be venerated by Hindus as a partial incarnation. The full incarnations are rarer, numbering only nine. There is a tenth still to come, Kalki, who will usher in the end of the present world era. Like a messiah figure, with his birth, a world of inner and outer harmony will prevail. The most venerated avatars of Vishnu are the seventh and eighth, Rama, the hero king of the *Ramayana,* and Krishna, the hero of the Gita.

Krishna is usually depicted with dark bluish skin, suggesting he is of non-Aryan origin. A divine flute-player, surrounded by beautiful women, his is the most popular image. In Indian iconography and literature the flute is the sign of the human being who, unless played upon by the breath of the deity, is as good as dead. It appears frequently in Tagore's *bhakti* poetry:

> Thou hast made me endless, such is thy pleasure. This frail vessel thou emptiest again and again, and fillest ever with fresh life.

> This little flute of a reed thou hast carried over hills and dales and hast breathed through it melodies eternally new.

> At the immortal touch of thy hands my little heart loses its limits in joy and gives birth to utterance ineffable.

> Thy infinite gifts come to me only in these very small hands of mine.
> Ages pass, and still thou pourest, and still there is room to fill.[25]

Krishna, as heavenly flute-player, is the subject of much erotic verse and painting. His relationship with his mistress, Radha, is considered to be a mystical recounting of the soul's relationship to God, somewhat like the Song of Songs in the Hebrew Scriptures. Krishna is also worshipped as an infant. The infant image is very popular with Indian women, and stories are relished of the wonderful miracles and naughty pranks enacted by the loveable divine child.

Two stories in particular relate how Krishna can be vividly present to believers, speaking to the human heart with a face his devotees can see and love. In the first,

Krishna bestows 'a sight' of himself to his devotees, but it is a *darshan* (sight) related to their human capabilities. This story relates to Krishna's encounter with the indecisive Arjuna in the Gita. Arjuna has been patiently instructed in transformative disciplines of action but, in a final gesture, he pleads with Krishna: 'Krishna, Lord of discipline, if you think I can see it, reveal to me your immutable self' (Gita 11:2-4). In response, there follows the theophany of Krishna, which terrifies the warrior. He finds himself slipping into dissolution and begs Krishna, 'Shelter of the Worlds', to show him once again his human form. Yet the positive effect of the theophany was that Arjuna was confirmed in his faith and came to a decision to assume his duty as a warrior: 'By thy grace I remember thy light, and now gone is my delusion. My doubts are no more, my faith is firm, and now I can say "Thy will be done"' (Gita 18:73).

The second story is that of Yashoda, Krishna's simple village mother. Yashoda delights in her son. She loves her God as a mother loves her child, who is always with her. She does not have to search for meaning in the same way as Arjuna, but the unexpected still intrudes into her ordinary devotion. One day, some boys who have been playing with Krishna report to her that he has been eating dirt. Yashoda takes her son by the hand and scolds him. Seeing that he is bewildered, she asks him to open his mouth. When she looks inside, she sees 'the whole world in all its detail, every form and every living thing and time and nature and action and hope too, and her own village, and even herself'.[26] Frightened and unable to survive this heightened state of consciousness, Yashoda begged to 'take refuge in God' in the old way, and Krishna draws her back to her ordinary maternal devotion to him.

The many stories of Krishna are parables of divine presence, which either challenge a deepening of faith, or, as in the Yashoda story, affirm the divine consolations present in the ordinariness of the everyday. In his relationship to worshippers as father, elder brother, hero, lover, husband and son, Krishna is considered to be Hinduism's most complete expression of God's humanity and divinity. In fact, Krishna has always been a point of entry into Hinduism for Christian theologians who have found in him possible likenesses to Christ.

Shiva

Unlike Vishnu, Shiva is not generally believed to incarnate himself for the welfare of the world, but is said to have manifested himself temporarily in many disguises to help his devotees. The ancient pre-Aryan character of this god is apparent in his altars, which are straight vertical stones (*linga*), probably from old fertility cults. He is also the great ascetic, the remote meditating figure of the Himalayas, smeared with ash and accompanied with animals. Yet he is more popularly represented as Nataraja, representing the cosmic dance in its five activities of creation, preservation, destruction, embodiment and liberation. One dancing foot crushes the demon of ignorance; the other, raised high, symbolises the state beyond the senses. The garland of flames surrounding Nataraja depicts creation as a vibrant dance of natural forces.

Yet meeting Shiva in his totality can be shocking to non-Hindu sensibilities. It is beyond the reach of our minds to accept the wild remoteness of this figure and its ash-covered nakedness. In Shiva temples, we see the predominance of the *lingam*, the phallic symbol signifying his unshaken control of desire, which he neither represses nor allows to overwhelm him. His habits of self-flagellation, which are imitated by devotees, have given Hinduism a bad name. Shiva's image is a reliving of the terrifying, howling Rudra of the Vedas, and is the accretion of many narrative traditions. However, to see Shiva at only this level is to miss the point.

Francis X. Clooney asks us to be patient with this Lord of contradictions. In Hindu eyes, Shiva is the necessary antidote to our propensity to make a comfortable image of the living divine presence. He is more than humans can comprehend. In his sexual imagery, he embraces totally what we cannot look at. In his nakedness, he provokes us to uncover the false desires lurking in our hearts. As the mad Shiva, he shocks. The followers who are truly devoted to him sometimes appear deranged. He is the Lord of mystery in the sense of 'All and everything', and only the encompassing heart can know him.[27] He has been the object of some of the most exalted poetry, especially in southern India, where Tamil Shaivism is considered to be the highest form of devotional Hinduism.

Shaktism

Virtually every deity, from the Vedic gods on, have masculine and feminine aspects. Later developments describe the feminine as discrete characters, or as consorts, with their own rich life stories. Vishnu's consort is Lackshmi, a goddess of good fortune, patroness of the arts, learning and business. Her festival is the New Year celebration of Diwali, when she is invoked for blessings of wealth and prosperity. Two of the many consorts of Shiva are Durga and Kali. Durga, 'the unfathomable', is an ambiguous and sometimes terrifying figure, but in the great temple of Durga in Calcutta, women pray to her for children, especially the blessing of sons. Durga is sometimes merged with Kali, 'the black one', another terrifying consort worshipped in the Calcutta religion. The merging of these consorts of Shiva has led to a distinct mother-goddess cult, whose followers (*shaktas*), believe that 'to see' the goddess is to experience the immanent active energy (*shakti*) of the transcendental and remote Shiva. Shaktism is the epitome of holism in Hindu religion. The object of worship is turned into a totally experiential reality by the worshipper. The image of the goddess is focussed on with loving detail. In texts sometimes used in worship, she is visualised slowly and carefully from head to toe:

> Who the goddess is and how she relates to self and the world is gradually realised through this extended meditation on her physical form, each verse lingering in meditative enjoyment on one of her features.[28]

The whole self is engaged in worship, the feelings, the mind, the body and its sensations, the cosmic elements of earth, air, fire and water. In short, Shaktism, as a dimension of Hindu worship, engages primarily with the immanent presence of deity and is now broadly considered to be one of three modes of worshipping the Absolute Brahman in India, the other two being Shaivism and the Vaishnava tradition. However, in terms of total influence, the Vaishnava tradition is considered to be greater.[29]

Local Deities

Of the total population of India, over 80 per cent live in villages. One finds several small temples in villages, dedicated to high gods (*devas*) such as Rama, Krishna and Shiva, but by far the most numerous are the small wayside shrines that house the *grama devatas* – the village deities. In fact, if the various divine beings of devotional Hinduism were to be ranked in terms of importance or power, first would come Brahman or Bhagavan, the Godhead or Lord; second, the *devas*, the high gods; and lastly the *grama devatas*, the village deities. If the ranking were in terms of immediacy and the amount of attention received from the villagers, then the order would certainly be reversed. For the understanding of a substantial proportion of the village population, Brahman is too transcendent and remote, too concerned with the cosmos to be interested in their problems. While *devas* are too busy doing Bhagavan's work at a universal level, it is the *devatas*, or local deities, believed to have supernatural powers, that affect the villager's life and welfare. Some, comparable to saints in the Catholic tradition, have specialised functions, such as curing smallpox and other diseases. Others are associated with a specific part of a village, over which they are guardians. Not all have shrines; sometimes it is only possible to know that a *devata* is venerated because of pilgrimages to that place, or by rags tied to a thorn-bush as votive offerings. Yet, while it is generally held that no villager will confuse this type of supernaturalism with Bhagavan, it is also believed that the Supreme Lord will accommodate his devotees in their limitations in handling no deeper truth than what is presented by the graven image before them.[30]

Hinduism has the name of being tolerant and all-accepting, but to Western monotheistic eyes, it may seem just a flaccid tolerance. Yet it has its own critics and religious reformers. Reforming philosopher statesman, one-time President of India and Nobel Prize winner, Sarvepalli Radhakrishnan (1888–1975) describes the pluralism of Hindu worship practices, and evokes the unifying aspiration of the religion as follows:

> Hinduism accepts all religious notions as facts and arranges them in the order of their more or less intrinsic significance. The bewildering polytheism of the masses and the uncompromising monotheism of the classes are for the Hindu the expressions of one and the same force at different levels. Hinduism insists on working steadily upwards and improving our knowledge of God. 'The worshippers of the Absolute are the highest in rank; second to them are the worshippers of the personal God; then come the worshippers of the incarnations like Rama, Krishna, Buddha; below them are those who worship ancestors, deities and sages, and lowest of all are the worshippers of the petty forces or spirits.' Again, 'The deities of some men are in water (i.e. bathing places), those of the more advanced are in the heavens, those of the children (in religion) are in images of wood and stone, but the sage finds his God in his deeper self. 'The man of action finds his God in fire, the man of feeling in his heart, and the feeble-minded in the idol but the strong in spirit find God everywhere. The seers see the Supreme in the self, and not in images.[31]

Radhakrishnan recommends, as indeed did Gandhi, that Hindu leaders must hold aloft the highest conception of God and work steadily on the minds of believers to effect an improvement in their conceptions. He urges that temples, shrines and sanctuaries be used, not only as places of worship, but also as places of learning for the spiritual education of Hindus.

The Hindu Temple and Worship

During the Vedic period, priestly officiants performed major religious rituals at open-air altars. Architecture was not necessary, since the gods, who lived in their own supernatural sphere of cosmic influence, needed no shelter. The Upanishads and the Gita developed a more spiritual understanding of sacrifice and laid the ground for the personal images of deity that were to blossom in the various *bhakti* movements. Personal devotion, in turn, led to the proliferation of iconography and to the belief that the personal Lord, the Bhagavan, was close to believers in his/her various incarnate presences. This meant that deity required a place to reside amongst its devotees.

Jewish, Christian and Muslim places of worship are 'houses of the people of God', places to assemble for congregational prayer and, in many cases, for ongoing education. But in the Catholic tradition, in which the church building is primarily 'God's House' and a place of sacramental divine presence, we have a greater likeness to the Hindu temple. For the temple, or Mandir, is primarily 'God's House', 'the palace of the Lord', a place where the people visit as guests. The heart of the Mandir is the *garbhagriha*, the 'womb-house', where the image or form (*murti*) of the presiding deity is placed. This central space is usually windowless and dark, with only one entry and with a further space inside for the image and the officiating priest. Shiva temples usually have the *lingam* as their central *murti*; Vishnu temples have images of Vishnu and his *avataras*, such as Rama and Krishna in human forms. Their related images are usually placed in shrines around the temple walls.

The 'image worship' that features in most Hindu traditions may seem, to the Western mind, to be a kind of polytheism. Within these traditions, emphasis is placed on the image's proper ritual consecration and, once consecrated, it is revered as 'descent' of God. The image, however vulnerable the materials used, is the way in which God makes himself easily accessible to human beings.

Temples have both local and cosmic significance. Local traditions tell of the origins of the temple and of the special blessings the deity brings. Cosmically, the temple physically replicates the order of the universe, and so temple building is a sacred art. Ancient texts prescribe everything from the choice of a religiously appropriate site to the geometric mandala layout which symbolises the universe. The central space belongs to the presiding deity. Encircling this is the divine realm of supernatural beings, *devas* and guardians. Outlying this is the circle of human beings, and beyond the human realm is the sphere of the demonic and the worldly. Thus entering the temple means leaving the outer world behind; one is invited to shed all attachments. The surrounding images, which unite one with the powers of the cosmos, are there to help with this journey and the *garbhagriha* ultimately invites the devotee into the inner shrine of the Self, where God dwells in darkness.

In their architectural scale, some of the great temples appear like mountains of stone. The deities were traditionally said to have resided on the peaks of mountains – the Himalayas signifying God's remoteness and grandeur. Therefore, a visit to the temple was a substitute journey for a visit to the holy mountain. The conical dome or peak – the mountain-shaped *shikara* – extends to the sky over the *garbhagriha*. Its façade is variegated by many tiers or terraces, peopled with elaborate sculptures narrating the adventures of the heroes of the great epics. In this way, the Hindu temple may be said to represent in stone the reality of the remote high deity, deigning to come close, coming to the womb chamber, symbolising the inviolate cave of the heart of the devotee.

There is no formal obligation on Hindus to attend the temple, but there will hardly be any Hindu who will not go there once in a while to receive *prasada* (communion) as a support for his/her daily life. One will see large numbers of devotees, but they will be dispersed individuals reciting their prayers before icons in the ambulatories of the open part, or seated as families or groups performing a ritual. The core ritual is *puja*, the worship of the *murti*. It is usual for a group or family to engage a *pujari*, or professional priest, to make the offerings. The priest receives the offerings of the worshippers, performs the actions necessary for direct contact with the deity and returns to the devotees the *prasada* as a token of their communion with the divine.

Central to temple worship is *upachara* (honour offering), in service of the deity who presides. The governing idea is that the deity is a 'royal person', whose image needs to be treated with appropriate respect. Like royalty, the enshrined deity has his or her round of daily activities. It begins when the temple staff wakes up the deity and clears away the previous day's flower offerings. Bathing comes next, sometimes indirectly with the priest pouring water over the deity's image in a mirror. Many images are then clad in fresh garments. Worshippers then summon and welcome the deity and offer flowers. Then occurs the centuries-old and universal practice of circumambulation around the building, always with the right shoulder towards the sacred presence. This is followed by the presentation of gifts and the entertaining of the deity by waving bright lamps rhythmically before him or her. As the day ends, the worshippers bid farewell to the deity, who then returns to splendid solitude and rest. At some temples, the staff take the image out on procession through the neighbourhood. Through all these ritual activities, the overriding desire of worshippers is to be given a *darshan,* to see and be blessed by a 'glance' of the wide-eyed deity who sees everybody and knows their needs. *Darshan* is central to Hindu culture and disciples of revered teachers are said to seek *darshan* from those they follow or with whom they associate.

To Christians, for whom liturgy is a subdued and solemn affair, what goes on in a Hindu temple can appear to be chaotic. And yet there is a communal dimension. What brings worshippers together is not the individual rituals but the irrepressible festive spirit. John Renard explains that Hindu worship is joyous and has a light-hearted feel about it:

> ... whenever Hindus approach the divine presence, they tend to do so in the conviction that God enjoys the whole business and wants human beings to share in the delight. What most Christians think of as God's 'work', the Hindu tradition prefers to see as God's play.[32]

Domestic *puja* has many of the attributes of the temple tradition. The Hindu householder is expected to set aside a shelf or room for the household deities. A family may have many chosen deities and these are represented on the family altar with statuettes or pictures. Although men have a role on special occasions, daily *puja* is the responsibility of the mother of the family. The *puja* is performed before breakfast and all food prepared for the family is first offered to the deities. As in the temple, the chosen deities of the family are cared for like honoured guests.

Pilgrimage (*yatra,* 'going') is also a major form of Hindu worship. A pilgrimage site is a 'sacred crossing' (*tirtha*), where the divine and the human meet. Pilgrimages are governed by complex rules such as fasting, celibacy and ascetical practices like sleeping on the floor. In ancient times, the pilgrims undertook the whole journey on foot and, as in some Catholic sites such as Fatima and Compostela, they complete the last part on their knees. There are multiple pilgrim sites in India, but the seven listed by the *Mahabharata* are the most significant: Kashi (today Varanasi), Prayaga (today Allahabad), Mathura (the birthplace of Krishna), Ujjaini, Haridwar, Ayodhya and Gaya (where the Buddha was enlightened). Allahabad, associated with the Kumbh Mela festival, is one of the most sacred Hindu places because of the coming together there of the three rivers, the Ganges, the Yamuna and the invisible Sarasvati. A bath at the confluence of these rivers at the auspicious hour of sunrise on special days of the calendar assures the pilgrim freedom from the cycle of rebirth. Further along the Ganges is Varanasi, considered to be the centre of the cosmos and the holy city of India. To die there guarantees liberation, and the city has extensive cremation facilities for those who make the holy city their final place of pilgrimage.

As we have seen, Hinduism glories in multiplicity and diversity and there are many levels to being Hindu. Hinduism develops every doctrine to its extreme implication. There is the insistence on the extreme transcendence of the divine and on extreme immanence, which do not contradict each other, for both aspects are one. There is extreme intellectualism along with extreme devotionalism; extreme sensualism along with extreme asceticism. There is a certain ease with these contrasting traditions; nothing is excluded because it is not in the nature of Brahman to exclude. But the vitality of Hinduism – its capaciousness, its earthiness and joy – can be fully experienced only among the people of India and in their land, which is their sacred geography.

SUMMARY

Aware that scholars tell us there are many 'Hinduisms', we have been treading a way through the religion loosely and developmentally. At this stage, A. L. Hermann's philosophic synthesis of Brahminism, Brahmanism and Bhaktism can provide an overview:[33]

- Brahminism of the Vedic world rests on a realistic pluralism which holds that there are many real entities in the universe, such as gods and human selves who are in relation to one another, and that there is also disorder brought about by disobedience to the Eternal Dharma or by neglect of sacrifice. Hinduism is always context specific. The way forward is via righteous moral living and the observation of one's personal *dharma* of class and caste, within the support of the family and through cooperation with the gods in restoring the cosmic order through prayer and sacrifice. The Vedic Hindu turns to the divine in its various forms for success and wealth in this life, and desires to see God in a personal heaven after death.

- Brahmanism, the worldview of the Upanishads, probes more deeply who God is. This rests on a metaphysical oneness and mystical identity between transcendent Brahman and the *atman* (the self). That emphasis is not so much on caring for the world or restoring cosmic order as on overcoming the disorder of ignorance *within* the personal self. The transformation of the self becomes the basis for the restoration of the cosmos. Brahman, the ultimate *That*, is impersonal. There is no great emphasis on the survival of the individual personal self in a relationship to Brahman, since the only self that matters is the True Self as one with the Real. As we have seen, 'That Thou art … you, yourself, are that soul divine' is the outstanding thesis of the Upanishads. It was to become the basis for the *advaita* non-dual relationship to God that permeates Hindu thought to this day. There are divergent opinions on *advaita*. Brahmanism has often been identified with a pure monism, a non-dual simple equation of the world and the human God. Yet, following the teaching of the great Tamil philosopher, Ramanuja (1017–1137), Brahman is identified with the personal Lord of theism, and *advaita* with the non-dual differentiated relationship of the soul to God. Such an interpretation forges a link between the great *advaita* insight of the Upanishads and the devotional theism of surrender to divine grace of the *bhakti* tradition.

• Bhaktism, the highest expression of which is the Bhagavad Gita, pervades the later devotional scriptures of India. Here, God is personal Bhagavan or Lord. The beginnings of such development may be traced back to the indigenous religion of the Indus Valley, and to an extent is present in the Vedas. These Indus cults were dedicated to non-Aryan deities, such as the later Shiva and Krishna, and to the worship of the goddess. The worldview of Bhaktism is closer to the Christian, and indeed it has been said that a Catholic who believes in God's incarnation in Christ, and whose world of worship is the variegated one of rituals and sacraments, shrines and pilgrimages and communion with saints and holy persons, should feel at home in Hinduism. Bhaktism holds that the Bhagavan, such as Krishna, is ultimate and absolutely real, and that his disciples are called to personal union with him through loving devotion. Above all, the Bhagavan is gracious, capable of acting as a forgiving parent, of removing the burden of *karma*, of liberating from cosmic forces and of ensuring that his devotees will have eternal life with him in heaven. In Bhakti devotion, God is available to everyone: the householder and serf, as well as the Brahmin.

With the Gita and the literature that followed, from the opening centuries of the Christian era until the present, the decisive development has been that the Brahman experience of the past is being reinterpreted in terms of a personal supreme deity. Indeed, divine personality permeates the whole range of Hindu consciousness. The truth of who God is is multi-faceted and varied because it is truth-as-experienced. Eastern religions have given us a word for this: realisation. This quest to *realise* the divine in our lives is Hinduism's greatest gift to the West. As a kind of life experience and insight (*darshan*, 'seeing') into the nature of reality, Hinduism can appear inscrutable, challenging and even relativistic to the monotheistic consciousness of Western Christians who are accustomed to discriminating in our language about God. Hinduism tolerantly accepts all religions in their ceremonies and dogmas but as the 'eternal religion', it values other religions in terms of their capacity to draw the lives and minds of believers to what is essential – the realisation of God.

Further Reading

Berry, Thomas, *Religions of India: Hinduism, Yoga, Buddhism* (New York: Columbia University Press, 1996).

Bowen, Paul, ed., *Themes and Issues in Hinduism* (London: Cassell, 1998).

Clooney, Francis X., SJ, *Hindu Wisdom for All God's Children* (Maryknoll, NY: Orbis Books, 1998).

Cross, Stephen, *The Elements of Hinduism* (London: Element Books, 1996).

Demariaux, Jean-Christophe, *How to Understand Hinduism* (London: SCM Press, 1995).

Ellinger, Herbert, *Hinduism: The Basics* (London: SCM, 1995).

Ganeri, Martin, OP, 'Catholicism and Hinduism', *The Catholic Church and the World Religions*, ed. Gavin D'Costa (Edinburgh: T. & T. Clark, 2011), pp. 106–40.

Griffiths, Bede, *The Cosmic Revelation: The Hindu Way to God* (Illinois: Templegate, 1983).

Herman, A. L., *A Brief Introduction to Hinduism: Religion, Philosophy and Ways of Liberation* (Oxford: Westview, 1991).

Hinnells, John R., ed., *A Handbook of Living Religions* (London: Penguin Books, 1991).

Klostermaier, Klaus, *A Survey of Hinduism* (New York: State University of New York Press, 1994).

Renard, John, *Responses to 101 Questions on Hinduism* (New York: Paulist Press, 1999).

Ruland, Vernon, *Imagining the Sacred: Soundings in the World Religions* (New York: Orbis Books, 1998).

Zaehner, R. C., *Hinduism* (Oxford: Oxford University Press, 1966).

NOTES

1. For personal reading, I recommend Juan Mascaro's translations of the Upanishads (Penguin, 1970) and the *Bhagavad* Gita (Penguin, 1980), as he writes for Western readers and evokes the inner voice of the text in a way that goes beyond the boundaries of word and culture. Scriptural text citations herein refer to Mascaro, except occasionally, where R. C. Zaehner's translations are considered to be closer to the original Sanskrit: R. C. Zaehner, trans., *The Hindu Scriptures* (London: J. M. Dent, 1978); R. C. Zaehner, *The Bhagavad* Gita *with Commentary Based on Original Sources* (Oxford: Oxford University Press, 1986).
2. R. C. Zaehner, *Hinduism*, pp. 2–5. *Dharma* is akin to natural law in the Catholic tradition. It has its roots in the structure of the cosmos and the socio-ethical laws governing humankind are but one facet of this all-embracing law encompassing all beings. *Dharma* is its own justification. There is a Hindu maxim which states: '*Dharma* when violated destroys; *dharma* when preserved protects.' See K. Klostermaier, *A Survey of Hinduism*, p. 52.
3. A translation of the *Gayatri* mantra by Raimundo Panikkar, *The Vedic Experience: Mantrama-Njari: An Anthology of the Vedas for Modern Man and Contemporary Celebration* (Pondicherry: All India Books, 1983), p. 38.
4. Klaus Klostermaier, *A Survey of Hinduism*, p. 43.
5. John Bowker, *The Problems of Suffering in the Religions of the World* (Cambridge: Cambridge University Press, 1975), p. 199.
6. Thomas Berry, *Religions of India*, p. 11
7. Bede Griffiths, *The Cosmic Revelation*, p. 48.
8. Thomas Berry, p. 17
9. Bede Griffiths, *Essential Writings*, selected and introduced by Thomas Matus (New York: Orbis Books, 2004), p. 58.
10. John Renard, *Responses to 101 Questions*, p. 21.
11. R. C. Zaehner, *The Hindu Scriptures*, p.101.
12. Bede Griffiths (1906–93) was an English Benedictine who settled in India in 1955 and went on to become one of the great mystical teachers of our time. Assuming the dress and ascetic discipline of a Hindu *sannyasi*, Griffiths established a Christian community following the customs of a Hindu *ashram*. Shantivanam (which means 'Forest of Peace') still flourishes near the city of Tiruchirapalli in southern India. See Shirley de Boulay, *Beyond the Darkness: A Biography of Bede Griffiths* (London: Rider, 1998). Henry Le Saux (1910–73) was a Breton-born Benedictine monk who moved to India in 1948. His deep encounter with Hindu spirituality led him to live as a Hindu holy man and to pursue the challenging and adventurous path of *advaita* mysticism and the extraordinary search for God in the truth beyond opposites.
13. Bede Griffiths, *The Cosmic Revelation*, p. 57.
14. *Ibid.*, p. 61.

15. *Brihad-aranyaka Upanishad*, cited in J. Bowker, p. 211.
16. The Laws of Manu (c. 1500 BCE) are a particular and hallowed tradition of socio-ethical laws which apply *dharma* to the lifestyle of the classes. Hinduism has always had a place for the teaching and example of individual sages. Some of these sages have been revered by a very large number of followers as special manifestations of divinity and as worthy of universal acclaim. The laws are accepted as *smriti* ('remembered') commentaries on the primary revelations (*sruti*). They consist of twelve books, and the main body of the literature deals with the duties incumbent on individuals as the pass through the four traditional stages of life, with the greatest focus on householders, their wives and the duties of family. Other books deal with broader, even philosophical issues. Since the Manu tradition descends from Brahmanical circles, and endorses the power of Brahmins, many lower caste Hindus reject it altogether. See J. Renard, p. 57.
17. Huston Smith, *The World's Religions* (San Francisco: Harper, 1991), p. 17.
18. R. C. Zaehner, *The Bhagavad* Gita *with Commentary*, p. 275.
19. Bede Griffiths, *The Cosmic Revelation*, pp. 87–108.
20. Cited in A. L. Herman, *A Brief Introduction to Hinduism*, p. 14.
21. *Ibid.*, p. 28. For more detail on three modern sages – Gandhi, the Maharshi and Bhaktivedanta – see pp. 1–36.
22. Rabindranath Tagore, *Gitanjali: Song Offerings* (Boston: Beacon Press, 1992), pp. 34–5.
23. Thomas Berry, Chapter 3.
24. John Renard, p. 39f.
25. Rabindranath Tagore, *Gitanjali*, p. 13.
26. Francis X. Clooney, *Hindu Wisdom*, pp. 68–71.
27. *Ibid.*, pp. 72f.
28. *Ibid.*, p. 97.
29. Thomas Berry, p. 17.
30. Cf. John R. Hinnells, ed., pp. 222f.
31. Sarvepalli Radhakrishnan, *The Hindu View of Life* (London: Unwin, 1980), pp. 24–5.
32. On temple worship, see John Renard, pp. 49–52, and Klaus Klostermaier, Chapter 20.
33. A. L. Hermann's *A Brief Introduction to Hinduism* is structured around this threefold synthesis.

CHAPTER 6

Hindu–Christian Meeting Points

I have a definite feeling that if you want to feel the aroma of Christianity, you must copy the rose. The rose irresistibly draws people to itself, and the scent remains with them. Even so, the aroma of Christianity is subtler even than that of the rose and should, therefore, be imparted in an even quieter and more impenetrable manner, if possible.

GANDHI

Hinduism is a challenging interlocutor for Christians, challenging because of the very different culture in which the Hindu search for God is embodied. Yet God is always the Ever Greater, greater than any culture, and India's way of meeting God can be a gift if we do not pre-judge the gift in terms of Western biblical and philosophical categories. As we have seen, Hinduism is a complex of monotheistic beliefs and ritualised soul-making. But, above all, it is a mystical religion. Even the more dualistic popular Hinduism of the masses, the way of *bhakti*, is still a mysticism of devotion in ritual, pilgrimage, prayer and song to God whose unconditional love precedes all human loving. Not unrelated to *bhakti*, but distinguishable from it, is the current of non-dualistic Hinduism, known as Vedanta, which originated in the Upanishads and is centred on Brahman, the non-personal divine being. Possibly a more elite Hinduism, it is the religion of spiritual seekers, of monks and 'holy persons' (*sannyasins*), and is an aspect of the religion that has always attracted Western Christians.

In this chapter we will focus on Christianity's meeting points with Hinduism. Since God saves all peoples, the divine is mediated through the doctrines of the religions, with all their cultural and social ambiguities and strengths. While this will be a dialogue of differences, it will not be disputatious, but will aim to discern the points of contact between the biblical-prophetic religion of Christianity and the more cosmic Hinduism. But the fact that Hinduism is less concerned with doctrines as such and more with spiritual practice invites some reflection on contributions from spiritual seekers such as Bede Griffiths (1906–93) and Henri

Le Saux (1910–73): both Christian *sannyasins* in India and significant voices in interfaith exchange. We will look briefly at some Church teachings which formally acknowledge the spiritual gifts of Hindu religion and examine some experiences of 'dialogue-on-the-ground' as exemplified in the evangelising mission of Asian bishops and theologians. The chapter ends with a reflection on how Mahatma Gandhi related his deep Hindu faith to Christianity.

DOCTRINES, DIFFERENCES AND BEYOND

Here we bring to mind some of the key ways in which Hinduism differs from Christianity. Hindu theology speaks of Brahma, Vishnu and Shiva, the *Trimurti* ('three forms'). The Trimurti is a manifestation of a single deity in three forms, each omnipotent, and each associated with a characteristic work of creating, destroying and re-creating/sustaining. Sometimes the three in their ultimate ground are named Being, Awareness, Bliss (*Sat, Cit, Ananda*), suggesting something of the essential impersonal nature of Godhead. Here one can be tempted to see a likeness between the Trimurti and the tri-personal understanding of God in the Christian tradition. However, the Trimurti represents Godhead in relation to the universe only. In Christian theology, the Trinity is about God's relation to creation – what theologians call the 'economic trinity' – yet unlike the Trimurti, it is also a truth about the inner life of God – the 'immanent Trinity' – which, in its very incomprehensibility, is a communion of love between persons.

Furthermore, Christians readily see in the Hindu *avatars* parallels to the doctrine of incarnation. On a relatively superficial level, both concepts describe the 'descent' of the divine into the world of humanity. Yet there are some major differences. The avataric manifestations of Vishnu are concerned with world order and mostly prevent the dissolution of the cosmos. For example, Vishnu's two principal avatars, Rama and Krishna, are intended primarily to save humankind from immorality and to punish evildoers. But since humanity is divine, Rama and Krishna do not assume the human condition in order to divinise it. Furthermore, there is no finality about the appearance of *avatars*. Each time righteousness declines, an *avatar* will appear in one form or other. In Christian revelation there is finality: the manifestation of the divine in Jesus – the incarnation – does not occur in mythical and cyclic time, but once only in history. It occurs among a historic people – the Jews – and is indissolubly linked with the historic figure of Jesus, in whom it is brought to finality once and for all.

What becomes apparent in a dialogue of differences, however, is that in understanding doctrines we cannot divorce them from their contexts. Hindu doctrines can only be fully understood within their own religious and philosophical landscape, the general character of which is quite different from the Judeo-Christian.

Hinduism is a cosmic religion. In the Vedic tradition creation is an emanation of the divine Brahman. God did not create the world out of nothing; therefore, unlike the God of the Hebrew Scriptures, Brahman is not absolutely distinct from the world. Yet it must be said that Hinduism is not a Pantheism, in which the world is simply equated with God. Many Hindus describe their faith with the formula: 'One in all and all in One.' The word 'in' here is important. More appropriately, they are speaking of a monism, in which the world is *in* God and the impersonal Brahman is mysteriously *more* than world. This is the source of the propulsion toward unity – the monistic tendency in all things Indian – and it has been said that 'unless we experience within us the great attraction of monism we cannot even understand and enter into dialogue with Hinduism'.[1]

In this orientation of human beings toward the 'more' of Brahman, lies the good order (*rta*): the salvation of the world and human beings. Hindu time is cyclic. Existentially, the world is experienced as real and must be dealt with; yet the great struggle of the Hindu saint is to escape from this wheel of time, space and matter, from *samsara* and rebirth. Despite his great empathy for Hinduism, this is one of the problems Bede Griffiths is particularly sensitive to – salvation as 'escape':

> I cannot help feeling that the present situation of India, with its masses of poor, illiterate people, of people suffering from disease and being left to die in the streets, really stems from this basic philosophy … If one can help somebody else to have a better birth, if one can help him on his way, that is good; but there is no obligation to do it. *Karma* is working itself out.[2]

The fatalism we note here – what seems like a 'play' or lack of engagement between the divine and the human – Griffiths attributes to the mythological character of Hinduism.[3] The Epics and Puranas, as stories of deities, are mythologies rather than history. Admittedly, the mythical and symbolic are congenial for the understanding of religious truths, but since mythology arises from the archetypal imagery of the unconscious, and lives in the world of imagination, the danger is that universal principles can be symbolised by anything that comes to hand, with an indifference to the power and influence of the particular symbol chosen. The mythological character of Hinduism is due then to the cyclic nature of time and to Hinduism's apparent indifference to linking the 'seeing' (*darshan*) of deity to time and place and history.

Cardinal Joseph Ratzinger (now Pope Benedict XVI) in his analysis of the cosmic and prophetic development of religions, brings precision to the question. He clarifies the difference between a 'Christian personal understanding of God' and an 'Asian mysticism of identity'. Since monotheism in India is an evolutionary development, in practice, the gods are never overthrown. A peaceful balance between various forms comes about, between God and gods, between monotheistic and polytheistic beliefs – all of which are recounted in Indian mythologies. In contrast, the monotheism of Israel has its origin by way of the revolution of a few religious persons who were filled with a new religious awareness of the divine as a transcendent personal being, and so the question ultimately became

> whether the divine 'God' stands over against us, so that religion, being human, is in the last resort a relationship – love – that becomes a union ('God is all in all': 1 Cor 15:28) but that does not do away with the opposition of I and Thou; or, whether the divine lies beyond personality, and the final aim of man is to become one with, and dissolve in the All-One.[4]

What is being highlighted here, in contradistinction to Asian religions, are some of the key characteristics of biblical Christian religion: that it is historic and has an 'event' quality. That it is not the product of our experience only but of 'encounter' and 'otherness' impinging on us from without.[5] That 'without' is the Creator God, who transcends the world and yet is a loving personal presence declaring himself in creation and history and giving direction to human lives. When human experience enters, it is simply the form our faith-response takes in relation to the Divine as Love, who meets us in the here-and-now and takes us out of ourselves to create with us something new.

While Benedict XVI's profiling of religions as cosmic and prophetic can be seen in terms of progressive religious development, leading to the event of the more historical Judeo-Christian revelation of a personal God – nevertheless, he generously reminds the reader that his words 'must not be seen to serve as a handy rational justification of Christian faith in the controversy between religions'.[6]

We must not forget what unites us, he says, that we are all part of a single history of peoples in many different fashions on the way to God, and that we must be open to Eastern religions in order to determine more clearly the place of Christian faith and practice in world faiths as a whole. Once again, the message is that by looking at other religions we come to see our own way more clearly.[7]

As an Asian religion, Hinduism has been characterised as a transcendental wisdom, the salvific goal of which is 'illumination', which, in effect, means the retrieval of the lost truth of oneness with the hidden ground of reality itself – the famous *tat tvam asi* ('That thou art') of the Upanishads. The relation to God in Christianity, however, is one of a greater astringency. Faced with the holiness of the divine who reveals Godself, the relationship is also redemptive. It is elevation to a new order; it is *transformation* of the mind (Rm 12:2) in relation to the divine holiness which is God's will for us.

Hindu truth then is totalising and paradoxical. Negative and positive are held together in a both-and synthesis. From one perspective, the world order as supported by the divine is Brahman's manifestation. From another, the world and human existence are *maya*: appearances which seem to have no intrinsic value in themselves. As 'the eternal religion', Hinduism is highly inclusive and presents itself as capable of drawing all religions to it. Hindu–Christian theologian Mariasusai Dhavamony writes:

> The household of Hinduism is aware of itself as a community which can absorb all religious values and which alone is thought to be capable of doing so in the names of tolerance and peace.[8]

He goes on to speak of an 'intolerant tolerance', a not listening on the part of the educated Hindu, which can be a subtle exclusivism.[9] Since religion, at its core, is the realisation of union with God through experience of truth, freedom and non-violence, many Hindus hold that it should not be restricted to dogmas, to a particular cult or a particular authority. Thus, popular presentations of Christianity that make clear divisions between God and the universe, heaven and hell, and operate with a fondness for distinguishing, are alien to Hindu thinking and convey to the Hindu mind that Christians have trapped the divine in fixed forms and in a historically datable figure.

Yet the popular religions in India are also very much characterised by the 'without'. Worship is often clothed in outward, sometimes even trivial, forms.

However, the focus on the 'without' is only a 'play of the divine', because what matters to the Hindu is realisation of the divine mystery 'within'. Despite differences in doctrines and worldviews, we must acknowledge that the special grace of India is the call to interiority, and

> no message from the West, even were it gathered up and sent by the Word of God, will ever succeed in awakening a deep echo in the soul of India, unless it is presented in the guise of the 'within'.[10]

This seems to be the opinion held by Christian communities in India and by spiritual seekers who have spent time there.

THE CAVE OF THE HEART

Henri Le Saux and Bede Griffiths were monastics attracted and committed to the ultimate impulse behind Hindu religious practice: the interior one of experiencing the reality of God. Their writings, sapiential rather than theological, speak especially to those who feel there must be one Unity, one reality at the heart of all religions, a reality that is the Beyond and yet interior to the human heart.

Henri Le Saux was born in Brittany in 1910. After studying for several years as a diocesan seminarian, he entered the Benedictine community of Saint-Anne-de-Kergonan, not far from his family home. A letter he wrote to the novice master a year before his eventual entry sounds the theme that would characterise his deepest desire for the rest of his life:

> What has drawn me [to the monastery] from the beginning, and what leads me on, is the hope of finding there the presence of God more immediately than anywhere else.[11]

Following ordination, Le Saux expressed the desire to go to India, to help Christianise that land in the same way the Benedictine monks had fashioned a Christian Europe centuries earlier. He was finally accepted by a bishop in the southern Indian state of Tamil Nadu. There he was welcomed by French diocesan priest Jules Monchanin, who saw in him a kindred spirit with whom he could start an ashram: a religious retreat centre where disciples would gather around a teacher or guru. The two men began living in simple huts at a site called Shantivanam ('Forest of Peace') along the banks of the river Carvery, not far from the city of Tiruchirapalli in the Tamil Nadu state. It was at this time that Le Saux took the Indian name Abhishiktananda ('Bliss of the Anointed One'), by which he increasingly became known. The emphasis on silence was innately congenial to him. He also felt called to visit Hindu holy places and to enter more deeply into the Hindu religious experience. His meeting with the saintly Hindu mystic Sri Ramana Maharshi, who lived with disciples at the base of the sacred Mount Arunachala, deeply impressed him. As time went on, feeling that Shantivanam had failed his spiritual needs, he spent more of his life in the mountains of northern India and, in 1957, built a hermitage at the base of the Himalayas, where he lived for sixteen years, praying, meditating, writing and receiving visitors, until his death from a heart attack in 1973. Le Saux's ideal was to become a Hindu monk *and* a Christian monk. Having been initiated as a Hindu *sannyasin*, he felt an overpowering sense that his self at its inmost core was ultimately one with the Absolute. He claimed that such experience, so prominent in the advaitic 'non-dual' texts of the Upanishads, was likewise present in the gospels, as in Jesus' words, 'The Father and I are one' (Jn 10:30). 'The experience of the Upanishads is true – *I know!*' he wrote enthusiastically, and all the time he celebrated the Eucharist and recited the breviary with fidelity and devotion.[12] An intrepid spiritual explorer, this struggle of dual identity was to cause him heart-rending anguish, something we do not find in the more urbane Bede Griffiths.

Born Alan Griffiths in 1906, into a middle-class English family, Griffiths' spiritual journey took him from a vague agnosticism during his teens to nature mysticism (or what he called a 'kind of worship of nature') while at Oxford University, to the Anglican Communion and eventually to Catholicism, a journey described by him in his first book.[13] Shortly after being received into the Catholic Church, he entered the Benedictine monastery at Prinknash Abbey, Gloucestershire, later remarking that this was the only place in England where he really felt at home. It was here that he took the name Bede. His study of the Bhagavad Gita and Upanishads enkindled in him a desire to go to India. The deeper motivation was not primarily missionary but, as he himself often said, 'to find the other half of … [my] soul'. This 'half of the soul', drawn to the intuitive and the imaginative, was oppressed, he believed, by the excessive rationalism and activism of the West, which he felt led to a 'dumbing down' of the spiritual journey for many people.

Griffiths' dream came to fruition in the mid-1950s, when he accepted the invitation of an Indian priest to help establish a monastery in Bangalore. Although this experiment failed, he remained on in India, first at a Cistercian ashram in Kerala state, and then at Shantivanam, as the successor of Henri Le Saux. Whereas Le Saux had been unable to bring any permanent members into the community, Griffiths did attract vocations; by the time of his death in 1993, the community had about fifteen members, all of whom were Indian. Griffiths' twenty-five years at Shantivanam were quiet and focused. He officiated as a kind of monastic superior in the ashram, training the novices and welcoming the continuous stream of guests, mostly from Europe and Australia. Always desirous to keep his links with his Benedictine origins, the opportunity came in 1980, when the ashram established affiliation with the Italian Camaldolese Benedictines and became the Hermitage of the Holy Trinity, as it still is today. Griffiths' final years were filled with writing, world travels and lectures, although the three years before his death were limited by debilitating strokes. He concluded his life's journey in May 1993.

Many Catholics met with Bede at Shantivanam, and their stay there led to a revitalisation of their faith. In his writings, he makes this plea to the Church: he says the Christian experience of God is of unfathomable depth, but it has come across to religious Hindus in particular, as superficial and locked up in words and formula, some of which have lost their meaning for many Christians. Only when the Catholic Church opens itself to the immeasurable riches of Asian religion will we be able to answer the needs of the new generation, which flocks to India and other parts of Asia every year in search of God.

Bede Griffiths and Henri Le Saux have, each in their own way, opened up paths to these riches. Like other pioneers of interreligious dialogue, they have had their critics and detractors, but their contribution is considerable and they have had an influence on the dialogical tone of the Church's pastoral practice in India.

Advaita and Interiority as Meeting Point

Both Griffiths and Le Saux show that to truly meet any religion, we must do so at its source – where the truth lies. 'Deep calls unto deep' as the psalmist says (Ps 42:7), and Asian religions evoke depth for Christians. These writers find the springboard of Hinduism in the Upanishads especially, in the truth that *atman* is Brahman, that the soul in its depth is God, and that in terms of experience, the fine point of the soul or spirit, the *guha* or 'cave of the heart', is the privileged place where God dwells. That God is known, not just as an object out there but subjectively in our very experience, is the path of *advaita*. It sets primacy on the non-dual relationship of the soul to God.

Henri Le Saux

Much has been written on *advaita* but it would be hard to improve on Le Saux's definition for clarity and brevity.

> *Advaita* means precisely this: neither God alone nor the creature alone, nor God plus the creature, but an indefinable non-duality which transcends at once all separation and confusion.[14]

He says the real stumbling blocks do not lie in *advaita*, but in the extremes of thinking, such as, on the one hand, a monistic identification between God and the human spirit which *advaita* is not and, on the other, a dualistic understanding of God as over-and-against. Le Saux says that such dualism in the way Christians speak of their faith often misleads Hindus. It can give the impression that the Christian experience is hopelessly superficial. Ultimately, he says, the challenge of *advaita* is not addressed to the essentials of Christian faith as such, but to the laziness and pride of Christians, to their reluctance to accept once and for all Jesus' inexorable law for the spiritual life that 'the seed must fall into the ground and die' (Jn 12:24).[15]

Yet the path of *advaita*, as the Chandogya Upanishad reminds us, is 'narrow as the edge of a razor'. Indeed, *advaita* was a 'razor's edge' for Le Saux and in wrestling with it he experienced the tension of exposure to the difference of another religion.[16] However, in his later years he was more at peace with his double belonging, and came to believe that the advaitic experience, although rare, was not uniquely Indian; that it lay at the heart of Christian faith and had been undergone by Christian mystics in Europe, such as Meister Eckhart and John of the Cross, although they had expressed it inadequately at times due to the fetters of a language dependent on distinctions (as in Hellenistic and Scholastic thought).

The gift of the Upanishads, according to Le Saux, is the radical 'emptying out' – the *neti, neti*, 'not this, not this' – the very purification of language and of consciousness itself. All this is of relevance to the Christian, because no Christian should ever forget that beyond and behind the manifestation of the Word of God and the effusion of the Spirit is the silence of the Father from whom Word and Spirit proceed. For Le Saux, the man of silence, Hindu *advaita* was to become a radical support for his calling to apophatic mysticism:

The Christian of the West and the East, whom a temporary acculturation has all too often cut from the well-springs of his prayer, must relearn this silence of his soul before God from eternal India ... Only when the soul has undergone the experience that the Name beyond all names can be pronounced only in the silence of the Spirit, does one become capable of this total openness which permits one to perceive the Mystery in its sign.[17]

Those who knew Le Saux and visited him at the hermitage have said that the predominant signs of the Mystery for him were the Bible – to which, after meditating on the Upanishads, he turned 'with eyes remarkably unsealed ... capable of a wholly new penetration into the mystery of the Lord' – and the Eucharist, which for visiting groups at the hermitage was an unforgettable contemplative experience.[18]

Bede Griffiths

The advaitic experience was also important for Griffiths, but due possibly to his Anglican background and intellectual capacity for synthesis, he was more capable of enunciating paradox than Le Saux. However, in line with Le Saux, he believed that *advaita*, like Christianity, is not an idea or intellectual discovery; it is something that touches the spirit in its deepest centre and from there takes complete control of everything in it. It is a fundamental attitude of soul, a total gift of self, and a complete surrender to the mystery that reveals itself within.[19]

Bede is at pains to clarify that *advaita* is not a state of identity with God, but a quality characterising our relationship to the divine being – the fundamental tenet of Christian faith. Thus he speaks frequently of the Trinity, holding that only in its light can the Christian embrace *advaita*; *advaita* in turn enabling surrender to the Triune Mystery. In *A New Vision of Reality*, considered by many to be his most masterful synthesis, Bede writes:

The Hindu in his deepest experience of *advaita* knows God is identity of being. 'I am Brahman,' 'Thou art that.' The Christian experience is a communion of being, a relationship of love, in which there is nonetheless perfect unity of being.[20]

Thus the stance of the human being before God is not a dualism of 'over-and-against'. It is a relational unity of love, because 'God is love' (1 Jn 4:7f). In relation to the personal freedom of God as love, one does not lose personality; one finds it in a new and more profound way, as the gospel teaches: 'Those who lose their life for my sake will find it' (Mt 10:39).

This losing and finding was to be played out in a dramatic way during the final three years of Bede's life, when the gift he truly longed for – to know God in the other part of his soul – was given to him. Early on the morning of 25 January 1990, while he was meditating on the veranda of his hut, there occurred the first of a series of strokes which, over time, were to lead to a profound inner transformation. Although he recovered, Bede became more grounded and earthed in a way that was unfamiliar to him. During this time, one of the most powerful experiences he had was of the Black Madonna. She did not appear as an image, more as a sense of the feminine in all its forms – as the Mother of God, as Earth Mother, as the feminine divine energy in God (the Hindu *Shakti*), as the feminine in nature and the Church, as motherhood itself. A further experience, also felt as a physical onslaught, left Bede with the greatest gift of his life – a profound sense of being engulfed by love: 'It was the unconditional love of which I had often spoken, utterly mysterious, beyond words.'[21] During this experience, Bede knew that he was being changed radically; that he was being favoured by one of the gifts of India, a gift that meant he had grown more in the two years after his stroke than in the previous eighty-four:

God is not simply in the light, in the intelligible world, in the rational order. God is in the darkness, in the womb, in the Mother, in the chaos, from which the order comes. So the chaos is in God, we could say, and that is why discovering the darkness is so important. We tend to reject it … [but] the darkness is the womb of life.[22]

The lives and teachings of these spiritual masters have become milestones in our dialogue with Hinduism. In the book *Hindu–Christian Meeting Point*, Le Saux reiterates that there is but one fundamental point of meeting with Hinduism – interiority:

Only a Church which has fully actualised her own experience of faith and has attained to that inner depth where the authentic spiritual life of India is lived, will be capable of entering into a true religious dialogue with her. Those who are to be Christian apostles in India should prepare themselves for this dialogue by serious study of the thought of India and by personal contact with her living spirituality. Their preparation will be even more effective if prayer and contemplation hold the chief place in their life. In all this they should not neglect the methods of spiritual discipline recommended by Indian traditions for quietening the senses and the mind.[23]

Griffiths, ever the visionary and pragmatist in the forward thrust of his thought, insists that the Church needs to be in dialogue with representatives of other religions today because, to one degree or another, the great religious traditions – Christianity included – can become fossilised. The religions need each other, and being in relation is their way to renewal:

> We are not seeking a syncretism in which each religion will lose its own individuality, but an organic growth in which each religion has to purify itself and discover its inmost depth and significance and then relate itself to the inner depth of the other traditions. Perhaps it will never be achieved in this world, but it is the one way in which we can advance today towards that unity which is the ultimate goal of mankind.[24]

The Witness of Holy Persons

Both Le Saux and Griffiths became convinced that Hindus are more open to the witness of persons than to doctrines. Both were doubtful about the fruitfulness of dialogue, if being Christian in India was mainly about the communication of doctrines. Hindus, whose minds are formed in a system which is philosophic and all-encompassing, do not easily reach out to the 'other', but tend to co-opt the other into their own beliefs. Griffiths reports that over twenty-five years in India he 'hardly ever found an educated Hindu who is really open to dialogue, who really wanted to understand the Christian faith as something "other"'.[25]

Both he and Le Saux recommend that the meeting of religions be at a deeper level of personal witness to the experience of God. Hindus, with their many deities and *avatars*, their 'holy persons' (*gurus*) and renunciants (*sannyasins*), respond to concrete exemplars of faith. The *guru* is most certainly not some master, professor, preacher or spiritual guide who has learnt what he says from books or from others. He is one who has himself first attained the Real, who knows from personal experience the way that leads there and is capable of bringing about the disciple's own personal experience of the Real.

Griffiths observed that lifestyle is also important for ministering in India. In his early years in Kerala, he lived a rather enclosed Western monastic life in a Cistercian monastery. He saw that this kept him apart from the Hindu people spiritually. By moving to Shantivanam, it became possible for him to live more simply and be a Christian *sannyasin* for his Hindu neighbours, the majority of whom were materially poor.

ECCLESIA IN ASIA

The seeds for openness to Asian Eastern religions were sown by *Nostra Aetate* in 1965, which speaks of Hinduism in two important sentences:

> In Hinduism men contemplate the divine mystery and express it through an unspent fruitfulness of myths and through searching philosophical inquiry. They seek release from the anguish of our condition through ascetical practices or deep meditation or a loving, trusting flight towards God. (NA 2)

These words unfold the very core of Hinduism: (i) that it is a monotheism; (ii) that it shows a keen awareness of the existential estrangement of the human condition; and (iii) that the Hindu desires release through union with the divine as the absolute mystery. The text also implicitly endorses *karma yoga, jnana* and *bhakti*, the classical Indian practices of spirituality and liberation. Later, in relation to Asian religions, *Nostra Aetate* exhorts Catholics to

> prudently and lovingly, through dialogue and collaboration with the followers of other religions, and in witness of Christian faith and life, acknowledge, preserve and promote the spiritual and moral goods found among these men, as well as the values of their society and culture. (NA 2)

The call for dialogue with this ancient and major Asian religion becomes stronger and more focused in John Paul II's magisterial encyclical *Fides et Ratio* (1998). Speaking of inculturaltion in the preaching of the gospel, he writes: 'Christianity first encountered Greek philosophy; but this does not mean that other approaches are precluded.' When Christianity meets new cultures, it faces problems not unlike those faced by the early Church. He continues: 'My thoughts turn immediately to the lands of the East, so rich in religious and philosophical traditions of great antiquity' (FR 72), putting his finger on the very core of the Indian spiritual experience when he says:

> Among these lands, India has a special place. A great spiritual impulse leads Indian thought to seek an experience that would liberate the spirit from the shackles of time and space and would therefore acquire absolute values. The dynamic of this quest for liberation provides the context for great metaphysical systems. (FR 72)

Needless to say, John Paul II does not advocate total acceptance of Hindu (and Buddhist) religious experiences. Nor does he hesitate to remind us that 'the Church cannot abandon what she has gained from her inculturation in the world of Greco-Latin thought' (FR 72). And while he appears to canonise the experiential-interior dialogue of pioneers in Indian spiritual practice, he places this dialogue in a wider intercultural context and suggests that Western Christianity must deal with and learn from Indian philosophy as a different cultural reality, and that Indian Christianity must equally retain its links with the cultures of Greece and Rome that have shaped Christianity in the West.

Fides et Ratio was published six months after the Asian Synod which met in Rome in April–May 1998. *Ecclesia in Asia*, the Apostolic Exhortation of the Pope following the Synod, was promulgated by him in New Delhi in November 1999. *Ecclesia in Asia* is a more pastoral document, primarily concerned with evangelisation, and begins by expressing the hope that

> just as in the first millennium, the Cross was planted on the soil of Europe, and in the second, on that of the Americas and Africa, we can pray that in the Third Christian Millennium, *a great harvest of faith* will be reaped in this vast and vital continent. (EA 1)

Citing his earlier apostolic letter *Tertio Millennio Adveniente*, John Paul II goes on to point out specifically that 'the issue of encounter of Christianity with ancient local cultures and religions is a pressing one', and that 'this is a great challenge for evangelisation, since religious systems such as Buddhism or Hinduism have a clearly soteriological character' (EA 2). The document later recognises the challenges to proclamation of the gospel posed by the philosophical and cultural differences of these religions, deeply intertwined as they are with specific worldviews (EA 20). Yet it strongly recommends the need for inculturation in order to appreciate Asia's gift. It lists the characteristics of the Asian soul – 'its love of silence and contemplation, simplicity, harmony, detachment, non-violence, spirit of hard work, discipline, frugal living, the thirst for learning and philosophical enquiry' and 'its innate spiritual insight and moral wisdom' – and recommends that the Church relate to these values, not in a confrontational way, but in a spirit of harmony and complementarity (EA 6).

In respect for the Asian gift and temperament, it emphasises that in dialogue it is imperative 'to revitalise prayer and contemplation' and to also give witness to 'the great Christian traditions of asceticism and mysticism' (EA 31). Recognising 'the pressing need of the local churches in Asia to present the mystery of Christ to their peoples in accordance with their cultural patterns and ways of thinking' (EA 20), it suggests that in 'contemplating Jesus in his human nature, the peoples find their deepest questions answered' (EA 14). In light of Asia's complexities – home to 85 per cent non-Christians and widely underdeveloped – the document urges that dialogue must be holistic, and encompass a preferential love for the poor, care for health, education, peacemaking, Asia's foreign debt and the environment (EA 34–41). It also acknowledges the fact that the Church has been looked upon as foreign and as allied with colonial powers (EA 9), though use of the past tense here has been criticised by commentators for whom Christianity's association with colonial powers is still a reality in India.[26]

Though praiseworthy as a holding document, *Ecclesia in Asia* has evoked numerous responses from Asian bishops and theologians. A significant response to its direct evangelisation thrust came from the President Delegate of the Synod of Asia, Cardinal Julius Darmaatmadja. Accepting the document's core message that 'the Church's unique contribution to the peoples of the continent is the proclamation of Jesus Christ' (EA 10), Darmaatmadja purports to expand this view, urging that Christian mission is also about discovering Jesus present and working in the world of Asia, rather than proclaiming him as if he were not there before. Thus, he advocates that the 'new evangelisation' of which *Ecclesia in Asia* speaks must also be a 'new way of being Church in Asia'. He presses for an inculturated Church, a Church with 'an Asian face'. In the document, inculturation is for the purpose of understanding Asian people in their culture, so that the Church can then begin 'the dialogue of salvation' where 'she can offer, respectfully but with clarity and conviction, the Good News of the redemption to all who freely wish to listen and respond' (EA 21). In the Cardinal's view, inculturation implies that the Church, if it is to minister in a meaningful way to Asian society, is *in need* of the living water the religions and cultures in Asia alone can give (see EA 50). Therefore, he encourages an immersion of the Church that will allow it to 'grow more in an Asian appearance'. Darmaatmadja emphasises that evangelisation must be carried out in dialogue with the religions and the cultures – as only then will it answer the deep yearnings of the Asian people.[27]

PROCLAMATION THROUGH DIALOGUE

We know that in the past the problem with Christian mission was its seeming lack of respect for the cultures it came to serve. Lacking subtlety of approach, or even a basic curiosity about Hinduism, it interpreted it simply as polytheism, idolatry and superstition. In the spirit of 'error has no rights', the Church kept itself apart from those who were not Christian. It was an all or nothing approach: there must be total conversion or the 'other' remains forever outside the walls. The new Christian had to give up the Vedas and the Upanishads, as well as Hindu social manners and customs, and assume a very un-Indian way of life. This generated a fear among well-meaning Hindus, something that has been strongly voiced by Gandhi, who had studied the gospels and identified with Jesus – particularly as the sublime teacher of the Beatitudes – but felt that the Christian missionary motive precluded the elemental openness and willingness necessary for understanding the other as an equal partner in dialogue.

In Asia, where, after four hundred years of mission, Christians still form a minuscule part of the Asian population (2.5 per cent) and non-Christian religions have recently staged a vigorous revival, the prospect of massive conversion to the Christian faith seems highly unlikely. The Church in Asia is now coming to terms with this, and also with the fact that it is destined to remain, for the foreseeable future, a 'small remnant', where Christians must journey in friendship with adherents of other religions toward the eschatological kingdom of God.

Indian Jesuit theologian, Michael Amaladoss, whose ancestors were Hindu, warns that the Church can no longer afford to be a self-enclosed, self-sufficient belief system with no interest in Indian culture.[28] In support of this, he points to the current conflicting elements in Hindu–Christian dialogue, particularly the tensions coming from the Hindutva movement which has gained dominance in recent years.[29] Claiming to be a cultural nationalism, Hindutva teaches that India belongs to all those who are culturally Hindu, who consider India their motherland and their holy land. As cultural Hindus, they may practice different religions. Though positive in intent, Hindutva itself is not unified and tends to group itself around the dominant stream of Brahminism of the Vedic and Vedantic traditions. It thus treats the many believers of cosmic and folk religions as subordinates. Though the majority of Hindus today are not followers of the extreme forms of this ideology, they are defensive of their religion as a cultural identity. But some extreme forms tend to make Hindutva a political entity, and we have heard and read in the media that Hindu groups have indulged in violence against Christians. In light of this, Amaladoss advises that if the Church is to be a presence in India, and not attract hostility, it cannot afford to be apart as a foreign import. It must become an Asian Church, a Church embracing the culture of India. The proclamation of Christian faith can no longer occur without dialogue. Neither will it occur if dialogue is simply an accompanying strategy to show respectful awareness of the different other. The Christian witness can only be proclamation *through* dialogue – proclamation and dialogue being one integral activity. Proclamation-dialogue, as a pastoral and prophetic activity, is all-encompassing, involving all the activities of the Church, including interreligious dialogue. Edmund Chia, commenting on the documents of the Federation of Asian Bishops Conference (FABC) from the 1970s on, makes the interesting point that earlier publications always gave specific paragraphs to interreligious dialogue. But in their later statements in response to *Ecclesia in Asia*, interreligious dialogue is no longer spelt out; it is now taken for granted as integral to the Church's Mission of Love and Service:

> For thirty years we have tried to re-formulate our Christian identity in Asia, we have addressed different issues, one after another: evangelisation, inculturation, dialogue, the Asian-ness of the Church, justice, the option for the poor, etc. Today after three decades, we no longer speak of such distinct issues. We are addressing present needs that are massive and increasingly complex. These are not separate topics to be discussed, but aspects of our integrated approach to our Mission of Love and Service.[30]

A TRIPLE DIALOGUE

Governing the Asian Bishops' integral approach to proclamation-dialogue is a triple dialogue: (i) dialogue *with the culture*, so that the local Church will be truly present within the life of the people; (ii) dialogue *with the great Asian religions* so that God's Word in them may come to further flowering in contact with the gospel; and (iii) dialogue through *engagement with the poor*, uniting with them in the struggle for a more humane world. In all this, FABC sees the culture and the religions as inseparable. Since Asia is the womb of great scriptural religions, the psyche of the average Asian is still shaped by a language of spiritual experience that is grounded in a sense of divine immanence. The bishops write:

> The ancient religions of the orient … have been for us in Asia the doorway to God … God's saving will is at work in many different ways in these religions … God has drawn our people to himself through them.[31]

Accepting the religions as significant and positive elements in the economy of God's salvation, the bishops carry forward the vision of Vatican II, but they also go beyond the theological framework of an older Western theology, which has been reluctant to accept believers of other religions as equal partners. Christians are encouraged to study the religions – not just to analyse and dissect them, but to love and respect their texts and rituals as alternative expressions of God's Word and of the universal action of the Spirit. With this approach, FABC asserts that irreconcilable, doctrinal differences need never be an obstacle to dialogue. Witnessing to Christ will instead call for experimental adjustments in framework and language and it will be an enrichment, a bringing forth from the gospel new things and old. FABC publications accentuate again and again the following meeting points in the Christian encounter with Hindu and Asian beliefs.

Jesus with an Asian Face

It is against the background of a Triple Dialogue that Asian theologians press forward to ask how we must speak of Jesus, for since he was Good News for the poor of his time, he cannot but be good news for Asia. Can this Jesus have an Asian face? There is, in fact, concern for this question in *Ecclesia in Asia* itself, wherein the exhortation recounts that 'Jesus is often perceived as foreign to Asia. It is paradoxical that most Asians tend to regard Jesus – born on Asian soil – as a Western rather than an Asian figure', and goes on to urge theologians to find ways 'to present the mystery of Christ to their peoples according to their cultural patterns and ways of thinking' (EA 20).

The experience of the Church in India is that proclaiming Jesus to Hindus has to be primarily a listening process. The all-encompassing nature of Hinduism, the natural tolerance of a religious psyche that resonates with pluralism, means that Hindus already have some knowledge of Jesus and even include him in their pantheon of saviour figures. That being the case, it is also to be expected that they will respond to Jesus in a plurality of ways. It is interesting to note that the first persons to 'theologise' about Jesus from an Indian perspective were not Christians but Hindu reformers, such as Ram Mohun Roy (Jesus as the supreme guide to happiness), Keshub Chunder Sen (Jesus as true Yogi), Swami Vivekananda (Jesus as Jivanmukta, the one who achieved advaitic liberation while alive), Rabindranath Tagore (Jesus as the Son of Man seeking the 'poor' of the earth), and Mahatma Gandhi (Jesus as the supreme Satyagrahi, the lover and fighter for truth).[32]

What all these Hindu reformers have in common is a manifest interest in Jesus as saviour. And one also finds that Asian theologians on the whole put similar emphasis on this more salvific approach. As Sebastian Painadath writes:

> The Christ we proclaim cannot be the royal Christ of imperial Christianity but the Divine Master who washed the feet of his disciples: the Christ in whom God's *kenosis* was revealed and God's compassion was embodied.[33]

This Christ is known more through a 'pedagogy of encounter' with the other, which, when the other's religious experience is included, will yield to an amassing of experimental truths: 'Jesus fragments'. Rather than belittling them in light of classical Christology, these fragments of truth must be seen for what they really are – 'adumbrations of the whole', 'interior illuminations and revelations'; because, ultimately, the Spirit is the inner master who teaches from within in a pedagogical way.[34]

Ontological and classical underpinnings of Christology are not denied; they are simply bracketed. Experience in relating to Hindus has shown that when the reality of Jesus is restricted to a language of dogmatism, he can sometimes be perceived as just another god to believe in, another *deva* of the Hindu pantheon. In this context, Felix Wilfrid warns against a socially irresponsible Christology that could divide people on the basis of the purity of their grasp of doctrine:

> … formulations and claims in exclusive terms about Christ do not remain simply in the realm of thought. They can have serious *political consequences*, especially in view of the Asian colonial history, identified with the religion of the colonisers.

He adds that such an approach cannot be true to Jesus as the Christ of Asia, an Asia which gives primacy of place to inclusiveness and harmony between peoples and indeed with all of nature.[35] Thus, Christians in dialogue will not simply 'preach' a doctrine they have heard or learnt, but will primarily be witness to the Good News – how Christ has been saving in their life, and how he can also be saving for the other.

Given the pluralism of the Asian religious psyche, it is possible there will be a variety of responses to the proclamation of Jesus. Michael Amaladoss provides examples of groups of people in certain parts of India who cannot become Christian for whatever reason, but who remain *Christbhaktas,* or devotees of Christ. They form a community of dialogue with Christians because the Church no longer sees itself as excluding them.[36] Asian theologians also tell us that these people find it easier than Western Christians to hold together the divine and the human in Jesus. With our basis in the Chalcedonian foundation for Western classical Christology, we still have tendencies in theology and private devotion to emphasise either the divinity or the humanity of Jesus one-sidedly. For Asians, to come to Jesus as divine is to come to his saving divine power, but it is also to come to him concretely as born of a woman, God-made poor, God-with-us, our Peace, our teacher, prophet, healer, person of harmony, suffering-servant, liberator: the divine in Jesus not being a concept but a call to faith, to a more intense realisation of the divine in the human.[37]

Divine, Self-Emptying Love

The experience of God as love is not unknown in Hinduism. The main thrust of Dhavamony's writing is to affirm with an in-depth account the presence of the holy in *bhakti* religion. Yet of the *avatar,* he writes: 'An *avatar* may enter human life but he does not share it. He is over and above it, always God, helping, guiding, instructing, but as God.'[38] One does not get the sense that Hindu theism is about the divine personally active in history, or, alternatively, that the non-personal Brahman, in whom Krishna of the Gita is ultimately sourced is, in itself, love. The New Testament moves beyond this ambiguity to proclaim that the Absolute with whom Jesus is identified *is* love (1 Jn 4:8). The God of Jesus Christ is not a monad, but a communion of Persons. This God is not an 'I' but a 'we' – the 'we' of the Father, Son and the Holy Spirit in interrelation. The new perspective that the mystery of the Trinity opens up is that the ground of being itself is a communion of love. In his historical person, in the self-emptying (*kenosis*) of his death and resurrection, in his on-going presence in our lives as the Christ, Jesus is the event of this love. Not dominating or powerful, God as love in Jesus decisively locates the Divine Presence where it seems most absent – in the uncertainties and sinfulness of human beings in history. An illuminating and consoling love of being-with, it is a free gift to contemplate in gratitude. But it is also a prophetic and challenging love, inviting us to engage with God in the drama of history where faith becomes way of transformation. Thus the divine presence in Christ attests that the One who overwhelms in non-personal *advaita* or comforts through *bhakti* devotion is also the Crucified One whose engagement in love with human beings is *the* mode of divine action in the world. Here lies the challenge to Hinduism – a religion in which love, especially outside family, tends to be over-ridden by duties in relation to caste – to allow that the Absolute and Universal Brahman is a call and power for a love that is transforming and universal in scope. Here also lies the source of human dignity and freedom.

Jesus, the Freedom of God

In a highly ritualistic religion such as Hinduism, where religious and social existence are interwoven, the total patterning of life is governed by *karma*, rebirth and the hierarchy of the caste system. The masses of people, especially the uneducated, are precluded from finding in their religion the source of their dignity and freedom as persons. We know that inequalities are not absent in Christian societies, but at least they cannot be justified by a Christian faith embraced in truthfulness. The Bible teaches that the human being is in the image of God and one's status as a Christian is not determined by birth, class or gender. Therefore, to speak of Jesus in India today is to announce news of the freedom of God and the freedom of human beings.

It has been acknowledged by commentators that the Christian presence in India has helped to move society to a greater recognition of the dignity and freedom of persons.[39] In a pre-papal article, Benedict XVI acknowledges this, noting that the neo-Hindu movement desires to bring about reforms in social customs, such as the abolition of caste laws and the immolation of widows. Indian society is beginning to see that the religious theory bolstering these customs – that salvation lies in losing one's identity to dissolve in the All-One – is not always consonant with the dignity and freedom of persons. This means that the profound 'That Thou Art' of the Hindu needs to be complemented by the Christian truth that the Absolute is a Person who draws us into a relationship of freedom and love. Hopefully, Pope Benedict opines, the search for correct 'praxis' regarding the inviolability of persons will move neo-Hinduism to correct its underlying 'theory'.[40]

As well as Mahatma Gandhi, many of the great reformers of the *bhakti* tradition seemed to have been aware of this and turned to the gospel as a resource and complement.[41] Michael Amaladoss, writing from his Indian experience, tells us that it is in their quest for equality, for personal dignity and freedom, that many Dalits (members of the lowest class) and tribals, who are outside class, are attracted to the Church, in that it is there they feel they have some standing as persons and are given the support to justly resist the oppressive religio-cultural systems to which they are subject.[42]

God's Pact with the Poor

That the Church of Asia is the 'Church of the poor' has become the *cantus firmus* of Asian theologians and indeed of FABC teachings and practice. The distinctive teaching of the Judeo-Christian tradition – that God is antagonistic to mammon (material wealth) and is irrevocably on the side of those who have been deprived of life – is not clearly expressed in Eastern religions and so can be prophetic for them. Sri Lankan Jesuit Aloysius Pieris speaks of the need for an Indian Liberation Theology, baptised in the Jordan of Asian religiousness and the Calvary of Asian poverty.[43] And while the Church in India will be concerned with the freedom and dignity of persons, and as far as possible the betterment of material conditions, it does not mean that the person of Jesus in whom God's presence is incarnated is presented as a social reformer. Indeed, the Asian sensibility, as Pieris suggests, would not be drawn to receive him in that way, no more than they are drawn to the imperial Jesus. Rather, when the Church, in the inclusive Spirit of Jesus, reaches out to the poor, the dialogue will cut both ways, and Christians will receive as much as they give. They will be given another 'Jesus fragment'. They will discover that it is the quality of being poor in spirit that enables the communication of the Word of God in India. But it is not just the poverty of spirit of those who witness to Jesus that speaks; it is also the poverty of Jesus himself, in that it is as 'renunciant' and 'Poor Monk' that for Asians he becomes a doorway to God.[44]

Spirit of God as Liberating Power

The Asian Bishops take a definite pneumatological perspective on the plurality of religions. When they say the religious traditions of Asia are expressions of the universal action of God's Spirit, they are not speaking about a divine Spirit other than the Holy Spirit, who is the Spirit of Jesus. The Spirit of Christ is active outside the bounds of the visible Church: the ways of the Spirit are mysterious and unfathomable, and no one can dictate the direction of the Spirit's grace. This means that in matters of religious experience we cannot expect, or even demand, that people of another culture will interpret our truth in terms of our categories only. It is the Spirit who enables the realisation of truth.

In this context, Felix Wilfrid draws our attention to a common characteristic of Asian thought – its flexibility and porousness. He asks us to accept that a grey zone in dialogue and even in proclamation need not necessarily be a failure in communication. It can be positive and enriching. It can be the deepest place of dialogue, because it is where we truly encounter the other as subject of his/her own spiritual quest.[45] It is the acknowledgement of the presence of God's Spirit as the inner master who teaches believers from within. It is also the basis for our tolerance of other ways to God who is mystery.

Kingdom of God as the Universal Horizon

What the Spirit of God brings about is the Kingdom of God. FABC sees the Kingdom as the *raison d'etre* of the Christian presence in Asia; it becomes the meeting place of the religions. Christians perceive the emergence of the Kingdom in and through Jesus, since the core of Christ's proclamation is the Reign of God. Christians also believe that the Church exists as 'sign' or 'instrument' of God's Kingdom. But Kingdom is far wider than the Church's boundaries. FABC acknowledges this and speaks of God's Kingdom as also being brought about by way of the cultural and religious traditions of Asia. Thus the call to the Church is to move out of itself into fellowship with all people of goodwill to join in building the Kingdom, whose completion is ultimately in God's hands. Such thinking, which calls for an acceptance in principle as well as in fact of the plurality of religions, places the Asian Bishops at the front line in the work of interreligious dialogue:

> The plurality of religions is a consequence of the richness of creation itself and of the manifold grace of God. Though coming from the same source, peoples have perceived the universe and articulated their awareness of the Divine Mystery in manifold ways, and God has surely been present in these historical undertakings of his children. Such pluralism therefore is in no way to be deplored but rather acknowledged as itself a divine gift.[46]

Harmony as the Goal

A central theme which has evolved in FABC seminars over the years is *Samanvaya*, or harmony – a very Hindu theme. Harmony, as the Bishops understand it, is beyond the extremes of exclusivism and inclusivism. It is a subtle form of pluralism; a resting with totality; the generous holding together of diversity in a larger unity, as the following text implies:

> *Samanvaya* is the spiritual pursuit of the totality of reality in its infinite diversity and radical unity. Since the ultimate ground of being is unity-in-plurality, the divergent forms of reality are perceived in the convergent rhythm that harmonises them. Harmony evolves by respecting the otherness of the other and by acknowledging its significance in relation to totality. Consequently the unique significance of every religion is gratefully and critically perceived within the context of the universal spiritual evolution of humanity.[47]

FABC teaches that the great religions of Asia – with their respective creeds, cults and codes – reveal to us diverse ways of responding to God, whose Spirit is active in all religions. Therefore diversity is not something to be regretted or abolished but to be rejoiced in and promoted, since it represents richness and strength. For Western Christians, shaped as we are by linear and monopolar thought processes that tend to distinctions and exclusions, all this can be confusing to say the least. And yet this sense of a harmonious pluralism seems to be *the* gift which the Asian Bishops and theologians are bringing to the Church as a whole. FABC believes that the plurality of religions is the decisive question for the Church at large. The Christian of the future will be an interreligious person: rooted in their own faith and branching out towards other believers with generosity and receptivity. When we see great love of humanity and earth in people of other religions and, above all, when we meet believers who pray, we will want to know God from their side too. Gandhi is one such person, a Hindu voice who speaks to us from that other side.

GANDHI AND CHRISTIANS

Gandhi is acknowledged as being a major influence in Hindu–Christian dialogue and was one of the first to claim that Jesus was Asian. To affirm Gandhi's knowledge of the gospels and devotion to Jesus is not to claim him for Christianity, nor is it to see the full meaning of Christ through him. He remained a Hindu all his life and yet the purity and freedom of his theocentric faith has been a source of inspiration for Christians. He reflected the energy and thrust of Jesus' message of the Kingdom in Mark 1:14 when he said: 'Jesus preached not a new religion, but a new life. He called men to repentance.' Gandhi separated Jesus from the Church. He rejected the milieu-Christianity of the West and the Church doctrines associated with it:

> Today I rebel against orthodox Christianity, as I am convinced that it has distorted the message of Jesus. He was an Asiatic whose message was delivered through many media, and when it had the backing of the Roman Emperor it became an imperialist faith as it is today.[48]

Critical as he was of direct conversion work, Gandhi's view of evangelisation must be seen in the politicised context of the India of his time. He welcomed Christian mission work particularly for its service to people, but he felt it needed to extricate itself from the exploitative structures of Western imperialism and from the untenable ideology that one religion has superiority over another. He reminded Christians that God is already in India and missionaries must meet him there, and that 'conversion is a heart process known only to and by God' and 'purity of character and salvation depend on purity of heart'.

When the Church proclaimed that Jesus is God's Son and communicates this doctrine in an exclusive way, Gandhi's response was

> I do not deny that Jesus is God's Son, the Anointed of Humanity, but I do need a more experimental test of that truth – as 'a felt experience', 'a spiritual birth'. Jesus' own life is key to the nearness of God; he expresses as no other could the spirit of the will of God. It is in this sense that I see and recognise Him as the Son of God.[49]

Mohandas Karamchand Gandhi (1869–1948), a Gujarati, was born into a family of Vaishnavites, specially devoted to the Vishnu manifestation in Rama and Krishna. His father was a businessman; his mother, a devout Vaishnava, paid daily visits to the Temple, fasted regularly and kept many vows. She imbued the young Mohandas with her religious sensibilities. A shy boy, he was married by the arrangement of his parents at the age of thirteen to Kasturba, who was to be his life-long partner and friend for sixty-two years. They raised four sons. At the age of eighteen he was shipped to a law school in England, where at first he tried to become the perfect westerner. Returning to India in 1891, he was unable to find work and encouraged by his relatives to pursue an offer to practice law for an Indian Company in South Africa, he left in 1893. Some fifty years later, when asked what was the most transforming experience of his life, Gandhi told the now well-known story of his first week in South Africa. He was travelling by train to conduct a case in Pretoria, quietly reading in a first-class compartment, when a white conductor ordered him to move immediately to third-class or be thrown off the train. He refused to move, was thrown off the train and sat all night at the cold station weighing his options.

> The creative experience comes there. I was afraid for my very life. I entered the dark waiting room. There was a man in the room. I was afraid of him. What was my duty, I asked myself? Should I go back to India or should I go forward with God as my helper, and face whatever was in store for me? I decided to stay and suffer. Active non-violence began from that date. And God put me to the test during that very journey. That was one of the richest experiences of my life.[50]

Returning again to India, Gandhi brought with him the Satyagraha (Truth-Force) movement, the political-religious form of active non-violence it expressed, and the communal way of living he had developed in South Africa. Practically minded, he was a skilful negotiator; and though frail in appearance, he had tremendous endurance. All his restless activity and endless travels, sometimes to the poorest and most remote places, were motivated by his faith. His ultimate aim was not the welfare state but the Ramrajya, the restoration of the kingdom of 'the rule of justice' and the 'realisation of God', which Hindus associate with the blessed reign of the *avatar* King Rama and his wife Zita. In the minds of religious Hindus, Rama and Zita are the ideal Hindu holy family. The India Gandhi envisaged was a holy land that had to purify itself through suffering in order to be made acceptable to God.

Gandhi's interest in the religions was not in the particularities of their creeds. Living in a world where his partners and adversaries were Hindus, Muslims, Christians, Jews, Sikhs, Parsis and Jains, he saw himself first of all as a human being in dialogue with human beings, as a friend with other friends:

I am a believer in the truth of all the great religions of the world. There will be no lasting peace on earth unless we learn not merely to tolerate but even to respect the other faiths as our own.[51]

Simple and one-pointed in his desire to serve all of humanity, he aspired to a plural Ramrajya, a place beyond sectarianism, in which people of all religions had a place and a right to flourish. But the bedrock of his desire was to 'see God', which was inseparable from 'purification of self':

What I want to achieve – what I have been striving for and aiming to achieve these thirty years – is self-realisation, to see God face to face, to attain *moksha* [liberation]. I live and move my being in pursuit of that goal.[52]

In naming God as Ultimate, Gandhi draws on the Hindu *sat* (Truth). 'God is Truth', he said, although in later years he stated in one of his most potent formulas 'Truth is God'. Realising Truth, he wrote shortly before his death, 'means realising that Truth is Love and that all human beings are one'.[53]

Gandhi was, by temperament, an experimenter. It was in the practical and in action that the meaning of Truth shone out for him – both in his spiritual ascetical experiments and in his service of humanity. In 1927 he wrote to a friend: 'I am endeavouring to see God through the service of humanity, for I know that God is neither in heaven nor down below, but in everyone.'[54] In terms of the classic paths of Hindu spirituality, he is a *karmayogi*. His is not the calling to find God in a Himalayan cave. His vocation is modelled on Krishna's call to Arjuna in the Bhagavad Gita – to bring about God's kingdom of justice and peace through a life of service. The three paths Krishna describes – *karma, jnana* and *bhakti* – are spiritually complementary and in no way exclusive. Yet in the Hindu tradition, human gifts, temperament and social standing can shape one's destiny, and one may be called to excel in one rather than the other.

Gandhi also believed that God-realisation was impossible without identifying with the poorest:

There is only one joy for me and that is to get a glimpse of God. This will be possible when I become one with the poor. I can become one with the poor if I merge myself with the poor people of a poor country.[55]

Indeed his lifestyle was one of solidarity with the poor and oppressed: he gave away his money and possessions, renounced his career, moved to a communal farm, made his own clothes, dressed like the poorest Indian peasant and shared their meagre diet of fruit and vegetables. His willingness to go to jail and his defence of 'Untouchables' was another way of sharing the poverty of the masses. Gandhi's solidarity with the poor echoes the Hebrew prophets and the Beatitudes of Jesus and his teaching on the 'union with the least' as outlined in Matthew 25. Gandhi conveys the absoluteness of this teaching in a well-known Talisman for moving beyond confused self-centredness:

> Whenever you are in doubt or when the self becomes too much for you, apply the following test. Recall the face of the poorest and weakest person you have seen, and ask yourself if the next step you contemplate is going to be of any use to that person. Will that person gain anything by it? Will it restore that person to a control over his or her life or destiny? In other words will it lead to freedom for the hungry and spiritually starving millions? Then you will find your doubts and your self melting away.[56]

He further adapted the Hindu vow of non-stealing to mean *aparigraha*, or 'non-possession', refraining from owning more than one needed. The spinning-wheel for making his own homespun clothes, which he carried everywhere, became the symbol of this radical commitment. Labour for the poor, he said, is always a question of survival; it is 'bread labour' and it is salutary for us to remember that for the poor God most often appears in the form of bread.

It was in the public sphere, through his teaching and practice of non-violence, that Gandhi exerted the greatest influence. Non-violence – *ahimsa* – is, he said, not original. It is in the Hindu scriptures, the Qur'an and especially in the gospels. Living during the Second World War and the horror of the extermination camps in Europe, Gandhi knew that non-violence does not come easily to human beings. Echoing the gospel, he said non-violence is the largest and purest of loves – the love of enemy. It is not simply a negative helplessness in face of the other, nor is it just refraining from revenge; it is an active force – it is what Truth becomes when it makes itself felt as love. *Ahimsa* is the shining forth of Truth itself; it is the way God himself works in the world.

In the political sphere, the Mahatma's Satyagraha movement was the context, training ground and public face for the practice of *ahimsa*. In 1908, while organising the movement for social justice and racial equality in South Africa, he coined the word *satyagraha* to describe this mass pursuit of Truth by entire peoples and nations. Satyagraha is 'holding to the Truth', 'truth-force', 'steadfast, non-violent, direct action for truth'. It results in active non-violent resistance to injustice or oppression of any kind.

It is interesting to note that the teaching of the Hindu Gita shapes Gandhi's teaching here. The *satyagrahi*, like the Warrior of the Gita, realises God in and through the battles of life. This entails sacrifice. The Gita, interpreting the ancient Vedic tradition where sacrifice is offered to propitiate the gods and restore the order of the universe, teaches that the sacrifice to make is of the ego, the greedy self. One's actions are 'consecrated actions' when they are detached from results and rewards and made over to God for God's sake. One's actions must be fearless in the face of loss, violence or oppression, for the *satyagrahi* must be willing to give his life even unto death. It is no wonder that Gandhi, the man of Truth, came to see the face of Christ in these Hindu scriptures. He once spoke of Christ as the Prince of Satyagrahis and the aspect of Jesus' life as Suffering Servant held a special meaning for him. He believed that it was through his self-abnegation, his willing embrace of suffering, that Jesus evoked the nearness of the long-suffering God – something that must be a badge of any servant of the divine. Or rendered in Hindu terms, through Jesus' non-violent sacrificial life and death, God has been realised, a world order has been restored and a template was laid down for those who would be servants of the Kingdom.

Only months before his assassination, anguished by what was failure for him – the partition of India – Gandhi wrote what reveals his heart best:

> By my fetters I can fly, by my worries I can love, by my tears I can walk, and by my cross I can enter the heart of humanity. Let me praise my cross, O God.[57]

Gandhi's experience of Christianity enabled him to transform Hinduism in at least three significant ways. Firstly, his restoration of the divine Hindu Ramanuja order embraced a radical inclusiveness: because divine truth is also Love and all persons had human dignity, especially the poor and 'Untouchables'. Secondly, in his focus on social justice issues he reinterpreted *karma* as more than an isolated individualised relationship with God. Seeing it also as the inexorable weight of sinfulness generated by social and communal expressions, he validated people's freedom to liberate themselves from so-called 'religious' yet sinful structures. Thirdly, he discerned that the cross or suffering love (*ahimsa*) is the way God works in the world, not only in personal spiritual growth but in the God-realisation of people and nations. And coming to Christ as one who was Hindu, he invited us to more lateral explorations of Jesus, to draw out of the gospel new things as well as old. He turns us to the non-violence and radical love of Jesus to contemplate God's presence as active and vulnerable love amongst us.

As always with Gandhi, one's own heart had first to be put right with God. And this was through continuous prayer. 'Let God disarm your heart,' he writes:

> I have no strength save what God gives me. I have no authority over my compatriots save the purely moral. If God holds me to be a pure instrument for the spread of non-violence in the place of the awful violence now ruling the earth, God will give me the strength and show me the way. My greatest weapon is mute prayer.
>
> I can give my own testimony and say that heartfelt prayer is undoubtedly the most potent instrument that humanity possesses for overcoming cowardice and all other bad habits.[58]

Absolute renunciation is not to be found even on the peaks of the Himalayas. The true cave is the one in the heart. People can hide themselves within it and, thus protected, remain untouched by the world even while living and moving freely in the world and taking part in all those activities which cannot be avoided.

During the last years of his life, Gandhi spoke on prayer every evening during his daily public services. He gave a number of hours to prayer, but the way forward for him was not always one of clarity and light. It is not surprising to read that Cardinal Newman's hymn, 'Lead Kindly Light, One Step Enough For Me' was his favourite Christian prayer. Since God is the mystery of mysteries, he said, why should we expect everything to be clear?

> The impenetrable darkness that surrounds us is not a curse but a blessing. God has given us the power to see the steps in front of us, and it would be enough if heavenly light revealed that step to us.[59]

The purpose of this reflection on Gandhi is not to 'claim' him for Christian faith nor subject his views on Christianity to theological critique. It has been said that he resisted with good humour those Christians who held the opinion that 'if only he accepted Christ' his example would be perfect, and by the same token he never sought to convert others to Hindu faith.[60] His contribution to dialogue owes little to his specific comments on Jesus or Christianity. He was not concerned with doctrines and believed that interreligious understanding must not be separated from issues of liberation, peace and the good of the earth. In living the purity of Hindu faith in a life of dedication and sacrifice, Gandhi retrieved its moral truth of non-violence and went on to link this with the gospels. Truth is God, he said in one of his most potent formulas, and Truth is Love, and love is non-violence because non-violence is the way of God. Gandhi's challenge to Christians is to see the suffering Christ with new eyes and in interreligious dialogue to let the gospel shine out with greater purity.

SUMMARY

Hindu monotheism is a cosmic religion of extremes – the remote impersonal Brahman and yet the personal deity and deities present in the cosmos and in all aspects of life. It is primarily a religion of divine immanence, in which the final aim of the human person, whose *atman* is Brahman, is to become one with and dissolve in the All-One. In contrast to the evolving ambit of Hinduism, the Judeo-Christian religion is a revolution. A prophetic religion, it is a decisive engagement of a transcendent Creator God with history, immersing human beings in a transforming relationship of love. Whereas union with God for the Hindu is a mysticism of identity, for the Christian it is a personal union in which I and Thou are not done away with. It is against this background that we can understand more fully the differences between beliefs that nominally are common to both religions: God as creating and sustaining the world, a triad in God, and incarnation and *avatars*.

However, Hinduism's monistic tendencies are not to be denigrated and its millennia-old methods of meditation and asceticism in relation to the soul and God have always been respected by Western Christians. Spiritual seekers such as Griffiths and Le Saux have strongly affirmed that the gift of India is not primarily doctrines but interiority or realisation, and that Indian sensibility looks for the same in Christians. When Christian truth is communicated as realised, Hindus are more easily drawn into dialogue.

Since Vatican II, the teaching Church has shown positive regard for Eastern religions. *Nostra Aetate* (1965) sees Hinduism as concerned with the Divine

Mystery, as aware of the estrangement of the human condition and of the desire for release and recourse to God in confidence and love. In *Fides et Ratio* (1998) Pope John Paul II extols the great Indian metaphysical systems, and in the more pastoral *Ecclesia in Asia* (1999) he calls for a proclamation of the gospel in a spirit of harmony and complementarity with Asia's special gifts of spiritual insight and moral wisdom.

In the pastoral approach of the Asian Bishops in India we meet with a more 'working dialogue'. Living in a multi-cultural situation, they recommend a 'proclamation *through* dialogue', the dialogue being a Triple Dialogue with the culture, the religions and the poor. Such proclamation through dialogue will be a giving and a receiving – a sharing of the Word of God in Jesus, but also a receiving of new insights into the Christ mystery, called 'Jesus fragments' by theologians. It will also be a dialogue that resonates with the *bhakti* devotion and practices around the theism of the majority of Hindus. It will ask what we mean when we say 'God is love'. The Christian presence in India has always been an ethical one and Hindus have acknowledged its reforming influence in relation to inhumanities, such as the caste system, widow-burning and temple prostitution. However, Hindus have resisted asking the question why this is so. The Christian in dialogue attempts to show that this transforming love of the other is ultimately sourced in the nature of God who *is* love and in the incarnation of God in Jesus, whose life and death manifest the self-emptying and vulnerability of this love in history.

Mahatma Gandhi was not a Christian. However, through his reading of the gospels, especially the Beatitudes, he seems to have come to an intellectual and personal appreciation that God is Love. As a Hindu, he invariably speaks of God as Truth, whom he, as a *karmayogi*, knows through prayer and his selfless service of the oppressed. Yet in later life he affirms that Truth is Love, and that the signature of Truth as Love is non-violence. Suffering love (*ahimsa*) is the way God works in the universe, not only in personal growth but in the God-realisation of people and nations. Gandhi came to believe that through the Cross of Christ, a world order was restored and a template laid down for all who would be servants of the Kingdom.

Differences of doctrine always arise when we dialogue with Hinduism, as with any Eastern religion. But Christians who live in India are inevitably led to a more inductive dialogue 'from below', more like the pastoral dialogue evidenced in the publications of Asian Bishops and theologians. Jesuit Hindu scholar, Francis X. Clooney, in a lecture on Hinduism, spoke of another kind of dialogue: the dialogue of sensibilities. Despite our differences, he proposed that the sensibility of Catholics – nurtured as it is by a plurality of experiences such as sacramental practices, cult of saints and love of pilgrimage – is already equipped to enter without judgement into the 'God-all-and-everything' experience that is Hinduism.

FURTHER READING

Abhishiktananda, *Hindu–Christian Meeting Point: The Cave of the Heart* (Delhi: ISPK, 2005).

Amaladoss, Michael, SJ, *Beyond Dialogue: Pilgrims to the Absolute* (Bangalore: Asian Trading Corporation, 2008).

————, 'Dialogue Between Religions in Asia Today', *East Asian Pastoral Review (EAPR)* 42 (2005), pp. 45–60.

————, *Making All Things New: Dialogue, Pluralism and Evangelisation in Asia* (New York: Orbis Books, 1990).

————, 'Hindu–Christian Encounter: Challenge and Promise,' *EAPR* 44 (2007), pp. 187–201.

————, 'Who Do You Say That I Am? Speaking of Jesus in India Today', *EAPR* 34 (1997), pp. 1–7.

Barker, Gregory A., *Jesus in The World's Faiths* (Maryknoll, NY: Orbis Books, 2005).

Coward, Harold, ed., *Hindu–Christian Dialogue* (Maryknoll, NY: Orbis Books, 1990).

Dear, John, ed., *Mohandas Gandhi's Essential Writings* (Maryknoll, NY: Orbis Books, 2002).

De Mesa, Jose M., 'The Quest for Truth in Asia', *EAPR* 35 (1998), pp. 356–63.

Dhavamony, Mariasusai, *Hindu–Christian Dialogue: Theological Soundings and Perspectives* (New York: Rodopi, 2002).

Ellsberg, Robert, ed., *Gandhi on Christianity* (Maryknoll, NY: Orbis Books, 1995).

Griffiths, Bede, *The Cosmic Revelation: The Hindu Way to God* (Springfield, IL.: Templegate, 1983).

————, *A New Vision of Reality: Western Science, Eastern Mysticism and Christian Faith* (Springfield, IL.: Templegate, 1990).

Painadath, Sebastian, 'Theological Perspectives of FABC on Interreligious Dialogue', *Jeevadhara* 27 (1997), pp. 272–88.

Phan, Peter, *Christianity with an Asian Face* (Maryknoll, NY: Orbis Books, 2003).

Pohlmann, Horst Georg, *Encounters with Hinduism: A Contribution to Inter-Religious Dialogue* (Norwich: SCM, 1996).

Pieris, Aloysius, 'Inter-religious Dialogue and Theology of Religions: An Asian Paradigm', *EAPR* 29 (1992), pp. 1–8.

Sugirtharajah, R. S., ed., *Asian Faces of Jesus* (Norwich: SCM, 1993).

Wilfrid, Felix, 'Jesus Interpretations in Asia: Fragmentary Reflections on Fragments', *EAPR* 43 (2006), pp. 334–58.

NOTES
1. George Gespert-Sauchm SJ, 'The Two-Edged Dialogue: Reflection After Fifty Years', *The Way Supplement* 104 (2002), pp. 39–40, citing his Hindu mentor, Professor G. C. Jhala (1907–72).
2. Bede Griffiths, *The Cosmic Revelation*, p. 118.
3. *Ibid.*, pp. 115f.
4. Cardinal Joseph Ratzinger, *Truth and Tolerance: Christian Belief and World Religions* (San Francisco: Ignatius Press, 2004), p. 45.
5. *Ibid.*, pp. 87–8.
6. *Ibid.*, p. 44.
7. *Ibid.*
8. Mariasusai Dhavamony, *Hindu–Christian Dialogue*, pp. 184–5.
9. *Ibid.*
10. Henri Le Saux, cited in Shirley du Boulay, *Swami Abhishitananda, Essential Writings* (Maryknoll, NY: Orbis Books, 2006), p. 92.
11. Letter, 4 December 1928, in James Stuart, *Swami Abhishiktananda: His Life Told Through His Letters* (Dulhi: ISPK,1989), p. 3.
12. See William Johnston, *Arise My Love: Mysticism for a New Era* (Maryknoll, NY: Orbis Books, 2000), p. 123.
13. Bede Griffiths, *The Golden String: An Autobiography* (London: HarperCollins, 1979). Shirley du Boulay's *Beyond the Darkness: A Biography of Bede Griffiths* (London: Rider, 1998) is a clear and inspiring biography. For a selection from Griffiths' writings, see Thomas Matus, *Bede Griffiths, Essential Writings* (Maryknoll, NY: Orbis Books, 2004).
14. Henri Le Saux, *Hindu–Christian Meeting Point*, p. 98.
15. *Ibid.*, Chapter 7.
16. Le Saux journeyed further into Hindu mysticism than any other Westerner. In one of his last papers, he writes of the advaitic identity as moving to a state where there is no longer 'Thou' nor 'I', where the gulf between has vanished, where *advaita* means 'there is no face to face, for there is only That-which-Is, and no other to name It'. In short, *advaita* is the experience of that which just *is*. There is no need for prayer in this state: for to Whom does one pray, and who is she/he who prays? ('Experience of God in Eastern Religions', *Cistercian Studies* 9 [1974], pp. 151–2). Le Saux came under criticism for seeming to suppress our relation to God, and God's to us, which are at the heart of the Christian mystery. It has been considered that the antinomy he placed between the Christian experience of God and the Hindu (and which was a source of suffering to him) was due to a rigorist French theological training, which led to an inability to communicate the 'both-and' character of God's relationship to

us (see William Johnston, *Arise My Love*, pp. 123f). Yet in practice, Le Saux continued to pray the breviary and the Eucharist daily. One cannot doubt his authenticity, because when he writes of the inexpressible, it is obvious that he has lived in communion with it.

17. Cited in James Wiseman, *Spirituality and Mysticism: A Global View* (Maryknoll, NY: Orbis Books, 2006), p. 170.
18. Cited in William Johnston, *Arise My Love*, p. 193.
19. Abhishiktananda, *Hindu–Christian Meeting Point*, p. 103.
20. Bede Griffiths, *A New Vision of Reality*, p. 220.
21. Cited in Shirley du Boulay, *Beyond the Darkness*, p. 249.
22. Cited in *ibid.*, p. 250.
23. Le Saux, *Hindu–Christian Meeting Point*, p. 110.
24. Bede Griffiths, cited in *Spirituality and Mysticism*, pp. 173–4, from *The Tablet* (9 March 1974).
25. Bede Griffiths, *The Cosmic Revelation*, p. 113.
26. *Ecclesia in Asia* has been criticised for not being Asia's voice. See Peter Phan, *Christianity with an Asian Face* (Orbis Books, 2003), Chapter 8; Edmund Chia FSC, 'Of Fork and Spoon or Fingers and Chopsticks: Interreligious Dialogue in *Ecclesia in Asia*', *Horizon* 28.2 (2001), pp. 294–306. The author's main point is that the Vatican does not appreciate Asia's cultural differences. Asian Bishops and theologians are of one mind with the Vatican that Christ must be proclaimed, but they differ as to the mode of proclamation. They press for a methodology of communication that respects the culture and deep spiritual yearnings of the peoples of Asia.
27. See Edmund Chia, *ibid.*, for response of Cardinal Darmaatmadja, pp. 298–300.
28. Michael Amaladoss, 'Hindu–Christian Encounter: Challenge and Promise', pp. 188–90.
29. *Ibid.* The word *hindutva* means 'the quality of Hinduism' and has come to summarise a fundamental belief in the merit and worth of all things Indian. Its greatest theoretician was V. D. Sarvarkar (1883–1996), who fought in countless speeches and publications for a violent liberation of India from everything foreign and a complete restoration of Hindu ideas and society. India's independence from British rule in 1947 was not enough for him, he bitterly opposed Nehru's secular state concept and continued agitating for the total Hinduisation of India. In his essay 'Hindutva' he developed the outlines of the new Hindu India, distinguishing between Hindu-Dharma (Hinduism as a religion) and Hindutva (Hindudom as the unifying socio-cultural background of all Hindus). The political implication of Hindutva was promoted by the RSS – 'the organisation of national volunteers' – of whom Gandhi's assassin, Nathuram Godse, was a member. The RSS later gave rise to the founding of the BJP (Bharatiya Janata Party) in 1980, for whom the belief in Hindutva is fundamental. The BJP held office from 1998–2004. Hindutva is a belief that has changed India – and by implication Pakistan as well. Extremist leaders, in the spirit of Hindutva, justify their anti-Christian campaigns on the grounds that missionaries should be punished for trying to convert lower-caste Hindus to Christianity, a charge denied by Church leaders of different denominations.
30. Cited in Edmund Chia, p. 303.
31. For unreferenced texts of the FABC, see Sebastian Painadath's 'Theological Perspectives of FABC on Interreligious Dialogue'.
32. Samuel Rayan, 'Hindu Perspectives of Christ in the Nineteenth Century', *Concilium* 2 (1993).
33. Sebastian Painadath, p. 277.
34. Felix Wilfrid, 'Jesus Interpretations in Asia', pp. 335–41.
35. *Ibid.*, p. 343.
36. Michael Amaladoss 'Hindu–Christian Encounter: Challenge and Promise', p. 194.
37. Michael Amaladoss, *Beyond Dialogue: Pilgrims to the Absolute*, p. 22; F. Wilfrid, p. 343.
38. Mariasusai Dhavamony, *Hindu–Christian Dialogue*, p. 29.

39. Cardinal Ratzinger cites scholar Hans Burkle on changes in modern Hinduism: 'the experience of identity found in the Upanishads ... offers no adequate basis for the enduring validity and dignity of the uniqueness as an individual of every single person. This cannot be reconciled with the notion that this life is merely a transitory phase in the rhythm of changing levels of reincarnation ... The modern reforms of Hinduism are thus quite logically committed to asking about the dignity of man. The Christian concept of the person is taken over by them in the Hindu context as a whole, without its foundation in the context of God' (p. 47).

40. Cardinal Ratzinger, 'Introduction to Christianity: Yesterday, Today and Tomorrow', *Communio* (Fall 2004), p. 491.

41. Most of the reformers looked upon Christ as liberator from social and religious oppression; some finally came to an orthodox ecclesial view of Christ. See Samuel Rayan, 'Hindu Perspectives of Christ'.

42. Michael Amaladoss, 'Hindu–Christian Encounter: Challenge and Promise', p. 199f.

43. Aloysius Pieris, *An Asian Theology of Liberation* (Edinburgh: T. & T. Clark, 1988). The writings of this Sri Lankan theologian focus mainly on Buddhist–Christian dialogue. He is director of the Tulana Research Centre in Sri Lanka and interprets Latin American Liberation Theology from an Asian perspective.

44. Aloysius Pieris, *An Asian Theology*, pp. 56–8.

45. Felix Wilfrid, p. 349f.

46. Cited in Michael Amaladoss, *Beyond Dialogue: Pilgrims to the Absolute*, p. 16.

47. Sebastian Painadath, pp. 287–8.

48. John Dear, *Mohandas Gandhi: Essential Writings*, p. 79.

49. Cited in Robert Ellsberg, p. 27.

50. John Dear, p. 20, pp. 54f.

51. *Ibid.*, p. 78.

52. Gandhi, cited in Francis X. Clooney, *Hindu Wisdom For All God's Children* (New York: Maryknoll, 1998), p. 114.

53. John Dear, pp. 72f.

54. *Ibid.*, p. 34.

55. *Ibid.*, p. 55.

56. *Ibid.*, pp. 190–1.

57. Klaus Klostermaier, *A Survey of Hinduism* (New York: State University New York Press, 1994), p. 460.

58. John Dear, pp. 140–1.

59. *Ibid.*, p. 142.

60. Robert Ellsberg, p. xv.

CHAPTER 7

Buddhism: The Way of Wisdom

Now thou art seen, thou builder of the house,
Never again shalt thou build me a house.
All my rafters are broken, shattered the roof-beam;
My thoughts are purified of illusion;
The extinction of craving has been won.

DHAMMAPADA, 154

Buddhism began with a Hindu, Siddhartha Gautama, who was born at the foot of the Himalayas around 566 BCE in what is now Nepal. When his followers asked him 'Who are you? A god? An angel? A saint?' Gautama replied, 'I am awake.' This answer was to become his title – the Buddha, the Awakened or Enlightened One.

Between 800–500 BCE, Indian society witnessed a growing dissatisfaction with the ritualism of ancient Vedic religion. Centred on the Four Vedas, this religion was under the tight control of the priestly Brahmins. This elite class was the source for both religious and secular authority. Remote from the realities of human life and ensconced in the social structures which supported them, their religion was becoming fossilised. Allied to Brahminism was the Hindu caste system, which robbed people of room for manoeuvre. Already in the sixth-century Upanishads, we see intimations of this social ferment. Here we find the individual emerging as a centre of knowledge and power; we find a turning inward in search of life's meaning and a consequent refinement in the understanding of the person and of God.

Against this spiritual and social background, reform-minded seekers such as the Jainist founder, Mahavira, and the Buddha emerge. Much of the language of Buddhism reflects its Hindu origins; yet we will see that the Buddha formulates the religious question in a radically new manner. He was known as one of the *nastikas* – the 'nay-sayers'. Since the accepted Hindu doctrines of the human soul (*atman*) and the existence of God (*Brahman*) do not feature in the Buddha's teaching, the Christian may wonder if they share any common ground with Buddhism. Strangely, however, the best training in the dialogue between the religions can occur when the engagement is with what is most 'other'. Buddhism in itself is a totally intelligible, life-enhancing and attractive worldview. Since it offers more radical exposure to 'otherness' and 'unlikeness' than the Abrahamic religions, the questions Buddhism poses tend to be quite fundamental and can stimulate us to reflect more deeply on what we believe and why.

It is customary for Buddhists to begin a meditation period with a prayer of taking refuge in the Three Jewels – the Buddha, the Dharma and the Sangha. It is prayer of trust in the Buddha, the great physician of the human condition; in the Dharma, or Truth, the sure remedy; and in the Sangha, the community of practising Buddhists who will administer the remedy and offer support and challenge on the way. The exploration of the Three Jewels will form the basis of this chapter.

Firstly, we will consider the founder, Siddhartha, since his life is the concrete embodiment of Buddhism. Neither a prophet, nor an incarnate son of God, nor a saviour, he was a pathfinder and pointer to the Middle Way. Secondly, we will reflect on the main elements of the Buddhist worldview and the *dharma* path which is its core. Space does not allow a treatment of the Sangha as such, which is the practice of everyday Buddhism, monastic and lay, but here it will be explored in a broader sense, encompassing the levels of Buddhist development. As we shall see, the religion has a capacity for integrating itself with different cultures and religions, and for transforming itself while still remaining true to its core teaching. While accepting as foundational the basic historical figure of the Buddha and the teachings that grew around him as developed in the Theravada tradition, we will go on to consider the more expansive Mahayana and its offshoot, Zen, whose subtle and highly wrought system of practice is of great interest to Christian theology and spirituality.

THE BUDDHA

The Buddha, Siddhartha (literally 'soul attained') was born into the Gautama family, who were members of the Kshatriya ruling class. His father, Suddhodana, was the elected head of the aristocratic Shakya people. Though Gautama is historical, there is little precise information about his life and he left no personal writings – the numerous inspiring tales and legends about him emerged much later. These records are quite simple and direct and the personality of the Buddha comes across with surprising clarity: his experiential approach to life, his sympathy for the afflicted masses of people, his certitude concerning his mission, his moderation, modesty of bearing and depth of insight, his independence of judgement and capacity to mark out and communicate a new spiritual path to humankind. It is understandable that his followers would be over-awed by such a life and would embellish it with legend. We are told that the worlds were flooded with light at his birth, that even the cries of beasts were hushed as peace encircled the earth. Only Mara (literally 'destruction'), the Evil One, did not rejoice.

Before Siddhartha was born, Hindu seers informed his father that if the child remained attached to the world, he would be a great king; but if he withdrew from the world, he would be a redeemer. Suddhodana determined to steer his son toward worldly glory and ensured that he would live a life of luxury, without contact with the suffering of life. At sixteen Siddhartha married and at twenty-eight had a son called Rahula. Yet he was not happy. In the Legend of the Four Passing Sights, we touch on the beginning of Siddhartha's awakening. One day, as he was driving outside the royal park, he noticed an aged man 'bowed like the gable of an old house', a man afflicted with leprosy and bent to the ground in pain, a corpse being carried to a burning pyre and a wandering mendicant whose face was filled with joy and peace. On enquiring, he was told that the mendicant was one of the many ascetics who had gone forth into the homeless life. After these experiences, Siddhartha resolved to go forth on the supreme quest. Buddhist art and legend tell of the Great Going Forth, when, aged twenty-nine, he left his wife, son and palace in the middle of the night – the *devas* cushioning the hooves of his horse to make good his escape. In the forest Siddhartha made acquaintance with hermit mendicants, who taught him about *atman* and the sacred knowledge of the Upanishads. Yet this was not what he wanted and after six years he left the Hindu seekers. Joining a group of five ascetics, he practised bodily austerities to an extreme degree, but also discovered that this was not his way. Finally at Gaya (today Bodhgaya in the state of Bihar) Siddhartha had the experience he was seeking: sitting beneath a large pipal tree (the Bo tree) he vowed not to rise until he had come to true wisdom. The legends at this time tell of the struggles he went through. For forty-nine days he sank deeper and deeper into meditation. The Dhammapada, one of the earliest collections of the Buddha's sayings, describes his feelings at the time of Enlightenment:

Now thou art seen, thou builder of the house.
Never again shalt thou build me a house.
All my rafters are broken, shattered the roof-beam;
My thoughts are purified of illusion;
The extinction of craving has been won. (Dham 154)[1]

I have conquered all; I know all, and my life is pure.
I have left all and I am free from craving.
I myself found the way.
Whom shall I call Teacher?
Whom shall I teach? (Dham 353)[2]

But the evil spirit, Mara, foreseeing what was happening, tempted him: 'Nobody will listen to you!' he said. But Siddhartha replied: 'If even one will listen, that is enough'. Finally, the highest deity, Brahman, invited him to go forth to teach people. He did so and became an itinerant teacher for forty years around the mid-region of the Ganges. At Sarnath, a short distance north of the Hindu holy city of Varanasi, he was reunited with the five ascetics (*bhikkhu*) who became his followers. Tradition tells us that these were the first companions with whom he set in motion the Wheel of the Dharma, the Four Noble Truths and the Eightfold path.

The answer of the Buddha to the question, 'What do you teach?' is laconically given by the Dhammapada: 'Do not do evil. Do what is good. Keep your mind pure. This is the teaching of Buddha' (Dham 183). And to the question, 'What is the core of your teaching?' he is said to have replied: 'Brethren, the mighty ocean has but one flavour, the flavour of salt, even so, brethren, my teaching has but one flavour, the flavour of release.'[3] During the forty years, the Buddha had not only generated a body of teaching, he also established a mendicant community (*sangha*) of men and women. In the class-ridden and patriarchal Hindu society, he was classless, proclaiming that the spiritual life was possible for everybody.

At the age of eighty, after eating a meal of dried boar's flesh in the home of Cunda, the smith, he became fatally ill. Even on his deathbed, his mind moved toward others and towards Cunda especially, who felt responsible for his death. His last request was that Cunda be informed that of all meals he had eaten during his life only two stood out as having blessed him exceptionally: the meal which gave him strength to reach enlightenment under the Bo Tree, and the meal which opened the final gates to *nirvana*.

Two statements from the Buddha's valedictory have echoed through the ages: 'Be lamps unto yourselves. Rely on yourself and do not rely on external help' and 'All compounded things decay. Work out your salvation with diligence.' The Buddha's entire life was saturated with the conviction that, having attained wisdom, his mission was to be compassion for the world.

Titles for him vie with each other, but he remained half light, half shadow, defying complete intelligibility. He was Shakyamuni, the 'silent sage' (*muni*) of the Sakya clan; the Truth-Winner; The Perfectly Enlightened one; the Trainer of Untamed Minds. In Mahayana Buddhism, Shakyamuni is one of the great Bodhisattvas, the enlightened beings who defer final *nirvana* out of compassion for the world so caught in suffering. He is the Sage of Nothingness. Possibly the most exalted title is the Tathagata, the One-Who-Has-Thus-Come. As we shall see, the appeal of this very abstract Mahayana title lies in its unplumbed depths. It is paradoxical, conveying both 'emptiness' and 'this-worldliness'. It is one of the many titles which acts as a raft for Christians to the shore of Buddhism.

Buddhist art, also a rich resource on the identity of its founder, moves between the abstract and concrete. The most aniconic and abstract representations occur in the early period. Here extant images leave the representational figure of Shakyamini out altogether and use symbols to evoke his presence. Like the early Christians who used a fish or a plain cross to evoke Christ, the Buddha is symbolised by a parasol (a symbol of royalty and authority), a riderless horse, a wheel, an empty throne beneath a tree or footprints on the earth. Even under Hellenistic influence in north-west India, the first anthropomorphic images of the Buddha made no attempt to portray a likeness, but communicated an elegant, idealised version. Image makers were obliged to include his cornrow hair, the monk's robe draped over the left shoulder, the meditative lotus posture, the various hand gestures (*mudras*) of teaching and witnessing by pointing to the earth – all providing a pedagogy for believers, while at the same time evoking a reverence for the Buddha figure.

The most common architectural symbol of Buddhism is the *stupa*. One of the great royal patrons of Buddhism in India was the third-century King Ashoka, who converted to the *dharma* and declared it the state creed. During his forty-year reign, the building of *stupas* became his project. These colossal earth and masonry reliquary mounds were built on sites associated with the Buddha's presence. The *stupa* is a purely exteriorised structure. It consists of a round mass, an 'egg' or 'womb', which contains relics of the Buddha. It is often raised slightly on a square or circular base and is surmounted by a square box-shape, which in turn is crowned by a vertical shaft that supports two, three or five discs of decreasing diameter. The box-like forms, around which the pilgrims walk, recall the enclosed village altars of Vedic Hinduism. The disc-bearing pillar is a stylised reminder of both the sacred Bo Tree and the multi-tiered parasols that were long the symbol of royalty in India. In fact, the subsequent history of the *stupa* shows Buddhism's adaptability to various cultures. As Mahayana Buddhism transforms the Shakyamuni from earthly teacher to eternal spiritual power with numerous forms and titles, the solid earth mound gradually melts away and the tree/parasol gains independent existence as the multi-tiered pagodas of Far Eastern countries.

BASIC BUDDHIST CONCEPTS

Superficially, Buddhism might appear to be pessimistic but on reflection it is a carefully nuanced Middle Way between a repudiation of human existence and an inordinate attachment to the composite and impermanent selves that we are. The Buddha was a radical empiricist. He experienced human nature as it *is*, empirically and with great tenderness. He received no divine revelation from without. Through the austerity of mental concentration 'within the house of the body' he arrived at the transforming knowledge of wisdom. The Dalai Lama, also a rational empiricist, cites Shakyamuni as saying:

> It is within our body itself, mortal in itself and only six feet that we find the world and the origin of the world, and the end of the world and, in a parallel fashion, the path that leads to *nirvana*.[4]

We will now consider what the Buddha found through prolonged mental concentration within 'the house of the body'.

Dukkha

Dukkha is a word of far greater depth and complexity than the usual limp translation as 'suffering'. It is true that its immediate meaning refers to the ordinary sufferings of life, experienced by child and adult alike – sickness, old age, death and the frustration of our desires. It is suffering because we keep thinking life is not supposed to be that way. It is the view that these more immediate experiences are the *dukkha* the Buddha speaks of that has led to the view that Buddhism is pessimistic. But this is not so. In fact, the whole thrust of the religion is to enhance the happiness of life, its *sukkha* moments. In the Dhammapada we read sections on joy such as the following:

> O let us live in joy, in love amongst those who hate! Among men who hate let us live in love … O let us live in joy, although having nothing! In joy let us live like spirits of light. Health is the greatest possession. Contentment is the greatest treasure. Confidence is the greatest friend. *Nirvana* the greatest joy. (Dham 197, 200, 204)

Theravadin scholar Walpola Rahula emphasises that the Buddha, like any good physician, is neither pessimistic nor optimistic but realistic about life. *Dukkha* is more than painful symptoms. Rather, it underlies them as an unsatisfactoriness. It is one of the three marks of the human condition and of all living things, the other two being impermanence and the insubstantiality of things.[5]

Anicca

Anicca is the impermanence of things. We suffer acutely when we find that what we most desire to hold on to – health, beauty, success and friendship – are transitory. The Dhammapada remembers the Buddha as comparing impermanence to a 'burning fire'. 'How can there be laughter, how can there be pleasure when the whole world is burning?' (Dham 146). This image of fire, which is ever changing, is a powerful link between impermanence and suffering.

Pratitya-Samutpada

This third signature of all living things lies at the very heart of the *dharma* and is unique to Buddhism. 'He who sees dependent origination sees *dharma*; who sees *dharma* sees dependent origination.'[6] Since Buddhism makes no appeal to a Creator God and things are not self-creating, the question is how do phenomena arise? The answer is that they arise as a result of preceding causes and in turn become causes of future phenomena themselves. This chain of causation should be seen as a circle, not as a straight line. Samsaric existence is a chain reaction of twelve conditioned and conditioning links which inexorably keep the human life-cycle on the merry-go-round of *samsara*. If one must select one link as the fundamental propulsion in the wheel of life, it is ignorance – *avidya*, or false views. Ignorance gives rise to craving and impels human existence towards endless rebirth. The Buddha faced this with devastating directness:

> Monks, I do not see any other single obstacle which has so hindered mankind and caused man for so long to fare up and down and endlessly wander on like the obstacle of ignorance.[7]

The full implications of dependent origination are not easily grasped. When the Buddha's favourite disciple, Ananda, was unwise enough to declare to the Master that he understood it, the Buddha rebuked him sharply:

> Say not so, Ananda, say not so! Deep is this doctrine of events as arising from causes … It is through not understanding this doctrine, through not penetrating it, that this generation has become a tangled skein, a matted ball of thread … unable to overpass the Constant Round [of Transmigration].[8]

Raimundo Pannikar says that dependent origination is the Buddha's way of expressing the contingency or dependence of being. But it is not the contingency of things in terms of dependence on a Creator God:

> The Buddha did not speak of the 'beyond' in the sense of a divine reality other than the world. He speaks rather of an interdependency *within* the totality of what is 'right here'.[9]

Such a totality (which in Mahayana is *sunyata* – emptiness), being beyond the grasp of reasoning, is an ineffable and mystical experience. The Buddha presented this teaching as a Middle Way between two extremes: on one side are eternalists, for whom reality is a complex hierarchical strata of substances which extend all the way to a Supreme Being; on the other are the nihilists, for whom there is sheer nothingness, or a pure materialism which also does not portray reality. The view of the Middle Way is that things both are and are not. *I am* and things around me *are*. At the same time *I am not* because my existence is a momentary dependence which I cannot hold on to. The same is true of what is around me.

According to the Buddha, the eternalist is subject to craving, to 'building his house'. But the nihilist also craves, in that he desires non-existence. In understanding this complex insight, it is helpful to realise that the Buddha's teaching is always about salvation. With dependent origination he is teaching his followers to leave aside constructs of permanence and to stay with human experience, which is always of the self and the universe, arising and passing away at each moment. To see in this way is to overcome cravings for permanence; it is to be on the way to release from *dukkha*.

The Five Aggregates – The *Khandas*

It is against this background of a universe as a conditioned and relational chain of causality that Buddhism understands the human person as made up of many parts, and also as conditioned and relative. The person is an aggregate or compound of existences (*khandas*), a flowing together of the energies of matter into particular shapes and forms. There are five *khandas*, different energies of attachment, popularly referred to as 'Groups of Grasping':

Matter: What we call matter is not a substance, but a bundle of energies, cravings, desires. The human body is in this category.

Sensations: Every sensation is a form of contact, pleasant or neutral with the physical world. There are six kinds of sensing. Buddhists do not make a distinction between spirit and matter, and mind is just another organ of sensation, except that it responds to mental objects or ideas rather than to the physical.

Perceptions: Like sensations, our perceptions occur from contact with objects, physical or mental, but it is the organs of perception that recognise objects. They perceive a rose as a rose and a scorpion as a scorpion. But according to the Buddhist view, perception does not record an object with the impartiality of a camera. The sense organ in the act of perception sees a rose as beautiful and the scorpion as dangerous.

*Mental Formations (*Samskaras*)*: These refer to the emotional and volitional energies in the human person, whose function is to direct the mind toward good, bad or neutral actions. The senses and perceptive organs record reality objectively, but it is at this level one says: 'A rose, I love it, I want it; a scorpion, how dangerous, I hate it'. Most people use their volition and will-power to go against the stream and try, by mental effort, to rescue something substantial from the flow of change. The Buddha attached much import to the *samskaras* as the root of *karma*. At the *samskara* level, the person clings to their desired object (such as wealth) and, in making it their refuge from the chain of existence, the clinging deepens the very bondage they long to escape from. Because it is at this level that the Buddha locates the deepest need for deliverance, one cannot but think of the text of Paul in Romans 7:21-25, where he too cries for deliverance from the 'law in his members' which hinders him in doing good. And while the cry of human need is the same in both religions, for Paul the need is met in Christ the Deliverer, in Buddhism there is no saviour.

Consciousness: A form of rational knowledge that does not exist apart from being fed by the other four groups. It is not an entity in itself; is not spirit nor soul. It is always *this* consciousness, either visual, auditory or mental, depending on a person's desires and volition at any time. Sometimes spoken of as the storehouse or memory of a person's life as a whole, it is consciousness that is considered to be passed on to rebirth in another life.

Anatta

The features of Buddhism we have considered so far lead on to the difficult but vital question of who or what the 'self' is. Who is the 'self' that becomes aware of the reality of *dukkha*? Who is the 'self' embedded in the world of arising, passing away and conditioned becoming? What is the 'self' that has tasted the impermanence of all things? And, more importantly, is it the 'self' that holds the aggregates of personality together? The doctrine of *anatta* – the not-self – is the most original of the Buddha's teachings. It is especially difficult for westerners – our religious and philosophical traditions commit us to the reality of soul, an inner principle that gives to the human being his distinct essence. Allied to this is the acceptance that the soul of the human person is indestructible, that we will survive physical death in a transtemporal order and will continue in relationship with the personal Creator on whom our existence depends. It is also interesting to note that the Buddha differentiates his teaching from Hinduism, where *atman* is ultimately destined for union with a divine being.

To arrive at the conclusion of *anatta* is to understand the importance of the third level of suffering associated with the *samskaras*, the volitional emotional energies of the human being. Dwelling on this leads one to realise that the aggregates that constitute the human being are no more permanent than a tree or blade of grass. 'All flesh is grass, and all goodness therefore is as the flower of the field' (Is 40:6); but whereas the prophet of Israel could say this, knowing that he was supported by the Word of God which endures forever, the Buddha frankly says that it is folly and ignorance to try and read permanence into the 'bundle' of aggregates of which we are made. There is nothing that can be disentangled from the body or isolated from the inexorable process of decay and death.

The Buddha was aware that this teaching was 'against the current'. Among his disciples were people with false views: 'annihilationists', for whom *anatta* meant despair, and 'eternalists', who in a desire for self-preservation built their houses on soul (*atman*) that would live forever. Thus the Buddha, with an eye to the liberation of his followers, taught the middle ground doctrine of *anatta* as an *upaya*: a 'skilful means' to cross to the other shore of *nirvana*.

It must be mentioned that in Buddhism there are two kinds of truths: conventional and ultimate. When we use expressions such as 'I', 'you' and 'being' in reference to persons, we are speaking conventional language, a functional language that helps us get by. But truth is also ultimate, it is the 'Beyond', which the Buddha does not deny, cannot be designated as 'I', 'you' or 'being'. In a much repeated illustration, a Buddhist teacher, the Venerable Nagasena, answers the Greek King Menander's objections to *anatta*:

> The Venerable Nagasena addressed the King. 'Your Majesty, how did you come here – on foot, or in a vehicle?'
> 'In a chariot.'
> 'Then tell me what is the chariot? Is it the pole of the chariot?'
> 'No, your Reverence.'
> 'Or the axle, wheels frame, reins, yoke?'
> 'None of these things are the chariot.'
> 'Then all these separate parts taken together are the chariot?'
> 'No, your Reverence.'
> 'Then is the chariot something other than the separate parts?'
> 'No, your Reverence.'
> 'Then, for all my asking, your Majesty, I can find no chariot.'
> 'The chariot is a mere sound.'
> 'Surely what your majesty said is false! There is no chariot.'
> 'What I said was not false,' replied the King. 'It's on account of all these various components, pole, wheels … that the vehicle is called a chariot. It is just a generally understood term, a practical designation.'
> 'Well said, your Majesty! You know what the word "chariot" means! And it's just the same with me. It's on account of the various components of

my being that I am known by the generally understood term, the practical designation Nagasena.'[10]

Thus the Five Aggregates of human existence are a recognisable and perceptible object to which I can point when I say 'I'. Walpola Rahula explains that the persistent feeling of 'I am' that naturally accompanies one in life must not be attributed to any one of the aggregates, and especially not to the more evanescent 'mind' or 'consciousness'. The Buddha taught that since the physical body has more density and stability, it is better to designate it as 'self' rather than designating consciousness as self.[11] Indeed, I once heard the Dalai Lama say with a chuckle, 'When I am not sure who I am, I pinch myself'!

Nirvana

The certainty of *nirvana*, the hope of Buddhist religion, is based on the fact that the Buddha has attained it. Rahula tells of an enlightening conversation between a group of monks and the *bhikkhu* (monk) Klemaka. When Klemaka said that he did not experience in the Five Aggregates anything pertaining to a self, the monks responded, 'If so, then you must be an *arahant* free from all impurities.' Klemaka disclaims this high spiritual state, saying that within the Five Aggregates he still has the feeling of 'I am'. This feeling he describes somewhat like the smell of a flower, though later on, with progression in enlightenment, he knows it will fade away. This fading away of the 'I am' is a taste of *nirvana*.[12] Buddhist texts are high in praise of this experience, and Buddhist writers tend to take flight when speaking of it. In the words of the Shakyamuni Buddha, *nirvana* variously means 'the extinction or blowing out of desires', the Absolute Noble Truth which is Reality or, very simply, 'the Truth'. In all this, Rahula says it is incorrect to think of *nirvana* as the natural result of the extinction of craving. *Nirvana* is not the result of anything. It is beyond cause and effect. Like Truth, it *is* and it can only be realised. Faithfulness to the Eightfold Path does not cause it, no more than climbing a mountain causes the mountain to be. 'One lives the holy life,' says Rahula, 'with *nirvana* as its final plunge (into Absolute Truth), as its goal, as its ultimate end'.[13]

To avoid the false idea that *nirvana* is an acquisition, negative language is often used in describing it, as we see in these oft-quoted words of the Buddha:

Monks, there is an unborn, unoriginated, unmade and unconditioned. Were there not the unborn, unoriginated, unmade and unconditioned, there would be no escape from the born, originated, made and conditioned. Since there is an unborn, unoriginated, unmade and unconditioned, there is escape from the born, originated, made and conditioned.[14]

Thus *nirvana*, beyond name, 'the other shore', is the window on the hope and grace that suffuses Buddhist practice.

Afterlife

A related question often asked is what happens to the *arahant* after death? This is one of the questions that the Buddha is recorded as leaving aside because it is not conducive to liberation. Nevertheless, since such questions have persisted, commentators have come up with clarifications. A distinction is made between *nirvana*, which can be experienced before death (although this is a rare experience) and *parinirvana*, which refers to the historical death of a realised person, when they shed their conditioned body and move beyond the process of rebirth. As we shall see, in Mahayana Buddhism there is the tradition of the Bodhisattvas, enlightened figures who have entered into *nirvana* but who choose to remain in the world of *samsara* to relieve human suffering. Then there is the historical death of an *arahant*, which is often compared to a fire being extinguished when the supply of wood runs out, or to a flame going out when the wick and oil of a lamp are finished.

Buddhists are particularly reticent to speak of the 'afterlife' of the Founder, the Shakyamuni Buddha. They say that if the true nature of what he discovered under the Bo Tree some forty-five years previous is so great a mystery that it cannot be fully expressed in conventional terms, then how much more so the final fulfilment of the *Tathagata*:

As a flame blown out by the wind
Goes to rest and cannot be defined,
So the wise man freed from individuality
Goes to rest and cannot be defined.
Gone beyond all images –
Gone beyond the power of words.[15]

However, for the majority of people, there is some continuity in the afterlife, although not in the sense of Hindu reincarnation, which is the view that there is a soul or subtle essence imprinted with an enduring personal stamp that transmigrates from body to body down through the aeons. While Buddhism rejects the Hindu view, it does admit some causal connection between one life and another. The connection is like a light passing from one candle to another, where what is passed is not substantial or personal, but an en-kindling of still extant karmic energies in another becoming, so that a new round of desires and attachments are perpetuated and with them a new round of ego-illusion.

Rahula reminds us that rebirth isn't just something that bridges the abyss between one's physical life and another life. Rebirth and death are occurring daily: 'When the aggregates arise, decay arises, O Bhikkhus, every moment you are born, decay and die.'[16] Present life and afterlife are on a continuum of transference of energies, so that the difference between death and rebirth is only a thought moment, the last thought moment in this life conditioning the first thought moment in the next. One could say that, in a sense, that other person who carries your unexpiated *karma is* you and yet that person *is not* you, no more than the flame of a candle is the same as the flame from which it has been lighted. Life and afterlife are one moving process of arising and rebirthing, and to Buddhists the afterlife is not a great mystery. It is said that Buddhists do not fear death. The Tibetan Lamas tell us to prepare for death: 'Do not let death take you by surprise.' Their work in hospice movements throughout the world is evidence of this fact and is a witness to their skills in helping people to die at peace with themselves.

THE BUDDHADHARMA

Communicated in the Deerpark in Sarnath to the first five disciples, 2,500 years ago, the Four Noble (*Aryan*) Truths and Eightfold Path stand as the creed of Buddhism. These are truths to be believed in 'in the marrow bone'; only then will they liberate. The Buddha once engaged a member of the *sangha* in a discussion of the seductive nature of speculation. It seems that a disciple had threatened to leave unless the Buddha responded to his queries about the nature of the world, body, soul and life after death. 'You,' replied the Buddha, 'are like a person who has been shot by a poisoned arrow, yet fends off the ministrations of his friends and will not allow them to remove the shaft until he first knows the name of his assailant, his caste, place of origin, and the material from which the weapon was made. Such a one will die before solving these speculative questions.'[17]

The *dharma* aims to keep one from such distractions. It is likened to a raft that will convey its travellers from the shores of ignorance to the shores of enlightenment. The Buddhist scriptures record that the first disciples experienced enormous relief at this good news. They thought of the Buddha as a physician, who in the Four Noble Truths diagnosed the human condition and prescribed the Eightfold Path as a way for healing.

The Four Noble Truths
The First Truth is the fact of *dukkha*, the unsatisfactoriness of existence and the suffering that transience (*anicca*) brings.

The Second Truth is the cause of *dukkha*. Transience would not matter if we did not seek to deny it or even try to undo it. More seriously, the cause of *dukkha* is our thirst or craving (*tanha*), which clings to life and forgets that life is a moving stream. Fuelled by the Tree Fires of Existence – greed, hatred and illusion/ignorance – we eagerly grasp at possibilities of permanence; we pull back in resentment of the flow of life and desire annihilation. More commonly, we simply do not know what to do. Such delusion is what gives rise to greed and hatred in the first place. Buddhist awakening is a dispelling of ignorance and the Buddha faces this with devastating directness:

> Monks, I do not see any other single obstacle which has so hindered mankind and caused man for so long to fare up and down and endlessly wander on like this obstacle of ignorance.[18]

The Third Truth is that *dukkha* can cease. It is here that Buddhism offers hope to its followers, and points to the Buddha in whom the liberation of *nirvana* has occurred.

The Fourth Truth is obedience to the Path that leads to the goal.

The Eightfold Path
1. Right Understanding
2. Right Thought
3. Right Speech
4. Right Action
5. Right Livelihood
6. Right Effort

7. Right Mindfulness
8. Right Concentration

Buddhists are at pains to point out that, in terms of practice, the steps inhere and have a simultaneous presence in each other. Yet viewed as a path of formation for the beginner, there is a discernible progression from the basic moral level (3, 4, 5) to the level of mental culture (6, 7, 8) and to the level of wisdom (1, 2).

Morality (*Shila*)

Buddhist texts emphasise virtue as the base – it is like the earth on which one stands. Anyone who wishes to practice the *dharma* with a view to liberation from suffering must not act in a disconnected, unwholesome way. Actions such as falsity of speech or violent behaviour of any kind shatter the interdependence of all living things and contribute in general to suffering. These actions are also harmful to oneself, agitating the mind and hindering one's progress in insight. Lay persons may, as a token of their commitment to the Buddha, subscribe to Five Precepts as an essential moral minimum, undertaking to:

Refrain from taking life.
Refrain from taking what is not given.
Refrain from misuse of the senses.
Refrain from telling lies.
Refrain from self-intoxicating substances.

Finally, the path of Right Livelihood mandates that the livelihoods and professions of Buddhists should, as far as possible, promote rather than hinder life. While *shila* is a practice of wholesomeness in behaviour toward ourselves, others and sentient creation, it still bears on extrinsic behaviour. The Eightfold Path directs the disciple to a deeper cleansing of unwholesome tendencies, which spring ultimately from within. Therefore the mind must also be cleansed if our actions are to be wholesome. And so great emphasis is placed on *bhavana*, or mental culture.

Mental Culture (*Samadhi*)

Right Effort advocates the self-reliant ethos of the Buddha's teaching. The word 'right' is important here, indicating that the energy of effort should be strictly regulated according to the ability of the practitioner. One is not trying to obtain anything.

Proper effort is not the effort to make something particular happen. It is the effort to be aware and awake in each moment, the effort to overcome laziness and defilement, the effort to make each activity of our day a meditation.[19]

It has never been suggested that the Turning of the Wheel is easy. The Buddha speaks of it as 'unwearied digging'.[20] Right Effort is skilfully proactive about purifying the mind. 'Find joy in watchfulness; guard well your mind. Uplift yourself from your lower self, even as an elephant draws himself out of a muddy swamp' (Dham 327). It prevents evil and unwholesome states from arising; it abandons them immediately when they arise; it generates new wholesome states not already existing and it nourishes their further development. Right Effort has the one-pointedness of faith. It is the surest way to offset the doubts and anxieties that weaken the will of spiritual seekers of all religions.

Central to this question of mental culture is the breath as instrument. Focusing on the breath, we develop the ability of the mind to focus on a single object and resist distraction – two essential qualities for concentration. The breath is appropriate as a single object of attention, since it is natural and neutral and it does not arouse in us cravings and aversions. The breath, like the body, is where we are at any moment. In Buddhist meditation, breath is always returned to as the best place to begin.

The relation between Right Mindfulness and Concentration is subtle and is variously interpreted. In the light of spiritual growth in other traditions, and indeed in psychology, a meaningful interpretation would be that mindfulness is the general awareness or attentiveness one brings to living in the here and now; and if we are to detail it in Buddhist fashion, it is a live presence to oneself in body, sensations, feelings, mind and thought. We know that the beginnings of a remarkable freedom are in this kind of mindfulness. Closely observed anger, for instance, need not erupt with disastrous effects. Its energy may even be used for positive purposes. An interesting book on the spirituality of Buddhism, *After the Ecstasy, the Laundry*, asks how, after a prolonged period of meditation or retreat, one can bring the fruits of this experience to daily life.[21] The answer lies in the practice of mindfulness. But if one is to nourish a daily mindfulness, one must give some time to meditation, which deepens concentration.

This meditation is known as *samadhi*. With the purpose of Right Concentration and with the aid of the breath, a *mantra* or any other neutral object, it aims to concentrate the mind and make it a more subtle instrument for the attainment of wisdom (*prajna*). Neither *shila* nor *samadhi* are unique to Buddhism. It has been observed that the Buddha taught a number of states of *samadhi*, as instruments to sharpen the mind and to examine reality in a deeper way. While the practice of concentration confers great benefits, it is a partial solution only, since it still works at the level of the conscious mind and not at the depths where the roots of impurities lie. This seems to be a unique element in the Buddha's teaching – the discovery, twenty-five centuries ago, of the existence of the unconscious mind. He is reported as saying:

> If the roots remain untouched and firm in the ground,
> a felled tree still puts forth new shoots.
> If the underlying habit of craving and aversion is not uprooted,
> suffering arises anew, over and over again.[22]

Wisdom (*Prajna*)

In themselves, morality and mental culture are valuable but their real purpose is to lead to wisdom (*prajna*), for wisdom penetrates the reality within and frees one from ignorance and attachment. It is not a received wisdom, though the seeker is advised to avail of the guidance of a master; nor is it a theoretical wisdom, though an intellectual investigation may inspire and be its motivation. It is an experiential wisdom, a personal realisation of truth. Ultimately, no one else's realisation of truth will liberate us. The Buddha pointed away from himself and emphasised the necessity for each disciple to undertake the work for themselves alone: 'You have to do your work; those who have reached the goal will only show the way.' The truths to be realised in the attainment of wisdom are simply what are proclaimed in the Four Noble Truths and the three marks of existence which follow from them – *dukkha*, *annica* and *anatta*. It has been said that the Buddha's spiritual life, as a model for the disciple, began with awareness of these three realities. In enlightenment, he returned once again to see these three aspects of human existence without aversion and with equanimity. This was the state of wisdom or *prajna* – quite rare for most human beings – and it is what Buddhists aspire to.

Buddhist Meditation

In Theravada Buddhism the technique of *vipassana* meditation attempts a direct realisation of wisdom in a patient and methodic way. *Passana* means 'seeing' and *vi* denotes a special kind of seeing. It is a seeing of *dukkha, anicca* and *anatta* through a dispassionate observation of sensations within oneself. In the practice of awareness and *samadhi*, the effort is to observe natural breathing, without controlling or regulating it. In *vipassana*, we simply observe bodily sensation, and through these we observe the mind. One commentator on the Buddha's teaching on meditation tells us that:

> Sensation is indispensable in order to explore truth to the depths. Whatever we encounter in the world will evoke a sensation in the body. Sensation is the crossroads where mind and body meet ... Just to rid a garden of weeds one must be aware of the hidden roots and their vital function, similarly we must be aware of sensations, most of which usually remain hidden to us, if we are to understand our nature and deal with it properly.[23]

Vipassana

Vipassana meditation (also called insight meditation) is not overtly religious. It has little to do with prayer, worship or ceremony. It is based on the belief that by noting one's physical sensations one observes the mind, in that every thought, emotion and mental act has a corresponding sensation in the body. Meditators move attention systematically to different parts of the body. They take sensations and feelings as they come to them, simply observe them in a detached way and do not judge them. They examine how a sensation arises – its cause – and how it disappears – its cessation. They do not engage, because these sensations are empty. As this meditation deepens, unpleasant sensations may arise, long-lost feelings, memories bringing with them mental or physical discomfort, even pain. It is possible that some deeply buried conditioning, a tasting of *samskara* or karmic residue, will be stirred up and start to appear at the conscious level. Once again, the task is simply to observe objectively, and gradually, with sustained effort and without tension, the mind will come to tranquillity and one-pointedness. Coming to *vipassana* from the Christian tradition of prayer can provide a sharp taste of the sheer physicality of Buddhist effort and how the one-pointedness of its faith can engage one's person as a whole.

Metta

Metta (loving-kindness) meditation is particularly engaging and shows a surprisingly different side of Buddhism. Less clinical and introspective and more other-centred than *vipassana*, it has an extrovert energy and a lighter feel. In retreat centres, participants in *vipassana* often spend one week on *metta* as a kind of break. *Metta* is a meditation on the virtues, the *Brahma Viharas* or Four Sublime States of the Bodhisattvas, the virtues which elevate the human and call us beyond ourselves: loving-kindness (*metta*), compassion (*karuna*), sympathetic joy (*mudita*) and equanimity (*upekkha*). This meditation portrays the intimate, deeply affectionate and indeed joyous side of Buddhism, an aspect that gets less attention than it deserves. The *Discourse on Loving-Kindness*, one of the spiritual treasures of Buddhist culture, expresses this very depth of the tradition. A selection from it reads:

> May every creature abound
> In well-being and peace.

> May every living being weak or strong
> The long and the small
> The short and the medium-sized
> The mean and the great ...

> May all attain peace.

> Just as a mother with her own life
> Protects her son, her only son, from hurt,
> So within your own self foster
> A limitless concern for every creature.

> Display a heart of boundless love
> For all the world
> In all its height and depth and broad extent
> Love unrestrained, without hate or enmity.

> And as you stand or walk or sit or lie,
> Until overcome by drowsiness
> Devote your mind entirely to this;
> It is known as living here a divine life.[24]

Metta presents a warm-hearted concern for the well-being of all persons. Like Christian *agape*, it is not sentimental or erotically based, nor is it selectively applied to congenial people only. *Metta* extends outwardly in ever-increasing circles and yet expresses itself locally in concrete acts. As though to emphasise the centrality of *metta*, the Dalai Lama has often declared: 'My religion is kindness.' Speaking of his daily *metta* practice he says:

> To engender altruism or compassion in myself, I practice certain mental exercises which promote love toward all sentient beings, including especially my so-called enemies. For example, I remind myself that it is the actions of human beings rather than human beings themselves that make them my enemy. Given a change of behaviour that person could easily become a good friend.[25]

The practitioner then meditates on *karuna* – a highly regarded virtue and the motivation of the Bodhisattvas in Mahayana Buddhism. As the hard carapace of the 'I' breaks down, the sense of the interdependence of all living things deepens, and eventually their suffering comes to be regarded as one's own. *Mudita* is the very antithesis of the hard-hearted competitiveness that is so prevalent today. The 'normal view' can be to experience the success and happiness of others as threatening to one's 'legitimate interests'. The quality of *mudita* joyously celebrates the achievements of others and their successes become one's own. Finally, *upekkha*, a very Buddhist virtue, is the capacity to accept the vicissitudes of life calmly and dispassionately. Even in showing compassion for others one must be balanced. This is not a numbed indifference, nor is it sheer neurotic dissociation from life. Rather it arises from the insight that all events are neutral and that if one is not biased by desire or craving, one can be at home in the world whatever the conditions.

Note on *Dana* (Giving)

Westerners are often attracted to the moral precepts and the meditation and mindfulness offered in Buddhism, but we tend to forget that giving is foundational to this religion. Buddhist texts and sermons are fulsome in praise of *dana* because it reduces possessiveness and selfishness and encourages sensitivity to others. The altruism of *dana* becomes the motivation for observing the precepts. *Dana* may be demonstrated in charitable acts or hospitality towards others, but in its true Buddhist sense it is a religious act, performed with care, a sense of purpose and frequently with ritual. For lay people, *dana* is exercised in giving food to the monks of the Sangha. Commentators say that in his instructions on giving, the Buddha obviously wishes to retain some of the values and power of Brahmanical sacrifice.[26] Giving is sacrificial, not in the sense of the placating of gods, but as a 'beyond-self' transformative spiritual practice. Simple, short-lived gestures of *dana* as sharp attacks on the ego are characterised by a truthfulness – a foretaste of the mindset needed for the Four Noble truths, and for an emptying of self that anticipates *nirvana*.

Mahayana Buddhism

A whole trend of schools came into being as Buddhism developed. One can reduce the development to three vehicles ('vehicle' because the *dharma* is conceived of as a ship or raft to ferry believers across the ocean of suffering to the other shore of *nirvana*). The foundational, orthodox tradition is Hinayana, the Small Vehicle. The term *Hinayana* is rarely used today, but the tradition survives in an extensive scale as Theravada Buddhism, the Way of the Elders, the main religion of Sri Lanka, Burma and Thailand. Theravada teaching remains fundamental for all Buddhists. The later development of Mahayana, called the Great Vehicle because of the universality of its beliefs, is found mainly in Tibet, Mongolia, China, Korea and Japan. A third vehicle, Vajrayana, the Thunderbolt, is also Mahayanan, yet quite distinctive in its strong cultic character. It is found mainly in the Himalayas, Tibet and Mongolia.

Mahayana is characterised by diversity. It is not a single school of Buddhism in the sense of Theravada, but a convenient label for a whole variety of teachings and practices suitable for different cultures and levels of spiritual development. It is sometimes claimed that Mahayana is more lay oriented that Theravada; yet the monastic *sangha* is still central, most notably in Tibet. Even from its beginnings, the *sangha* was 'the fourfold *sangha*' of 'monks, nuns, lay men and lay women'. However, the democratic ethos of Mahayana – its natural expansiveness and ability to adapt to cultures, its openness to a heavenly presence of Buddha figures who are worshipped as powerful saviour beings – are among the many developments which make it more inclusive of lay people. From the *Lotus Sutra* of Mahayana, the highest message of the Buddha to humanity is: 'Forsake all doubt and uncertainty; you shall become Buddhas. Rejoice!'[27]

There are and have been western authors who praise Theravada as the pure, original and unfalsified version of the *dharma*, and as safeguarding the contemplative rationalism and empiricism of original Buddhism. They believe that final spiritual liberation requires a steady going forth into the homeless state of a strict asceticism and that, ideally, the calling is best lived in a monastic setting. They believe that there is only one wholly enlightened one in each world cycle, so the furthest anyone can advance in the present cycle (since the Shakyamuni Buddha has already appeared) is to become an *arhat*, not a Buddha. An *arhat* is one who has passed beyond the fetters of samsaric existence and rebirth, and who has reached his goal. The Buddha is a real historical figure for Theravadins, and he is revered and loved for the universal nature of his mission as Teacher. He is not an object of devotion or a saviour, nor is he in any way elevated to divine status.

It is of interest to note that the development of Buddhism in its Mahayana forms coincides with the beginnings of the Christian era. Loving knowledge and compassion, which remind one of Christian charity and which were subordinate virtues in the older Buddhism, have now moved to the centre. Bodhisattvas people the heavens as a kind of communion of saints and descend upon earth to do good. There is the belief that Buddhas existed for many aeons before becoming historical and that they assumed bodily forms as a means of salvation.

While the question of God is not addressed by the self-reliant Theravadins, being simply 'laid aside', Mahayana is more overtly theological, offering a 'trackless track' of transcendence which teases and fascinates. The gift of the Buddha nature *within* all beings is at its heart. Scholars are eager to point out the weaknesses of the 'Lesser Vehicle' – that it was primarily a way of merit, that the goal of arahatship was for monks only and that, in its practice, the laity were inferior. The highly popular teachings of Vimalikirti (c. 400 CE) portray the learned Theravada monks as baffled by the wisdom of a mere layman who playfully reveals the higher truths of Mahayana.[28]

The Bodhisattva Ideal

In Mahayana, supreme wisdom (*prajna*) flows outward in compassion (*karuna*). A new type of hero different from the *arhat* appears. The central notion is that Buddhas are saviours, selflessly devoted to the salvation of others. From this developed the notion of Bodhisattva, which refers to those many beings who, on the last stage to enlightenment, turn back to help those in the world who are still in pain and ignorance. These aspirants to Buddhahood have generated the 'wisdom heart'. They seek rebirth for compassionate reasons and are voluntarily reborn into the world of *samsara*. If the *arhat* rejects the world and seeks cessation in an ineffable *nirvana* beyond the world, the Bodhisattva maintains an enlightened quiescence amid the hurly-burly of life.

In Mahayana, all people have the potential and calling to become Bodhisattvas and even Buddhas. Buddhahood is not a distant goal, it is within all beings waiting to be claimed. Bodhisattvas do not redeem as Christ does; they are the 'good friends' of all beings. Operating out of the 'wisdom heart', their energy flows over into compassion, and they shirk no task, however difficult, however impossible. The scriptures give us the four vows of the Bodhisattva:

However innumerable sentient beings are I vow to save them!
However inexhaustible the defilements are I vow to extinguish them!
However immeasurable the *dharmas* are I vow to master them!
However incomparable Enlightenment is I vow to attain it![29]

These celestial figures, who have reached the higher stages of enlightenment, are thought of as enormously powerful beings, virtually identical with the Buddha in his heavenly form. They are many in number. The most popular Bodhisattvas in Mahayana devotion are Avalokiteshvara, Manjusri and Amitabha. Avalokitesh-vara, 'Regarder of the Cares of the World', is often shown with many arms extended in compassion or with a thousand faces, reflecting all the sufferings of the world. In Tibet he is known as Chenresi. It is no surprise that he is guardian of this country, where people live in unimaginably harsh conditions in their land on 'the roof of the world'. The Dalai Lama is believed to be his incarnation.[30]

Manjusri, beloved of scholars and students, is more severe. He is represented with a book in one hand and a sword in the other. The weapon serves to dispel the clouds of ignorance which bedevil the understanding of the *dharma*. He is often portrayed in terrifying forms as the 'conqueror of death' or 'guardian of doctrine'. The rituals related to this terrifying iconography are held in special rooms, which are usually reserved for monks who have attained certain levels of spirituality.

In China we find devotion to Amitaba (Amida, in Japan), the 'buddha of infinite light', who inhabits the magnificent paradise of the Pure Land. Pure Land Buddhism is distinguished by its complete trust in the Bodhisattva's saving grace and power. Faith and devotion are held to be particularly productive of merit and great things are expected from prayer to Amitaba and the offering of flowers and perfumes at his shrines.

Pure Land Buddhism offers more immediate and tangible results. Commenting on the development of this popular Buddhism, Conze tells us that a natural reaction developed against the belief that Bodhisattvas had to go through aeons to reach the Buddhahood. People felt the aim was so distant that it could not provide a motive for action, and they drifted into lassitude and despair. In the Pure Land tradition, which is often likened to Christianity, the near goal of rebirth after death into the paradise of Amitaba is sufficient for salvation.[31]

Mahayana Buddhism also became gradually more profuse in rituals, prayers of devotion, temples and officiating priests. Furthermore, the historical aspect of the Shakyamuni Buddha appeared to have receded in importance. On this matter, Conze cites a Mahayana text which seems to disparage devotion to the Shakyamuni: 'From the Buddha arise only the disciples ... but from the Bodhisattva the perfect Buddha is born.' Yet we must remember that what attracted followers to the historical Buddha from the beginning was that he was different. As supreme embodiment of the *dharma*, no human being could have gone further. He is reported to have said to a disciple, Vakkali: 'What is there in seeing this vile body of mine? Who so sees the spirit Dharma, he sees me; who so sees the Dharma sees me ...'[32]

Trikaya – The Three Bodies of the Buddha

Yet Mahayana does not see Buddhahood as floating above or apart from worldly reality. How Buddhahood and the world meet is creatively addressed by the rather abstruse doctrine of the Three Bodies of the Buddha. It has been said that this doctrine has parallels with the forms of Christ in the Christian tradition – the eternal *Logos* in whom all things are created; the Risen and glorified presence of Christ in sacramental signs and in the body of believers; and the historical Jesus, the divine in human form. In Mahayana we find the Dharmakaya, the '*dharma* body', which is the Buddha as Absolute Truth underlying all things. In itself, the Dharmakaya is beyond conventional language. The Sambhogakaya, the 'bliss body', the Buddha in his glorious celestial form, as object of devotion and visualisation on part of believers. The Nirmanakaya, 'transformation body', is the assumed form, or how the celestial Buddha appears as a human being. Mahayana speaks of the pre-existence of a Buddha. Not pre-existence in the eternal sense of the *Logos*, but in Buddhist time, which means that it takes aeons for a human being to arrive at Buddhahood. Thus, in sixth-century India, the Shakyamuni Buddha was an 'appearance' of his glorious body. He was the Dharmakaya then on the earth. His life story and enacted journey toward enlightenment was *upaya*, a 'skilful means' which the Dharmakaya manifested in history for the salvation of people. The Three Bodies are a seamless unity. On the level of ultimate truth, only the Dharmakaya is real as Absolute and source of salvation.

Sunyata-Tathata

Here we touch on the higher wisdom of Mahayana, an overwhelming subject, vast in scope and sublime in its basic insight. Mahayana maintains that our linguistic sources are hopelessly inadequate for making positive statements about the Absolute and that the Buddha's 'roaring silence' is the only answer. *Sunyata* (pronounced 'shunyata'), with its negative connotations of 'emptiness' is used, and is complemented by the more positive *tathata*, which means 'thusness' or 'suchness'. Both words, operating in a paradoxical way, intuit an Ultimate Reality, which is at once an Emptiness and a Fullness.

Rather than attempting to explain the inexplicable (*sunyata-tathata*), we will turn to the parable of a twelfth-century Chinese Zen monk, Kakuan, called 'The Ox-Herding Pictures'. This story, with ten pictures and corresponding verses, is very popular with Zen Buddhists. Although the original text is believed to be lost, it is available today in many versions. The ox stands for that tremendous life energy that is the Buddha nature in all persons and things. We are usually unaware of it and may even fear it. The sequence of pictures attempts to depict the story of the ox herder, as he claims the inexhaustible treasure of Buddha nature or, as the story tells, he tames the ox. The circle surrounding each picture symbolises the non-beginning, non-ending quality of *sunyata-tathata* or the ever presence of the Buddha-nature. So the herder sets out on his journey, drawn by his desire.

First picture: *Searching for the Ox*. His awakened desire for the truth.

Second picture: *Seeing the Traces*. Encouraged by pointers on the way.

Third picture: *Seeing the Ox*. The herder sees the black ox disappearing through the trees.

Fourth picture: *Catching the Ox*: Catching the ox by the tail, the herder struggles.

Fifth picture: *Herding the Ox*. Patiently, he tames the ox and enters upon a period of learning through living with the animal.

Sixth picture: *Coming Home on the Ox's Back*. Riding the ox and playing the flute, he looks happy, at home with himself. (In pictures five and six, the Ox gradually loses his blackness and becomes more transparent.)

Seventh picture: *The Ox Forgotten*. Shows the man in meditation. No sign of the ox. In the distance the mountain and the moon. The ox is 'emptied' and now the herder is without function. He is 'the Man'.

Eighth picture: *Ox and Man both Gone out of Sight*. Only an empty circle here signifying *sunyata* or the truly 'emptied Man'.

Ninth picture: *Returning to the Origin/Source*. Picture shows natural things, water, trees, flowers. No sign of the Man who has now returned to who he naturally is. Lines from Kakuan's original verse read: 'Behold the streams flowing whither, nobody knows;/And the flowers vividly red – for whom are they?'

Tenth picture: *Entering the City with Bliss Bestowing Hands*: A common, everyday occurrence is portrayed in which an old man with a protruding belly, like a laughing Buddha, is greeted by a curious young man. The belly signifies whole-body thinking. He is happy and playful in demeanour. Kakuan states:

> Carrying a gourd he goes into the market, leaning against a staff, he comes home. He is found in company with wine-drinkers and butchers, he and they are all converted into Buddhas.

The activity of *sunyata* is symbolised by the gourd he carries. 'Home' for him is being right there in the world. Propelled by compassion he goes anywhere he likes. Friendly with the most unlikely people he brings them to the *dharma*.[33]

In this Zen-Buddhist parable, we get a glimpse of the transformation in the ox-herder; it is the experience of *sunyata-tathata*. The source of this teaching is the *Prajnaparamita*, the Sutras of 'the Perfection of Wisdom'. Legend says they were discovered by the supreme Buddhist philosopher, Nagarjuna (second century CE), having been suppressed until someone of his perception providentially appeared. Nagarjuna made these obscure texts the basis of his metaphysics of *sunyata*, known as *Madhyamika*, which translated is 'middlemost'. It is not a metaphysics of being in the classical western sense; it is a metaphysics of awareness. The fundamentals of Buddhist thought are nevertheless still there. The Buddha taught that all things in the phenomenal world are conditioned in nature, in process of becoming and governed by causes and conditions. They are thus in a state of constant flux and destined to pass away. They may therefore be designated as 'empty' because they lack any permanent characteristics by which they might be described, changing as they do from instant to instant. At best, they can be delineated by what they are not – not permanent and not self.

The formulators of Mahayana preferred to emphasise the positive aspects of emptiness rather than the negative. Since emptiness is the quality of all things, it is an abiding reality. Beyond distinctions and dualisms, it is what holds all beings in equality together without fusion. The tradition says that Buddha was not 'tight fisted' as a Teacher; he kept nothing back of the truth. He offered the whole truth if people could see. But a truth such as this is not available to the conventional mind – habitually overlaid as it is with emotions, desires, ideas, beliefs and pre-formed habits of thought – which makes 'things' of what it sees. This truth is the pure perception of Right Wisdom. Its 'object' needs no conceptual explanation. It simply *is*.

Thomas Berry designates this wisdom of the higher reaches of Mahayana as 'homeless wisdom'.[34] It is the wisdom of the one who has truly gone forth into a nakedness, having shed all names and forms, even Buddhism itself. The ox-herder simply becomes 'the Man'. And yet, emptiness must also be emptied. *Sunyata* is 'non-*sunyata*'. Even in one's desire to know Absolute Truth, there must be no clinging, however noble the object. Mahayana truth lies in the middle, beyond the dualism of 'it is not' and 'it is'. This zigzagging logic of ascending negation issuing in descending affirmation is what lifts the mind beyond discriminations and concepts into silence, emptiness and joyful assent to earthly existence. We find this paradox of negation- affirmation in the words of the famous Heart Sutra of the *Prajnaparamita* literature: 'Form is emptiness and emptiness is form.' All forms are empty, and yet emptiness as such is not a nothingness; it is form.[35]

Thus, *sunyata*, as the true wisdom experience, does not take the enlightened person out of the world:

> Within this mystery the world is lifted up towards the transearthly, this in turn descends to become as ordinary as daily life, as common as carrying water and chopping wood. Indeed, the difference between the chopping of wood and quiet meditation no longer exists. Both become spiritual disciplines, ways of perfection ... The sublime and the holy meet in the one reality of simple human living.[36]

The Ox-Herder returns to the marketplace with bliss-bestowing hands. *Sunyata* is *samsara*. The experience of emptiness is the realisation of *Tathata*, the 'thusness' or 'suchness' of things. It means 'things as they are in their primordial and fundamental naturalness'. It means 'ordinary existence' seen, not instrumentally in service of an agenda, but simply as 'thus'. A beautiful Zen story illustrates this point:

> 'There are three stages in one's spiritual development,' said the Master.
> 'The carnal, the spiritual, the divine.'
> 'What is the carnal stage?' asked the disciple.
> 'That is the stage when trees are seen as trees and mountains as mountains.'
> 'And the spiritual?'
> 'When one looks more deeply into things. Then trees are no longer trees and mountains are no longer mountains.'
> 'And the divine?'
> 'Ah, that's enlightenment,' said the Master. 'When trees become trees again and mountains mountains.'[37]

The first person is caught in the *khandhas*, he is the naïve realist who sees the mountain in terms of his preoccupations, programmes and desires. The second realises that things are not what they appear to be – a Platonist or possibly a religious person. The mountain is functional, it is a sign of the 'yonder side' to which he aspires. He is the Buddhist who has not yet emptied the emptiness he so fervently desires. The third person just sees the mountain in its *suchness* as mountain. Here 'the yonder side is this side'. Buddhists do not speak of mystery, but they do speak of Wondrous Being.[38] This is *tathata*, the other side of *sunyata*, where the void is experienced as 'fullness' (*plenum*). It is in this context that we understand the most honorific title of the Shakyamuni Buddha, the Tathagatha – literally 'the One who is thus come'.

Japanese philosopher, Keiji Nishitani, in writing on emptiness, repeatedly speaks of this great affirmation of worldly reality at the heart of Buddhism:

> On that field of emptiness each thing comes into its own and reveals itself in a self-affirmation, each in its own possibility and *virtus* (Jap. *toku*) of being, each in its own shape. The conversion to and entrance into that field means, for us men [sic] the fundamental affirmation of the being of all

things (of the world), and at the same time, of our own existence. The field of emptiness is nothing but the field of the great affirmation.[39]

Buddhism, says the same author, is 'the religion of the absolute this-side'.[40] And yet *sunyata* as *plenum* can only be appreciated through what is often called the Great Death, the death of the discriminating mind. It is the moment of conversion and breakthrough. The Great Death is at the heart of Zen Buddhism. Zen is not a metaphysics but a practice, and is the premier school of meditation in Mahayana.

ZEN BUDDHISM

The legendary history of Zen goes back to the Shakyamuni Buddha, who is said to have once taught the *dharma* by holding up a single flower and turning it in his hand. Only one of his disciples, Kasyapa, understood the message and smiled. This direct grasp of reality was passed down from masters to pupils in India as an alternative tradition to that recorded in the Sutras. Eventually (c. 520 CE), an Indian master, Bodhidharma, came from India to China and began the line of Chinese Ch'an masters (*Ch'an* being a translation of the Indian *Dhyana* (meditation); the Japanese parallel is *Zen*). Bodhidharma is a partially legendary figure, who is said to have commenced his preaching by facing a wall for nine years until his legs fell off, and who insulted the emperor by telling him that his sponsoring of Buddhist monasteries and copying of scriptures would gain him no merit. Here he symbolises the Ch'an opposition to a Buddhism of metaphysical speculations and outward observances. He stressed the need for a practical exertion in the quest for purity of mind.

Zen has a long and varied history. Developed by the Ch'an masters, it spread to Japan in the twelfth century, where it thrives today. The Chinese brought to Zen the Confucian practical mind. Eschewing the soaring Mahayana speculations on *sunyata*, the Chinese Zen Patriarchs cultivated the ordinary mind, naturalness, the concrete and particular which they expressed in image and anecdote and in the intuition of 'Wondrous Being' rather than in abstraction. Like the ox-herder, the enlightened one is found in the market-place in the midst of the hurly-burly of life.

However, when Zen was introduced into China, most Buddhists were addicted to discussion of highly metaphysical questions, satisfied with observing the moral precepts of the Buddha or leading lethargic lives entirely absorbed in the transience of things worldly. In response to this pitiful state of affairs, the early Ch'an masters proclaimed Four Great Statements of Zen:

1. A special transmission outside the scriptures.
2. No dependence upon words and letters.
3. Direct pointing to the soul of man.
4. Seeing into one's nature and the attainment of Buddhahood.[41]

Outside scriptures, words and letters, the truth of Zen is transmitted directly from mind to mind. Hence the importance of the master–pupil relationship, because only a person already enlightened knows how best to accompany another to the experience of *satori* (Jap. 'enlightenment'). In Japan, a Zen master is called a *roshi* and pupils are expected to submit without question to his authority. It is traditional to have periodic private interviews with the *roshi*, who will question the pupil and gauge his development. In one of modern Japan's major sects, Rinzai, founded by Hakuin (1685–1768), the master–pupil relationship can be unpredictable and traumatic. Rinzai seeks an instant understanding of the truth gained by a sudden revolution of consciousness. This is brought about by dramatic methods and severe discipline. Masters are known to have shouted at pupils, slapped them and even cut off fingers.

Dogen (1200–53), the founder of the more popular Soto, is a revered saint of the tradition. He taught that the true Buddhist life is a simple and selfless one, and that we do not have to go to dramatic extremes to achieve *satori*. In fact, we should not desire it at all. His teaching was that simply sitting (*zazen*) and having faith in one's teacher was sufficient; that by doing so, the Buddha nature, which one already possesses, would unfold in undramatic ways. Dogen was less adverse to scriptural study than his Rinzai counterparts and left various influential writings behind, from one of which come the following lines, written in his characteristically terse and direct style:

To study the way is to study the self.
To study the self is to forget the self.
To forget the self is to be enlightened by all things.
To be enlightened by all things is to remove the barrier between self and others.

In Japanese culture these methods are appropriate for different personalities: Rinzai, with its military origin, for the leaders in world affairs and Soto for the farmer.

Elements of Zen
The Direct Method

The truth of Zen is the truth of the fact of living, which one apprehends with a freshness and newness by getting in touch with the workings of one's inner nature. Human life means to live, to move and act, not merely reflect. It is as if when I raise my hand thus, there is Zen, but when I assert that I have raised my hand, Zen is no more. Zen is caught where life is fleeting, not where life has flown. Zen is not directed to our memories or regrets about the past, nor to our plans for the future, but to the living fact: the fleeting, unpredictable, unrecoverable character of life now. Like a watercolour painting, Zen must be executed once and for all without hesitation, no corrections being permissible, as the following tale demonstrates:

> A disciple who was an attendant to a Master, once said to him: 'Since I came to you I have not at all been instructed in the study of mind.'
> Replied the master, 'Ever since you came to me I have been pointing to you how to study mind.'
> 'In what way, Sir? When you served me with food, did I not partake of it? When you made bows to me, did I not return them? When did I ever neglect in giving you instructions?'
> The attendant kept his head hanging for some time, when the master told him, 'If you want to see, see directly into it; but when you try to think about it, it is altogether missed.'[42]

Zazen

'Sitting meditation', or its Sanskrit equivalent *dhyana*, is the prevailing method of spiritual discipline in all forms of Zen. Here again, the direct method prevails. All outer details are controlled so as to bring the mind into the most favourable condition in which it will gradually rise above the turbulence of passions. Eating and drinking are properly regulated; sleep is not overly indulged; the body is to be kept in an easy position, but straight and erect. And the meditator faces a bare wall.

Satori

This is the raison d'etre of Zen. In itself, Zen must be distinguished from the more trance-like Hindu dhyana, which quiets the mind; from Theravada meditation on transience; and even from Mahayana reflection on emptiness. Neither is it seeing

God as God is. In such a sense of God, there is implied a dualism of 'no-God', and in Zen, any dualism is a limited and incomplete knowledge. *Satori* is an inclusive and unitive way of knowing. It is an upheaval of the logical mind, a pushing beyond naming of any kind, beyond A is A, and beyond A is not A. When the word 'beyond' is used, it is not as designating an other-worldly reality objectively. It is rather an unmediated experience beyond our more conventional and dualistic way of knowing. Words such as 'Absolute Unity' or the 'One' may be used of *satori*, but unfailingly such abstractions are debunked by the Zen masters:

> A monk asked Chao-chou, 'All things are reducible to the One; but where is the One reducible?'
> Chou said, 'When I was in the district of Ch'ing I had a robe made that weighed seven *chin*.'
> A monk asked Hsuan-sha, 'I am a new-comer in the monastery; please tell me how to go with my study.'
> 'Do you hear the murmuring stream?'
> 'Yes Master.'
> 'If so, here is the entrance.'[43]

To the logical mind, these responses are baffling. Yet their homely this-worldliness endeavours to bring the disciple down to where the fullness of life really is – under his nose.

> 'What is Zen?' a disciple anxiously asks.
> 'The cypress tree in the garden,' replies the Master.
> To the monk who seeks to be instructed in Zen, the Master asks: 'Have you had your breakfast or not?'
> 'Yes, Master, I have,' the monk replied.
> 'If so wash your dishes', is the immediate response, which opens the monk's mind to the truth of Zen.[44]

Zen Masters do not wait patiently for *satori* to come by itself to their disciples. In their earnestness, they forcefully indicate the way with contradictions, paradoxes, affirmations and exclamations – *koans*. *Zazen* and the *koans* are the two great handmaids of Zen, *zazen* being the meditative context for struggling with the *koans*.

Koans

In master–pupil interviews, the pupil may be asked to explain a *koan*. *Koan* means literally 'public document' or 'authoritative statement'. In practice, it is a paradoxical riddle-like saying, question or response to the disciple's queries, drawn from the tradition of the old Zen masters. The following, according to Suzuki, are some which are given to the uninitiated:

> When a monk overtook the fugitive Hui-neng, who was to become the Sixth Patriarch, he wanted him to give up the secret of Zen. Hui-neng replied, 'What are your original features which you have even prior to your birth?'
> When Chao-chou came to study Zen under a master, he asked, 'What is the Tao [the Way]?' The Master replied, 'Your everyday mind, that is the Tao.'[45]

The *koan* aims to debunk the everyday discriminating mind which distinguishes between subject and object. The truth of the *koan* is not grasped by struggling for a meaning in the arrangement of its words or images. Nor does Zen yield its truth by keeping the mind in an attitude of waiting for *satori*. Zen is not a passive, meditative activity. It is a frontal attack, a pole to leap over the stream of relativity to the side of the Absolute. It implies a struggle with the depths of personality, because the affective and cognitive centres which are really the foundation of personal character are charged to do their utmost in the solution of the *koan*. So the Zen Master says: 'Unless once you have been thoroughly drenched in perspiration you cannot expect to see the revelation of a palace of pearls on a blade of grass.'[46] All *koans* are utterances of what cannot be named, hence their uncouthness and incomprehensibility. Yet without what cannot be named (*satori*), there is no Zen. The illogicality of the *koans* propels the student forward to a reality beyond logic, which is experienced as living fact. When the disciple fails to respond, the Zen master may give him a sharp slap on the face. Now everything is blotted out except the stinging sensation of his flesh, and in this upheaval there occurs for some a taste of Zen.

Zen is the 'emptiness' of all classifications and dualisms experienced in the vibrancy of the living fact of one's own 'suchness' and of the 'suchness' of all things – the cherry tree in the garden, the mountain as mountain. It is ordinary mind, simple naturalness.

D. T. Suzuki (1869–1966), a foremost Zen scholar and its chief emissary in the West, warned that unless one has had a Zen experience, it is not possible to understand it, no more that one can know the sweetness of honey if you've never tasted it. Yet this area of Buddhism is the most familiar in the West. Its very neutrality has made Zen a suitable companion for many Christians in their spiritual practice, something that was happening long before Buddhism began to be addressed in the field of interreligious dialogue.

SUMMARY

Buddhism arose from the awakening of Siddhartha Gautama (b.c. 563 BCE) a prince of a royal family in Nepal. Buddha means 'awakened one', one who experiences reality as it truly is, in its 'thusness', without constructs. The Buddha taught that the way to awakening lay not in the worship of gods or salvation bestowed by gods or cultic religion. He did not call himself a saviour, he said: 'I show the way.' Buddhists affirm that we have lost 'the way', which is the source of our true identity – hence the constant experience we have of the unsatisfactoriness of existence. This key concept of *dukkha*, or 'suffering', is the springboard of Buddhism, which, as a religion, is concerned with release from suffering. Buddhism is a religion of hope and a way of deliverance. There is release from suffering (the teaching in the Four Noble truths) and there is a way toward that release (the Eightfold Path).

The foundational Buddhist tradition is Theravada, in which the Path is practised mainly in a monastic setting. The Buddha – the Truth Winner and Tamer of Minds – taught that the human mind is prey to 'three fires of existence': hatred, false craving and illusion. The heart of Theravada is that the mind can be tamed by moral life and meditation, and that it can come to wisdom or the truth of things; that all life is transient, that the self is not a permanent entity, and that our relation to the universe is one of on-going causal interdependence.

In the wider tradition of Mahayana, Buddhism assumes more religious elements and appeals to the faith and devotion of the lay person. While the historical figure of Gautama is still central, he is also seen as a celestial being, one of the many beings who people the heavens and who descend to earth to bring release from suffering. The Buddha and those who surround him are called Bodhisattvas. As objects of popular devotion, they have links with geographical areas and have temples dedicated to their honour with officiating priests. Mahayana also teaches that the 'buddha' nature is within everybody, waiting to be developed. Mahayana has a creative intellectual tradition which distinguishes between our conventional constructs of the Absolute and the Absolute itself, which is beyond explanation. Mahayana does not deny transcendence, but teases the mind with a 'trackless transcendence', to which it gives the word *sunyata* (emptiness).

It is said that the Buddha observed 'a roaring silence' when it came to questions of ultimacy. Following the logic of his thinking, mental constructs are not to be trusted because they freeze the nature of ultimacy and put a screen between us and truth. It is apparent here that Buddhism is not a theistic faith like Judaism, Christianity, Islam or even Hinduism. As in its parent, Hinduism, there is in Buddhism a going forth from the unsatisfactoriness of existence toward a beyond. While the *sannyasin* remains supported by Hindu ritual and belief, Buddhist going forth is more intellectual and methodic and addresses the abandonment of mental and emotional enslavement to a transient and unsubstantial world. For the theist and the Christian, dialogue with this very different way of salvation can be fruitful. It does not offer pre-packaged answers, but enables us to touch base with human questions in our own desire for salvation-liberation.

FURTHER READING

Barrett, William, ed., *Zen Buddhism: Selected Writings of D.T. Suzuki* (New York: Doubleday, 1996).

Bercholz, Samuel and Shebab Chodzin Kohn, *Entering the Stream* (London: Rider Books, 1993).

Berry, Thomas, *The Religions of India, Hinduism, Yoga, Buddhism* (New York: Columbia University Press, 1996)

_____, *Buddhism* (New York: Columbia University Press, 1996).

Bowker, John, *Problems of Suffering in the Religions of the World* (Cambridge: Cambridge University Press, 1995).

Cush, Denise, *Buddhism* (London: Hodder & Stoughton, 1993).

Ellinger, Herbert, *Buddhism* (London: SCM Press, 1995).

Fernando, Antony and Leonard Swidler, *Buddhism Made Plain: An Introduction for Christians and Jews* (Maryknoll, NY: Orbis Books, 1985).

Harvey, Andrew, *An Introduction to Buddhism: Teachings, History and Practice* (Cambridge: Cambridge University Press, 1998).

Keown, Damien, *Buddhism* (Oxford: Oxford University Press, 1996).

Rahula, Walpola, *What the Buddha Taught* (Oxford: One World, 1997).

Renard, John, *Responses to 101 Questions on Buddhism* (Mahwah, NJ: Paulist Press, 1999).

Snelling, John, *The Buddhist Handbook* (London: Rider Books, 1997).

Suzuki, D. T., *Studies in Zen* (London: Unwin, 1986).

The Dhammapada: The Path of Perfection, trans. Juan Mascaro (London: Penguin, 1980).

NOTES

1. Translation, cited in Thomas Berry, *Buddhism*, p. 23.
2. *The Dhammapada: The Path of Perfection*, trans. Juan Mascaro (London: Penguin, 1980). Texts from the Dhammapada will be taken from this publication, unless otherwise stated. References will be in verses only.
3. Cited in Thomas Berry, *Buddhism*, p. 19.
4. Cited in Anthony Fernando and Leonard Swidler, p. 53.
5. Walpola Rahula, pp. 29–34.
6. Cited in I. B. Horner, 'Buddhism: The Theravada', R. C. Zaehner, *The Hutchinson Encyclopaedia of Living Faiths* (Abingdon: Helicon, 1998), p. 278.
7. Cited in Thomas Berry, *Buddhism*, p. 14.
8. Cited in John Snelling, p. 75.
9. Raimundo Pannikar, *The Silence of God: The Answer of the Buddha* (Maryknoll, NY: Orbis Books, 1990), p. 55.
10. Cited in John Bowker, p. 243.
11. Walpola Rahula, p. 65.
12. *Ibid.*, pp. 65–6.
13. *Ibid.*, p. 41.
14. Cited in John Snelling, p. 54.
15. Cited in John Snelling, p. 40.
16. Walpola Rahula, p. 33.
17. *Ibid.*, p. 34.
18. Cited in Thomas Berry, p. 14.
19. John Snelling, p. 61.
20. Cited in John Bowker, p. 257.
21. Jack Kornfield, *After the Ecstasy, the Laundry: How the Heart Grows Wise on the Spiritual Path* (New York: Bantam, 2000).
22. S. N. Goenka, 'Moral Conduct, Concentration, Wisdom', *Entering the Stream*, p. 109.
23. *Ibid.*, p. 115.
24. Cited in Thomas Berry, *Buddhism*, pp. 40–1.
25. Dalai Lama (Tenzin Gyatso), *Freedom in Exile: The Autobiography of the Dalai Lama* (NY: Harper Collins, 1990), p. 271.
26. L. S. Cousins, 'Buddhism', *A Handbook of Living Religions*, ed. John Hinnells (London: Penguin, 1991), p. 301.
27. Cited in Thomas Berry, *Buddhism*, p. 93. The *Lotus Sutra* is used especially by Tendai Buddhists in Japan. It is considered a 'precious' *sutra*, because the Buddha's presence is felt in the world more than any other.
28. *Vimalakirti Sutra*, trans. Burton Watson (NY: Columbia University Press, 1983). One of the most famous and influential works of the Mahayana canon, this sutra is outstanding in the eloquent and orderly way in which it presents the basic tenets of Mahayana, the liveliness of its episodes and its humour. It is unusual in that its central figure is not a Buddha but a wealthy townsman of Shakyamuni's time, who, in his religious understanding and practice,

became an ideal for the lay believer. For this reason, and also for the sutra's literary appeal, it is particularly popular among lay Buddhists in China and Japan and especially in the Zen sect.

29. Cited in Edward Conze, 'Buddhism: Mahayana,' R. C. Zaehner, *The Hutchinson Encyclopedia of Living Faiths* (Abingdon: Helicon, 1998), p. 304.
30. The common description of the Dalai Lama as the 'god-king' is misleading since Tibetans do not see their head of state as a god in the sense of our understanding of God. For them, he is an incarnation, an 'earthly birth' of the Bodhisattva Avalokiteshvara. The Tibetans also lovingly call him Kundun, which means 'presence'.
31. Edward Conze, p. 316.
32. *Ibid.*, p. 306.
33. *Gentling the Bull: The Ten Bull Pictures, A Spiritual Journey* (Boston: C. E. Tuttle, 1988); *Entering the Stream*, Chapter 21; Philip Kapleau, *The Three Pillars of Zen* (London: Doubleday, 1989), pp. 313–25.
34. Thomas Berry, *Buddhism*, Chapter 14.
35. Text and commentary in Thomas Berry, Chapter 14. See also Mu Soeng, *The Heart Sutra* (Rhode Island: Primary Point Press, 1991).
36. Thomas Berry, *Buddhism*, p. 126.
37. Adapted from William Barrett, p. 14.
38. Phrase taken from Hans Waldenfels, *Absolute Nothingness: Foundations of a Buddhist–Christian Dialogue*, trans. J. W. Heisig (Mahwah, NJ: Paulist Press, 1980), p. 73. This book is a study of the Japanese philosopher Keiji Nishitani. Here, the phrase used by the author is from Masao Abe, a Japanese philosopher who has contributed much to Buddhist–Christian Dialogue.
39. Cited in Hans Waldenfels, p. 94.
40. *Ibid.*, p. 99.
41. Cited in William Barrett, ed., p. 9.
42. Cited in Barrett ed., p. 132.
43. *Ibid.*, p. 152.
44. *Ibid.*, p. 91.
45. *Ibid.*, pp. 134–5.
46. *Ibid.*, p. 139.

CHAPTER 8

Christian–Buddhist Conversations

You depend on God; does God depend on you?

DALAI LAMA

I believe that as far as religion is concerned, the present age will have to decide ultimately between the Asiatic worldview and the Christian faith. I have no doubt that both sides have a great deal to learn from each other. The issue may be which of the two can rescue more the other's authentic content.

POPE BENEDICT XVI

My first exposure to the Buddhist tradition was through a study seminar and some *Vipassana* retreats in the US. Participants in the seminar were mostly Americans, ex-Catholic and Jewish as well as a young Burmese Buddhist monk. I remember, to my shame, that I was an awkward participant. When the Zen teacher spoke of *sunyata*, I raised conceptual issues about God as Creator and Revealer – all of them true in their own context, but proving that I was not really listening at the level of his communication. One of the other participants turned and said, 'Jo, if you could let go of your constructs, you would come into such freedom.' Gradually, I began to discover that the truths of Buddhism are realities 'one reaches into', not objects of thought. But the Theravadin monk, Vimala, was curious and asked me to tell him about this God I spoke of, especially the Trinity. Conscious of the 'no-God' in Buddhism, I tried to evoke rather than describe who God is; speaking of the Trinity was even more daunting. Vimala, however, was not impressed. The next day, he baldly informed me: 'I cannot believe in God; I would cling.' This was my first lesson: that clinging in any form activates the 'original sin' of Buddhism. The second lesson was my own awakening to that special 'clinging' that sustained me during the tough *vipassana* retreat. The days were spent in silence, marked by periods of meditation (sitting), walking and household chores, with times for eating and resting. In the beginning, I found it very demanding. It was a taste of the 'effort' the Eight-Fold Path speaks of. After five hours' daily sitting, we were encouraged to go late at night to the meditation hall for yet another session. As I looked at all the others making their way, I reasoned that what is good for them is good for me, and so I took off my shoes. Then I found myself saying: 'I do it for you, Lord.' I often return to this moment, because in a simple movement of the heart, I was naming for myself what differentiates Christian faith from Buddhism, which is, belief in a *personal* Absolute, with whom one is in relationship.

Woven through this chapter are these two insights: the non-clinging of Buddhism and the clinging of Christian faith. If the writing appears to vacillate at times as to conclusions, it is in the interest of fairness and concern for truth, because I believe that Christian faith can be questioned and renewed by the humane wisdom of the Buddha.

Of all the Eastern religions, Buddhism is the most refined and subtle. The *dharma* touches on the fundamentals of being human; one cannot engage with it in bits and pieces. One either goes over to it in its totality or one remains a Christian, but somehow more open to the totalising questions of one's faith. Good conversations are a mutual search for truth. They are patient with resonances and differences. They seldom end with vanquishing the opponent, as in debate.[1] To begin, we will briefly look at some tensions between the Vatican and Buddhism especially as understood and expounded by Pope John Paul II. Following this, there will be three conversations. Firstly, the foundational one about God and 'no God'; secondly, the influence of Buddhism on Christian spiritual practice; and thirdly, by way of an overview, a reflection on Jesus and Buddha.

DEVELOPMENTS SINCE VATICAN II

Buddhism was dismissed as nihilistic and atheistic by nineteenth-century missionaries. It was presumed that a non-theistic religion could hardly be a religion or a way of salvation for people, but this was a misunderstanding of the type that arises when one takes the determining categories of one's own beliefs as the measure for the beliefs of others. A more real and generous acknowledgement of Buddhism occurs in Vatican II, where *Nostra Aetate* ranks it as a religion alongside Hinduism, Islam and Judaism:

> Buddhism in its multiple forms acknowledges the radical insufficiency of this shifting world. It teaches a path by which men, in a devout and confident spirit, can either reach a state of absolute freedom or attain supreme enlightenment by their own efforts or by higher assistance. (NA 2)

This short inchoate statement is positively placed within 'the ray of Truth' that *Nostra Aetate* affirms is present in the great World Religions. What is at least implied in this statement is that Buddhism is more than a nihilism, that it is a religion with a soteriological dimension, and that it offers answers to the profound human questions enunciated by *Nostra Aetate* in its opening paragraph.

However, a crisis occurred in 1994, due to a controversial chapter on Buddhism in Pope John Paul II's *Crossing the Threshold of Hope*. This led to the boycott of his visit to Sri Lanka by the Buddhist leadership who objected to the book's description of Buddhism as 'an almost exclusively *negative soteriology*', as 'in large measure an *atheistic system*'. It goes on to say: 'We do not free ourselves from evil through the good which comes from God; we liberate ourselves through detachment from the world which is bad.' 'Union with God' is replaced by a detachment from the world which leads to *nirvana*:

> *To save oneself* means, above all, to free oneself from evil by becoming *indifferent to the world, which is the source of evil.* This is the culmination of the spiritual process.

Furthermore, the chapter concludes by issuing a warning to those Christians who '*enthusiastically welcome certain ideas in religious traditions of the Far East.*' One misses from the papal responses the 'rugged directness' and honesty of John Paul II, and wonders whether his responses are preempted by the leading questions of the interviewer, Vittorio Messori.[2]

In the aftermath of the Pope's publication, Sri Lankan interreligious journal, *Dialogue*, published a complete issue of responses. Editor Aloysius Pieris SJ affirmed the already sound record of John Paul II in the area of interreligious dialogue, saying that the publication was not about 'Pope bashing' but he hoped that the damage caused to Buddhist–Christian relations in Sri Lanka might be repaired in the event of the responses of some Buddhist scholars, monks and Christian writers being made public. Some felt that the leader of the Catholic Church should have been more careful in expressing his views about another religion. The majority of writers believed that the Pope did not misrepresent Buddhism out of disrespect but that he was badly briefed and that his understanding of the religion dated back to nineteenth-century missionary misinterpretations, hence his presentation being less irenic than Vatican II. Finally, some commentators suggested that the Pope's tone when speaking about

Buddhism expressed fear and apprehension at the growing popularity of the religion in the West.[3]

Yet there was a positive outcome from John Paul's altercation with the Theravadin tradition of Sri Lanka. A decision was taken by a representative group of Buddhist and Catholic leaders from around the world to hold a colloquium on the theme 'Buddhists and Christians: Convergences and Divergences'. Held in a Buddhist monastery in Taiwan in spring 1995, it was chaired by Cardinal Francis Arinze of the Pontifical Council for Interreligious Dialogue. It was not a discussion of the Pope's book or of the boycott of his visit to Sri Lanka, but a dialogue on the fundamental beliefs raised by the situation that sought to foster mutual understanding of and respect for both religions. The colloquium led to the document *The Taiwan Buddhist–Catholic Statement*, which presented the fundamentals of both religions under four headings:

> *Both religions recognise that the human condition is in need of liberation*: prior to the Taiwan meeting, Buddhists had expressed concern that the Pope's statement implied that the world is the source of evil and suffering. The joint statement makes it clear that evil originates in the human being. For Buddhists, it is a karmic energy rooted in ignorance and selfish attachment and is the cause of human suffering and evil. For Christians, it is sourced in the original sinfulness of the human being.

> *God and* nirvana *were discussed in terms of the ideals of perfection pursued in each religion*: for Buddhists, the ideal is the subtle selfless, pure and unattached state of balance between awakened wisdom and compassion for the world; for Catholics, it is ultimately the state of relational union with a personal God.

> *In relation to the Buddha and Christ, the greatest divergences between the two religions emerged*: It was brought out clearly that the Buddha is an enlightened human being who shows us the perfection of Buddhahood (perfect selflessness manifested as purity, compassion and wisdom) and gives people the hope that they can themselves attain the ideal. From the Buddha and his first disciples a great historical movement was born (the Sangha) with a message of spiritual liberation for all sentient beings. It was understood clearly that for Christians, Jesus Christ as the incarnation of

the second person of the Trinity was the manifestation of God's will; that he brought the light of salvation into the world for all humankind once and for all; that through the grace of this event, he brought the enlightenment of all persons (Jn 1:9) and human history.

Personal detachment and social commitment: This is the area of the inner and outer, of wisdom and compassion, love of God and love of neighbour. It is proposed as the most fruitful area of Buddhist–Christian dialogue, because what holds true for the Buddhist – that 'the more the mind is purified, the deeper becomes one's wisdom and compassion' – is also true for the Christian.[4]

Within a month, this document, now considered to be a reference point for future dialogue with Buddhists, was published by the Vatican.[5] In it we see truths which were of the highest value to participants being placed in contiguous relation to each other. The spirit of the document is one of conversation, respect and encounter with difference. However, it is significant that praise is also given to John Paul II, who, in keeping with his genuine commitment to interreligious dialogue, said that 'what unites us is much *greater* than what separates us' and that it is 'necessary … to rid ourselves of stereotypes [and] old habits. And above all it is necessary to recognise the unity that exists.'[6] We need only to return to *Nostra Aetate* to know what that unity is: it is the unity of the human family, all with the same questions of meaning about life and death. And it is the unity around our search for and naming of the absolute, 'that ultimate and unutterable mystery which engulfs our being, whence we take our rise and whither our journey leads us' (NA 1).

NAMING THE ABSOLUTE

Ludwig Wittgenstein's dictum 'Whereof one cannot speak, thereof one must be silent' always comes to mind when we think of Buddhism. Siddhartha Gautama was a man of tremendous silences. Speaking only of what can be humanly experienced, he excluded language about the Absolute, because to put words on the Absolute is to make it a construct of the mind, to bring it within the human sphere of 'beings'. At this level of constructs, intellectual debate goes on forever and it becomes natural to cling. Holding such speculative views is not the Middle Path of the Buddha. The Middle Path avoids 'yes' or 'no' in order to clear away arguments that keep the mind 'on fire'. What matters is the awakening to truth.

Those who are faithful to the path will renounce all attachments, even to the Buddha and to *nirvana*. Enlightenment will be found in apprehending reality with the 'right view'. For the practising Buddhist, it will be a journey in faith and hope, characterised by elements of graciousness which in Christian eyes make interesting correspondences.

Correspondences
The Grace of Bodhicitta

Even in the sober Theravadin tradition there is the mysterious grace of *bodhicitta*, *in* which the monk has faith. *Bodhicitta* is the seed of the Buddha nature. The task of the Buddhist is to let this potential (the *citta*) dawn on the mind, to affirmatively confess and develop it. A classic text enunciating this gift and task (and a favourite of the Dalai Lama) is *The Way of the Bodhisattva*, by the eighth-century Indian monk Shantideva. In relation to the line, 'This noble jewel-like state of mind arises truly wondrous, never seen before', the commentator writes:

> Even in the throes of *samsara*, the mind is never alienated from *bodhicitta*, the first stirrings of which are profoundly mysterious. One is moved to ask its origin, for it appears to come from outside.[7]

The *citta*, as Aloysius Pieris suggests, has yet to be given due consideration in Buddhist–Christian dialogue.[8] May we not say with Rahner that since divine grace is a universal dimension of all human experience, its reception in human historical consciousness will be situated and pluriform. If grace exists at all, it exists as a reality of human experience.[9] It will be variously the 'divine spark' (the Spirit) or *citta*. In all, it is experienced as a gift from the outside, initiating a transcending of the self; it is the evidence of God's will to save all people and the 'ray of that Truth' of which *Nostra Aetate* speaks.

The Surprise of Nirvana

The Theravadin also has faith in the reality of *nirvana* as the goal of life. Variously spoken of as deathlessness, immortality, 'the blowing out of desires', it is soteriological in thrust. The significant early text which relates this liberated state to the reality of the Unborn is worth citing again:

Monks, there is an unborn, unoriginated, unmade and unconditioned. Were there not the unborn, unmade, unoriginated and unconditioned, there would be no escape from the born, the originated, made and conditioned. Since there is an unborn, unoriginated, unmade and unconditioned, there is escape from the born, originated, made and conditioned.[10]

At this basic experiential level, Buddhism is a religion of salvation and hope. The Tibetan Buddhist scholar, David Snellgrove, puts it clearly:

The Buddhists are rather the supreme optimists for while regarding the world as essentially nothingness, without any belief in a Creator God, they nonetheless have faith in the realisability of that transcendent immortal state, which just such a God, if one but knows, might happily represent. Having no term for God, they identify the nirvanic state as the essence of buddhahood, as realised in the moment of perfect enlightenment.[11]

We note a further correspondence, in that nothing and no one can cause *nirvana*. It is considered that a Pelagian interpretation of *nirvana* – which sees enlightenment as gained by one's own efforts – has not been in the tradition from its earliest inception.[12] One must observe the *dharma* as if all depended on oneself; and one must have faith as if all depended on the *dharma*. For *nirvana*, of which nothing final can be said, may not be construed as if it were not, for 'it is distinct and not an aspect of the mind that glimpses it'.[13] When it comes to *nirvana*

man's part in [the] ... whole process is that he learns to observe and not to obstruct ... but in the decisive and ultimate moment, his will cannot make the blessed, salvific event. It is the *dharma* alone that upholds protects, sustains, and transforms.[14]

Thus, there is a certain gracious surprise in the forms of *bodhicitta-nirvana*. Though no Giver is explicitly acknowledged, the Dharma Path enables its followers to live out of existence as surrounded by gift.

But can these experiences that point to Buddhism as more than a materialism or a nihilism be articulated in a more systematic way? Is there a Buddhist metaphysics? This has been the contribution of the great Mahayana philosopher, Nagarjuna – the most influential thinker in the Asian world in his time (c. 150

CE) Nagarjuna taught his disciples to use philosophy not as *theoria* but as *upaya* (skilful means) in the service of liberation from the fetters of existence. Attributed to him is the Mahayana development that *nirvana* is *sunyata* (emptiness), and also the remarkable teaching that to the enlightened mind the state of *sunyata* is not separable from *samsara*. *Samsara* is *sunyata* and *sunyata* is *samsara*.

Emptiness and the Absolute

Sunyata as emptiness or absolute nothingness is open to misunderstanding in the West. In itself, it transcends objectification. In the experience of *sunyata*, one moves *beyond* the spheres of both existing 'beings' and 'non-being' (nihilism). One moves into absolute emptiness, which transcends both. But absolute emptiness is a positive reality. It is *sunyata-tathata*, 'Wondrous Being'. The immediate challenge of *sunyata* is its radical negation of language in relation to the Absolute. Many have said that from this 'religion of silence' we can learn to purify our language for God. And it is true that, at times, Christians can be wordy, self-assured and even garrulous when we speak of God. But it is also true that in reaching out to *sunyata*, we become excited by this new language and are tempted to equate it with the hidden God, the *Deus Absconditus* of the Judeo-Christian tradition. But this is to unthinkingly disrespect the Buddha's silence and to dishonour the process of dialogue. David Tracy's reminder that 'to understand is to understand differently' is helpful here.[15] Even if we feel drawn to correspondences and the play of likeness, the more rewarding play, in the sense of opening up truth, is the play of difference. The greater challenge lies in naming our differences and doing so in a way that does not obstruct how we learn from each other.

Differences – Buddhist and Christian

Pannikar has said that at the heart of Buddhism is an 'ontological apophaticism'.[16] Buddhism does not attest to 'being' with the realism of classical western philosophy or theology. This follows logically from the religion's governing idea, which is not the creation of the world by a Creator but the empirically based teaching that all that is is this world of mutually dependent horizontal relations in which things arise from each other ('dependent origination'). Since all things are things-in-relation, they are *empty* and no-self. And since the Absolute is within the stream of relationships, the Absolute is also empty. This means that the Absolute cannot be objectified or spoken about as a reality out there. There is a clear consensus among scholars today that the Buddha was not an atheist, and to declare *nirvana-sunyata* to be utterly godless is to abuse the Buddha's language – or lack of language. He was simply silent about the nature of ultimacy. This silence is the Buddhist way to that which is totally other than what can be known by contingent human beings. Scholars, such as Heinrich Dumoulin, see a genuine recognition of 'transcendence' here.[17]

Yet, while the reality is totally other, it is totally and absolutely the same as what is observed and experienced. This 'transcendence' is primarily an 'immanence', Buddhism being the religion of 'the Absolute This Side.' *Sunyata* is an existential and grounded experience. It is *sunyata-tathata*; a 'rich emptiness', which one may say is analogous to the Christian experience of the *pleroma* of the Reign of God.[18]

However, in being over-hasty with comparisons we may deny ourselves the real gift of Buddhism. Pannikar reminds us that the Buddha is primarily a religious practitioner who, as the parable of the poisoned arrow attests, wants to resolve a practical problem, not pose a new religious theory; and that his teaching is primarily *upaya* – a skilful means toward liberation.[19] As he says, the very silence of the Buddha is also *upaya*. It is a warning that conceptual questions about *sunyata* are null questions: we do not know what we are asking when we ask them, so how can we understand the reply?[20]

Sunyata, therefore, is a profound sense of non-dual reality in the here and now; a reality reached into, not thought. As we saw in the Zen story of the ox-herder, it is *sunyata-tathata*, a world-affirming experience; a profound 'yes' to things as they are. The self-emptying of the ox-herder encompasses all things as 'Wondrous Being'. Of *sunyata*, Masao Abe, a Japanese veteran of Buddhist Christian dialogue, says: 'You and I and everything else are included without losing our particularity in the dynamic structure of *positive* Nothingness.'[21] It is a *positive* nothingness, in that in *sunyata* 'particularity really exists'.[22] It is a *dynamic* nothingness in that the Absolute is in every particular, and yet there is only one Absolute. This is truly mind-boggling if we think of it as an invitation to stretch our minds towards a fuller appreciation of the immanence of God. One commentator even detects in Buddhism the immanent God of the Johannine writings, which, in defining God as love, portray God not as *doer* but as the *doing* (in us) of something, a God whose 'reality … is not to be sought beyond the phenomenal'.[23] Obviously there is an invitation here to a deeper exploration. But at least one milestone has been established: what matters to the Buddha is not the reality of an Absolute divine being, God, with which we are in relationship, but rather the 'godly' state of emptiness which overflows in wisdom and compassion.

Basic affirmation characterises the movement toward the Absolute in Christian faith since it is grounded in belief in God as Creator. The divine is known within the ambience of relationship, the relationship of the creature to a Creator distinct from the world and to the Father who revealed Godself as redeeming in the saving history of Israel and in the Person of his Son. In the Judeo-Christian tradition the Creator is *there*, thus we come to know God mainly in affirmative ways through the language of the Bible, symbols, images, words and gestures in worship, and through creation itself and our relationships with people. However, the relationships played out in the drama of salvation history are always relationships to a transcendent other. Biblical language reminds us of this: 'No one has ever seen God' (Jn 1:18). The Fourth Evangelist has in mind here Yahweh of the Hebrew Bible who is mysterious, unknowable and ineffable, unlike anything made by human hands. He is the 'hidden God' (Is 45:15), the one whom Moses meets only in the thick darkness (2 Chr 6:1). He is 'the abyss of the abyss' (Ps 72:8), the Holy Mystery.

Therefore the 'yes' to God must also be expressed in a nescience of language (an epistemological apophaticism), which is not a denial of the divine reality as Being. To use Karl Rahner's phrase, God is the known unknown.[24] In the unknown we touch the very divine transcendence itself. This does not mean that God is the bleak ever-withdrawing horizon of our knowledge, ever receding from us. Rather it is the very positivity of Holy Mystery coming towards us experienced as hiddenness and darkness, as void or absence. Yet we may say 'emptiness', though the non-knowing and silence about God are at heart an affirmation. They are simply the emptying of words, images and symbols in the 'yes' to Holy Being.

The Play of Correspondences and Differences

Similarities and differences are constantly at play in Christianity's dialogue with Buddhism. The most obvious correspondence is that the two religions are salvational in thrust and that there is a loose parallel between the 'religion of the Absolute this side' and the very structure of Christian existence itself, which is also 'this side' of God, God incarnate 'with us and for us' in the world. The experience of salvation as 'wondrous Being here and now', as a participatory field of realised immanence, might also be named as the Reign of God and the 'new creation' enunciated by Paul (2 Cor 5:17). In both religions, what is being named is the Absolute as experienced here and now. In Buddhism it is the realised experience of Ground Luminosity, one may say, an anthropological mysticism. In

Christianity it is the realised experience of Trinitarian community in the Reign of God.[25] Undoubtedly, the gift of Buddhism, as we shall see later, is that it offers Christians many practical ways of awakening to this identity, to what Ignatius of Loyola calls the presence of 'God in all things'.

Correspondences and differences also arise when the relationship of the incomprehensible God to Absolute emptiness is further explored. It has been said that, for Buddhists, Christianity's personal theism is limiting and 'offensive', not only to the Ultimate but to human beings. This critique is of the popular theism of the masses, where Buddhists see belief in God as inducing fear (since so many believers are at the mercy of their own images of the divine being), or as limiting human growth and supporting immature clinging. From a Christian point of view, it must be admitted that belief in a personal God has sometimes led to an anthropomorphised Deity, to a totally-Other who controls our lives or who can be used by us to control each other. Whatever the limitations of this theism in the past, with a return to the experiencing subject in theologies and with the retrieval of mystical insight in our language about God, we are now moving to a place where dialogue with the 'no-God' of Buddhism need no longer be out of bounds.

Buddhists also would understand the language of Karl Rahner when he says that the core of biblical revelation is that the *deus abscondituus* is radically present as an abiding mystery.[26] And that the incomprehensibility of God is not just one of God's attributes among others, it is the 'attribute of attributes', the point from which we recognise God as the all-illuminating answer to our search for meaning.[27] Nagarjuna says that it is the fall into emptiness that evokes true wisdom and compassion in the Buddhist; and in Christian theology, it is the divine incomprehensibility that teaches us the banality of looking for a controlling knowledge of God in favour of a loving knowledge, in which we entrust ourselves to the Divine Mystery.[28] In short, in both religions it is apparent that what is most ultimate and most transformative of the human is also most mysterious and beyond our grasp.

Though mysterious, Buddhist emptiness and the incomprehensible God of the Judeo–Christian tradition are not the same. The *dharma* which comes out of the silence of the Buddha is 'skilful means'; it is the raft to the other shore of unnameable emptiness and wonderous being. The raft of Christian belief is a positive naming of the other shore. The shore is *Who* and it just *is*. In the Judeo–Christian tradition, the transcendent being is not just a remote master designer.

It is also being as personal and rational as attested to in the biblical statement 'God is love' (1 Jn 4:8). The Christian's relationship with the Absolute, then, has an I–Thou dimension.

Indeed it has been said that this concept 'person', especially in its application to God, is perhaps the most difficult point in dialogue between Christianity and Eastern religions.[29] It also raises a question too large to fully attend to here: whether it is ever appropriate to prise a religion out of its cultural base. It is interesting to note that the Dalai Lama, who in the West symbolises the emergence of Buddhism from the Himalayas, discourages Christians from thinking that one can totally espouse Buddhism and remain a Christian. A well-known saying of his is: 'You cannot put a yak's head on a sheep's body.' However it does not mean that the gap between Christians and Buddhists is unbridgeable. *The Good Heart,* a publication of his commentaries on the New Testament, shows him creatively eliciting and affirming the innate *bodhicitta* of the gospel texts.[30] Participants who heard him speak from the silence of a deep religious experience felt they were at the receiving end of a living sapiential commentary. In all his teachings, the Dalai Lama has emphasised the need to appreciate the distinctiveness of different paths but he has also taught that we must not let diversity alienate us from the common ground, where words are less explicit and where our meeting in silence can be more fruitful. In his innovative and radical book on the silence of the Buddha, Pannikar concludes that 'Buddhism cannot be really and truly "spoken of". It must be prayed.'[31] And for the Buddha, noted for his detachment from 'isms' and even from Buddhism itself, the Middle Way was *upaya*, a 'skilful means'. It is in this spirit that many religious people today believe they can make best common ground with the Middle Way, when we hitch a ride on its raft of spiritual practices of self-emptying and awakening.

THE AWAKENED HEART

Interestingly, Thich Nhat Hanh, a Vietnamese Buddhist who has given such great leadership in work for peace, says that in dialogue with Christian faith, he can more easily identify with the Spirit of God working in all things than with God himself.[32] Indeed with Asian religions generally, the most fruitful exchanges have been in the area of spiritual practice – how God is with us – and so it is from monastics and spiritual writers of East and West that leadership in Buddhist–Christian dialogue has come.

Thomas Merton and the True Self

The journey to the East, in December 1968, of the American Trappist monk, Thomas Merton (1915–68), still stands out as epochal in the history of dialogue. His journey was an acknowledgement of the universalism of the 'monastic archetype' and the fact that there are believers in all religions who will endeavour to appease in a singular way the cravings of the human heart for the Absolute and eternal. Merton travelled to the East to meet the ancient non-Christian monasticism, about which he had written and spoken so much, on its own soil. His accidental death, which occurred on the second day of the conference sponsored by an international Benedictine group in Bangkok (8–15 December 1968), had the same effect as the seed which in dying produces much fruit. Monasticism was singled out as the institution of the Church that is closest to the non-Christian religions of the East and as being the most appropriate context in which to meet them.[33]

Merton was aware of Tibetan Buddhism through his friendship with the Dalai Lama, but it was through his correspondence with D. T. Suzuki that Zen became his greatest interest. Merton's Zen commentaries are still considered the best that a westerner has produced. His writings were widely influential because in his search for God he repeatedly threw light on what it means to be truly human, and when Christian faith meets Zen at his hands, all these interesting fundamental questions arise to illuminate each other. Only a few hours before his death, Merton uttered what may well be his central insight:

> Christianity and Buddhism agree that the root of man's problems is that his consciousness is fouled up and does not apprehend reality as it is … Christianity and Buddhism alike, then, seek to bring about a transformation of man's consciousness … [and] to transform and liberate the truth in each person, with the idea that it will communicate itself to others. Of course the man par excellence to whom the task is deputed is the monk. And the Christian monk and the Buddhist monk – in their sort of ideal setting and ideal way of looking at them – fulfil this role in society … The whole purpose of the monastic life is to teach men to live by love.[34]

Merton affirms the existential quality of Zen, where it aims at inner meaning and direct experience. In its neutrality, Zen is no threat to Christians. It promulgates no new doctrines. It simply points to the soul of the human being from where springs the 'living fact' of one's life now. While Zen is not revelation and not the 'good news' from the Father of Jesus Christ, it is perfectly compatible with Christian belief. What it communicates is awareness of the ontological ground of self. Merton calls this the True Self. The goal of the spiritual life is to shift our identification from the illusory false self, the privately owned small self where we live apart from God, to the self as *imago dei*, where we can taste eternal life. While Merton equates original fallenness (which hides the face of God from us) with Buddhist *avidya* (illusion), he also expands on this theme with cultural comment.[35] He says we in the West are plagued by a narrowing of consciousness and that the East can help us:

> Modern man in so far as he is still Cartesian … is a subject for whom his own self-awareness as a thinking, observing, measuring and estimating 'self' is absolutely primary. It is for him the one indubitable 'reality' and all truth starts here.[36]

He believes that the 'bubble' of self-consciousness from which we relate limits truth. It governs the manner in which we know the world; it estranges us from the True Self and from God, who becomes a 'God-object', manipulated for our self-centred ends. We become detached observers of the fullness of truth that is our life and we suffer from 'spiritual homelessness'. Like the Dalai Lama, Merton believes that one cannot attain anything in the spiritual life without total dedication and discipline, and his interest in Buddhist meditation appears to be a practical one in that all that one needs to do is meditate with a desire for the real. Yet as a Catholic monk, he never suppresses the differences between Christian prayer and Zen; as he writes in *New Seeds of Contemplation*: 'The only one who can teach me to find God is God himself, alone.'[37] Merton's writings also show that he was particularly drawn to the mystical tradition of prayer and the apophaticism of St John of the Cross, yet his creative mind saw parallels with Zen as a neutral, religionless, 'skilful means' of accessing the wisdom of self-emptying.

William Johnston and the 'Third Way'

Irish Jesuit William Johnston (1925–2010) lived for over thirty-five years in Japan and was a widely read populariser of Christian spirituality in dialogue with Zen. With a background in the richly incarnational mysticism of Ignatius of Loyola, the 'mystic of moods and thoughts', and as a master of discernment of spirits, Johnston was to find numerous parallels in the precise spiritual methodology of Zen. His significant work on the dark, silent, imageless and apophatic mysticism of *The Cloud of Unknowing* provided him with a Christian analogue for understanding the path of Zen self-emptying. While Merton, in the 1960s, wrote of Zen as a 'transformation of consciousness' – an opening of the door to Christian grace – Johnston saw Zen as a 'graced mysticism' in itself, culminating in the undifferentiated unity of *sunyata-tathata*, in which all is one and yet not one. Supported by the existential quality of Vatican II documents and the teaching of Karl Rahner that all people of all faiths, in virtue of their grounding in God's grace, are called to contemplation, Johnston writes in an inclusive and non-contentious way. He draws parallels between Zen and Christian faith; Christianity, for example, has its own *koans* – meta-rational puzzles – which can only be solved through becoming more deeply one with Christ. The crucifix, Trinity, incarnation, and the Bread and Wine are but a few of the examples. The Rosary, Gregorian Chant, the Jesus Prayer and ejaculatory prayers all make use of basic human psychomatic rhythms to promote deep, silent, contemplative prayer. Prayer before the Blessed Sacrament is a type of *yoga* (union) that fixes the person's attention on one point, the light or the tabernacle. Pondering on texts or phrases of the Bible, one's feelings are refined to a deeper mystical level. Without diminishing the differences of Christianity, Johnston's writings show that he lived what some commentators have called for: a Christianity stretched beyond itself.

In his survey of East–West dialogue on spirituality, Johnston outlined a new mysticism, or 'third way'. Beyond the great classic mysticisms of the tradition, he advocated a contemplative access to the gospel of Christ for *all* believers and seekers:

> Everywhere we see Christians of all ages and cultures sitting quietly in meditation. Some sit before a crucifix or an icon in one-pointed meditation. Others sit and breathe as they look at the tabernacle. Others practise mindfulness, awareness of God in their surroundings. Others recite a mantra to the rhythm of their breath. Others, influenced by Zen or yoga or *vipassana* open their minds and hearts to the presence of God in the universe. Others just talk to God. We hear of many new approaches to the living God.[38]

What is common in all this is that the practice of prayer and the pursuit of a spiritual life are no longer considered to be beyond the competence of the ordinary person, immersed as they are in the daily tasks of living. Traditionally, contemplative prayer has been associated with a monastic lifestyle – with its renunciation and ambience of silence – and so was not thought possible for the average person. More suitable was a more discursive informative mediation, 'beginners' prayer', which was considered the necessary grounding for a more contemplative relationship with God. On this point, Johnston made an interesting observation:

> Discursive meditation of the old style presupposes belief in the existence of God; it was popular in the age of faith when atheism was rare. But this age of faith is no longer with us ... Must we, then, resolve people's doubts before we encourage them to pray? I think not. Eastern contemplation ... can begin as reverence toward a God in whom we believe, but it can also be a search for God who is the great unknown.[39]

The influence of Buddhism led him to favour the introduction of meditation to people from the very beginning, because he saw firsthand how those practising Eastern forms of meditation made progress in the spiritual journey, whether it was a deepening of their relationship to God or even a first tentative movement beyond agnosticism.

Buddhist meditators, given their rootedness in the body and experience, bring many gifts to Christians. They model a way of relating to the divine, demonstrating that by virtue of one's desire for the Absolute, one has entered into at least the beginnings of an active presence to the Real. As spiritual writers have said often since Vatican II, this capacity for contemplation is the prerogative of everybody. Buddhism's gift to Christians is that it provides a simple method of spiritual practice and of presence to the Divine, known or unknown, that is possible for people of all ages and cultures.

The Simple Mechanics of Practice

When we think of prayer as 'the elevation of the soul to God' it can be daunting. Do I have to be a holy person? How does one move beyond a sporadic turning to God in moments of need to definite times of prayer or continuous prayer (1 Th 5:17)? More simply, how does one form the habit of living in the Divine Presence? Here the Buddhist is very matter of fact. Monks confidently knows where to begin because they do so with the body and the breath. Sitting (*zazen*) is not spiritual; it is a physical skill. Sitting upright and attending to one's breathing are tangible physical practices that discipline mind and heart. Johnston tells us that, for Zen, the body is not just flesh. The body (the Japanese *hara*) is 'the sea of energy', the source of creativity and the principal locus of religious experience. This energy is released when one sits in the correct posture, with back straight and eyes slightly open.[40] The physical ability of posture is supported by breath and abdominal breathing is key. Breath is participation in the most basic gift of all – that of life itself. In the Judeo-Christian tradition, breath is the symbol of the Holy Spirit who fills the universe and envelops it with its presence. In Zen, the great root of faith is that one lives by the spark of the *bodhicitta* within, and 'sitting' is the unsurpassed way of trapping the tremendous power with which one is endowed, in order to draw on it in faith. There is a 'can-do' energy to this piece of advice. No matter how I feel I can be there and sit. There is no mystery to sitting; as the great Zen Master, Dogen, once said: *zazen* is for *zazen's* sake. To simply sit is to be enlightened. The bodily gesture of *zazen* is a posture that evokes Absolute Reality and no matter what my feelings are, the Absolute will not go away. Therefore, Zen Masters say to praying Christians, 'sit with confidence'.

The Centring of the Mind in the Heart

'We move spiritually not by our feet but by our desire,' said St Augustine, and the simple bodily gestures of disposing oneself activate the desire in the whole person, however inchoately and fleetingly. What we desire is God – the Real – whether we know it or not. For the Christian, its chief characteristic is the sense of presence to Another. It is the will reaching out to God, not as we imagine God to be, nor as he is in any of his works, but as God is in himself. It is also the emptying out of thought and conversation; the purification of self. A different kind of knowledge rooted in love is entered into, which, as an awareness of God's presence, however fragile, suppresses the awareness of self and our inveterate tendency to place ourselves at the centre of the universe. Spiritual writers proficient in Eastern meditation tell us that Zen can be a catalyst here. Zen sitting plunges one into the contemplative act in which there is neither subject not object. Its method directly assists and confirms the being-present and self-emptying aspects of prayer for the Christian.

American Trappist monk, Thomas Keating, tells us that it was the impression Eastern Buddhist monks and Zen *roshis* made upon him when they visited his monastery in the 1970s that led to his participation in the founding of the Centering Prayer Movement and Contemplative Outreach.[41] He believed that people must be introduced to the ways of contemplative prayer early on. Such prayer, he said, was a 'divine therapy' of the whole person, which initiates a process of growth over time.[42] Prayer is learnt by plunging into the act of praying itself. The superficial ego is negated and the true self, the hidden mysterious and desiring heart-person, is drawn into the presence of God. In time, the person who prays will feel the need to avail more deeply of the great supports for prayer – such as the *lectio* of the Word of God and a renewed sacramental life. The simplicity of such prayer and its suitability is that it is not about acquisition or success; its 'goal' is the practice of prayer itself, or as the Zen masters say, 'simply sitting'. Its effect, if one is faithful, is the beginning of a deeper union with God, which will enable one to live in a freer way and with more effectiveness in work and ministry.

While the Zen contribution is evident in the confident bodily choice to be present and in the use of a word (*mantra*), there is a subtle difference in the way the sacred word is used. In Eastern meditation, it is mainly a focus of attention, its continual repetition as a *mantra* helping to 'block out' all other thoughts. In centring prayer it is also used with intention, to express our loving consent to be present to God and to his action upon us.[43] Describing centring prayer, American Trappist monk, Basil Pennington, writes:

> You have to get settled comfortably at first and turn to God who is dwelling in the depths of your being. Then you take a little word of love, and use that word to stay quietly with God. Whenever you become aware of anything else, just use the little word to come back again. And at the end of the time you can finish with the Lord's Prayer.[44]

The Gift of No Mind

The Zen experience of sitting encourages 'being there' in the present moment – the state of 'no-mind' – something that is also, to an extent, the Christian experience. Both Zen and Christian spirituality prize a purity of heart and an emptying of constructs, feelings and attachments, however noble. Zen calls it the Great Death, liberating one into *tathata* – the love of all things without desire. The Spanish mystic, John of the Cross, calls it the 'dark night'. Coming to know God, he said, is like ascending a mountain; one must shed everything on the way.

Apart from the Creator, all things are nothing and I am nothing. When I come to realise the nothingness of my separate being, I can, in a moment of enlightenment, realise that God *is*. The 'nothingness' of John is proverbial:

> To reach satisfaction in all, Desire its possession in nothing. To come to the knowledge of all, Desire the knowledge of nothing. To come to possess all, Desire the possession of nothing.[45]

This nothingness is the reason for the 'dark night', the 'darkness' felt as a shattering inflow of God into the soul. Where there is Great Death, where there is 'dark night', there is 'nothingness'. For the Christian, such purification is a deepening of faith in one's relationship to God.

The Gift of Self-Reliance
Jesuit Zen roshi, Robert Kennedy, makes the following interesting statement: 'Those who are uncomfortable with "not-knowing" will never be self-reliant.' He is not here discounting the Christian attitude of childlike dependence on God, nor is he belittling a mode of prayer where feelings and images of God matter. He is alerting us to unhealthy spiritual childishness. He says Zen masters speak of the disciple whose cloak 'sweeps the grasses', who goes from master to master looking for answers. He is like a 'rice bag with holes'. But when he learns to empty himself and be content with unknowing, he becomes joyful and self-reliant: he realises that what he seeks is what he already has and is, and he comes to *zazen* with a back like 'a rod of steel'.[46] In the Christian tradition we call this living by faith. Moving beyond dependencies where God ceases to be a crutch, those who exemplify it are like the strong woman of scripture or champions about to run the race (1 Cor 9:24). We live in a cluttered age, says Johnston, and it is the freedom and purity of this unknowing that inspires the resilience we find in the many people today who, despite a secular environment, consciously pursue a spiritual life.[47]

The Christian 'For You, Lord'
'Emptiness', 'True Self', 'centring', 'no-mind', 'not clinging', 'self-reliance', 'awakening' – many of these words are Eastern in origin and have now come to complement the language of Christian spirituality. Many are confused by the

seeming rationalisation of Christian truths and weary of the number of beliefs to be adhered to. They desire the experience of faith behind the beliefs or a relationship to God that would give life meaning. And so they are drawn to Eastern religions because their gift is the simplicity of realisation. Still we must ask, what is the experience that is being realised? In any religion, Eastern or Western, realisation will, to an extent, be governed by the structures of the religion itself. The articulation of this truth seems to be the main concern of the much maligned 1989 letter On Certain Aspects of Christian Meditation (*Orationis Formas*), published by the Congregation for the Doctrine of the Faith. In a preamble, the letter acknowledges the interest of Christians in Eastern methods and says this is due to many factors: exposure to exchanges between religions and cultures; the spiritual restlessness of our times arising from a life subjected to the driving pace of technology, encouraging many to seek methods of prayer as paths to interior peace and psychic balance; and the fact that, in recent times, many traditional ways of meditation, including Christian, have fallen into disuse (OF Intro.). The letter acknowledges that the majority of the great religions seek union with God and point out ways to achieve it. We may be supported and guided by these ways, but always with the understanding that Christian prayer has the 'intimate nature of a relationship'. Ultimately it is guided by the Holy Spirit and cannot be totally programmed. The letter is not against serious instruction in Eastern methods, but it warns against those that can lead people astray – such as thinking that one has 'arrived', that one has achieved enlightenment; the mistaking of bodily sensations or psychic peace for spiritual experience. The particular difference of the Christian journey is that it is grounded in the sense of being addressed by Another, by the 'meeting of two freedoms, the infinite freedom of God with the infinite freedom of man' (OF Intro.). Its ultimate tutor is the Spirit of God, who, as Paul tells us, renews the mind in the light of God's will (Rm 12:2). Once more, the play of differences arises and it returns us to our earlier conversation on the nature of the Absolute, where we attempted to hold together in resonance two profound truths – the Absolute as Emptiness and the Absolute as Personal Creator. We now turn to Jesus and the Buddha for another angle on the conversation.

JESUS AND THE BUDDHA

Much has been written on the Buddha but hitherto unsurpassed from a Christian perspective is Romano Guardini's appreciation:

A single man has seriously attempted to lay hands on being itself: Buddha. He wanted more than merely to become better or, starting from the world, to find peace. He undertook the inconceivable: while standing in existence, to shake existence to its foundations. What he meant by *nirvana*, by the final awakening, by the cessation of illusion and of being, no one on the Christian side has yet understood and judged. Whoever should will to do so would have to become perfectly free in the love of Christ but be united in deep reverence to that mysterious one in the sixth century before the birth of the Lord.[48]

Hans Waldenfels SJ writes: 'The claim must be conceded to Buddhism that it orients man towards the absolute decisive point from which light falls on the whole of reality.'[49] The legend of St Josaphat, which enjoyed widespread popularity in medieval Europe, recounts a story of wisdom gained through renunciation and self-denial. Josaphat, a young prince with much going for him, decided to give up his wealth and position in order to find wisdom through a life of ascetic self-denial. Many scholars agree that the legend is actually a version of the life of Siddhartha Gautama. Josaphat is probably a garbled Greek version of the Sanskrit word *Bodhisattva*. In the legend, Prince Siddhartha becomes a Christian with his story remarkably intact. As James Fredericks observes:

> That the Buddha's teachings on impermanence and renunciation, however disguised in the journey from India into Christendom, should hold Christians in their thrall for so many centuries is testimony to the power of this man's life to sustain the religious imagination.[50]

Guardini, however, writing in pre-Vatican times, is said to have warned that when it comes to making an impression, the man from Nazareth comes second best to the Buddha.[51] It is possible he foresaw that the Buddha, once the 'naysayer' in sixth-century India, who challenged the conventions of Brahmanical religion and its priestly mediations, still had the power to do the same today; and that Buddhism would come into its own as a discourse about the Absolute in a secular mode. With its implied absence of God as the West understands God, it would be a this-worldly religion. In its rationality and skilful engagement of the whole person, it would appeal to the post-modern sensibility of individualism, nurturing human confidence and autonomy in the domain of one's chosen religious practice.

And so Buddhism would move into the vacuum left by the traditional concept of a theistic God, who in the minds of many has been associated with a reality that was anything but self-effacing or humbly relational.

While this is to name the problem of the weakening of faith in the West, it is also a challenge to probe more closely the nature of God. Theologians of interreligious dialogue are saying that we do not have to see Buddhism as our competitor, but rather as our reminder that we have a common language with it in the very radicality of God's self-emptying in Jesus' death on the cross. If we could imagine a conversation between Jesus and the Buddha, Jesus too would speak of an absence of God. His words on the Cross, 'My God, my God, why have you forsaken me?' (Mk 15:34), witness to the transcendent Father who has 'emptied himself into the world, transformed his substance in the blind mechanism of the world, a God who dies in the inconsolable pits of human affliction.'[52] The image of the *kenosis* (self-emptying) of God, who lovingly renounces any claims to domineering omnipotence, has great explanatory potential. This image fulfils our deepest longings for love and compassion and also liberates us to responsibly partner God in bringing about the Kingdom. Yet it is an image that we continually resist in daily living and spirituality. There we want God to be potentate who does it all, to be magician who intervenes, and even frequently to be somebody we can manipulate. And yet the divine reality in the gospels is revealed in the mystery of the death and resurrection of God's son. In a rare foray into a theology of interreligious dialogue, Cardinal Ratzinger (now Pope Benedict XVI) speaks of the divine self-emptying as the new form of the cloud of mystery in which God hides and at the same time shows himself. And in his conclusion that 'God's *kenosis* is itself the place where the religions can come into contact without arrogant claims to domination', one finds a language that need not discount Buddhism.[53]

It is mainly this language of divine self-emptying that has opened a way for Buddhists, such as the distinguished Japanese scholar Masao Abe, who tells us that, for him, the most touching and impressive passage in the Christian scriptures is the following from Paul:

> Have this mind among yourselves, which is yours in Christ Jesus, who though he was in the form of God, did not count equality with God a thing to be grasped, but emptied himself, taking the form of a servant, being born in the likeness of men. And being found in human form he humbled himself and became obedient unto death, even death on a cross. (Phil 2:5-8)

The familiar phrases 'he emptied himself, taking the form of a servant' and 'he humbled himself and became obedient' have become commonplace to us, and it is possible that the Pauline adaptation of this hymn from the early Christian community may be heard as an exhortation to the Philippians to be humble and empty as Jesus was. But we also know that in Paul God's action in the death of Jesus, when viewed through the eyes of conventional wisdom, is 'foolishness' (1 Cor 1:25). Abe's interpretation is that through the *kenosis* of incarnation and death of Jesus, God the Father reveals Godself as unconditional love beyond discriminatory justice.[54] He goes on to say that if the Son of God empties himself, we should also speak of the self-emptying of the Father whom the Son reveals: 'Without the self-emptying of God the Father the self-emptying of the Son is inconceivable.' And that 'only through this total *kenosis* is God truly God.'[55] That is, God is not God by virtue of a monarchical sovereignty over the world, but by virtue of creation and incarnation, which manifest God's emptied-out self-giving. Abe concludes that when we bring to realisation the kenotic God of Christianity and dynamic *sunyata* of Buddhism – without eliminating the distinctiveness of either religion – we find that what is common and binding them together is what is spiritually communicable: the inexpressible reality.[56]

Buddhism and Christianity invite each other to let go in different ways. Like Buddhism, Christianity, as a religion of incarnation, is also a religion of 'the Absolute This Side'. Christianity as sourced in the transcendent will of the 'Free in Love' to become incarnate, even more radically immanent and this-worldly than Buddhism.[57] Buddhists have acknowledged this and shown a willingness to learn from the socially transformative dimensions of Christian faith, as one commentator attests:

> This aspect for me is one of the most appealing of the legacy of Jesus. I consider my Christian brothers and sisters fortunate in having at the very core of their tradition – in the very life of their founder – such a clear and superb model for what it means to be a just and socially responsible person, a person of integrity in the world.[58]

The longstanding critique that Buddhism is weak on social issues has been said to arise from its view that the pain of the world is seen subjectively only. The *dharma* enables the Buddhist to live in such a way that suffering – the 'unsatisfactoriness of existence' – will gradually cease for each of them personally, and although

Buddhists live in community, each individual is responsible for his own journey in liberation. Allied to this is the contention that compassion is not the same as Christian charity.[59] This was brought home to me once in a simple incident: on thanking a Buddhist nun for a kind act, she replied: 'No problem. I did it for my *karma.*' Is it that the altruism of Buddhist practice, however ardent, is simply a procedure for getting rid of one's desire? Or is it that compassion (*karuna*), the most sublime virtue in the higher regions of the practice, is not a response to an individual other (since 'individual' does not really exist), but a love which is pity for the universal condition of *samsara* in which all living creatures are mired? Does the Buddhist not tangle with the real as the historical here and now?

It is not possible here to go into any depth on these issues, and to treat them lightly is offensive in the face of meeting with Buddhists and experiencing their disinterested service. Indeed Christians have much to learn from Buddhist loving-kindness and equanimity on how to temper the tactless zeal that sometimes characterises our charity. Living religions are in constant development and it is well known that Buddhists have become more socially concerned and prophetic. The Dalai Lama is such a modern prophet. He has often expressed his patience in the face of the massive injustice suffered by his country and religion at the hands of the Chinese, a patience that can live with not expecting the full resolution of Tibet's crisis during his lifetime. Such patience is supported by several factors: his Buddhist equanimity; his compassion, which also extends to the enemy; his spirit of joy; his belief that the global community will see the nobility of the Tibetans' largely non-violent, patient endurance more clearly and the justice of their cause, and thus a fair resolution will eventually be reached; and his firm belief that a non-violent approach is the only one that will truly resolve the conflict at its roots. Like the Dalai Lama, there are many engaged Buddhists today whose patient endurance and movements they have founded stand as witness to the special gift the religion brings to social action – the non-violence and patience that are at the heart of the tradition.[60]

Summary

The figure of the serene and smiling Buddha sitting in a position of meditation and the figure of the helpless, suffering Christ hanging upon the Cross, each in their different ways mediate the realities of *sunyata* and the Father God. Each calls for our response. One common response is that they complement each other as Love meeting Wisdom (Aloysius Pieris). Another, that it is in the chasm between them that the tension of being fully human is played out, because the One Spirit addresses us through them in different ways. I suggest that it is in this latter sense that the Buddha and Christ are not totally separate and will always be a word for each other. The Buddha is beyond suffering and beyond the world. Suffering has ceased; it has reached its true meaning as emptiness in that it never had reality in the first place. In Christ, suffering is willingly embraced as part of the historical human condition. He is redeemer, in that the suffering ends in him; he does not pass on its bad *karma* to others. The Buddha manifests the peace of emptiness and the value of becoming no-thing. The Cross manifests the sacrifice of emptiness and the value of transcending the self for the other. Buddha symbolises the equanimity of wisdom and compassion. The Crucified One dramatises horrifically the personal engagement of love. The serene figure of the Buddha discourages his disciples from clinging, even to his own person. He says: 'Be lamps to yourselves.' The Christ figure engages with us, drawing us to himself: 'Come to me all you who labour and are burdened'. Yet he challenges us: 'Take up your cross and follow me.'

The persistent attraction of the Buddha is that he symbolises the ideals of being fully human, of having a certain nobility and religious perfection, and who would not want these qualities and virtues? It is in this that Buddhism pushes us to the limits of interreligious dialogue because the Buddha, of all religious figures, is the one who best acts as a foil to the identity of Jesus. As Guardini once said, to praise Jesus as a great religious figure or the summit of perfection is inappropriate; such praise is purely incidental to the One who is the Son, in whom the omnipotent Word has entered into our human existence and whose invitation to us is not to imitate him but to open ourselves in faith to the divine mystery in him.[61]

It is only in the existential experience of Buddhism that one can transcend the Cartesian mind. A true meeting with Buddhism must be also one of 'no words', of meditation and prayer. What we should seek to experience in this meeting is not a message, not a word, not even good news, but a self-emptying through which we might touch the ground of being and rise up to run with the Word of God in confidence. The ground we share and the awakening to the living quality of that ground, to its 'truth and grace', are the most fundamental of the many gifts of Buddhism.

FURTHER READING

Fitzgerald, Michael L. and John Borelli, *Interfaith Dialogue: A Catholic View* (New York: Orbis Books, 2006).

Fredericks, James L., *Buddhists and Christians: Through Comparative Theology to Solidarity* (New York: Orbis Books, 2004).

Gross, Rita M. and Terry Muck, eds., *Christians Talk About Buddhist Meditation* (London: Continuum, 2003).

Henry, Patrick, ed., *Benedict's Dharma: Buddhists Reflect on the Rule of Saint Benedict* (London: Continuum, 2002).

Johnston, William, *Arise My Love: Mysticism for a New Era* (New York: Orbis Books, 2000).

_____, *Christian Zen* (Dublin: Gill & Macmillan, 1979).

_____, *Mystical Theology: The Science of Love* (London: HarperCollins, 1995).

_____, *The Inner Eye of Love: Mysticism and Religion* (London: HarperCollins, 1978).

Mitchell, Donald and James Wiseman, eds., *The Gethsemani Encounter: A Dialogue on the Spiritual Life by Buddhist and Christian Monastics* (New York: Continuum, 1998).

Pannikar, Raimundo, *The Silence of God: The Answer to the Buddha* (New York: Orbis Books, 1989).

Schmidt-Leukel, Perry, *Buddhism and Christianity in Dialogue* (London: SCM, 2005).

Waldenfels, Hans, *Absolute Nothingness: Foundations for a Buddhist–Christian Dialogue* (New York: Paulist Press, 1980).

NOTES

1. David Tracy, *Dialogue With the Other: The Inter-Religious Dialogue* (Louvain: Peeters Press, 1990), pp. 40–1.
2. Pope John Paul II, *Crossing the Threshold of Hope* (London: Jonathan Cape, 1994), pp. 84–90. See Denis Carroll, 'Review of *Crossing the Threshold*', *Studies* 84 (1995), pp. 197–204.
3. *Dialogue: New Series* 22 (1995), pp. 5–95. For other responses to Pope John Paul II, see *John Paul II and Interreligious Dialogue*, Byron L. Sherwin and Harold Kasimow, eds. (New York: Orbis Books, 1999).
4. Cf. Donald Mitchell, 'The Making of a Joint Buddhist–Catholic Statement', *Buddhist–Christian Studies* 16 (1996), pp. 203–8.
5. *Origins* 25.14 (September 1995), pp. 222–4.
6. *Crossing the Threshold of Hope*, pp. 147–9. Dr Havanpola Ratanasara interprets the Pope's remarks to apply to interfaith dialogue. He says he does not agree with everything the Pope says in the book but these disagreements are eclipsed by the points with which consensus seems attainable, as well as by the Pope's breadth of vision and his genuine concern for a continuing dialogue with other faiths. See *The Gethsemani Encounter*, pp. 9–10.

7. *The Way of the Bodhisattva*, revised trans. by Padmakasa Group (Boston: Shambala Classics, 2006), p. 4.
8. Aloysius Pieris, *Love Meets Wisdom: A Christian Experience of Buddhism* (New York: Orbis Books, 1988), p. 132.
9. Karl Rahner, *Spiritual Writings*, Philip Endean, ed. (New York: Orbis Books, 2004), p. 14.
10. Cited in John Snelling, *The Buddhist Handbook* (London: Rider, 1997), p. 54.
11. David Snellgrove, 'Theological Reflections on the Buddhist Goal of Perfect Enlightenment', *Bulletin: Secretariat for Christian Unity* 17 (1971), p. 91.
12. Edward Conze, *Buddhism: Its Essence and Development* (New York: HarperCollins, 1959), p. 40.
13. Joseph Roccasalvo, 'Toward an Atheism of Reverence: The Special Case of Buddhism', *Chicago Studies* 14.2 (2002), p. 214.
14. *Ibid.*, p. 215, citing Dr Palihawadana of the University of Sri Lanka.
15. *Ibid.*, p. 44.
16. Raimundo Pannikar, *The Silence of God*, p. 102.
17. Heinrich Dumoulin, *Christianity Meets Buddhism* (LaSalle, IL: Open Court, 1974), pp. 97–8.
18. William Johnston, *The Still Point: Reflections on Zen and Christian Mysticism* (New York: Harper & Row, 1970), p. 33.
19. Raimundo Pannikar, *The Silence of God*, p. 89.
20. *Ibid.*, p. 152.
21. Masao Abe, 'Self-Awakening and Faith in Zen and Christianity', *Masao Abe: Zen and Western Thought*, W. B. La Fleur, ed. (London: Macmillan, 1999), p. 187.
22. Heinrich Dumouli, *Zen Enlightenment: Origins and Meaning* (New York: Weatherhill, 1979), pp. 102–14.
23. J. Edgar Bruns, *The Christian Buddhism of St John* (New York: Paulist Press), 1971, p. 24.
24. Karl Rahner, *Theological Investigations*, Vol. 11 (London: Darton, Longman & Todd, 1961–91), p. 68–114.
25. William Johnston, *Arise My Love*, p. 107.
26. Karl Rahner, 'The Hiddenness of God', *Theological Investigations*, Vol. 16, p. 238.
27. *Ibid.*, Vol. 18, p. 92.
28. In *Buddhists and Christians: Through Comparative Theology to Solidarity*, James Fredericks explores emptiness/incomprehensibility through the lens of Aquinas and Nagarjuna. He says that both these religious thinkers are concerned with 'purification of views' of the Ultimate. For the Buddhist, words and constructs, indeed views of any kind, are always false and must be renounced in the quest for liberation. For Aquinas, not all views are false but they are always inadequate, even the orthodox ones, since divine incomprehensibility means God has an infinite capacity to be known.
29. Walter Kasper, *The God of Jesus Christ* (London: SCM Press, 1982), p. 153.
30. Robert Kiely, ed., *The Good Heart* (London: Rider, 1996). This book explores the gospels with the commentary the Dalai Lama gave to participants in the John Main Seminar, held in London in 1996. In addition to capturing the proceedings of the seminar, it contains contextual materials that enhance its use in Christian–Buddhist dialogue.
31. Raimundo Pannikar, *The Silence of God*, p. 155.
32. *Thich Nhat Hanh: Essential Writings*, with introduction by Sister Annabel Laity (Maryknoll, NY: Orbis Books, 2001), pp. 142f.
33. In 1973, the Vatican formally encouraged this dialogue. Cardinal Pignedoli, representing Pope Paul VI and the Secretariat for Non-Christian Religions (now the Pontifical Council for Interreligious Dialogue), formally invited Abbot Primate Weakland of the Benedictines to consider how Catholic monastics could serve as a bridge between religions of the East and West. Following this, conferences were held, exchange visits between Catholic and non-

Christian monks were arranged, and the boards of Monastic Interreligious Dialogue (MID) in the US and Dialogue Interreligieux Monastique (DIM) in Europe were established.

34. *The Asian Journal of Thomas Merton*, Naomi Burton, Patrick Hart and James Laughlin, eds. (New York: New Directions, 1973), pp. 332–3.

35. *Ibid.*, p. 332f. On the topic of the Fall, see Donald Mitchell, *Spirituality and Emptiness: The Dynamics of Spiritual Life in Buddhism and Christianity* (New York: Paulist Press, 1991), Chapter 2.

36. Thomas Merton, *Zen and the Birds of Appetite* (New York: New Directions, 1968), p. 22.

37. Thomas Merton, *New Seeds of Contemplation* (London: Burns & Oates, 1999), p. 34.

38. William Johnston, *Mystical Theology*, p. 134.

39. William Johnston, 'Oriental Mysticism and Christian Prayer', *Review for Religious* 29 (1970), pp. 125–7, p. 274.

40. William Johnston, *Mystical Theology*, pp. 125–7.

41. The Centering Prayer Movement in the US was initiated in the monastery of the monks of Spencer Abbey, Massachusetts, and was largely lead by Thomas Keating and Basil Pennington. For resources on centring prayer and for informative discussion on its links with Eastern meditation, see Murchadh O'Madagáin, *Centering Prayer and the Healing of the Unconscious* (New York: Lantern Books, 2007). Also well-known in Ireland is the Christian Meditation Movement, initiated by Benedictine John Main. A direct simple prayer with a mantra, its origin lies in Main's experiences of meditation in India. It has continued to flower worldwide (in my opinion now showing more Buddhist influence) under Benedictine Laurence Freeman's direction and is available on the World Community for Christian Meditation website: www.wccm.org.

42. Thomas Keating, *Invitation to Love: The Way of Christian Contemplation* (New York: Continuum, 2000).

43. For a more detailed discussion on this distinction, see Murchadh O'Madagáin, *Centering Prayer*, pp. 40f.

44. Basil Pennington, *Gethsemani Encounter*, p. 208.

45. For a more extensive commentary on links between the apophatic mysticism of John of the Cross and Zen apophaticism, see William Johnston, *The Inner Eye of Love*, pp. 106–25, and *Mystical Theology*, pp. 166f.

46. Robert Kennedy, *Zen Gifts for Christians* (New York: Continuum, 2000), see Chapter 3 on 'Self-Reliance'.

47. William Johnston, *The Inner Eye of Love*, p. 85.

48. Romano Guardini, *The Lord* (London: Longmans, 1953), pp. 355–6. Trans. of text in Hans Waldenfels, 'Buddhism and Christianity in Dialogue: Notes on the Intellectual Presuppositions', *Communio* 15 (Winter 1988), p. 421. In *The Lord*, Guardini implies that it is through a Christian sensibility that we can truly appreciate the greatness of the Buddha.

49. Hans Waldenfels, *op cit.*, p. 411.

50. James L. Fredericks, *Buddhists and Christians*, pp. 114–15.

51. Romano Guardini, *op. cit.*, pp. 424f.

52. Cited in Louis Dupres, 'Spiritual Life in a Secular Age', *Daedalus III* 1 (1982), p. 26.

53. Cardinal Joseph Ratzinger, *Many Religions – One Covenant* (San Franscisco: Ignatius Press, 1999), p. 108.

54. Masao Abe, 'Kenosis and Emptiness', *Buddhist Emptiness and Christian Trinity*, Roger Corless and Paul Knitter, eds. (New York: Paulist Press, 1990), p. 12.

55. *Ibid.*, p. 16.

56. *Ibid.*, p. 24. Abe has not just been an academic; William Johnston, who was acquainted with him, tells us that Abe practiced Zen assiduously and that he sat with him in *sesshin* (sitting meditation) in Kyoto. From knowing him, he concludes that 'when he speaks of emptiness he is talking about something he has experienced at the depths of his own being'; *Mystical Theology*, p. 165. It is at this level of realisation that Abe claims a oneness

between the emptiness of *sunyata* and the emptiness of God in Jesus Christ. Much has been written on this line of dialogue between the Buddha and Christ, *sunyata* and God, but it is apparent that Abe, as a Buddhist, would overlook the distinction between God and world in implying that God is totally emptied out in the world, as *sunyata* is *samsara*. And so the question David Tracy (who is sympathetic to Buddhism) put to Abe a long time ago still holds: how can *sunyata* be 'dynamic' unless it is also personal freedom and love in relation to the world? See 'Kenosis, Sunyata and Trinity', *The Emptying God: A Buddhist–Jewish–Christian Conversation*, John B. Cobb and Christopher Ives, eds. (New York: Orbis Books, 1990), pp. 135–54.

57. 'The Free in Love' is the felicitous phrase used by Walter Kasper in his naming of the God of Jesus in *The God of Jesus Christ* (London: SCM, 1983).

58. Jose Ignacio Cabezon, 'Buddhist Views of Jesus', *Jesus in the World Faiths*, Gregory A. Barker, ed. (New York: Orbis Books, 2005), p. 18.

59. While in practice it seems patronising and offensive to consider Christian charity superior to Buddhist compassion, nevertheless this was the contention of Henri de Lubac, who, before the Vatican Council, laid the groundwork for Christian–Buddhist dialogue in the scholarly study *Aspects of Buddhism* (New York: Sheed & Ward, 1953). Lubac draws a sharp distinction between the Judeo-Christian tradition, which is dynamic and other-centred, and Buddhism, as belonging to Asian wisdom traditions that encourage inertia and withdrawal from the world. See also de Lubac, 'Buddhist Charity and Christian Charity', *Communio* 15 (Winter 1988), pp. 49–51.

60. See Sallie B. King, 'Buddhism and Social Engagement', *The Sound of Liberating Truth*, Paul O. Ingram, ed. (Richmond: Curzon, 1998), pp. 159–80. King comments on the work of the Dalai Lama and the numerous monks and nuns who have participated in the Tibetan Liberation Movement; on Aung San Suu Kyi of Burma; Thich Nhat Hahn of Vietnam; and on Ghosananda, a monk of Cambodia who emerged as a leader after the Cambodian purge to bring healing to the suffering Cambodian people.

61. Romano Guardini, p. 359.

Conclusion

Truth in Christ and Making Room

The challenge of religious pluralism invites us to a new understanding of Christianity as the religion of the gospel.

Claude Geffré

For Christ plays in ten thousand places,
Lovely in limbs, and lovely in eyes not his
To the Father through the features of men's faces.

Gerard Manley Hopkins

Some time ago, I heard the Dalai Lama speak of heaven and of God. It was in the context of a multi-faith gathering and he was urging his listeners to move beyond their differences and beyond the constructs that shape them, since the quest of all the religions is finally an ultimate and unutterable mystery that is One in itself. He added, uncharacteristically, 'in heaven there will only be One God'. While it is true that the question of God is the foundational one for all religions, it is also true that *how* we perceive and articulate the divine mystery is integral to religious faith. It is this articulation that gives rise to our differences. The originality of each religion lies in what it says about the Absolute, toward whom it is a path, and the originality of Christianity lies in the way God is conceived. So what distinguishes Christian belief is not God's grace, which is given to all, but the expression of that gift of grace in Jesus Christ, crucified and risen and in his Spirit.

Despite the demands of the more radical pluralists, there can be no level playing field in the dialogue between the religions. Each religion will tend to evaluate and judge the other in the light of its own non-negotiables. Indeed there is a tendency toward inclusivism in all religions. And so our question becomes: can there be an inclusivism that is truly open and respectful of the other? This short chapter attempts to probe this question, and the tentative reflections offered have been stimulated by theologians who push the boundaries of inclusivism in different ways.[1] They show how it is possible to hold in dialectical tension the constitutive character of Christ as universal saviour *with* and *within* a broader understanding of God's design for humankind. And that it is within that broader design, in which the positive values of the religions are endorsed, that we must formulate how Christ is related to these other faiths. The text of 1 Timothy 2:3-5 is thought to express these two incontrovertible principles of Christian dialogue – the universal salvific will of God and the uniqueness and universality of Christ's mediation:

> God [is] our Saviour, who desires everyone to be saved and to come to the knowledge of the truth. For there is one God: there is also one mediator between God and humankind, Christ Jesus, himself human, who gave himself as a ransom for all.

In line with this text, the saving design of God will be looked at through *two* lenses, both of which refract each other and are indissolubly linked – the lens of the Absolute Saviour, the Father God, who in the Word and Spirit enacts the broader expanse of divine salvation, and the lens of the historical person of Jesus the Christ, who as incarnate Word is the visible sacrament God of what God does in the world. In the process, we will note some factors contributing to the ongoing debate on interreligious dialogue before concluding with some reflections on the particularity of divine revelation in Christ and the decisiveness of its significance in the world of faiths.

THE UNIVERSALITY OF GOD'S REIGN

> Humanity forms but one community. This is so because all stem from the one stock which God created to people the earth, and also because all share a common destiny, God. (NA 1)

This mystery of unity which unites all human beings, whatever their differences, is an important aspect of the broader foundation of interreligious dialogue. No aspect of the world is 'without' God; and no human lives are untouched by the divine presence. In biblical terms, this mystery of unity is the Reign of God.

Belief in the Reign of God is found in the Hebrew scriptures. Distinctive to Israelite faith is the belief that Yahweh, as sovereign Creator, is also present as transformative power in the history and events of Israel. The Kingdom of Yahweh encompasses creation and the hearts of human beings. The gospels tell us that when Jesus speaks of God, he rarely speaks of God per se, but of God as Father and as Kingdom. We know that the personal experience of God as *Abba* was the source and origin of his being and message. In relation to *Abba,* he was the Son. Spelt out socially, this relationship was communicated as God-with-us, God's Reign. The gospels testify to this in Jesus' teaching and actions; in his parables and healing ministry he manifested God's Reign. He was the personal embodiment of the Kingdom, as Luke tells us, the kingdom in our midst (Lk 17:21).

Not so long ago, the Catholic Church simply identified the Kingdom with itself. But since Vatican II, a distinction has been made between Church and Kingdom and there is an explicit recognition that God's Reign extends beyond the communion of Church members to include the whole of humankind. In the encyclical *Redemptoris Missio* (1990), Pope John Paul II intimates this new relationship between the Church and the Kingdom:

> It is true that the inchoate reality of the Kingdom can also be found beyond the confines of the Church among peoples everywhere, to the extent that they live 'gospel values' and are open to the workings of the Spirit who breathes when and where he wills (Jn 3:8). But it must be immediately added that this temporal dimension of the Kingdom remains incomplete unless it is related to the kingdom of Christ present in the Church and straining towards eschatological fullness. (RM 20).

This is tantamount to saying that while the Kingdom is present in a more concentrated way in the Church, it also extends beyond the limits of Church. Such is the implication of Vatican II's definition of the Church as 'the universal sacrament of salvation' (LG 48). As sacrament, the Church stands in the world as witness to God's universal reign but it also exists as servant and enabler of God's Reign, working in collaboration with other believers whose lives and religious practices are also an operative presence of the divine in the world and history. It is in this latter inclusive sense that Jacques Dupuis says one can transform the ancient controversial axiom 'outside the Church no salvation' to 'outside the world, no salvation'.[2]

The opening up of the distinction between Church and Kingdom has importance for interreligious dialogue. With it we are moving beyond an understanding of Church as a closed self-serving reality to Church as a witnessing sacrament of God's Reign, a servant Church journeying in pilgrimage with persons of other faiths towards fulfilment of that Reign. When we think of the Church in this way, we allow a space for what has been called the 'surplus of meanings' that have always been there, continuously buffeting us and resisting our tendencies to total inclusion. Such are the plurality of religions out there which also contribute in their own ways to the Kingdom and, furthermore, the eschatological nature of truth itself, which is evoked by the continuous presence of a 'surplus' of meaning. This dimension of Christian eschatology is particularly relevant for dialogue since much of Christian triumphalism and arrogance towards other religions in the past has derived from the tendency to identify the historical Church with the Kingdom of God. But as *Redemptoris Missio* says, the Church as 'seed, sign and instrument' of the Kingdom is also straining toward its eschatological fullness (*RM* 18, 20). It is not surprising then that Christian theologians engaged in dialogue have eagerly appropriated the notion of eschatology as the basis for a greater theological openness and receptivity. On this matter, Dupuis writes:

> There is, perhaps, nothing which provides interreligious dialogue with such a deep theological basis, and such a true motivation, as the conviction that in spite of the differences by which they are distinguished, the members of different religious traditions, co-members of the Reign of God in history, are travelling together toward the fullness of the Reign of God, toward the new humanity willed by God for the end of time, of which they are called to be co-creators with God.[3]

Thus the space of the Reign of God makes room for the possible truth that the divine presence in the world *does* manifest itself in a plurality of ways.[4] That Christ's play in the world can be lovely in eyes and limbs *not* his, and that close contact with the religious life of other believers, as Pope John Paul II recognised in his first encyclical, *Redemptor Hominis*, can indeed 'make Christians ashamed' (RH 6). The dictum of Jesus, 'By their fruits you shall know them ' (Mt 7:16, 20), is a criterion of authentic spirituality in all the religions. Within the context of the universality of salvation and God's reign, Christian theologians continue to probe how we can say that *every* religion, in its positive elements, is part of God's plan to lead *all* people to Christ. A number of interesting factors contribute to this debate.

The Religions as Gifts of God?

Experience of living in multi-religious situations has led Dupuis, who has worked for many years in India, to say we can no longer look upon non-Christian religions as solely and primarily representing a natural human effort to search for God, or as being more akin to cultures or philosophies. Nor can we say that the continual flourishing of Islam and Asian religions is due simply to the failure of Christian mission. Back in 1961, when Rahner tentatively probed the whole area of interreligious dialogue with his theory of the 'anonymous Christian', he proposed that there is but one economy of salvation which is God's self-gift in Christ to the world.[4] He gave clear expression to this as his theology of revelation-salvation when he wrote:

> As God's real self-communication in grace … the history of salvation and revelation is coextensive with the history of the world and of the human spirit, and hence also of the history of religion.[5]

The expansive spirit of Rahner's non-dualist thinking was to enrich Vatican II documents, especially *Ad Gentes*, where even the phrase 'truth and grace', signifying 'a sort of secret presence of God' (AG 9) outside the Christian economy, can be said to echo the theologian's writings.

In the 1961 article he also went on to speak of the 'lawfulness' of the religions.[6] Because humans are historical and social beings, the saving and universal grace of God is mediated to them in and through the social and cultural institutions to which they belong. If Christian theology holds that we must work out our salvation in a religious institution, then the same must be true for Muslims, Hindus and Buddhists. It must be possible to say that their religious institutions are providential mediations of grace for their adherents. Yet while the early documents of Vatican II generously affirmed the seeds of 'truth and grace' in the religions, they showed little interest in the institutions as 'ways of salvation' for their members.

Dupuis is one of the many theologians who vouches for a more pluralist and differentiated view of God's presence in Christ. At the level of experience, so many factors contribute to make us think along these lines. Firstly, in a more globalised world we are faced with a pluralism of cultures and a multitude of religious believers whose very presence among us is an invitation to relate and reflect more deeply on the meaning of divine revelation and how God communicates with humankind. Secondly, we must accept that of the seven billion of the world population, approximately 2.2 billion are Christian. Thirdly, as Christians we believe that the God who created all humans is not partial (Deut 10:17; Rm 2:11; Acts 10:34), that God 'is greater than our hearts' (1 Jn 3:20) and that he wills the salvation of all peoples (1 Tm 2:14). And so in light of these truths, Dupuis would say that we are being invited to open ourselves to a greater variety in God's communication with us. And he proposes the hypothesis that if the variety of divine communication is providentially *in principio* as well as *de facto*, we must begin to accept that religions other than Christianity are more than 'stepping stones'.[7] Being providential gifts of God (AG 11), it becomes possible to say that in relation to the Christ event, they have saving value in themselves and manifest in their very multiplicity the superabundant richness of divine revelation.

God's Unrevoked Covenant with the Jews

On this question of the plurality of religions, it is interesting to note how theologians turn to the asymmetrical relationship of Christianity and Judaism for support. French Dominican, Claude Geffré, surmises that the 'irreducibility' of Israel gives Christian theology permission to speak in an analogous way of the irreducibility of other religions and to resist in their regard any temptation to totalitarian fulfilment:

> Even if it is a matter of a simple analogy, the relationship of Christianity to Judaism has a paradigmatic value with regard to the relationship of Christianity to the other religions. Just as the church does not integrate or replace Israel, in the same way it cannot be said to integrate or replace the religious truth that may be present in another religion.[8]

It was St Paul who first struggled with the link between the nascent Christian faith and Jewish forms of otherness (Rm 11:11-32). Paul maintains that the Jews remain very dear to God for the sake of the patriarchs, 'since God does not take back the gifts he has bestowed or the choice he made' (Rm 11:28). The covenant with Israel endures today no less than it did in biblical times.

As we have seen, *Nostra Aetate* (1965), *Guidelines* (1974) and *Notes* (1985) point out that Jews practising Judaism are to be honoured, revered and supported by Christians and by the Church as a whole that needs the witness of the people of the Torah. The former speaks of the 'spiritual bond' that links Christians with

'Abraham's stock' (NA 3). Christian self-understanding needs the witness of the Jews, for since New Testament revelation is in continuity with the Hebrew scriptures, we continue to 'draw sustenance from the roots of that good olive tree onto which, as wild olive branches, we have been grafted' (NA 3). Yet God's ways confound our propensity for human neatness and, mysteriously, we are learning that there is sustenance also to be drawn from the fact that the Jews, as people of the Torah, are different from us. *Nostra Aetate* is quite humble on this subject and ends on an eschatological note:

> ... who knows the mind of God but only God? Together with the prophets and the same apostle [Paul], the Church awaits the day, known to God alone, when all people will call on God with one voice and 'serve him shoulder to shoulder' (Sop. [Zech] 3:9; Is 66:23; Ps 65:4). (NA 4)

The Jews, 'Our fathers in the faith', therefore continue to stand as a providential reminder that Christianity and indeed the Church must not close in on themselves. Given the nature of biblical revelation, whose culmination is in Christ, who was a Jew, it goes without saying that our relationship with Israel is of a different order to our relationship with Islam, Hinduism and Buddhism. Nevertheless, Israel invites us to be open to the hypothesis of a possible providential and mysterious pluralism within the divine plan of salvation for all peoples.

As a way of interpreting an *in principio* pluralism in the divine relation to Christianity, Dupuis proposes that while God's revelation to human beings is one, it is also differentiated. He speaks of this differentiation as three stages, which strictly speaking do not represent a chronological sequence, but partially overlap:

> In the first stage, God enables seers to hear in their hearts a secret word, at least traces of which are found in sacred scriptures of the religious traditions of the world. In the second, God speaks 'officially' to Israel through the mouth of its prophets, and the entire Old Testament is a record of this word and of human responses to it. In both of these stages, the word of God is ordered, although differently in each, to the plenary revelation that will take place in Jesus Christ. In this, the third stage, God utters his decisive word in him who is 'the Word', and it is to this word that the whole New Testament officially bears witness.[9]

Here Dupuis is moving beyond the old distinction of Christianity as the religion of grace, in which God searches for human beings and the religions as purely human strivings toward God but not systems of salvation. Obviously influenced by Rahner's move beyond the dualism of nature and grace, Dupuis goes on to emphasise that it is not religious systems, Christianity or otherwise, that save, but God alone who as author of grace is the Absolute and gracious saviour in all religions. While the accomplishment of universal salvation as God's work is beyond systems, Dupuis, as a Christian theologian, professes that it is in the person of Jesus the Christ that this saving work is decisively mediated for humankind. How this is enacted in such a way that does not suppress the divine gift in other religious systems remains an open question.

The Universal Activity of God's Spirit in All Believers

More recently, the emphasis placed on the presence of the Holy Spirit in all religions is also opening us to their reality as providential gifts. Dermot Lane, in his recent work *Stepping Stones to Other Religions*, makes a significant contribution here. Lane is aware of the reticence of theologians traditionally concerning pneumatology, such as the fear that it can provide a way to opt out of a more reasonable probing of theological truths – that when the going gets tough we leave it to the Holy Spirit to explain. And he rightly questions whether, as members of a global culture that is industrial, market-driven and capitalistic, we too have been infected unconsciously in our thinking by the 'Spirit-stifling practices' of the times we live in.[10] Lane's grounded and critical unfolding of pneumatology goes a long way to allaying these fears. Promoting a Spirit Christology that is beyond exclusivism, he warns that 'without attention to the dynamic presence of the Spirit of God in history, there is the danger that the Christian revelation of God becomes frozen in time.'[11]

It is helpful to remember that John XXIII, in convening the Second Vatican Council, expressed the hope that it would be a 'new Pentecost' for the Church. A number of Vatican documents attest to the presence and action of the Spirit in the world and other religions. The *Pastoral Constitution on the Church in the Modern World* (1965) says: 'We must hold that the Holy Spirit offers to all the possibility of being made partners, in a way known only to God, in the Paschal Mystery' (n. 22) and *Ad Gentes* (1965) makes a reference to the presence of the Spirit at work in the world *before* Christ was glorified (AG 4). That we must not think of the Spirit of God as the preserve of the Church only is given singular emphasis by John

Paul II. In his encyclical on the Holy Spirit, *Dominum et Vivificantem* (1986), he reminds us that the Holy Spirit was active in influencing the course of history, people, cultures and religions before the coming of Christ (DV 53). And a text from the later encyclical letter, *Redemptoris Missio* (1990), states:

> The Spirit manifests himself in a special way in the Church and her members. Nevertheless, his presence and activity are universal, limited neither by space nor time … [The Spirit] is at the very source of the human person's existential and religious questioning which is occasioned not only by contingent situations but by the very structure of his being. The Spirit's presence and activity affect not only individuals but also society and history, peoples, cultures and religions. (RM 28)

Furthermore, we find in John Paul II's address to the Roman Curia on prayer the implication of an existential link between the human spirit and the Holy Spirit. Recalling the World Day of Prayer for Peace which was held at Assisi on 17 October 1986, two months earlier, the Pope marvelled at the greater unity that bound so many participants of diverse traditions together, and in his discourse on prayer he spoke of the Holy Spirit as the agent of this unity, 'every authentic prayer being called forth by the Holy Spirit, who is mysteriously present in the heart of every person.'[12]

The theological basis for this link had earlier been established by Karl Rahner. Arising from his non-dualistic theology of nature and grace, he had written:

> God … has already communicated Himself in his Holy Spirit always and everywhere and to every person as the innermost centre of his existence, whether he wants it or not, whether he reflects on it or not, whether he accepts it or not.[13]

While the Divine Spirit as gift of God transcends the human spirit, yet it is always received as mediated in the deepest recesses of the human spirit, from which, though distinct, it is inseparable. This existential grounding of God's Spirit in the human spirit is of special interest for interreligious dialogue. We have seen how in Hinduism the 'cave of the heart' is the place where God is known, not just as an object out there, but inwardly in the depths of the self. For Asians, whether Hindu, Buddhist or Christian, the 'fullness' to which all divine truth tends is called 'realised truth'.[14] It is not surprising then that the official Church teaching in Asia and its theologians have given such prominence to the Holy Spirit – the Advocate – as the One who *realises* truth in all human lives, Christian and other. Asian Christians live and minister in cultures where it is obvious that the spirit of the people is already attuned to religious search. We have seen how the special gift of members of Asian religions is their witness to divine truth as having heart-searching and Spirit-filled qualities. The following lines from the Federation of Asian Bishops Conference (FABC) are worth citing in full:

> Its experience of the other religions has led the Church in Asia to positive appreciation of their role in the divine economy of salvation. This appreciation is based on the fruits of the Spirit perceived in the lives of other religious believers: a sense of the sacred, a commitment to the pursuit of fullness, a thirst for self-realisation, a taste for prayer and commitment, a desire for renunciation, a struggle for justice, an urge to basic human goodness, an involvement in service, a total surrender of the self to God, and an attachment to the transcendent in their symbols, rituals and in life itself, though human weakness and sin are not absent.[15]

Indeed we may say that such gifts or fruits of the Spirit are manifestations of the universality of divine grace and that the agent of divine grace is God's Spirit operative in the hearts of people, the majority of whom are supported in their faith by institutions and rituals other than Christian.

In Christian theology, the primordial mediation of God's Spirit is Christ who is the Word. In the early Church, Irenaeus, when referring to the saving actions of God in the world, spoke of the 'two hands of God', Word and Spirit, both of which work together for the same goal of God's reign.[16] Word is, of its nature, clarifying. As *Logos,* it is the truth of all things, the light that enlightens everything (Jn 1:9). It is the Word that gives focus to the universal outreach of God's Spirit. Elements of such truth have always pervaded the human heart and creation, waiting to be discerned (Rm 1:20-21). God's Holy Spirit, the Advocate, is the discerner of truth in us and in the Church, and it is the Spirit who enables us to say of the Word incarnate that 'Jesus is Lord' (1 Cor 12:3).

Thus, Yves Congar writes that 'The Spirit is the way God exists outside God.'[17] But he also intimates a certain surprise in the Spirit's workings in the lives of people. For it is characteristic of the Spirit of God to lead us on, to act freely and in mysterious and unpredictable ways. The Fourth Gospel symbolises this mysterious activity of the Spirit: 'The wind [Spirit] blows where it chooses, and you hear the sound of it, but you do not know where it comes from nor where it goes' (Jn 3:8). There is at least one instance in Acts of this mysterious divine freedom, where the Spirit was poured out on people before they were baptised (Acts 10:44–11:18) causing Peter to declare during the Jerusalem Council: 'And God who knows the human heart, testified to them [though not yet baptised] by giving them the Holy Spirit, just as he did to us' (Acts 15:8). The outpouring of the Spirit in the Cornelius incident took place while they were listening to Peter preaching (Acts 10:44), and in this sense the receiving of the Spirit may be said to be associated with the hearing of the good news. While one of the purposes of that incident is to affirm Peter as the head of the Church, he and the Jewish Christians also come to realise that they must not consider the gentile 'others' profane, unholy or outside the Reign of God.

It is within this context of the universal and dynamic presence of the Holy Spirit that we can become attuned to the utter freedom of God in his relationship to us, and so come to rest more easily with challenging truths such as the 'unrevoked covenant' of the Jewish people; the religions as 'gifts of God'; and the possible view that as God's gifts they are providentially and, *in principio*, part of the divine plan of salvation. Yet, this latter point is still an ongoing question for Catholic interreligious dialogue.

'Participated Mediations'

Current Church teaching is more reserved on the issue of the religions as part of God's plan of salvation in the sense of having a divine origin in themselves. *Dominus Iesus* (2000), a major critique of any possible relativising of Christian faith, seems to have put paid to the issue.[18] It asserts unambiguously that 'The Church's constant missionary proclamation is endangered today by relativistic theories which seek to justify religious pluralism, not only *de facto* but also *de jure* [or in principle]' (DI 4). It goes on to elaborate:

> Certainly the various religious traditions contain and offer religious elements which come from God, and which are part of what 'the Spirit brings about in human hearts and in the history of peoples, in cultures, and religions. Indeed, some prayers and rituals of the other religions may assume a role of preparation for the gospel, in that they are occasions or

pedagogical helps in which the human heart is prompted to be open to the action of God. One cannot attribute to these, however, a divine origin or an *ex opera operato* efficacy, which is proper to the Christian sacraments. (DI 21)

If we think of it as a document for dialogue, *Dominus Iesus'* problem is dogmatic *a priori* thinking in relation to the religions in that all are lumped together as 'other religions', 'religious traditions', or 'non-Christians', whereas we know that Judaism in its relation to Christianity is in a category of its own, and that the Abrahamic theism of Islam is very different from Hindu theism or Buddhist non-theism. The document acknowledges that the followers of other religions can receive divine grace, but goes on to say that 'it is also certain that *objectively speaking* they are in a gravely deficient situation in comparison with those who in the Church, have the fullness of the means of salvation' (DI 22). Taken alone and unrelated to fact or experience, this sentence is offensive to real people of other religions, whose living faith, as John Paul II once said, often 'puts Christians to shame'.

Admittedly, the major purpose of *Dominus Iesus* is not to explain approaches to other religions but to affirm Christian belief in Jesus Christ as the universal saviour. And while this positive affirmation is welcome to Christians, it can give rise to a negative rhetoric that unfortunately smacks of pre-conciliar exclusivism. However, we cannot discount the fact that in other magisterial documents since Vatican II, a door had been opened. *Redemptoris Missio* (1990) does not theorise *a priori* about plurality as such, nor does it pre-empt how God might think or act in relation to others. In it, it seems as if evidence of the values in the religions has led Pope John Paul II to speak of them as 'participated mediations' in the salvation of their members:

Though participated forms of mediation of different kinds and degrees are not excluded, they acquire meaning and value *only* from Christ's own mediation, and they cannot be understood as parallel or complementary to his. (RM 5)

It is not actually clear if the Pope is speaking of the religions themselves or of their adherents, but the later *Dialogue and Proclamation* (1991), a document of the Joint Commissions of Interreligious Dialogue and Evangelisation, definitely moves beyond a theology emanating from first principles by engaging with the practical reality of a Church already in dialogue. Indeed the document speaks to and of other believers:

> The mystery of salvation reaches out to them, in a way known to God, through the invisible action of the Spirit of Christ. Concretely it will be in sincere practice of what is good in their own religious tradition and by following the dictates of their conscience that the members of other religions respond positively to God's invitation and receive salvation in Jesus Christ, even while they do not recognise or acknowledge him as their Saviour. (DP 29)

In this passage, *Dialogue and Proclamation* seems to be making more room for the religions, implying a more dynamic view of the active presence of Christ as mediated by other traditions themselves rather than a simple inclusivist understanding of Christianity as totally absorbing these traditions.

John Paul II's 'participated mediations', which in a way hearkens back to Rahner's 'lawfulness' of the religions, makes a gesture toward the pluralist theologians' concern that other religions are truly gifts of God, and that our dialogue with them can be real and can lead to reciprocal benefits. 'The Christian gives but also receives,' say Dupuis. 'While wanting to share his or her own experience of Jesus Christ and of His Spirit, the Christian will be quick to discover new aspects of the mystery of Christ and of God in the experience of the other.'[19] The word 'mediations' recalls a significant dimension of Christian faith, which is that of sacramentality, implying that the divine presence is in all things, that God takes time and space seriously, and that the finite, the human and historic are the ways of divine *mediation*.

So far we have considered the first part of 1 Timothy 2:3-5, which focuses on the 'universality' of salvation and on 'God our Saviour, who desires everyone to be saved and to come to knowledge of the truth'. Now we turn to the second part of the text: 'there is one God; there is also one mediator between God and humankind, Christ Jesus, himself human, who gave himself as a ransom for all'. Here it is the very time-bond and mediated character of Christian faith that claims to be a universal truth. When the Buddhist tradition states that the enlightened experience of wisdom and compassion has universal import for all people, no one disagrees. But when Christianity claims that the particular historical event of the life of an itinerant Jewish rabbi possesses saving significance for peoples of all times and places (including those who lived before Jesus), it is considered unseemly that the human and the divine should be found in each other so easily. From the earliest times, theologians have called this 'the scandal of particularity'. Such is the doctrine of the incarnation.

JESUS THE ONE MEDIATOR

Jesus as the one mediator of God is more than an instance of God's saving presence; more than a representation of a universal love-ethic; more than the human form of a universal ideal, whose story must be made to serve that ideal. In short, Jesus is more than a cipher of the divine. Christians believe that in Christ God broke into the world, bringing about a decisive event of revelation-salvation, and that in his personal identity as incarnate Son, Jesus draws us into the mystery of a God who is a triune communion of persons – Father, Son and Holy Spirit. The gospel values that Jesus promoted, the Kingdom of God he proclaimed, his option for the poor and marginalised, his message of universal love – all these attributes contribute to the difference and specificity of his historical Jewish personality. Yet the uniqueness and universal significance of Jesus for humankind lies not just in his words and deeds. The real truth of Jesus is not a doctrine but his very person as the Son of the Father and Word Incarnate. Not a philosophical truth, not even a doctrinal truth in the sense of being totally explicable, but a truth attested to in faith in a Person who is the Way, the Truth and the Life (Jn 14:6).

Our challenge today, in a plural world, is how to attest to this truth without resorting to totalising meanings that exclude or reduce the beliefs of others. There must be a way of reflecting upon Jesus as True God and True Man that is sensitive to these questions. Since all religions are, in some form or other, mediations of the reality of God, religious people expect to hear something of the distinctive reality of God as mediated by Jesus. But it is also true that they are adverse to explanations that pre-empt the truths of their own religious systems. Thus theologians are advising that we must not begin with the 'high' Christological and classically conceived doctrines of divinity, the Incarnation or Trinity; these great truths will always stand, but they are points of arrival. Instead we need to return to the departures within the New Testament itself, to which these doctrines were a response.[20] Such Christology will not be 'a cause for wielding the big stick of Christian universalism', but will arise rather from the 'the crushed reed' of the particularity of Jesus himself.[21] It will be a more fragmentary and tentative theology, functioning as a light on the Divine Mystery in a way that is invitational, questioning and making room.

The God of Jesus Beyond Ideology

It is in this spirit that the Italian theologian Bruno Forte says that we must go behind our classical doctrines to refresh ourselves in their source, which is the gospel as revelation in Word and Spirit.[22] We must recall that the true meaning of revelation is *re-velatio* – the unveiling of what is hidden and the veiling of what is revealed: the 'unveiling' of what is hidden because in Jesus the Son we now say that God has truly shown his face, we don't have to search in agnosticism as 'We have been brought near' (Eph 1:13) to taste the mystery of God; and the 'veiling' of what is revealed because Jesus as the Word made flesh in a sense hides God, his human presence a veiling of the Word in sacrament among us. While the special witness of Christians is the very concreteness of the divine presence in Jesus as something we can lay hold of in history, we must not forget that the person of Jesus remains suffused with the hiddenness of God, the hiddenness of the Father from whom the Word comes, the hiddenness of the sacramental humanity of Jesus of Nazareth himself, and the hidden eschatological nature of Jesus the Christ, toward whom we still journey with the guidance of the Holy Spirit (Jn 16:13).

Thus Forte would say that to believe in Jesus as Son is also to believe that the Father of Jesus is the God who resists being turned into an ideological formula. Simply put, we must not use the God of Jesus to explain everything. If we acclaim, as in the Fourth Gospel, that Jesus is the Word and Truth (Jn 1:1-14) and, as in later developments, that he is the universal *Logos* of all things, it does not mean that the truth of who Jesus is ceases to be a claim on our faith. Indeed, he himself was 'the pioneer and perfecter of our faith' (Heb 12:2), having lived his life in a constant climate of surrender to the Father. Forte writes:

> The faith of the Son incarnate is the radical negation of every ideological, logic-centred reduction of Christianity, which would presume to explain all things. If Christianity is the religion of the *revelatio*, by which God communicates God-self without eliminating the excess of the divine mystery in relation to human reason and history, then no all-embracing formulas, either ideological, political or even moral must be smuggled into it.[23]

Truth in Christ – Divine Gift and Question

Similarly, Archbishop Rowan Williams proposes that our task as Christians in relating to other religions and systems of meaning is not to construct a meta-theory around Christ as container of all meanings, but to explore the identity of Jesus as God's ongoing question to all meanings, including our own Christian religiousness.[24] The God of the New Testament is not 'our' God in the sense of a tribal God. The difference of God is beyond all words and institutions in which it is (inevitably) articulated, and through which it is often turned into a means of control. To make his point, Williams draws on a rough paraphrase of the Pauline text of 1 Corinthians 1:25, where Paul, referring to the weakness and folly of God, evokes the beyond and the new in ways that go further than the expectations of human reason:

> We do not have omnipotence of meaning; we do not proclaim to you the totality of meaning; we have nothing to proclaim but Jesus dead and risen; we have only this news which has no value as a response to everything or as the totality of meaning, but has value in itself.[25]

Therefore, when we speak to the religiousness of other believers, it will not be about excluding or totally including, about winning arguments for good and all, or about having all the answers. The God who is revealed in the Son is not an answer to human expectations. The God of Jesus on the Cross, as 'a value in itself', is the subversion of all answers.

As a truth also held in faith, Christianity is not comparable to any other religion, even though it comprises all the identifying features of religion at the level of institution, rituals and doctrines and codes. Christianity, as Geffré points out, is defined essentially in reference to the gospel – that is, the 'good news' of salvation from every religious code, morality or ritual which claims to be pleasing to God or make God the supreme utility for human needs.[26] As the good news responded to in faith, it transcends religion and Christianity itself, which is replete with the elements of religion. Elsewhere, Geffré speaks of Christian faith as the 'leaven' for all the religious traditions of humanity.[27] Therefore, theologians are saying that we must begin to think of the truth of Christ in relation to other religions as 'a relational truth' or 'a-truth-in-relation-to'. Since all religions are in themselves providential forms of divine communication, they hold elements of truth and grace, but the particular gift of Christianity is that it is the pre-eminent witness to divine truth and grace in all religions.[28] Thus the gospel truth of God in Christ is not another block of meaning over and against other belief systems. Rather it is a call to conversion to the 'truth and grace' within all theistic and non-theistic ways of salvation. Alternatively, Rowan Williams puts it that the gospel truth of the revelation of God in Christ to the world is always God's gift, God's 'question', no more, no less. Being a Christian is being held to that question in our relation to all religious discourse.[29]

Meeting in the *Kenosis* of God

What is the question the God of Jesus Christ puts to the religions? What is the particular space in Christian faith that is amenable for encounter with the other? In his great encyclical *Fides et Ratio*, John Paul II shows that faith does not have to discount reason but rather purifies it in opening up its capacities to a larger concept of truth than arid rationalism:

> ... the prime commitment of theology is the understanding of God's *kenosis* [self-empting], a grand and mysterious truth for the human mind, which finds it inconceivable that suffering and death can express a love which gives itself and seeks nothing in return. (FR 93)

John Paul II was no theological radical, but here he is formally expressing what countless Christian theologians now agree is the radical message of the gospel. While this image of the humility of God has always been in the tradition, the contemporary experience of the eclipse of God, the aftermath of two World Wars and the horrors of the Holocaust mean that we are beginning to see, to use Bonhoeffer's phrase, that 'only a suffering God can help'. A number of theologians today, including Rowan Williams in his comment on 1 Corinthians 1:25, are focussing on the revelation of God in the death and resurrection of Jesus as an important resource in dialogue. John Haught attends to this question is some depth. He says it will bring into our relations with other religions a tolerant and humble approach in imitation of the self-abandoning Divine Mystery who lets the world be, in order that it many flourish in rich and luxuriant spontaneity. This truth can also nourish in us a healthy nescience (*docta ignorantia*) about the finality of our doctrinal statements.[30]

We know that Benedict XVI has been vigorous in opposing the current relativising of Christian truth and has warned against the propensity for this in a radically pluralistic approach to the religions.[31] If Christian faith is not true, he says, it has nothing to say to our living and dying and, we may add, nothing to say to other believers.[32] But having expressed the need for clarity in truth, he immediately sees the problem arising in the mind of the modern reader and goes on to ask whether dogmatic formulations of truths can so shape the Christian sensibility by making people intolerant of the 'other'? In a surprising move, Benedict implies that we also need the mystical in our understanding of God, so that 'one-sided' and 'hardened' statements on Christian faith are broken down. In relation to God, and indeed all aspects of Christian faith, there is always an unlikeness between what is known by us and the reality we know only obscurely, even darkly:

> In Christ, God becomes altogether concrete, he becomes something we can lay hold of in history. He comes bodily to men. But this very God who has become tangible is wholly mysterious. His self-chosen humiliation, his *kenosis* is a new form, as it were, of the cloud of mystery in which he hides and at the same time shows himself. For what paradox could be greater than that God is vulnerable and can be killed? The Word, which the incarnate and crucified Christ is, always far surpasses all human words; thus God's *kenosis* is itself the place where the religions can meet without arrogant claims to domination.[33]

It is as if Pope Benedict is saying that Christians in dialogue must not be limited by an exposition of doctrines only. They come to dialogue from a deeper place beyond arrogance and dominance. Since the last word about being is no longer the unnameable Absolute, but love, making itself visible in the *kenosis* of the crucified Christ, they enter dialogue in a spirit of self-emptying, being a word to others of that love. It is in this spirit that Christians can be truly confident in dialogue and tread the path lightly. And it is in imitation of the vulnerability and generosity of God made tangible in Christ, that they will transform the individualised pluralism of today into an inclusive plurality.[34] Although he does not say so, we may ask if Benedict's 'community of plurality', which is at once both gift and task, is not a description of the Reign of God at a time when the historic religions are also making their presence felt as meditations of the divine mystery.

SUMMARY

We have seen that the dialogue between Christian faith and other religious traditions hovers in a zig-zagging relationship between two truths: that God desires all people to be saved and that there is but one Mediator between God and humanity, himself a human being, Christ Jesus, who gave himself as a ransom for all (2 Tm 3:5). Now that we are more aware of the existence of other mediations of the divine mystery which have existed for centuries in institutions with their own identities, we ask how can we still attest to this truth without claiming dominance, without considering the 'other' inferior and indeed without unsubtle proselytising? Theologians of Christian interreligious dialogue have come at this question from numerous angles and continue to explore it.

Arising from the *de facto* plurality of religions as 'ways to God', some theologians have been pressing for an initial pluralism of approach (*in principio*) in God's dealings with humankind. Factors which have contributed in some way to this thinking are:

- The 'covenant never revoked' of the Jewish tradition, which implies a plurality of differentiation in the one divine revelation.

- The greater consideration now being given to the Holy Spirit as the agent of divine presence in Christ in creation, in all cultures and religions from the earliest times, and as the point of God's entry wherever and whenever God reveals and communicates himself. Indeed it is the recognition of the same Spirit at work in other believers that gives impetus to our sharing of gifts in dialogue.

- Since God alone is Absolute Saviour, it is within God's Reign that we must see salvation as mediated in differing ways by all religions. Accepting the Spirit's universal presence and the ambience of God's Reign as places of meeting for all the religions moves Christian dialogue beyond an exclusive ecclesiocentrism. But the particular originality that Christians bring to dialogue is God, to whom they witness in the person of Jesus Christ. Christians will continue to proclaim the universality of God's salvation, as most religions do, but their particular proclamation will also be about the difference of the Absolute God who saves. That is, the Absolute as the Triune God who has entered history, and through the incarnation of his Son manifests himself in the utter gratuity of crucified love. The Christian will also proclaim that it is in the very particularity of the Word made Flesh that the Spirit of God addresses the 'truth and grace' in all the religions.

One can say that all religions are inclusive, in that they tend to reach out to find their own treasured non-negotiables in other religions. Since Vatican II, the Church, through the dialogue experience of its theologians and members, is espousing a more *open* inclusivism, and in respecting the non-negotiables of other faiths is, hopefully, moving toward the transformed communion of plurality Benedict XVI has spoken of. As gift of God, invitation and question, Christian truth treads lightly. It is a 'truth-in-relation-to', best expressed in the language of sign, symbol and sacrament. We need only turn to the Fourth Gospel for such a language. I choose one symbol: Jesus is the light (Jn 1: 1f; 8:12). As light, the presence of Christ infiltrates but does not crowd out. It is a presence that illumines and seeks out the essence; it confirms, judges and shows up the dross in all human discourse about God; it purifies and transforms.

In line with the voice emerging in magisterial documents inspired by Vatican II's positivity toward the religions, it is a truth that recognises that while Christ is the one mediator, the 'participated mediations' of grace and truth in the beliefs and practices of other religions in relation to him can be concrete 'ways of salvation' for their adherents. This means that our interreligious relationships are real and that through these traditions we can come to see Christ newly radiant in different ways. As a truth that is ultimately known in faith, it is eschatological, and points us toward the future, 'to that day known by God alone, on which all peoples will address the Lord with a single voice and serve him with one accord' (NA 4). Therefore it is not about control, in the sense of 'This is the truth' or 'I have the truth'. We never have it; it at best has us because it manifests itself through its own power.[35] As Christians we are committed to being ready to give account of the hope its power gives to us, and to do so with gentleness and love (cf. 1 Pt 3:15).

FURTHER READING

Cornille, Catherine, *The Impossibility of Interreligious Dialogue* (New York: Crossroad, 2008).

Di Noia, Joseph A., *The Diversity of Religions: A Christian Perspective* (Washington D.C.: Catholic University of America Press, 1992).

Dupuis, Jacques, *Toward a Christian Theology of Religious Pluralism* (New York: Orbis Books, 1997).

————, *Christianity and the Religions: From Confrontation to Dialogue* (New York: Orbis Books, 2002).

Fitzgerald, Michael and John Borelli, *Interfaith Dialogue: A Catholic View* (New York: Orbis Books, 2006).

Fredericks, James L., *Faith Among Faiths: Christian Theology and the Non-Christian Religions* (New York: Paulist Press, 1999).

Hall, Gerard, 'Catholic Church teaching in its relationship to other Religions since Vatican II', *Australian E-Journal of Theology* 3 (2003), pp. 1–8.

Lane, Dermot, *Stepping Stones to Other Religions: A Christian Theology of Inter-Religious Dialogue* (Dublin: Veritas, 2011).

McBrien, Richard, *Catholicism* (London: Chapman, 1994).

Ratzinger, Cardinal Joseph, *Truth and Tolerance: Christian Belief and the World Religions* (San Francisco: Ignatius Press, 2003).

NOTES

1. I am particularly indebted to Jacques Dupuis. In *Toward a Christian Theology of Religious Pluralism* (1997), Dupuis attempts to develop a comprehensive theology of the religions which, while being avowedly Christian and inclusivist, also explores several avenues of Christian theology that could lead beyond the frontiers of a narrow inclusivist doctrine. Following its publication, there occurred a two-and-half-year Vatican investigation by the Congregation for the Doctrine of the Faith. The seventy-seven-year-old retired professor told reporters that the long inquiry had been a 'very great suffering'. Initially accused of 'errors' in his writing, this accusation was eventually dropped, but the Vatican published a *Notification* in relation to what it considered 'ambiguous' or 'potentially misleading' assertions. This *Notification*, signed by the then Prefect, Cardinal Ratzinger, has been appended to all later editions. Dupuis' willingness to address the question of whether the *de facto* plurality of religions might also be a plurality *in principio*, i.e. positively part of God's plan, perhaps explains the interest of the Congregation for the Doctrine of the Faith. Not surprisingly, in view of the many years he spent in India, Dupuis also has regard for the theological insights of Asian (especially Indian) bishops and theologians. He clearly situates himself in the inclusivist camp but, as he himself indicates, this camp is a diverse one. While the dialogue seems to move on a Western universalising perspective, and from there seems 'to know too much about God', Dupuis' work is nevertheless brave. It is a book that had to be written and a comprehensive resource for students of interreligious dialogue. It will undoubtedly remain a reference and stepping stone for years to come. See *Tablet* 21 November 1998 and 16 January 1999, in which Cardinal Franz König writes in defence of Dupuis; and *Tablet*, 3 March 2001. See also Terence Merrigan, 'Exploring the Frontiers: Jacques Dupuis and the Movement Toward a Christian Theology of Religious Pluralism', *Louvain Studies* 23 (1998), pp. 338–59, and Jacques Dupuis, 'The Truth Will Make You Free', *Louvain Studies* 24 (1999), pp. 211–63, for his response to the queries and criticisms of theologians.

2. Jacques Dupuis, *Christianity and the Religions*, p. 216.

3. Jacques Dupuis, *Toward a Christian Theology*, p. 346.

4. Karl Rahner, 'Christianity and the Non-Christian Religions', *Theological Investigations*, Vol. 5 (London: Darton, Longman & Todd, 1966), pp. 113–34.

5. Karl Rahner, *Foundations of Christian Faith: An Introduction to the Idea of Christianity* (New York: Crossroad, 1978), p. 139.

6. Karl Rahner, 'Christianity and the Non-Christian Religions', p. 121.

7. Jacques Dupuis, *Christianity and the Religions*, p. 257.

8. Claude Geffré, 'Double Belonging and the Originality of Christianity as a Religion', *Many Mansions: Multiple Religious Belonging and Christian Identity*, Catherine Cornille, ed., (New York: Orbis Books, 2002), p.102. Cf. Claude Geffré, 'The Christian View of Judaism', *Theology Digest* 44:1 (Spring 1997), p. 20; Jacques Dupuis, *Toward a Christian Theology of Religious Pluralism*, p. 228.

9. Jacques Dupuis, *Christianity and the Religions*, p. 133.

10. Dermot Lane, *Stepping Stones*, p. 184. Here a significant section is given to an exploration of the theology of the Holy Spirit and its relevance, indeed necessity, for interreligious dialogue.

11. *Ibid.*, p. 207.

12. Francesco Gioia, ed., *Interreligious Dialogue: Official Teaching of the Catholic Church: 1963–1995* (Boston: Pontifical Council for Interreligious Dialogue and Pauline Books, 1997), p. 366, n. 572.

13. Karl Rahner, *Foundations*, p. 139.

14. Jose Kuttianimattathil SDB, 'The Holy Spirit and the World Religions: The Meaning of God's Revelation', *Vidyajyoti* 63 (1999), nos. 4 and 5. Jacques Dupuis, 'The Spirit, Basis for Interreligious Dialogue', *Theology Digest* 46.1 (Spring 1999), pp. 27–31.

15. Cited in Jacques Dupuis, *Toward a Christian Theology of Religions*, p. 220.

16. Jacques Dupuis, *Christianity and the Religions*, p. 81, pp. 178–80.

17. Yves Congar, *I Believe in the Holy Spirit*, Vol. 3 (London: Chapman, 1983), p. 149.

18. See Gavin D'Costa, 'Catholicism and the World Religions: A Phenomenological Account', *The Catholic Church and the World Religions*, G. D'Costa, ed. (London: T. & T. Clark, 2011), p. 20. D'Costa sees an 'open door' in John Paul II's phrase 'participated mediations'.

19. Jacques Dupuis, 'The Spirit: Basis for Interreligious Dialogue', *Theology Digest* 46.1 (Spring 1999), p. 31.

20. Dermot Lane, 'Vatican II, Christology and the World Religions', *Louvain Studies* 24 (1999), p. 162.

21. Gerard Hall, 'Jacques Dupuis' Christian Theology of Religious Pluralism', *Pacifica* 15 (February 2002), p. 8.

22. Bruno Forte, 'Jesus of Nazareth, History of God, God of History', *The Myriad Christ: Plurality and the Quest for Unity in Contemporary Christology*, T. Merrigan and J. Haers, eds. (Louvain: Louvain University Press, 2000), pp. 100–20.

23. *Ibid.*, p. 113.

24. Rowan Williams, 'The Finality of Christ', *In Memoriam Charlotte Klein: Christology and Religious Pluralism*, Mary Kelly, ed. (London: Sisters of Sion, 1990), pp. 24–7.

25. *Ibid.*, p. 34. Here Williams cites Jacques Pohier's *God: In Fragments* (New York: Crossroad, 1985).

26. Claude Geffré, 'Toward a Hermeneutic of Interreligious Dialogue', *Radical Pluralism and Truth: David Tracy and the Hermeneutics of Religion*, Werner Jeanrond and Jennifer Rike, eds. (New York: Crossroad, 1991), p. 267. Geffré says that we need to abandon an image of God as the supreme utility of the human being, a kind of God of religion or the cosmos who corresponds too well to human needs. The originality of Christianity lies not in it being a theism (though it is that), but in it being a religion of the gospel, a 'good news' of divine grace in the world which is ultimately responded to in faith. Geffré takes his cue from the great evangelical theologian Karl Barth, who emphasises the distance between the God of religion and the God of faith, but he does not endorse Barth's sharp distinction between Christianity as a religion of grace and the religions as attempts by man to justify and sanctify themselves before God. C. Geffré, 'Toward a Hermeneutics of Interreligious Dialogue', p. 269.

27. *Ibid.*, p. 269.
28. The term 'relational', in itself abstract, is used by theologians to express the relation of the Christ event to other religions. Used explicitly by Jacques Dupuis in *Toward a Christian Theology*, p. 388, and by Claude Geffré, 'The Crisis of Christian Identity in an Age of Pluralism', *Concilium* 3 (2005), pp.18–19, and 'Toward a Hermeneutics', pp. 259–60, respectively.
29. Rowan Williams, 'The Finality of Christ', p. 35.
30. John Haught, *Mystery and Promise: A Theology of Revelation* (Collegeville, MN: Liturgical Press, 1993) where he says that in light of the eclipse of mystery, the aftermath of two world wars, theology needs to retrieve what has always been there in the tradition and could now be a generative image of revelation for our times – the image of the humility and self-abandonment of Divine Mystery. Haught says the image of the self-humbling generosity of God is also the key to the plurality of religions (p. 88). Other accessible sources include Thomas Norris, *A Fractured Relationship: Faith and the Crisis of Culture* (Dublin: Veritas, 2007), in which chapter VI reflects on 'Jesus Crucified as the Face of God for the Modern World', and Dermot Lane's 'Vatican II, Christology and the World Religions', in which he considers that the death of Jesus should be to the fore in the dialogue of the religions: 'The Christian ideas of divine *kenosis* and self-limitation, that God is at once revealed and hidden (*Deus revelatus et absconditus*), and the unity of emptiness and exaltation that derive from the Cross should be an important resource in this dialogue with the other religions' (pp. 166–7).
31. Joseph Cardinal Ratzinger, *Truth and Tolerance*, pp. 115–37. Ratzinger critiques the radical pluralistic stance of Hick and Knitter, for whom, he says, dialogue is authentic and possible only if it sets 'one's own position or belief on the same level with what the other person believes, ascribing to it, on principle, no more of the truth than to the position of the other person' (p. 120).
32. Joseph Ratzinger, *Truth and Tolerance*. See pp. 115–37, 'On the New Questions that Rose in the Nineties'. For an appreciative and critical view of Ratzinger's stance on the topic, see James Corkery, *Joseph Ratzinger's Theological Ideas: Wise Cautions and Legitimate Hopes* (Dublin: Dominican Publications, 2009), Chapter 7.
33. Joseph Ratzinger, 'Interreligious Dialogue and Jewish-Christian Relations', *Communio* (Spring 1998), pp. 29, 39, and *Many Religions – One Covenant* (San Francisco: Ignatius Press, 1999), p. 108.
34. Joseph Ratzinger, *Truth and Tolerance*, p. 83.
35. Benedict XVI, *Light of the World*, pp. 50–1.

Selected Glossary

JUDAISM

Am Yisrael People of Israel.

Bar Mitzvah Hebrew for 'son of the commandment'. A ceremony for boys who are about to assume religious duties. Generally observed at age thirteen.

Bat Mitzvah Hebrew for 'daughter of the commandment'. A ceremony for girls coming to adulthood. Celebrated in same manner as **Bar Mitzvah** in Liberal Congregations.

Brit milah Covenant of circumcision.

Eretz Yisrael Land of Israel.

Haggadah Jewish Torah contains both **halakha** and **haggada**. Haggadah is the collection of Jewish lore, the inspirational narratives that recount the love story between God and Israel. The Haggadah is also the ceremonial book read during the Passover **seder**.

Halakhah An umbrella term describing the entire body of Jewish law. Sourced in Hebrew *laleke* 'to go' (Ex 18:2).

Hanukkah The winter holiday commemorating the victory of the Maccabees over the Syrian Seleucids and the rededication of the Temple in Jerusalem (164 BCE).

Hanukkiah The Hannukah candelabra. It contains nine branches, one for each of the eight days of Hanukkah, and a ninth, a 'servant' candle used for lighting the other candles. Sometimes called the Menorah. The seven-branched menorah is used mainly for synagogue services.

Hashem Meaning 'the Name' in Hebrew. An accepted way of referring to God for Jews today.

Hasidism The ultra-Orthodox movement founded by the Ba'al Shem Tov in Eastern Europe during the seventeenth century.

Havdalah Hebrew for 'separation'. The evening service marking the end of Shabbat or other holidays.

Kabbalah Jewish mysticism based on the thirteenth century **Zohar** and other writings.

Kaddish Aramaic for 'holy'. The mourner's prayer. Although having nothing to do with death, it indicates faith, distress and submission to the will of God.

Kosher The term used to describe foods that comply with the biblical and rabbinical dietary rules.

Midrash (plr. *Midrashim*) Hebrew for 'investigation'. A collection of rabbinical questions, stories and commentaries on the Bible.

Mitzvah Hebrew for 'commandment'. **Mitzvot** (plr.) are prescriptions of **Halakhah**. In everyday usage means a good deed or kind act.

Pesach The Passover holiday celebrating the Exodus of the Jewish people from Egypt and their freedom from slavery. It is the celebration of redemption.

Purim Festival celebrating the story told in the Book of Esther, wherein the Jews are saved from destruction.

Qedushah Hebrew for ' holiness'. Holiness is the goal of Torah and Halakhah.

Qiddushin Hebrew for 'sanctification'. This is the word for marriage and expresses the sacredness of the relationship in which God is a third party.

Rabbi A seminary-trained and ordained member of the clergy who leads religious services, officiates at weddings and funerals, teaches classes through the synagogue. A spiritual leader of the synagogue.

Rosh Hashanah The Jewish New Year, one of the High Holidays (with **Yom Kippur**). It is marked by blowing the *shofar*.

Seder Hebrew for 'order'. Generally refers to the ceremony of the Passover meal.

Shabbat Hebrew for 'Sabbath'. The Yiddish word for Sabbath, Shabbos, is also commonly used.

Shavuot Hebrew for 'weeks', it is the holiday celebrating the spring harvest. It also celebrates revelation – the giving of the law to Moses on Mount Sinai.

Shekhinah The manifestation of God's presence. Used in Jewish theology today to refer to God's feminine attributes.

Shiva Hebrew for 'seven'. The seven-day mourning period after a funeral.

Shoah Hebrew for 'destruction'. It is preferred by some Jewish writers to 'Holocaust', a biblical word meaning burnt offering to God, and having a religious connotation that many object to as inappropriate for mass murder.

Simchat Torah A celebration with singing, dancing and procession to mark the end of the reading of the Pentateuch.

Sukkah The structure erected for the holiday of **Sukkot**.

Sukkot A celebration of creation occurring during the fall harvest and a commemoration of Israel's wandering and homeless existence in the desert.

Talmud The collection of commentaries, traditions and precedents that supplement the Hebrew scriptures.

Tanakh The Hebrew word for Bible. An acronym, made up of the first letters of the words **Torah** (Five Books of Moses), Nevi'im (Prophets) and Ketuvim (Writings).

Teshuva The dominant theme during the days between **Rosh Hashanah** and **Yom Kippur** Usually translated as 'repentance', but can also mean 'answer', 'apology' and 'return' to one's source in God.

Torah Specifically refers to the scroll containing the Five Books of Moses (Genesis, Exodus, Leviticus, Numbers, Deuteronomy) but to 'study Torah' can also encompass the **Talmud** and Jewish learning in general.

Yom HaShoah Holocaust Remembrance Day.

Yom Kippur The Day of Atonement; the holiest and most solemn day of the year characterised by an awareness of divine judgement and repentance (**teshuva**).

Zohar A book of Jewish mysticism and commentary on the Torah discovered at the end of the thirteenth century. It claims that hidden spiritual messages and the secrets of creation can be found by carefully examining biblical texts, although its authenticity is challenged by some authors.

ISLAM

Abd Slave, servant, especially of God (*Abd Allah*).

Al-Fatiha The Opening, meaning the first **surah** of the Qur'an. A prayer frequently uttered and considered to sum up Islam.

Allah God. A contraction of Arabic *il-ilah*, 'the God'.

Aya (pl. ayat) Sign of God in the created universe. Also verse of the Qur'an.

Ayat Allah Ayatollah. Literally 'sign of God'. Shi'ism in Iranian, the title of an especially revered member of the **ulama**.

Basmalah The opening of each **surah** of the Qur'an: 'In the Name of God the compassionate and the Merciful'.

Caliph Successor or deputy, especially of the Prophet.

Dar al-Islam The Abode (House) of Islam, meaning those territories of the **Umma** under Muslim control. The rest of the world is known as Dar al-Harb, 'The Abode of War'.

Da'wa Call, bidding to Islam. Islamic missionary activity.

Dhikr Remembering, mentioning God. The central Sufi form of spiritual discipline.

Din Religion, especially in practice.

Fitra The original human nature created by God. Sound and naturally disposed to the One God.

Ghaflah Forgetfulness, egocentricism. Human sinfulness in Islam.

Hadith Report, event, news. A literary form that communicates a **sunna** of the Prophet Muhammad. The *hadith*, as recording the behaviour of the Prophet, is second in importance to the Qur'an. Is a source of Islamic law. An individual narrative is also known as a *hadith*.

Hajj Pilgrimage to Mecca. A male pilgrim is known as a *hajji* and a female as a *hajja*. Terms of considerable honour.

Halal Permissible, lawful. Opposite is **haram**.

Hanif A pure or generic monotheist, such as Abraham, who was not Jew, Christian or qur'anic Muslim.

Haram Forbidden. Also means sacred space, sanctuary, what is off bounds.

Hijab Cover, curtain, veil. The Muslim practice of veiling women, either by covering the hair or entire head and face. In South East Asia, this is called *purdah*, which may also mean the seclusion of females.

Hijra Emigration, especially of the Prophet and his companions in Qur'an 622 from Mecca to Medina.

Id Festival. There are two canonical festivals recognised by Islamic law: the great Id al-Adha, 'the feast of Sacrifice', and the minor feast, Id al-Fitr, 'the feast of the breaking of the Ramadan fast'.

Ihram State of ritual purity achieved by renouncing certain activities and donning a special garb (also called *ihram*) as in commencing **hajj** to Mecca.

Imam Leader, as in daily **salat**. The Shi'is hold an exalted view of their *imams*, who have been invested with infallible guidance by God. An *imam* may also be a religious teacher with no special sacrality.

Iman Faith, a religious virtue that is more highly regarded by the Qur'an than Islam.

Injil Gospel.

Isa Jesus.

Ishan Doing what is beautiful. The third dimension of Islam.

Islam Surrender, submission. The name of the religion of the Qur'an. One who surrenders is an *uslim*.

Jihad Striving, exertion, especially in the religious path or holy war.

Ka'aba Literally 'cube'. The main Islamic sanctuary in Mecca.

Kitab Writing, book, scripture.

Masjid Place of prostration, mosque.

Mihrab Niche on the wall of the mosque marking the *qibla*, direction of Mecca.

Raka The basic cycle of postures in the **salat**, consisting of standing, bowing, prostrating and sitting.

Sadaqah Charity, freely given at any time. Not to be confused with *zakat*, which is a formal religious tax.

Salat The formal prayer-worship observed five times daily.

Sawm Fasting from dawn until dark during month of Ramadan.

Shahada The bearing witness to God's unity and Muhammad's messengerhood ('There is no God but God. Muhammad is the messenger of God'.) Saying the *Shahada* once in one's life, with belief, in the presence of an appropriate representative of Islam makes one a Muslim.

Shariah Literally 'the way to the watering hole'. Islamic law based on the Qur'an and **Sunna**.

Shi'a Party, faction, sect. The adherents of Ali who believe that Muhammad had chosen him and his descendents to be the rightful successors and rulers of the Muslims.

Shirk Association, especially of anything with God. The one unforgivable sin, according to Q 4:48.

Subha Muslim prayer beads, usually strung in a loop of eleven, thirty-three or ninety-nine, with suitable marker beads to aid in progressing through ritual repetitions of 'the beautiful names of God' and other prayers.

Sunna Custom, way of acting, especially of Muhammad. The Prophet's *sunna* are commemorated and transmitted by way of the **hadith**. *Sunna* is also a legal term that means 'recommended'.

Sunni Popular name for the Muslim majority. The name does not imply that Sunnis follow the Prophet's *sunna* more than the Shi'is.

Surah Chapter of the Qur'an.

Tariqa The Sufi 'way'. A Tariqa may be a method of spiritual discipline, or an actual order or organisation of Sufis.

Tawhid Maintaining God's unity and oneness. This is the central theological truth of Islam.

Ulama Revered teachers.

Umma A community having a common religion. The Muslim community.

Yathrib The oasis town to which Muhammad and his fellow Meccan Muslims migrated in the Hijra, 622 CE. Particularly known thereafter as *Madinat al-Nabi*, 'the city of the prophet' (Medina).

HINDUISM

Advaita The non-dualist version of Hindu thought, associated primarily with the eighth-century philosopher Shankara. It is non-dual in its assertion that the essential reality of the individual person is identical with **Brahman**, the Absolute Reality. Sometimes this view which is the dominant theme of the **Upanishads** is called **Vedanta** (end or goal of the Vedas).

Ahimsa Non-violent love.

Ashram Stage in life. The four stages are *brahmacarin*, the young boy whose chief duty is to study the Vedas; the *grihastha* or householder, who establishes a family; the *vanaprastha* or forest-dweller, who withdraws from worldly engagements to give time to prayer; the more radical *sannyasin* or *sadhu*, the wanderer who lives as a homeless person. *Ashram* also means place for spiritual exercises (*sadhana*) and simply lodgings.

Atman The 'divine self' in the human being that is one with **Brahman**.

Avatar Literally 'descent'. Incarnation of divine consciousness on earth. **Vishnu** is incarnate in ten avatars, one of whom is **Krishna**.

Avidya Greed, illusion.

Bhagavad Gita 'Song of the Lord,' one of the sacred scriptures of Hinduism. Written between 200 BCE and 100 CE. Has authority of 'remembrances' or tradition.

Bhakti Devotion to a personal deity, but also to all fellow creatures. One of the three ways to God (*bhakti-marga*, way of devotion; *jnana-marga*, way of knowledge; *karma-marga*, way of service). *Bhakti* is an essential ideal in Vaishnuism.

Brahma A deity in the Hindu *trimurti* ('three forms', trinity). God as creator of the universe.

Brahman The Absolute: the non-dual reality without properties, resting in itself. Inaccessible to human thought, it is *That*.

Brahmin Member of the priestly caste, occupying first place in the caste system.

Darshan Gaze, glance of the divine. A meeting with an esteemed *gur*. A system of Hindu philosophy.

Deva A Sanskrit word for God.

Devata A minor deity.

Dharma To hold, to maintain. The law of the universe; the foundation of morality. Hindus call their religion *Sanatana Dharma* – 'the eternal law'.

Garbhagriha The innermost room in a temple where the image of the deity is installed, the holiest part of the temple.

Ishta devata Beloved god. Often translated as 'chosen ideal', the personally chosen aspect of **Brahman**, the Absolute, that is to be worshipped.

Jnana The Hindu **marga** or **yoga** of non-dual knowledge which realises the union of the self with **Brahman**.

Karma The total effect of one's actions. The word also means 'action'/'service' and is one of the three dharmic paths described in the Gita, the others being **jnana** (knowledge) and **bhakti** (devotion).

Kshatriya A member of the second group in the class system – warrior or ruler.

Maharishi Great sage, a title of respect.

Mahatma Great soul, a title of respect.

Mandir Hindu temple.

Marga Path. The 'paths' of service, knowledge and devotion encapsulate Hinduism as an ethical and social system.

Maya The material world, the many as opposed to the One, which is ultimately deception, a prison.

Moksha Release from the bondage of the human condition; discovery of the true Self which lies beyond duality, and beyond rebirth and suffering. The highest end of life as union with **Brahman**.

Om The sound-symbol of the Absolute. The primordial sound from which the universe comes forth; recitation enables participation in **Brahman**.

Puja Worship.

Samsara Flowing together. The experience of the flux of individual existence in the phenomenal world and cycle of deaths and rebirth. Relativity.

Sanskrit Indo-European language from earliest times. Medium for much of Hindu religious and cultural expression.

Shaivism The worship of the god Shiva. A Hindu sect.

Shaktism Literally 'force', 'power', 'energy'. Feminine aspect of the divine. Worship of the divine mother, **Kali**.

Shiva A god of the Hindu trinity. Creator and destroyer. A principal god like Vishnu.

Shudra Caste of servants, workers.

Upanishads Sacred writings of the Hindus composed between 800–500 BCE. Have the authority of revelation.

Vaishnavism Worship of the god Vishnu. A Hindu sect.

Vaishya Caste of property owners, merchant class.

Vedanta The end of the Vedas, the school which seeks to systematise and develop the insights of the Upanishads. Its outstanding figure is the eighth-century philosopher, Shankara.

Vedas Literally 'body of knowledge'. Earliest sacred writings of the Hindus composed around 1000 BCE and later. Have authority of revelation.

Vishnu The sustainer of the world in the Hindu Trinity of Brahma, Vishnu and Shiva.

Yoga Union. The discipline leading to identity with the true self. There are many varieties of yoga, of which *hatha yoga*, known in the west, is one. Three dharmic paths described in the Gita are considered yogas of union with God.

BUDDHISM

Anatta Non-self, no soul. The Buddhist negation of the Hindu *atman* as the indestructible core of personality. In early Buddhism a strategic teaching to undercut all craving and attachments; later assumed the status of a metaphysical doctrine.

Anicca Impermanence, a mark of human existence.

Arhat One who is deserving of reverence. A monk of the Theravada tradition who has achieved freedom from the cycles of rebirth.

Avidya Ignorance, particularly of the Four Noble Truths; the root cause of **dukkha**.

Bhikkhu Mendicant, beggar – referring to a monk; *Bhikkuni* a nun.

Bodhi Awakening to the nature of conditioned reality and direct experience of the unconditioned.

Bodhicitta The potential or aspiration of enlightenment (**bodhi**). In **Mahayana**, the mental attitude the candidate arouses when aspiring to be a **Bodhisattva**.

Bodhisattva The ideal in **Mahayana**. Literally **bodhi** (enlightened), *sattva* (essence); one who foregoes final entry into **nirvana** out of compassion for all sentient beings.

Brahma-Viharas A meditation on the four types of love: loving-kindness, compassion, joy and equanimity.

Buddha Enlightened one. A historical person in Theravada tradition, Siddhartha Gautama; one of the innumerable beings in **Mahayana**, where each human being is a potential Buddha.

Dana Giving, generosity. The only meal in the day for Theravadin monks and nuns.

Dependent Origination Or 'dependent arising'. The Buddhist view of creation as ongoing genesis due to **avidya**, which continually brings about birth and death.

Dharma Truth or law. The teaching of the **Buddha**, or the Buddhadharma.

Dukkha Sorrow, dissatisfaction with the way things are. One of the three marks of human existence.

Hinayana Small, inferior vehicle. A pejorative **Mahayana** description of Buddhists who rejected Mahayana teaching, dating from the first to fourth centuries. Only one Hinayana sect, **Theravada**, survives today, mainly in Sri Lanka and Southeast Asia.

Karma Action, the cosmic law of cause and effect; every physical and spiritual action has long-range consequences.

Karuna Compassion for all sentient beings; what motivates the **Bodhisattva**.

Khandas The five constituents of the construct called 'personality'. Are the body, feeling, perception, thought formations, sensory consciousness – all are basis for clinging.

Koan A riddle, story or technique used for purification of the mind in Zen Buddhism.

Mahayana The Great Vehicle. The self-bestowed name for the teachings of the **Bodhisattva** path that began to appear between 100 BCE–100 CE.

Nirvana Literally 'blown out, no wind/breath'. The final goal or definitive liberation from the cycles of rebirth; the state of the unborn, or deathlessness in Theravada; emptiness in **Mahayana**.

Parinirvana Total passing into **nirvana** after death of a Buddha or **arhat**.

Prajna Pure intuited wisdom; complete insight into the way things are; the goal of Buddhism, often personified as feminine.

Roshi Japanese term for Zen master, often an abbot of a monastery.

Samadhi Concentration, absorption; a state of right concentration that leads to wisdom.

Samsara World of appearances and endless flux of becoming in death and rebirth.

Sangha Literally 'assembly', 'community'. Denotes the Buddha's followers, lay or ordained, who practice the **dharma** in some way; formally denotes the order of monks and nuns.

Satori Japanese term for full enlightenment in Zen.

Shila Morality; precepts of behaviour conducive to purification of the mind.

Sunyata Emptiness, void. The ultimate meaning of all things as a result of the three marks of existence – suffering, impermanence, dependent arising. A metaphysics developed in the *Madhyamika* (Middle Way) school by the early Indian Nagarjuna. Became a core teaching in **Mahayana**.

Sutra Literally 'thread'. Later written recollections of what the Buddha taught.

Tathagata Literally 'He who has come or gone thus' (on the path of the Buddhas); 'He who has reached or become what is really so, the True.' The term the Buddha used to speak of himself after Awakening.

Theravada The Way of the Elders. The foundational, orthodox tradition of Buddhism. Sometimes called Hinayana – 'the small vehicle'.

Vihara Buddhist monastery.

Vipassana 'Penetrating insight' into the marks of existence; a form of meditation practiced mainly in Theravada Buddhism.

Zazen Japanese term for 'sitting-absorption' in Zen.

Zen Japanese pronunciation of the Chinese *Ch'an* – a form of Mahayana Buddhism.